Operating Syr - DOS + WIN95 (System)

Applications { Word Perf
Lotus
Cornell
Database

(Application
Software)

COMPUTING

Larry Long
Nancy Long

Prentice Hall, Englewood Cliffs, New Jersey 07632

Library of Congress Cataloging–in–Publication Data

Long, Larry.
    Computing/Larry Long, Nancy Long.
        p.   cm.
    Includes index.
    ISBN 0-13-309956-3
    1. Microcomputers.   2. Computer software.   I. Long, Nancy
II.   Title
QA76.5.L6545   1995
004.16—dc20

                                                94-32975
                                                CIP

Acquisition Editor: P. J. Boardman
Production Editor: Nancy DeWolfe
Managing Editor: Joyce Turner
Interior & Cover Design: Rosemarie Votta
Design Director: Patricia H. Wosczyk

Copy Editor & Proofreader: Nancy Marcello
Page Layout: Diane Koromhas
Manufacturing Manager: Patrice Fraccio
Editorial Assistant: Amy Cohen

Cover Illustration: Don Baker

TO TROY AND BRADY, OUR SONS

© 1995 by Prentice Hall, Inc.
A Simon & Schuster Company
Englewood Cliffs, New Jersey 07632

Printed in the United States of America
10   9   8   7   6   5   4   3   2

ISBN 0-13-309956-3

Prentice-Hall International (UK) Limited, *London*
Prentice-Hall of Australia Pty. Limited, *Sydney*
Prentice-Hall Canada Inc., *Toronto*
Prentice-Hall Hispanoamericana, S.A., *Mexico*
Prentice-Hall of India Private Limited, *New Delhi*
Prentice-Hall of Japan, Inc., *Tokyo*
Simon & Schuster Asia Pte. Ltd., *Singapore*
Editora Prentice-Hall do Brasil, Ltda., *Rio de Janeiro*

OVERVIEW

Dr. Larry Long is a lecturer, author, consultant, and educator in the computer and information services fields. He has written over 30 books on a broad spectrum of computer/MIS-related topics from introductory computing, to programming, to MIS strategic planning. Dr. Long is actively involved in the production of multimedia-based interactive learning materials. He has addressed a breadth of management, computer, and MIS issues in his executive seminars.

Dr. Long has served as a consultant to all levels of management in virtually every major type of industry. He has over 25 years of classroom experience at IBM, the University of Oklahoma, Lehigh University, and the University of Arkansas, where he continues to be an active lecturer. He received his Ph.D., M.S., and B.S. degrees in industrial engineering at the University of Oklahoma and holds certification as a C.D.P. and a Professional Engineer.

Dr. Nancy Long has coauthored a number of books with her husband. She has teaching and administrative experience at all levels of education: elementary, secondary, college, and continuing education. Dr. Long received a Ph.D. in reading education and educational psychology, an M.S. in personnel services, and B.S. in elementary education at the University of Oklahoma.

CONTENTS

PREFACE

Computing is on a roll, especially personal computing. In the last five years, computers and computer software have experienced one giant leap in technology after another. The greatest changes, however, are not in technology but in the willingness of potential users to give computers a try. People *want* to achieve computer competency. In this text, we foster this learning momentum by giving readers a sense of discovery when they turn a page. Learning about computers and computing should be more than just an education—it should be an adventure!

Target Course

This text and its ancillary materials provide a foundation for computer competency. The target course for this text and its teaching/learning system

- Provides overview coverage of computing concepts and applications, with an emphasis on personal computing.
- Accommodates students from a broad spectrum of disciplines and interests.
- Can include a substantial laboratory component. (The teaching/learning system includes an extensive array of optional hands-on laboratory materials that can be packaged with the text to meet the needs of most lab environments.)

The text is also appropriate for abbreviated (one- and two-hour) survey courses that do not require a hands-on laboratory component.

Features

- *Brevity.* Important introductory computing concepts are covered in this brief, fast-paced text.
- *Applications-oriented.* The continuing theme throughout the text is applications. For example, Chapters 7, 8, and 9 give readers an opportunity to explore the applications potential of personal computing.

- *Informative boxed features.* Features focus on the growing importance of personal computing and on the many interesting ways in which computers are used.
- *Readability.* All elements (photos, figures, boxes, and so on) are integrated with the text to complement and reinforce learning.
- *Presentation style.* The text and all supplements are written in a style that remains pedagogically sound while communicating the energy and excitement of computers and computing to the student.
- *Currency-plus.* The material actually anticipates the emergence and implementation of computer technology.
- *Flexibility.* The text and its teaching/learning system are organized to permit maximum flexibility in course design and in the selection, assignment, and presentation of material.

Organization

Computing is organized in four parts.

- *Part I: Computers Today* (two chapters) places the world of computers into perspective and introduces concepts related to interaction with computers.
- *Part II: Hardware* (four chapters) exposes the reader to the inner workings of a computer, an array of input/output and storage devices, and networking.
- *Part III: Software* (three chapters) gives the reader an opportunity to explore the potential of personal computing by introducing popular productivity tools, along with graphics, multimedia, communications, and many other useful software packages.
- *Part IV: Opportunity, Responsibility, and Challenge* (one chapter) addresses ethical questions surrounding information technology, workstation ergonomics, and the emergence of the information superhighway.

The appendix shows readers how to interact with Microsoft's Windows, the dominant PC operating environment of the 1990s.

The *Computing* Teaching/Learning System

Computing is a small text with a big support package. The comprehensive teaching/learning system components are described here.

Prentice Hall CIS Multimedia Supplement The direct-access multimedia supplement makes a wide variety of source material available to professors during lectures. This supplement is organized into popular topic areas, such as I/O, word processing, and computer history. Each topic is supported by dynamic illustrations, summaries, colorful images, and full-motion video, all of which can be accessed directly. When used in conjunction with a computer, instructors can integrate the CIS multimedia material with their own source material to customize lectures. The *Instructor's Resource Manual (IRM)* contains cross-reference to all items in the supplement.

Instructor's Resource Manual (IRM) The *IRM* contains detailed teaching hints, chapter outlines with key terms and concepts, solutions to exercises, and instruction on the use of all of the teaching and learning materials, including the direct access CIS multimedia supplement. Embedded in the lecture notes are hundreds of teaching tips, interesting supplemental material, ethical concerns, in-class discussion questions and exercises, supplemental examples, warnings, quotes, cross-references to other components of the teaching/learning system, and much more.

Test Item File The *Test Item File* contains over 2000 multiple-choice, true/false, essay, and matching questions. The questions are listed by numbered section head. The *Test Item File* diskettes are distributed for use with PH DataManager software.

Test Item File Diskettes The *Test Item File* diskettes are used in conjunction with *Prentice Hall DataManager* software and the hard copy in *TIF.*

Prentice Hall DataManager *PH DataManager* is an integrated IBM-PC–compatible test-generation and classroom-management software package. The package permits instructors to design and create tests, to maintain student records, and to provide practice testing for students.

Computerized Testing Service The Computerized Testing Service is available free of charge to all instructors who adopt *Computing.* To take advantage of this service, professors simply call in their test order to Prentice Hall.

Study Guide The *Study Guide* is a supplementary book designed to support the student learning objectives in the text. It contains summaries, self-tests, and hand-in exercises.

CAPS (Computer-Assisted Presentation System)—Electronic Transparencies *CAPS* provides instructors with an integrated set of dynamic graphics, sometimes called *electronic transparencies.* Graphic displays are used in conjunction with a personal computer and a screen-image projector to enhance and facilitate classroom lectures. These computer-based "transparencies" enable the *dynamic* presentation of graphics, text, and animation. The transparencies contain key lecture points and appropriate graphics; they can be recalled from a menu and displayed as needed.

Color Transparency Acetates One hundred color transparency acetates, which support material in the text, are provided to facilitate in-class explanation.

The Prentice Hall/*New York Times*** Supplement** Prentice Hall, in cooperation with one of the world's premier newspapers, brings you and your students the Contemporary View Program. The program involves the periodic distribution of a *New York Times* supplement to you and your students. The supplement is the compilation of pertinent and timely *New York Times* articles on computers and automation.

*ABC News***/Prentice Hall Video Library** Prentice Hall and *ABC News* have joined forces to provide you with a video library that offers a variety of documentary and feature-style stories on computers and applications of information technology.

Essentials Skills Modules These booklets contain brief hands-on tutorials for combinations of MS-DOS, WordPerfect (5.X and 6.X), Lotus 1-2-3 (2.X), dBASE III Plus, and dBASE IV. You select the booklet that matches your lab environment. The short (20 to 35 pages), to-the-point, hands-on tutorials and exercises are carefully designed to introduce readers to the essential functionality of a particular package through guided learning, a fast-paced approach to building expertise with PC software.

Prentice Hall Source 1: Computing Essentials   This *Custom Lab Program* includes skills modules for MS-DOS, Windows, and a variety of popular word processing, spreadsheet, and database packages. Each skills module includes an *application description, step-by-step keystroke tutorials,* and *hands-on exercises.* You select the ones you need. Through custom publishing, Prentice Hall binds the applications software skills modules you selected with any college-specific lab material you supply. (Your Prentice Hall representative can provide details on publication deadlines.)

Laboratory Software and Support Materials   Prentice Hall is the largest and most prolific publisher of skills-oriented computer textbooks in the world. In many instances, full function and educational versions of commercial software (Windows 3.1, Microsoft Works, Microsoft Works for Windows, and Microsoft Office, for example) are distributed with these books. Prentice Hall also publishes a variety of programming texts.

Author Hotline   If you have questions about the text, its package, or course planning, call the authors on the hotline. The telephone number appears in the preface to the *IRM.*

Acknowledgments _____

During the conceptualization and writing of *Computing,* we talked personally with scores of professors about what they wanted in a brief introductory text. Catherine Brotherton (Riverside Community College), Thomas Byther (University of Maine), Stephanie Low Chenault (The College of Charleston), Cheryl Kiklas (Anoka Ramsey Community College), Barbara Mahring (Johnson County Community College), Domingo Molina III (The University of Texas at Brownsville), Bernie Straub (Trident Technical College), and Sandra Talbot (Naugatuck Valley Community Technical College) provided valuable insight on the manuscript. We deeply appreciate these dedicated professionals because their comments guided us in content and organization.

The people at Prentice Hall are to be congratulated for their fine effort on this project. We would like to give special thanks to P. J. Boardman, our editor, Nancy DeWolfe, our production editor, and Debbie Emry, our marketing manager, all top-the-line publishers and downright fun people. Also at Prentice Hall, we would like to extend our gratitude to Rich Wohl, Joyce Turner, David Shea, Anne Marie Dunn, Rosemarie Votta, Grace Walkus, Seth Reichlin, and Amy Cohen. The imagination and hard work of our colleagues, Henry Rowe, Stephanie Chenault, and Michael Padbury are evident throughout the *Computing* teaching/learning system.

People from dozens of companies have contributed source material and software to this text. We thank them, one and all.

LARRY LONG, PH.D.   NANCY LONG, PH.D.

1

THE WORLD OF COMPUTERS

OBJECTIVES

To grasp the scope of computer understanding needed by someone living in an information society.

To describe the implications of computer networks on organizations and on society.

To demonstrate awareness of the relative size, scope, uses, and variety of available computer systems.

To describe the fundamental components and the operational capabilities of a computer system.

To identify and describe uses of the computer.

1–1   THE INFORMATION SOCIETY

The Wake Up Call

The year is 2005. Computers are invisible; that is, they are built into our domestic, working, and external environment. Imagine this scenario. Your invisible computer is preprogrammed to awaken you to whatever stimulates you to
greet the new day. The wake up call could be the sound of your favorite music
artist, a vibrating bed, or any of hundreds of video information or entertainment options, such as your favorite network morning program, today's
weather, a stock report, a production status report for the evening shift at your
place of employment, the movie of your choice, or a to-do list for the day.
Suppose your wake up choice is the latter—a to-do list for the day. Besides
listing the events of the day, your invisible computer might *verbally* emphasize important events:

> *Computer:*   Shannon and Pat will arrive for dinner at 7:30. Shannon wants to
> know if you would like her to bring the bread or a dessert.
>
> *You:*   Please suggest possible Chinese cuisine.

In response, the nearest video display, which is prominent in every occupied
room in the house, is filled with a list and pictures of possible dishes. Just as
you notice that all dishes are meatless, your computer reminds you of an important consideration.

> *Computer:*   Remember, Shannon and Pat are vegetarians.
>
> *You:*   [select] Vegetable chop suey. Do we have the needed ingredients?

The system might respond by checking home inventory and ordering as
needed (all automatic).

> *Computer:*   To serve four, you will need a cup of fresh bean sprouts, a cup of
> fresh mushrooms, two large red onions, and a small bottle of peanut
> oil. Do you wish these delivered or will you pick them up?
>
> *You:*   I will pick up.

The system immediately orders the ingredients electronically and asks the retailer to hold them for pickup. By 2001, you, your invisible computer, and the
rest of the country will be linked via the information superhighway. The **information superhighway** is a network of high-speed data communications
links that eventually will connect virtually every facet of our society, both
public (perhaps the local supermarket) and private (perhaps to Aunt Minnie's
daily schedule).

Your home's computer system also prepares a hot, healthy breakfast. As
you begin to leave the house, your system prompts you again to respond to
Shannon's request.

> *Computer:*   What should I tell Shannon?
>
> *You:*   Please send this message to Shannon's office. Begin. Shannon, we are
> looking forward to having you and Pat for dinner. If you would like,
> please bring some of your delicious dilly bread, which would be
> delightful. End.

Before the door closes, Shannon's computer receives the message and prompts
her to read it.

Smart houses with home automation systems have progressed from science fiction to reality. Not only do smart houses exist today, but as the twenty-first century approaches, their prices should fall to where most of us can afford one. Computers and sensors enable the smart house to control security systems, entertainment centers, appliances, lights, blinds, heating and cooling systems, sprinkler systems, swimming pool systems, and other systems that can be activated by electrical apparatus. A central computer, called a controller, ties the threads together. We interact with the home automation system via telephone, hand-held remotes, keypads, touch screen televisions, and voice commands.

When you arrive at the supermarket, the store's system identifies your car as you drive to the pick up area and greets you by name.

> *Computer:* Good morning [your name], your order is in Bin 4. The amount is 12 dollars and 48 cents. Thank you for shopping ElectroMart.
>
> *You:* Good morning and you're welcome.

Polite conversation with computers is not required but is considered appropriate among well-mannered people in the age of automation. When you remove your order from Bin 4, all monetary transactions are completed automatically over the information superhighway. That is, funds are electronically transferred from your account to an ElectroMart account. (In the year 2005 we may be a cashless society.)

Soon after arriving at the office, Shannon reads the messages on the computer and immediately sends a message to the home computer.

> *Shannon:* Prepare one loaf of dilly bread to be ready by 7:00 P.M. today.

Shannon's contribution to the evening meal will be ready at 7:00. However, even in the year 2005, some tasks will continue to defy total automation. We will still have to cut fresh vegetables!

We are well on our way to the day when this scenario emerges as reality. Even today, millions of people carry computers with them much of the day. Millions more spend most of their day within arm's reach of a computer. Few will argue that we are rapidly approaching the age of automation, an era when invisible computers participate in or help us with nearly all we do. It may be sooner than you think. Much of this scenario is within the grasp of today's technology. This book is designed to help prepare you to better cope with and understand today's technology so you will be able to take your place in the age of automation.

Looking Back a Few Years

We have only to look back a few years to get some type of vision of what the future holds. Consider this.

- Fifty-five years ago, our parents and grandparents did everything from accounting to surgery without computers.
- In the 1960s, mammoth multimillion-dollar computers processed data for those very large companies that could afford them. These computers, the domain of highly specialized technical gurus, remained behind locked doors.
- In the mid-1970s computers became smaller and more accessible. This trend resulted in the introduction of commercially viable **personal computers,** or **PCs.** During the 1980s, millions of people from all walks of life purchased these miniature miracles. Suddenly, computers were for everyone!
- Today, one in four Americans has a general-purpose computer more powerful than those that did the processing for large banks during the 1960s. The widespread availability has prompted an explosion of applications for computers. Today, every computer-competent person is continually generating ideas about how computers can be used to enhance life.

What Is Computer Competency?

Not too long ago, people who pursued careers in almost any facet of business, education, or government were content to leave computers to computer professionals. Not so today. In less than a generation, computers have emerged in virtually every career from a background position to *an essential part of the learning experience.* The computer revolution has spawned an **information**

The computer revolution is changing every aspect of society, including the way we pass information and interact with one another. Traders at Sanwa Bank Ltd. in London have immediate access to securities markets around the world.

society where **knowledge workers** focus their energies on providing a myriad of information services. The knowledge worker's job function revolves around the use, manipulation, and dissemination of information. By the time you complete this course, you will achieve **computer competency** and have an understanding of computers. This will enable you to be an active and effective participant in the emerging information society. You and other computer-competent people will:

1. *Feel comfortable using and operating a computer system.*
2. *Be able to make the computer work for you.*
3. *Be able to interact with the computer—that is, generate input to the computer and interpret output from it.* **Input** is data entered to a computer system for processing. **Output** is the presentation of the results of processing (for example, a printed résumé or a tax return).
4. *Understand the impact of computers on society, now and in the future.*
5. *Be an intelligent consumer of computers and computer equipment, collectively called* **hardware.**
6. *Be an intelligent consumer of software and other non–hardware-related computer products and services.* **Software** refers collectively to a set of instructions that can be interpreted by a computer, called **programs.** The programs cause the computer to perform desired functions, such as flight simulation (a computer game), the generation of business graphics, or word processing.
7. *Be conversant in computerese.* The language of computers and information technology is sometimes called **computerese.** In this book, you will learn hundreds of terms and phrases that are the foundation of computer terminology.

The Computer Revolution

We are in the midst of a technological revolution that is changing our way of life. The cornerstone of this revolution, the *computer,* is transforming the way we communicate, do business, and learn. In our private lives, computers speed the checkout at supermarkets, enable 24-hour banking, provide up-to-the-minute weather information, and, of course, entertain us with computer-based games. Increasingly, the computer is the vehicle by which we communicate, whether with our colleagues at work through **electronic mail** or with our on-line friends through **bulletin-board systems** (**BBSs**). Both electronic mail and BBSs allow us to send/receive information via computer-to-computer hookups.

In our professional lives, the miniaturization of the computer has enabled us to take it with us wherever we go. The computer is the constant companion of millions of workers, whether at the office, in an airplane, or at home. Managers use word processing systems to compose memos and check spelling, grammar, and style. Geologists rely on an "expert" computer system for guidance in the quest for minerals. Stockbrokers examine up-to-the-minute securities information from their computers. Sociologists use computers to analyze demographic patterns. Computer artists have millions (yes, millions) of colors from which to choose.

In "the old days," through the 1970s, business computer systems were designed so a computer professional served as an intermediary between the **user** and the computer system. Users, who are sometimes called **end users,** are blue- and white-collar workers who use the computer to help them do their jobs better. **User-friendly** computer systems and software, which have played a major role in the computer revolution, reduce the need for users to go through an intermediary (the computer professional) and allow users to extract information directly from the computer system. User-friendly computer systems and software enable users to interact with them in a nontechnical, nonthreatening manner.

Data: Foundation for the Information Society

Up to now we have talked about *information,* but little about its origin—*data.* **Data** (the plural of *datum*) are the raw materials from which information is derived. **Information** is data that have been collected and processed into a meaningful form. Said in another way, information is the meaning we give to accumulated facts (data). Computers are very good at digesting facts and producing information.

Data are all around us. We, as members of the information society, are continuously generating data. When you call a mail-order merchandiser, the data you give the sales representative (name, address, product number) are entered directly to the computer. When you make a long-distance telephone call, your number, the number you call, and the length of the conversation are entered to a computer system. When you run short of cash and stop at an automatic teller machine, all data you enter, including that on the magnetic stripe of your bank card, are processed immediately by the bank's computer system. The computer system eventually manipulates the data to produce information.

The Computer Adventure

You are about to embark on an emotional and intellectual *journey* that will stimulate your imagination, challenge your every resource from physical dexterity to intellect, and, perhaps, alter your sense of perspective. Learning about computers is more than just education. It's an adventure!

This adventure will last a lifetime. **Information technology** (**IT**), the integration of computing technology and information processing, is changing every minute of the day. In a few years, hundreds of IT-related buzz words, concepts, applications, and hardware devices that do not exist today will confront you. Fortunately, you will have established a base of IT knowledge upon which you can build and continue your learning adventure.

1–2   NETWORKING: BRINGING PEOPLE TOGETHER

The Global Village

In 1967, Marshall McLuhan said,

> *The new electronic interdependence recreates the world in the image of a global village.*

A quarter of a century later, his insightful declaration is now clearly a matter of fact. At present we live in a *global village* in which computers and people

Today we are rapidly becoming an information society where "knowledge workers" depend on computer-generated information to accomplish their jobs. This knowledge worker at Southeast Paper Manufacturing Company in Dublin, Georgia, oversees an automated process that produces about a half million metric tons of recycled newsprint each year.

are linked within companies and between countries. The global village is an outgrowth of the computer network. Most existing computers are part of a **computer network;** that is, they are linked electronically to one or more computers to share resources and information. When we tap into networked computers, we can hold electronic meetings with widely dispersed colleagues, retrieve information from the corporate database, make hotel reservations, and much, much more.

On a more global scale, computer networks enable worldwide airline reservation data to be entered in the Bahamas and American insurance claims to be processed in Ireland. Securities are traded simultaneously on the New York Stock Exchange by people in Hong Kong, Los Angeles, and Berlin. The same is true of exchanges in Europe and Asia. A Japanese automobile assembled in Canada might include American electronics and Korean steel. Computer networks are the vehicles for coordination of the international logistics and communication needed to make a multinational automobile.

Workgroups

Computer networks allow the formation of workgroups that cooperate through **workgroup computing.** The workgroup is any group of people linked by a computer network: all people in a marketing department; corporate vice-presidents and the president; administrators and teachers in an elementary school; field sales representatives for a book publisher; and so on. Special software, tabbed **groupware,** helps in workgroup computing. Groupware is used with a computer network to enable workgroups to coordinate meetings, conduct electronic meetings, set priorities, do collaborative problem solving, share information, establish a library of rapidly changing policies and procedures, and much more. The workgroup is one of many ways that information technology can help bring people together.

The Federal Express COSMOS system uses advanced telecommunications to monitor the status of each shipment as it moves through key handling points in the system. Package whereabouts are monitored from pickup to delivery.

1–3   UNCOVERING THE "MYSTERY" OF COMPUTERS

The Computer System

Technically speaking, the computer is any counting device. But in the context of modern technology, we will define the **computer** as *an electronic device that can interpret and execute programmed commands for input, output, computation, and logic operations.*

Computers may be technically complex, but they are conceptually simple. The computer, also called a **processor,** is the "intelligence" of a **computer system.** A computer system has only four fundamental components: *input, processing, output,* and *storage.* Note that a computer system (not a computer) is made up of the four components. The actual computer is the processing component. When combined with the other three components, it forms a *computer system* (see Figure 1–1).

The relationship of data to a computer system is best explained by an analogy to gasoline and an automobile. Data are to a computer system as gas is to a car. Data provide the fuel for a computer system. A computer system without data is like a car with an empty gas tank: No gas, no go; no data, no information.

Input, process, output, storage

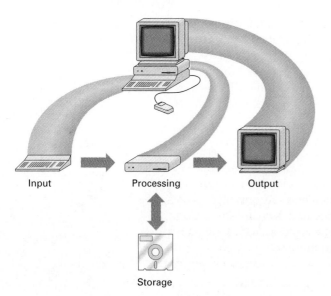

Input   Processing   Output

Storage

FIGURE 1–1 The Four Fundamental Components of a Personal Computer System   *In a personal computer system, the storage and processing components are often contained in the same physical unit. In the illustration, the disk storage medium is inserted into the unit that contains the processor.*

Categories of Computer Systems

The differences in the various categories of computers are very much a matter of scale. A good analogy can be made between airplanes and computers. Try thinking of a *wide-body jet* as a *supercomputer,* the most powerful computer, and a *commuter plane* as a *personal computer.* Both types of airplanes have the same fundamental capability: to carry passengers from one location to another. Wide-bodies, which fly at close to the speed of sound, can carry hundreds of passengers. In contrast, commuter planes travel much slower and carry about 30 passengers. Wide-bodies travel between large international airports, across countries, and between continents. Commuter planes travel short distances between regional airports. The commuter plane, with its small crew, can land, unload, load, and be on its way to another destination in 15 to 20 minutes. The wide-body may take 30 minutes just to unload. A PC is much like the commuter plane in that one person can get it up and running in just a few minutes. All aspects of the PC are controlled by one person. The supercomputer is like the wide-body in that a number of specialists are needed to keep it operational. No matter what their size, airplanes carry passengers and computers process data and produce information.

Computers can be found in a variety of shapes, from boxlike to U-shaped to cylindrical to notebook-shaped. However, the most distinguishing characteristic of any computer system is its *size*—not its physical size, but its *computing capacity.* Loosely speaking, size, or computer capacity, is the amount of processing that can be accomplished by a computer system per unit of time. **Minicomputers** have greater computing capacities than personal computers, also called **microcomputers. Mainframe computers** have greater computing capacities than minicomputers. And **supercomputers,** the biggest of all, have greater computing capacities than mainframe computers. Depending on their sophistication, a **workstation's** computing capacity falls somewhere between that of a micro and a mainframe. Some vendors are not content with pigeon-holing their products into one of these five major categories, so they have created new niches, such as *supermicros* and *superminis.* In this book, we will limit our discussion to these five major categories.

All computers, no matter how small or large, have the same fundamental capabilities—*processing, storage, input,* and *output.* Keep this in mind as you encounter these various types of computer systems in this book, at school, and at work (see Figure 1–2).

- Microcomputer system (personal computer or PC)
- Workstation
- Minicomputer system
- Mainframe computer system
- Supercomputer system

It should be emphasized that these categories are relative. What people call a minicomputer system today may be called a microcomputer system at some time in the future. In keeping with conversational computerese, we will drop the word *system* when discussing the categories of computer systems. Keep in mind, however, that a reference to any of these categories (for example, supercomputer) implies a reference to the entire computer system.

Micros (an abbreviation for microcomputers), workstations, minicomputers, mainframes, and supercomputers are computer systems. Each offers many input and output alternatives—ways to enter data to the system and to present information generated by the system. In addition, software for a variety of applications supports these computer systems. There are, of course, obvious differences in size and capabilities. Besides size and capability, the single most distinguishing characteristic of the various types of computers is the manner in which each type is used. The following summaries of system uses should give you insight into when and where a particular system might be used.

Microcomputer System   Most microcomputers are used by one user at a time. You will be the person who turns on the micro, selects the software to be run, enters the data, and requests the information. The micro, like other computers, is very versatile and has been used for everything from communi-

Size - refers to computing capacity.

- processing per unit of time

FIGURE 1–2 Categories of Computers

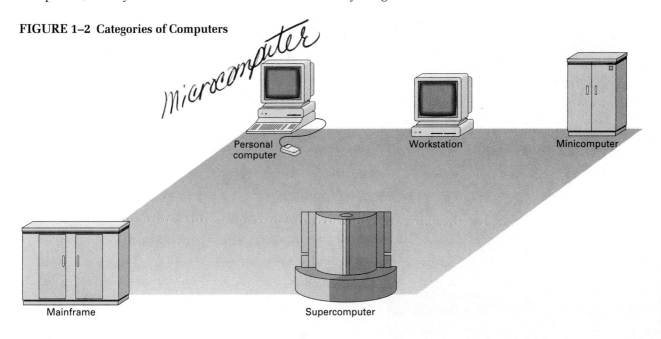

Microcomputer

Personal computer

Workstation

Minicomputer

Mainframe

Supercomputer

cating with business colleagues to controlling household appliances. Because the micro will likely be the center of your computing experience, it and its applications are discussed in more detail in this and other chapters. Throughout the book, we will discuss micro applications of a personal nature and those that involve the shared resources of a computer network. Remember, all computers perform essentially the same functions. Any PC concept you learn can be extrapolated easily to apply to the other types of computers.

Please note that the terms *personal computer, PC, microcomputer,* and *micro* are used interchangeably throughout the book, as they are in business and education. PCs come in many shapes and sizes.

Pocket, laptop, desktop, and tower PCs.   Personal computers come in four different physical sizes: **pocket PCs, laptop PCs, desktop PCs,** and **tower PCs.** The pocket and laptop PCs are light (a few ounces to about twelve pounds), compact, and can operate without an external power source. They earn the "portable" label. The smallest laptops, which weigh from four to eight pounds, are called **notebook PCs.** Notebooks are so named because they are about the size of a three-ring notebook. Desktop PCs and tower PCs are not designed for frequent movement and, therefore, are not considered portable. Typically, the monitor is positioned on top of the processing component of a desktop PC. The processing component of the tower PC is designed to rest on the floor, usually beside or under a desk. The tower PC resembles the processing component of a desktop PC placed on end.

The power of a PC is not necessarily directly related to its size. A few laptop PCs can run circles around some desktop PCs. Some user conveniences, however, must be sacrificed to achieve portability. For instance, the miniature keyboards on pocket PCs, sometimes called **palmtop PCs,** make data entry and interaction with the computer difficult and slow. The display screen on most laptop PCs is monochrome (as opposed to color). Portable computers take up less space and, therefore, have a smaller capacity for permanent storage of data and programs.

A recent innovation is the 2-in-1 PC that can be used as both a notebook and a desktop. The PC is in two parts: a fully functional *notebook PC* and *a docking station.* The docking station can be configured with a high-capacity disk, several interchangeable disk options, a tape backup unit, a high-resolution monitor, greater memory, and other features that may not fit within a notebook. Users of 2-in-1 PCs have the best of both worlds: portability and the expanded features of a desktop. The notebook, which supplies the processor, is simply inserted into or removed from the docking station, depending on the needs of the user.

Top: *This high-performance palmtop computer can run the same applications as its desktop cousin.* Second from top: *When searching for a personal computer, this executive identified portability as his primary criterion.* Third: *Desktop Macintosh micros are made available to library patrons.* Bottom: *Some of the more powerful desktop microcomputers actually sit under or beside a desk, thus providing more space for the keyboard, monitor, printer, and other peripheral devices.*

tickler file

Pen-based computers. Mobile workers in increasing numbers are using portable **pen-based PCs.** Pen-based PCs use electronic pens instead of keyboards. Users select options, enter data, and draw with the pen. The next time United Parcel Service visits your house, don't be surprised if the driver gives you a clipboard-shaped device, hands you an electronic stylus, and asks you to sign your name on a pressure-sensitive display screen. Congratulations! You've just entered the world of pen-based computing, where electronic pens replace the keyboards found on most portable PCs.

Pen-based computers are poised to make an entry into the world of mobile professionals who cannot or will not use keyboard-based portables. Many professionals cannot type, and in meetings, colleagues find the click-clack of a portable's keyboard an annoying distraction. In other situations, typing on a laptop is simply impractical. State Farm Insurance, for example, recently began testing notepads with agents and claims adjusters who need to work at accident or disaster scenes.

Personal digital assistants. The introduction of Apple's Newton served to move **personal digital assistants (PDAs)** to the forefront of the PC arena. PDAs are hand-held personal computers, like palmtop and pen-based computers, that take on many forms. Like the Newton, most PDAs are pen-based. They can include a built-in cellular phone. The cellular phone enables wireless sending/receiving of faxes and wireless sending/receiving of electronic mail and voice mail. PDAs can be carried in pockets, purses, and attache cases, or they can be strapped to parts of the body (a hand, an arm, a leg, or around the waist). Generally, PDAs support a variety of personal information systems, such as scheduling, phone number administration, to-do lists, tickler files, diaries, and so on. Of course, they can support a variety of PC-type applications. A beverage distributor equips its salespeople with PDAs, which enable them to better manage their territories. Technicians rely on their PDAs when they need information on how to make a particular repair. PDAs can store the equivalent of thousands of pages of technical manuals. Forecasters predict that some form of PDA may replace what we now know as textbooks.

Multiuser micros. **Multiuser micros** are configured with as many as a dozen VDTs. A **video display terminal (VDT),** or simply **terminal,** has a **keyboard** for input and a televisionlike (video) screen, called a **monitor,** for output. The VDTs are located in the user areas throughout the organization and linked to the multiuser PC via communications lines. These terminals, often located in the same office, share the microcomputer's resources and its input/output and storage devices. With a multiuser micro, a secretary can transcribe dictation at one terminal while a manager does financial analysis at another terminal and a clerk enters data to a database at yet another. All this can take place at the same time on the same multiuser micro. Multiuser microcomputer systems are installed in thousands of small businesses, from hardware stores to veterinarians' offices.

Workstation   What looks like a PC but isn't? It's a *workstation* and it's very fast. Speed, or computing capacity, is one characteristic that distinguishes workstations from micros. In fact, some people talk of workstations as "souped-up" PCs. The PC was fine for word processing, spreadsheets, and games, but for real "power users"—engineers doing computer-aided design,

MEMORY BITS
Types of Personal Computers

- Pocket PC or palmtop PC
- Laptop PC and notebook PC
- Desktop PC
- Tower PC
- Pen-based PC
- Personal digital assistant (PDA)

With the advent of user-friendly pen-based computers, insurance adjusters spend less time documenting the details of an accident.

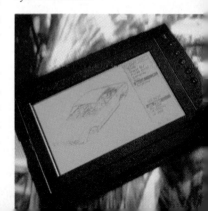

scientists, and other "number crunchers"—the PC fell short. Individual power users needed the speed of a mini or a mainframe at a fraction of the cost. The workstation, introduced in the early 1980s, filled this gap. Today's high-end workstations, which may service a single user, have processing capabilities similar to that of mainframe computers serving as many as 2000 terminals.

The capabilities of today's high-end PCs are very similar to those of low-end workstations. In a few years, the garden variety PC will have workstation capabilities. As the distinction between the two dims, the two will become one. Time will tell whether we call it a PC, a workstation, or something else.

Minicomputer and Mainframe Systems   The three larger multiuser computers, with their expanded processing capabilities, provide a computing resource that can be shared by many people. Minicomputers and mainframe computers are usually associated with *enterprise-wide systems.* For example, human resource management, accounting, and inventory management tasks are usually enterprise-wide systems handled by **minis,** mainframes, or a networked combination of the two. Depending on the size of the organization, a dozen people or 10,000 people can share system resources by interacting with their VDTs.

Supercomputer System   During the early 1970s, administrative data processing dominated computer applications. Bankers, college administrators, and advertising executives were amazed by the blinding speed at which million-dollar mainframes processed data. Engineers and scientists were grateful for this tremendous technological achievement, but they were far from satisfied. When business executives talked about unlimited capability, engineers and scientists knew they would have to wait for future enhancements before they could use computers to address complex problems. Automotive engineers were still not able to build three-dimensional prototypes of automobiles inside a computer. Physicists could not explore the activities of an atom during a nuclear explosion. The engineering and scientific communities had a desperate need for more powerful computers. In response to that need, computer designers began work on what are now known as supercomputers.

The workstations in the foreground are networked with the minicomputer in the rear.

Supercomputers primarily address applications that are **processor-bound.** Processor-bound applications, which are helpful to engineers and scientists, require little in the way of input or output. In processor-bound applications, the amount of work that can be done by the computer system is limited primarily by the speed of the computer. A typical scientific job involves the manipulation of a complex mathematical model, often requiring trillions of operations to resolve. During the early 1970s some complex processor-bound scientific jobs would tie up large mainframe computers at major universities for days at a time. This, of course, was unacceptable. In contrast, mainframe computers are oriented to **input/output-bound** applications; that is, the amount of work that can be performed by the computer system is limited primarily by the speeds of the I/O devices. Administrative data processing jobs, such as generating monthly statements for checking accounts at a bank, require little calculation and a great deal of input and output. In I/O-bound applications, the computer is often waiting for data to be entered or for an output device to complete its current task.

This supercomputer, which looks something like a space-age sofa, is installed at the Garland Division of E-Systems. The enormous speed of this Cray supercomputer helps E-Systems to lower the development costs of software and reduce development cycles for its customers.

Supercomputers are known as much for their applications as they are for their speed or computing capacity, which may be 10 times that of a large mainframe computer. These are representative supercomputer applications:

- Supercomputers enable the simulation of airflow around an airplane at different speeds and altitudes.
- Auto manufacturers use supercomputers to simulate auto accidents on video screens. (It is less expensive, more revealing, and safer than crashing the real thing.)
- Meteorologists employ supercomputers to study the formation of tornadoes.
- Hollywood production studios use advanced graphics to create special effects for movies and TV commercials.

All these applications are impractical, if not impossible, on mainframes.

Computer Makers

Hundreds of PC manufacturers build millions of PCs each year. By contrast, only a handful of companies build mainframe computers and fewer yet build supercomputers. PCs are simple to build compared to all other types of computer systems. Most PC companies simply assemble PCs from components that are readily available on the open market. The more successful PC companies add technological innovations and improved quality to differentiate their products from others on the market. Players in the PC arena include IBM and Apple (the market leaders), Compaq, Dell, Tandy/Grid Systems, Packard Bell Electronics, Gateway, Zenith, Toshiba, and many others.

The number of players drops quickly for makers of workstations, minis, mainframes, and supercomputers. The startup cost to develop a competitive mainframe computer could be billions of dollars. Major makers of workstations include Sun, Silicon Graphics, IBM, Digital Equipment, and Hewlett-Packard. Minicomputer makers include Digital Equipment, IBM,

MEMORY BITS
Categories of Computer Systems

- Microcomputer system
- Workstation
- Minicomputer system
- Mainframe computer system
- Supercomputer system

Hewlett-Packard, Data General, and Tandem. Manufacturers of mainframe computers include IBM, Digital Equipment, Hewlett-Packard, Unisys, Control Data Corporation, Fujitsu, Amdahl, and Bull. Cray Research, Hitachi, and others build supercomputers.

How a Computer System Works

Just about every organization that has employees and a computer maintains a computer-based payroll system. The payroll system enables input and processing of pertinent payroll-related data to produce payroll checks and a variety of reports. The payroll system in Figure 1–3 illustrates how data are entered into a personal computer system and how the four system components interact to produce information (a year-to-date overtime report) and payroll checks. Figure 1–3 illustrates the following steps.

1. At the end of each workweek, the supervisor manually records the number of hours worked for each employee on the Payroll Work Sheet, a **source document.** The source document is the original document from which data are entered.

2. The hours-worked data are keyed in, or *input,* to the system by the supervisor or a data entry operator.

3. The data are *stored* on the personnel **master file.** The master file is made up of **records,** each of which contains data about a particular employee (for example, name, hours worked, year-to-date FICA contribution, and so on). Files, records, and other data management concepts are discussed in Chapter 5, "Data Storage and Organization" and Chapter 8, "Data Management Software."

4. The payroll checks are prepared when the *processing* component, or the computer, *executes* a program. In this example, the employee records are recalled from storage, and the pay amounts are calculated.

FIGURE 1–3 A Personal Computer-Based Payroll System   *This microcomputer-based payroll system illustrates input, storage, processing, and output. The six steps are discussed in the section "How a Computer System Works."*

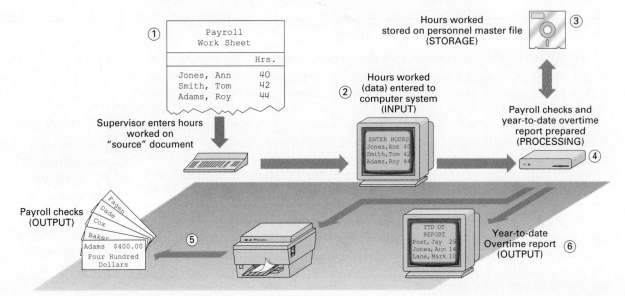

5. The *output* is the printed payroll checks.
6. Other programs extract data from the personnel master file to produce a year-to-date overtime report and any other *output* that might help in the management decision-making process.

The Hardware

The principles illustrated and discussed here apply equally to personal computers (Figure 1–1) and large multiuser mainframe computers. All computer systems, no matter how small or large, have four fundamental components and use data to produce information in a similar manner. The difference is that personal computers are more limited in their capabilities and are designed primarily for use by *one person at a time.* Mainframe computers can service *many users,* perhaps every person in the company, all at once.

In the payroll-system example of Figure 1–3, data are entered (input) and processed on a microcomputer. The PC has a typewriterlike *keyboard* and a **mouse** for input. The mouse enables the user to point and draw. The *monitor* provides for output such as the year-to-date overtime report. The output on a monitor is temporary and is often called **soft copy.** The payroll checks are output on a device called a **printer.** Printers produce **hard copy,** or printed output. Data are stored for later recall on **magnetic disk.** There is a variety of **input/output (I/O)** and storage devices. These and many other hardware devices that make up a computer system are discussed in detail in Chapter 4, "Input/Output Devices" and Chapter 5, "Data Storage and Organization."

There are more similarities than differences between a mainframe-based payroll system and a PC-based system. The main differences are that many people can use the mainframe system at the same time and their primary input/output device is the video display terminal (or VDT).

What Can a Computer Do?

Remember from our previous discussion that the *input/output* and *data storage* hardware components are connected, or *configured,* with the *processing* component (the computer) to make a computer system (Figure 1–1). Let's discuss the operational capabilities of a computer system a little further.

Input/Output Operations   The computer *reads* from input and storage devices. The computer *writes* to output and storage devices. Before data can be processed, they must be "read" from an input device or data storage device. Input data can be entered directly by end users or by professional data entry operators. Typically, data are entered on a VDT or PC keyboard or they are retrieved from data storage, such as a magnetic disk. Once data have been processed, they are "written" to a magnetic disk or to an output device, such as a printer.

Input/output (I/O) operations are illustrated in the payroll-system example in Figure 1–3. Hours-worked data are entered, or "read," into the computer system. These data are "written" to magnetic disk storage for recall later.

Processing Operations   The computer is totally objective. Any two computers instructed to perform the same operation will arrive at the same result. This is because the computer can perform only *computation* and *logic operations.*

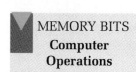

MEMORY BITS
Computer Operations
■ Input/output
  Read
  Write
■ Processing
  Computation
  Logic

■ *Computation operations.* The computational capabilities of the computer include adding (+), subtracting (−), multiplying (*), dividing (/), and exponentiation (^). The commonly accepted symbols used for conveying these computation operations to the computer are shown in parentheses. In the payroll-system example of Figure 1–3, the computer calculates the gross pay in a computation operation. For example, it does the calculations needed to determine the appropriate pay for someone who worked 40 hours and makes $15 per hour.

$$\text{Pay} = 40 \text{ hours worked} \times \$15/\text{hour} = \$600$$

■ *Logic operations.* The computer's logic capability enables comparisons between numbers and between words. Based on the result of a comparison, the computer performs appropriate functions. In the example of Figure 1–3, Tom Smith and Roy Adams had overtime hours since they worked more than 40 hours (the normal workweek). The computer must use its logic capability to decide if an employee is due overtime pay. To do this, hours worked is compared to 40.

$$\text{Are hours worked} > (\text{greater than}) \; 40?$$

■ For Tom Smith, who worked 42 hours, the comparison is true (42 is greater than 40). A comparison that is true causes the difference (2 hours) to be credited as overtime and paid at time and a half.

Computer System Capabilities

In a nutshell, computers are fast, accurate, and reliable; they don't forget anything; and they don't complain. Now, here are the details.

Speed Computers perform various activities by executing instructions. For example, they might multiply the hours worked times the rate of pay. These operations are measured in **milliseconds, microseconds, nanoseconds,** and **picoseconds** (one thousandth, one millionth, one billionth, and one trillionth of a second, respectively). To place computer speeds in perspective, consider that a beam of light travels down the length of this page in about one nanosecond. A millisecond can be sliced into a thousand microseconds, and a microsecond can be sliced into a thousand nanoseconds.

Accuracy Errors do occur in computer-based information systems, but precious few can be directly attributed to the computer system itself. The vast majority can be traced to a program logic error, a procedural error, or erroneous data. These are *human errors.*

Reliability Computer systems are particularly adept at repetitive tasks. They don't take sick days and coffee breaks, and they seldom complain. Anything below 99.9% **uptime,** the time when the computer system is in operation, is usually unacceptable. For some companies, any **downtime** is unacceptable. These companies provide **backup** computers that take over automatically should the main computers fail.

Memory Capability Computer systems have total and instant recall of data and an almost unlimited capacity to store these data. A typical mainframe computer system will have trillions of characters stored and available for instant recall. High-end PCs have immediate access to two or three billion characters of data. To give you a benchmark for comparison, this book contains approximately a million characters.

Computers are very reliable and may run for years without a problem. However, in many companies, work stops when they do go down. At Knight-Ridder Financial every effort has been made to keep the information flowing by minimizing response time to service calls.

1–4   HOW DO WE USE COMPUTERS?

For this discussion, we will classify the uses of computers into eight general categories:

- Information systems/data processing
- Personal computing
- Science, research, and engineering
- Process/device control
- Education
- Computer-aided design
- Entertainment
- Artificial intelligence

Figure 1–4 shows an estimate of how the sum of existing computer capacity is apportioned to each of these general categories.

Information Systems/ Data Processing

The bulk of existing computer power is dedicated to *information systems* and *data processing.* This category includes all uses of computers that support the administrative aspects of an organization. Example applications include payroll systems, airline reservation systems, student registration systems, hospital patient-billing systems, and countless others.

We combine *hardware, software, people, procedures,* and *data* to create an **information system.** A computer-based information system provides an organization with *data processing* capabilities and the knowledge workers in the organization with the *information* they need to make better, more informed decisions.

FIGURE 1–4 The Way We Use Computers   *This pie chart is an estimate of how existing computer capacity is distributed among the general categories of computer usage.*

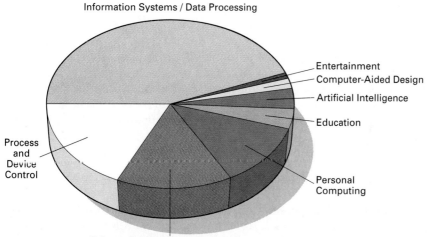

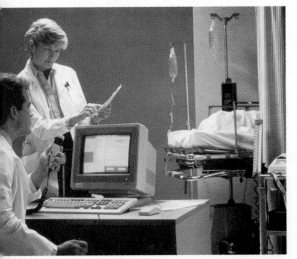

Bedside terminals enable doctors and nurses to enter patient data at the source. Doctors order blood tests, schedule operating rooms, and review medical records while interacting with the hospital's computer system.

An airline reservation system is a classic example of an information system that reflects an up-to-the-minute status. Airline reservation agents communicate with a centralized computer via remote terminals to update the database the moment a seat on any flight is filled or becomes available. An airline reservation system does much more than keep track of flight reservations. Departure and arrival times are closely monitored so that ground-crew activities can be coordinated. The system offers many kinds of management information needs: the number of passenger miles flown, profit per passenger on a particular flight, percent of arrivals on time, average number of empty seats on each flight for each day of the week, and so on. To give you an idea of the size and scope of these systems, American Airlines' Sabre System involves more than 100,000 terminals and printers and can process 1450 transactions per second!

The influence of computer information systems is just as pervasive in hospitals (patient accounting systems), government agencies (revenue administration systems), insurance companies (claims-processing systems), colleges (student registration systems), and other organizations. Can you think of an information system that has touched your life, directly or indirectly, during the past few days?

Personal Computing

Individuals and companies are purchasing small, inexpensive microcomputers for a variety of business and domestic applications. Micros vary in size from those small enough to fit in a coat pocket or a purse to those that sit on, under, or to the side of a desk. All can be controlled by one person. The growth of this general area, called **personal computing,** has surpassed even the most adventurous forecasts of a decade ago. Some high-tech companies actually have more personal computers than telephones.

Domestic Applications for Personal Computing   A variety of domestic and business applications form the foundation of personal computing. Domestic applications include maintaining an up-to-date inventory of household items; storing names and addresses for a personal mailing list; maintaining records for, preparing, and sending income tax returns; creating and monitoring a household budget; keeping an appointment and social calendar; handling household finances (for example, checkbook balancing, paying bills, coupon refunding); writing letters; education; creating graphic invitations and greeting cards; and, of course, entertainment. You can purchase software for all these applications, and you can probably obtain software for your special interest, whether it is astrology, charting biorhythms, genealogy, religion, composing music, cooking, or dieting.

Business Applications for Personal Computing   Inexpensive microcomputers have made automation financially feasible for virtually any business environment. As a result, microcomputer software is available to support thousands of common and not-so-common business applications. There is, of course, an established need for applications such as payroll, accounting, sales analysis, project management, and inventory control. There are also hundreds of industry-specific software packages for thoroughbred breeding, for medical laboratories, for professional football teams, for preowned car dealers, and for just about any other area of business.

The Microcomputer Family of Productivity Software   Microcomputer-based *productivity software* is a series of commercially available programs that can help people at home or knowledge workers in the business community save time and/or get information they need to make more informed decisions. The family of productivity software is the foundation of personal computing in the business world and in the home. Some of the most popular productivity tools include the following:

- *Word processing*. **Word processing software** enables users to enter text, to store it on magnetic storage media, to manipulate it in preparation for output, and to produce a hard copy (printed output).
- *Desktop publishing*. **Desktop publishing software** allows users to produce near-typeset-quality copy for newsletters, advertisements, and many other printing needs, all from the confines of a desktop.
- *Spreadsheet*. **Spreadsheet software** permits users to work with the rows and columns of a matrix (or spreadsheet) of data.
- *Database*. **Database software** permits users to create and maintain a database and to extract information from the database.
- *Graphics*. **Graphics software** facilitates the creation and management of computer-based images such as pie graphs, line drawings, company logos, maps, clip art, blueprints, and just about anything else that can be drawn in the traditional manner.

These software packages are general-purpose in that they provide the framework for many business and personal applications. For example, desktop publishing software can be used to create a company newsletter or a wedding invitation. The function and concepts of these and other productivity tools are described in Chapters 7, 8, and 9.

Information Network Services   Although personal computers are normally used as *stand-alone computer systems,* they can also double as remote *terminals.* This *dual-function* capability provides you with the flexibility to work with the PC as a stand-alone system or to link it with a larger computer and take advantage of its increased capacity. With a PC, you have a world of information at your finger tips. The personal computer can be used with the telephone system to transmit data to and receive data from an **information network.**

A growing trend among personal computer enthusiasts is to subscribe to the services of a commercial information network service, such as CompuServe, GEnie, America Online, or Prodigy. These information networks have one or several large computer systems that offer a variety of information services.

- *News, weather, sports*. Get the latest releases directly from the wire services. You can request general news or news about a specific topic. For example, you can request news about Australia, French politics, the plastics industry, or whatever interests you. You can request a short- or long-term weather fore-

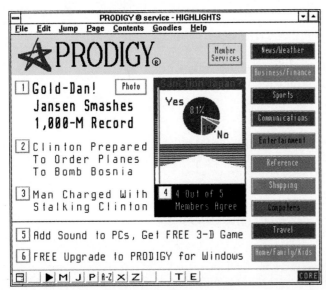

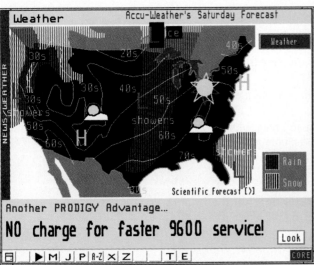

Prodigy, a popular information service, offers literally hundreds of services. The user navigates to a desired service by selecting from one of these families of services: News/Weather, Business/Finance, Sports, Communications, Entertainment, Reference, Shopping, Computers, Travel, and Home/Family/Kids. The highlights screen lets you know about fast-breaking events (top left). Seconds after Dan Jansen won an Olympic gold medal, Prodigy viewers knew about it (top right). Accu-Weather forecasts are continuously updated (bottom left). Movie buffs can get reviews of the latest movies (bottom right).

cast for any region in the world. You can obtain up-to-the-minute scores for college and professional sporting events, or, if you wish, only those of your favorite teams.

- *Entertainment.* Read reviews of the most recently released movies, videos, and records. Chart your biorhythms or ask the advice of an astrologer.

- *Games.* Hundreds of single-player games, such as digital football, and multi-player games, such as MegaWars, are available. You can even play a game of chess with a friend in another state! Or you might prefer to match wits with another trivia buff.

- *Home banking.* Check your account balances, transfer money, and pay bills in the comfort of your home or office.
- *Financial information.* Get up-to-the-minute quotes on stocks, securities, bonds, options, and commodities. You also can use this service to help you manage a securities portfolio and to keep tax records.
- *Brokerage services.* Purchase and sell securities 24 hours a day from your microcomputer.
- *Bulletin boards.* Use special-interest electronic bulletin boards as a forum for the exchange of ideas and information. Information services have hundreds of bulletin-board systems to choose from on topics ranging from gardening to IBM personal computers, to wine, to human sexuality, to computer art, to aviation, to graphics showing the FBI's most wanted fugitives.
- *Electronic mail.* Send electronic mail to and receive it from other users of the information service. Each subscriber is assigned an ID and an electronic mailbox. **E-mail,** another name for electronic mail, sent to a particular subscriber can be "opened" and read only by that subscriber.
- *Shop at home.* Select what you want from a list of thousands of items offered at discount prices. Unless you plan on ordering an automobile or a truck (which you can do), your order is delivered to your doorstep. Payment may be made via **electronic funds transfer (EFT)**; that is, money is exchanged electronically between your account and that of the shopping service.
- *Reference.* Look up items of interest in an electronic encyclopedia. Scan through various government publications. Recall articles on a particular subject from hundreds of newspapers, trade periodicals, and newsletters. Students seeking a college might want to query the service for information about schools of interest.
- *Education.* Choose from a variety of educational packages, from learning arithmetic to preparing for the Scholastic Aptitude Test (SAT). You can even determine your IQ!
- *Real estate.* Moving? Check out available real estate by scanning the listings for the city to which you are moving.
- *Cooking.* Use your micro to access thousands of culinary delights. For example, if you're hungry for a particular type of cuisine, enter appropriate descriptors to obtain a recipe (for example, entree, Spanish, rice, crab).
- *Health.* Address medical questions to a team of top physicians. Diagnose your own illness while interacting with a diagnosis system. Plan and monitor your next diet.
- *Travel.* Plan your own vacation or business trip. You can check airline, train, and cruise schedules and make your own reservations. You can even charter a yacht in the Caribbean, locate the nearest bed-and-breakfast inn, or rent a lodge in the Rockies.

The services provided by information networks are **on-line;** that is, once the user has established a communications link via his or her PC, the end user becomes part of the information network. When on-line, the user interacts directly with the computers in the information network to obtain desired services. When the user terminates the link, the user goes **off-line.** Information networks frequently are referred to as **on-line services.** On-line servces coupled with a vast array of applications software and the capabilities of microcomputer productivity software, eventually should make personal computers a "must-have" item in every home and business.

Science, Research, and Engineering

Engineers and scientists routinely use the computer as a tool in *experimentation, design,* and *development.* Aerospace engineers use computers to simulate the effects of a wind tunnel to analyze the aerodynamics of an airplane prototype. Political scientists collect and analyze demographic data, such as median income and housing starts, to predict voting trends. Computer scientists use software development tools to assist them in creating programs. Chemists use computer graphics to create three-dimensional views of an experimental molecule. Researchers in the field of agriculture use computers to determine the fertilization programs that optimize yields for various crops. Metallurgists rely on computers to analyze stress and shear data as they work to create stronger alloys. There are at least as many science and research applications for the computer as there are scientists and engineers.

Process/Device Control

The number of applications for computer-based **process/device control** is growing rapidly. For example, computers control every step in the oil-refining process and they control thousands of devices from dishwashers to drawbridges. Computers that control processes accept data in a continuous **feedback loop.** In a feedback loop, the process itself generates data that become input to the computer. As the data are received and interpreted by the computer, the computer initiates action to control the ongoing process. An automated traffic-control system is a good example of the continuous feedback loop in a computerized process-control system. Have you ever driven an automobile through a city with an automated traffic-control system? If so, you would soon notice how the traffic signals are coordinated to minimize delays and optimize traffic flow. Traffic sensors are strategically placed throughout the city to feed data continuously to a central computer on the volume and direction of traffic flow (see Figure 1–5). The computer-based control system that activates the traffic signals is programmed to plan ahead. That is, if the sensors locate a group of cars traveling together, traffic signals are then timed accordingly.

All around us (and even inside some of us), computers are controlling devices of every shape and size. Many domestic appliances are equipped with small computers. Your VCR has a small programmable computer. You are programming its computer when you set it to record several of your favorite TV shows during the coming week. On a larger scale, computers control robots that perform the materials-handling duties in five-acre warehouses. These robots, which navigate about the warehouse under computer control on a rail system, pick and place inventory items in bins.

Education

Computers can interact with students to enhance the learning process. Relatively inexpensive hardware capable of multidimensional communication (sound, print, graphics, and color) has resulted in the phenomenal growth of the computer as an educational tool in the home, in the classroom, and in business. Computer-based education will not replace teachers, but educators

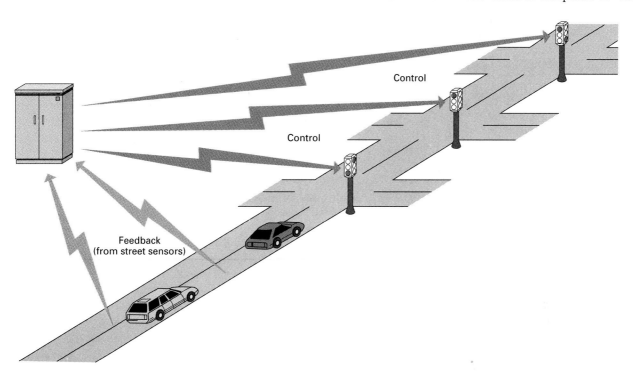

Control

Control

Feedback
(from street sensors)

FIGURE 1–5 An Automated Traffic-Control System   *In a continuous feedback loop, street sensors provide input to a process-control computer system about the direction and volume of traffic flow. Based on their feedback, the system controls the traffic lights to optimize the flow of traffic.*

agree that **computer-based training (CBT)** is having a profound impact on traditional modes of education.

Computers have been used for drill and practice for more than a decade. Only recently has sophisticated CBT been economically feasible. Now powerful personal computers have added a dimension that is not possible with books and traditional classroom lectures. The student controls the pace of learning and can interact directly with the computer system. Through interactive computer graphics, a CBT system can show certain concepts more effectively than can books or even teachers. The teacher–book–CBT approach has spawned a new era in education.

Available CBT programs can help you learn keyboarding skills, increase your vocabulary, study algebra, learn about the makeup of the atom, and practice your Russian. These are just the tips of the CBT iceberg.

Computer-Aided Design

Computer-aided design (CAD) is using the computer in the design process. CAD systems enable the creation and manipulation of an on-screen graphic image. CAD systems provide a sophisticated array of tools enabling designers to create three-dimensional objects that can be flipped, rotated, resized, viewed in detail, examined internally or externally, and much more. At a minimum, a CAD hardware configuration will include a high-performance computer, a large monitor, and a variety of point-and-draw input devices. High-end micros and all larger computers can run CAD applications.

Computer-aided design (CAD) has revolutionized the way in which engineers and scientists design, draft, and document a product. With CAD, most of the "bugs" can be worked out of a design before a structure is built.

CAD has all but eliminated the drawing table in many occupations. Engineers use CAD to design everything from toasters to locomotives. Architects use CAD to draw elevations and floor plans. Integrated circuit (chip) designers keep track of thousands of interconnected transistors with CAD. Software engineers use CAD to create graphic depictions of information systems. Chemists use CAD to examine the molecular structure of compounds. Photographs in this chapter and throughout the book illustrate a variety of CAD applications.

Entertainment

More applications are being created that tickle our fancy and entertain us.

- You can buy a computer chess opponent in the form of a board, chess pieces, and a miniature robotic arm that moves the pieces (you have to move your own pieces).
- The debonair thief, Carmen Sandiego, of computer games fame, thrills children with the chase to find her, while teaching them history and geography.
- For 85 years, going to the movies has been a passive activity. However, the interactive film is on the horizon. The first interactive film, *I'm Your Man,* premiered in 1992. Seats in the movie theater are outfitted with pistol grips, each with several buttons. At various times during the movie, the audience uses the buttons to vote on plot options, such as a character's fate and even the ending of the movie. The movie progresses based on the consensus opinion of the audience. By all accounts *I'm Your Man* is a big success. During the coming years we'll have a choice: We can go to traditional movies that do not involve the audience or we can be a part of the movie.

Artificial Intelligence

Human Beings Are Born, Not Manufactured   Today's computers can simulate many human capabilities such as reaching, grasping, calculating, speaking, remembering, comparing numbers, and drawing. Researchers are working to expand these capabilities and, therefore, the power of computers by developing hardware and software that can imitate intelligent human behavior. For example, researchers are working on systems that have the ability to reason, to learn or accumulate knowledge, to strive for self-improvement, and to simulate human sensory and mechanical capabilities. This general area of research is known as **artificial intelligence (AI)**.

Of course, computers will never be capable of simulating the distinctly human qualities of creativity, humor, and emotions! However, computers can drive machines that mimic human movements (such as picking up objects and placing them at a prescribed location) and provide the "brains" for systems that simulate the human thought process within the domain of a particular area of expertise (tax preparation, medical diagnosis, and so on).

Categories of Artificial Intelligence   Research in the field of artificial intelligence can be divided into four categories

Many traditional forms of entertainment are being made available for the computer. For example, if you wish to work a crossword puzzle, you can open the newspaper or you can turn on your computer.

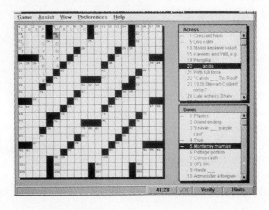

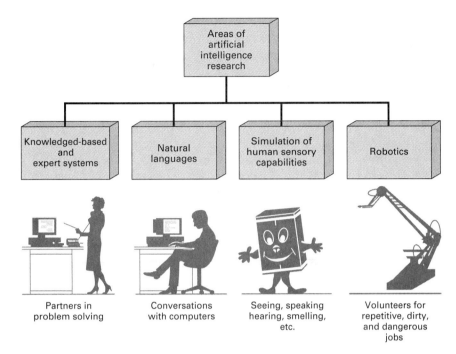

FIGURE 1–6 Categories of Artificial Intelligence

(see Figure 1–6): knowledge-based and expert systems, natural languages, simulation of human sensory capabilities, and robotics.

Knowledge-based and expert systems.   A **knowledge-based system** relies on a **knowledge base** filled with "rules of thumb" (intuition, judgment, and inferences) about a specific application area, such as automobile repair. Humans can use the knowledge-based system and the IF-THEN rules in the knowledge base to help them solve a particular problem. **Expert systems** are the most sophisticated application of a knowledge-based system. Once the knowledge of one or more human experts has been entered to an expert system's knowledge base, users can tap this knowledge by interacting with the system in much the same way they would interact with a human expert in that field. Both the user and the computer-based expert system ask and respond to each other's questions until a problem is resolved.

Expert systems are beginning to have a major influence on the way people in the business community make decisions. In recent years, expert systems have been developed to support decision makers in a broad range of disciplines, including automobile repair, medical diagnosis, oil exploration, financial planning, chemical analysis, surgery, locomotive repair, weather prediction, computer repair, trouble-shooting satellites, computer systems configuration, operation of nuclear power plants, newspaper layout, interpreting government regulations, tax preparation, and many others.

Natural languages.   **Natural languages** refer to software that enables computer systems to accept, interpret, and execute instructions in the native, or "natural," language of the end user, typically English. For example, the end user uses a natural language when he or she enters brief English commands such as "Show me a pie chart for regional sales" to a computer system. There are, of course, limitations on the complexity of the commands that can be in-

The precise, untiring movement of computer-controlled industrial robots helps insure the flow of work during production. Here a robot transfers materials in a pick-and-place application.

terpreted. The state of the art of natural languages is still primitive. Most commercial natural languages are designed to provide end users with a means of communicating with a corporate database or an expert system.

Simulation of human sensory capabilities.   One area of AI research involves computer simulation of human capabilities. This area focuses on equipping computer systems with the capabilities of seeing, hearing, speaking, and feeling (touching). These artificial intelligence capabilities are possible with current technology, to varying degrees. For example, some automobiles employ synthesized voice messages to warn the driver and passengers of problems: Have you ever heard, "A door is open"? Several of these capabilities are discussed in Chapter 4, "Input/Output Devices."

Robotics.   **Robotics** is the integration of computers and **robots.** Robots have many applications. In industry, industrial robots, which are usually equipped with an arm and a hand, can be "taught" to perform almost any repetitive manipulative task. These tasks could include painting a car, screwing on a bolt, moving material, and even such complex tasks as inspecting a manufactured part for defects. In medicine, surgeons use the precision of robots to help with brain and eye surgery. In law enforcement, police use mobile robots to remove and defuse bombs.

Summary

The amount of computing capacity in the world is doubling every two years. The number and sophistication of applications are growing rapidly with the increase in the number of computers and their capabilities. However, in the years ahead, look for personal computing, education, and artificial intelligence to become larger shares of the computer "pie."

*I*MPORTANT TERMS AND SUMMARY OUTLINE

artificial intelligence (AI)	electronic funds transfer (EFT)	input
backup	electronic mail (E-mail)	input/output (I/O)
bulletin-board systems (BBS)	end user	input/output-bound
computer	expert system	keyboard
computer-aided design (CAD)	feedback loop	knowledge base
computer-based training (CBT)	graphics software	knowledge-based system
computer competency	groupware	knowledge worker
computer network	hard copy	laptop PC
computer system	hardware	magnetic disk
computerese	information	mainframe computer
data	information network	master file
database software	information society	microcomputer (micro)
desktop PC	information superhighway	microsecond
desktop publishing software	information system	millisecond
downtime	information technology (IT)	minicomputer (mini)

monitor	personal computing	software
mouse	personal digital assistant (PDA)	source document
multiuser micro	picosecond	spreadsheet software
nanosecond	pocket PC	supercomputer
natural language	printer	terminal
notebook PC	process/device control	tower PC
offline	processor	uptime
on-line	processor-bound	user
on-line service	programs	user-friendly
output	record	video display terminal (VDT)
palmtop PC	robotics	word processing software
pen-based PC	robots	workgroup computing
personal computer (PC)	soft copy	workstation

1–1   The Information Society After the turn of the century we can anticipate traveling the **information superhighway,** a network of high-speed data communications links that eventually will connect virtually every facet of our society. Today, one in four Americans has a general-purpose computer, usually a **personal computer (PC).** This widespread availability has resulted in an explosion of applications for computers.

Computer competency is emerging as a universal goal in the **information society.** Computer-competent people know how to purchase, use, and operate a computer system, and how to make it work for them. The computer-competent person is also aware of the computer's impact on society and is conversant in **computerese.**

In an information society, **knowledge workers** focus their energies on providing a myriad of information services. The knowledge worker's job function revolves around the use, manipulation, and dissemination of information.

Software refers collectively to a set of machine-readable instructions, called **programs,** that cause the computer to perform desired functions. Computers and computer equipment, which accept **input** and provide **output,** are called **hardware.**

The computer revolution is transforming the way we communicate, do business, and learn. This technological revolution is having a profound impact on the business community and on our private and professional lives. For example, increasingly, we communicate with our colleagues at work through **electronic mail (E-mail)** or with our on-line friends through **bulletin-board systems (BBSs).**

Through the 1970s, **end users,** or simply **users,** would relate their information needs to computer professionals who would then work with the computer system to generate the necessary information. **User-friendly** computer systems and software minimize the need for users to go through a computer professional.

Data, which all of us create and use every day, are the raw materials from which information is derived. **Information** consists of data collected and processed into a meaningful form.

Learning about computers is an adventure that will last a lifetime, as **information technology (IT),** the integration of computing technology and information processing, is changing daily.

1–2   Networking: Bringing People Together We now live in a global village in which computers and people are linked within companies and between countries. Most existing computers are part of a **computer network,** the sharing of resources and information. Computer networks permit the formation of workgroups that cooperate through **workgroup computing** and the use of special software, called **groupware.**

1–3   Uncovering the "Mystery" of Computers The **computer,** or **processor,** is an electronic device capable of interpreting and executing programmed commands for input, output, computation, and logic operations.

The differences in the various categories of computers are very much a matter of scale. **Minicomputers (minis)** have greater computing capacities than personal computers, also called **microcomputers (micros). Mainframe computers** have greater computing capacities than minicomputers. And **supercomputers** have greater computing capacities than mainframe computers. Depending on their sophistication, a **workstation's** computing capacity falls somewhere between that of a micro and a mainframe. All **computer systems,** no matter how small or large, have the same fundamental capabilities—*processing, storage, input,* and *output.*

Personal computers come in four different physical sizes: **pocket PCs (palmtop), laptop PCs** (small ones are **notebook PCs**), **desktop PCs,** and **tower PCs.** Pocket and laptop PCs are considered portable. **Pen-based PCs** use electronic pens instead of keyboards. **Personal digital assistants (PDAs)** are hand-held personal computers that support a variety of personal information systems. **Multiuser micros,** which are configured with as many as a dozen VDTs, permit several people to use the system at once. A **video display terminal (VDT),** or simply **terminal,** has a **keyboard** for input and a televisionlike (video) screen, called a **monitor,** for output.

Besides size and capability, the single most distinguishing characteristic of the various types of computers is the manner in which each type is used. Although all computers can be networked with one another and share resources, generally, PCs and workstations service a single user and all others service multiple users. Users on multiuser computer systems interact via terminals.

Supercomputers primarily address applications that are **processor-bound,** where mainframe computers address **input/output-bound** applications.

The data are stored on the **master file,** which is made up of **records.** The **source document** is the original document from which data are entered.

Computer system capabilities are either input/output or processing. Processing capabilities are subdivided into computation and logic operations. A computer system has only four fundamental components: input (for example, via a point-and-draw device such as a **mouse**), processing (executing a program), output (via a **printer**), and storage (for example, **magnetic disk**). There is a variety of **input/output** (**I/O**) and storage devices. A monitor's output is **soft copy** and a printer's output is **hard copy.**

The computer is fast, accurate, reliable, and has an enormous memory capacity. Computer operations are measured in **milliseconds, microseconds, nanoseconds,** and **picoseconds.** For some companies, any **downtime** (versus **uptime**) is unacceptable. These companies provide **backup** computers that take over automatically should the main computers fail.

1–4 How Do We Use Computers? The uses of computers can be classified into eight general categories:

- *Information systems/data processing.* The computer is used to process data and produce business information. Hardware, software, people, procedures, and data are combined to create an **information system.**
- *Personal computing.* The single-user micro is used by individuals for a variety of business and domestic applications, including such productivity tools as **word processing software, desktop publishing software, spreadsheet soft-**ware, **database software,** and **graphics software.** This area of computing is often referred to as **personal computing.** The dual-function personal computers can be used with the telephone system to transmit data to and receive data from an **information network.** Information networks, or **on-line services,** permit such applications as **E-mail** and home shopping where payment may be made via **electronic funds transfer** (**EFT**). When the user terminates the link with an **on-line** service, the user goes **off-line.**

- *Science, research, and engineering.* The computer is used as a tool in experimentation, design, and development.
- *Process/device control.* Applications that involve computer-based **process/device control** accept data in a continuous **feedback loop.**
- *Education.* The computer interacts with students to enhance the learning process. **Computer-based training** (**CBT**) is having a profound impact on traditional modes of education.
- *Computer-aided design.* **Computer-aided design** (**CAD**) is using the computer in the design process. CAD systems enable the creation and manipulation of an on-screen graphic image.
- *Entertainment.* Every day, computer applications are being designed and created just to entertain us.
- *Artificial intelligence.* **Artificial intelligence** (**AI**) is the area of research that involves creating computer systems with the ability to reason, to learn or accumulate knowledge, to strive for self-improvement, and to simulate human sensory and mechanical capabilities. There are four categories of AI research: **knowledge-based systems,** which rely on a **knowledge base,** and **expert systems; natural languages;** simulation of human sensory capabilities; and **robotics** (the integration of computers and **robots**).

REVIEW EXERCISES

Concepts

1. What are the four fundamental components of a computer system?
2. Which component of a computer system executes the program?
3. Name the four categories of artificial intelligence research.
4. Associate the following with the appropriate category of computer usage: continuous feedback loop, experimentation, home use, CBT, synthesized

speech, architectural design, and business information systems.

5. Compare the information processing capabilities of human beings to those of computers with respect to speed, accuracy, reliability, and memory capability.

6. What term is used to describe the integration of computers and robots?

7. In terms of physical size, how are PCs categorized?

8. Describe the relationship between data and information.

9. Within the context of a computer system, what is meant by *read* and *write*?

10. Name five microcomputer productivity tools.

11. Which microcomputer productivity tool would be most helpful in writing a term paper? Explain.

12. List at least six information network services.

13. The operational capabilities of a computer system include what two types of processing operations?

14. What term is used to describe the integration of computers and information processing?

Discussion

15. The computer has had far-reaching effects on our lives. How has the computer affected your life?

16. What is your concept of computer competency? In what ways do you think achieving computer competency will affect your domestic life? Your business life?

17. At what age should computer-competency education begin?

18. Discuss how the complexion of jobs will change as we evolve from an industrial society into an information society. Give several examples.

19. The use of computers tends to stifle creativity. Argue for or against this statement.

20. Comment on how computers are changing our traditional patterns of personal communication.

21. Comment on how computers are changing our traditional patterns of recreation.

SELF-TEST (BY SECTION)

1–1 a. To be computer-competent, you must be able to write computer programs. (T/F)

b. A person whose job revolves around the use, manipulation, and dissemination of information is called: (a) a computerphobe, (b) a knowledge worker, or (c) a data expert?

c. _data_ are the raw materials from which _info_ is derived.

1–2 The _workgroup_ is any group of people linked by a computer network.

1–3 a. A printer is an example of which of the four computer system components? output

b. The four size categories of personal computers are miniature, portable, notebook, and business. (T/F)

c. The two types of processing operations performed by computers are _logic_ and _computations_

d. A microsecond is 1000 times longer than a nanosecond. (T/F)

1–4 a. Desktop publishing refers to the capability of producing _near type set_ copy from the confines of a desktop.

b. What type of computer-based system relies on a knowledge base to provide users with expert advice: (a) an expert system, (b) a master system, or (c) an intelligent system?

c. The greatest amount of available computing capacity is dedicated to the information systems/data processing category of computer usage. (T/F)

d. The microcomputer productivity tool that manipulates data organized in a tabular structure of rows and columns is called a _spreadsheet_

e. Artificial intelligence refers to an area of research that uses computers to simulate human capabilities. (T/F)

Self-test answers.   **1–1 (a)** F; **(b)** b; **(c)** Data, information. **1–2** workgroup. **1–3 (a)** output; **(b)** F; **(c)** computation, logic; **(d)** T. **1–4 (a)** near-typeset-quality; **(b)** a; **(c)** T; **(d)** spreadsheet; **(e)** T.

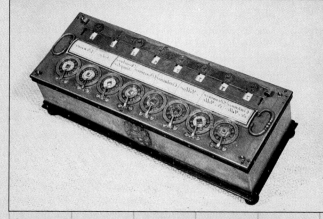

The Abacus The abacus was probably the original mechanical counting device, and its effectiveness has withstood the test of time. It is still used to illustrate the principles of counting.

The Pascaline Pascal's invention, the Pascaline, used gear-driven counting wheels to do addition. He built the Pascaline to help his father, a tax collector, calculate tax revenues. The numbers for each digit position were arranged on wheels so that a single revolution of one wheel resulted in one tenth of a revolution of the wheel to its immediate left.

Blaise Pascal French philosopher and mathematician Blaise Pascal (1623–1662) invented and built the first mechanical adding machine. Pascal's early work with mechanical calculators is recognized today by the popular computer programming language that bears his name.

Jacquard's Loom The Jacquard weaving loom was invented by the Frenchmen Joseph-Marie Jacquard (1753-1834) and is still in use today. It is controlled by cards in which holes are strategically punched. The punched cards are sequenced to indicate a particular weaving design.

Charles Babbage Concepts used in today's general-purpose computer were introduced over a century ago by Charles Babbage (1793–1871), an English visionary and Cambridge professor.

Difference Engine Charles Babbage advanced the state of computational hardware by inventing a "difference engine" that was capable of computing mathematical tables. Unfortunately, he completed only a part of his difference engine (shown here). While working on it, Babbage conceived the idea of an "analytical engine." In essence, this was a general-purpose computer. As designed, his analytical engine would add, subtract, multiply, and divide in automatic sequence at a rate of 60 additions per minute. His 1833 design called for thousands of gears and drives that would cover the area of a football field and be powered by a locomotive engine. Babbage worked on his analytical engine until his death.

Lady Ada Lovelace Lady Ada Augusta Lovelace suggested that punched cards could be prepared that would instruct Babbage's engine to repeat certain operations. Because of her suggestion, some people call Lady Lovelace the first programmer.

Punched-Card Tabulating Machine The U.S. Bureau of the Census did not complete the 1880 census until almost 1888. Bureau management concluded that before long, the 10-year census would take more than 10 years to complete! The Census Bureau commissioned Herman Hollerith to apply his expertise in the use of punched cards to the 1890 census. With punched-card processing and Hollerith's *punched-card tabulating machine*, the census was completed in just three years and his process saved the bureau over $5,000,000. Thus began the emergence of automated data processing.

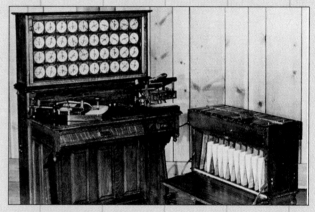

Dr. Herman Hollerith Herman Hollerith, a statistician, applied for a patent for a punched-card tabulating machine. Hollerith's idea for the punched card came not from Jacquard or Babbage but from "punch photography." Railroads of the day issued tickets with physical descriptions of the passengers. A conductor would punch holes in a ticket that noted a passenger's hair and eye color and the nose shape. Hollerith's daughter later said, "This gave him the idea for making a punch photograph of every person to be tabulated," which he later applied to taking the 1890 census. The patent was issued in 1889.

The EAM Era For decades through the mid-1950s, punched-card technology improved with the addition of more punched-card devices and more sophisticated capabilities. The electromechanical accounting machine (EAM) family of punched-card devices includes the card punch, verifier, reproducer, summary punch, interpreter, sorter, collator, calculator, and the accounting machine. Most of the devices in this 1940s machine room were "programmed" to perform a particular operation by the insertion of a prewired control panel. A machine-room operator in a punched-card installation had a physically demanding job. Punched cards and printed output were moved from one device to the next on hand trucks.

IBM's First Headquarters Building In 1896 Herman Hollerith founded the Tabulating Machine Company which, in 1911, merged with several other companies to form the Computing-Tabulating-Recording Company. In 1924 the company's general manager, Thomas J. Watson, changed its name to International Business Machines Corporation and moved into this building.

Dr. John Atanasoff During the years 1935 to 1938, Dr. John V. Atanasoff, a professor at Iowa State University, had begun to think about a machine that could reduce the time it took for him and his physics students to make long, complicated mathematical calculations. The decisions he made about such concepts as an electronic medium with vacuum tubes, the base-2 numbering system, memory, and logic circuits set the direction for the development of the modern computer.

The Mark I The first electromechanical computer, called the *Mark I*, was the result of IBM-sponsored research. Howard Aiken, a Harvard University professor, completed the Mark I in 1944. It was essentially a serial collection of electromechanical calculators and had many similarities to Babbage's analytical engine. (Aiken was unaware of Babbage's work.) The Mark I was a significant improvement in the state of the art, but IBM's management still felt that electromechanical computers would not replace punched-card equipment.

The ABC In 1939 Dr. Atanasoff and one of his graduate students, Clifford E. Berry, assembled a prototype of the ABC (Atanasoff Berry Computer), which by 1942 evolved into the working model shown here. However, Iowa State, the business world, and the scientific community showed little interest in the ABC. For example, when Dr. Atanasoff contacted IBM about what he called his "computing machine proper," the company responded that "IBM never will be interested in an electronic computing machine." A 1973 federal court ruling officially credited Atanasoff with the invention of the automatic electronic digital computer.

The ENIAC Dr. John W. Mauchly (middle) collaborated with J. Presper Eckert, Jr. (foreground), to develop a machine that would compute trajectory tables for the U.S. Army. The end product, a large-scale, fully operational electronic computer, was completed in 1946 and named the ENIAC (Electronic Numerical Integrator and Computer). The ENIAC (shown here), a thousand times faster than its electromechanical predecessors, signaled a major breakthrough in computer technology. It weighed 30 tons and occupied 15,000 square feet of floor space. With over 18,000 vacuum tubes, the ENIAC needed a huge amount of electricity. Legend has it that the ENIAC, built at the University of Pennsylvania, dimmed the lights of Philadelphia whenever it was activated. Because of its imposing scale, electronic components, and wide applicability, the ENIAC is generally considered the first functional electronic digital computer.

The Univac I and the First Generation of Computers The first generation of computers (1951-1959), which is characterized by vacuum tubes, is generally thought to have started with the introduction of the first

commercially viable electronic digital computer. The Universal Automatic Computer (UNIVAC I for short), developed by Mauchly and Eckert for the Remington-Rand Corporation, was installed in the U.S. Bureau of the Census in 1951. Later that year, CBS News gave the UNIVAC I national exposure when it correctly predicted Dwight Eisenhower's victory over Adlai Stevenson in the presidential election with only 5% of the votes counted. Shown here is Mr. Eckert instructing news anchor Walter Cronkite in the use of the UNIVAC I.

The IBM 650 Not until the success of the UNIVAC I did IBM make the decision and the commitment to develop and market computers. IBM's first entry into the commercial computer market was the IBM 701 in 1953. However, the IBM 650 (shown here), introduced in 1954, is probably the reason that IBM enjoys such a healthy share of today's computer market. Unlike some of its competitors, the IBM 650 was designed as a logical upgrade to existing punched-card machines. IBM management went out on a limb and estimated sales of 50, a figure that was greater than the number of installed computers in the United States at the time. IBM actually installed more than 1000. The rest is history.

The Honeywell 400 and the Second Generation of Computers The invention of the transistor signaled the start of the second generation of computers (1959–64). The transistor meant more powerful, more reliable, and less expensive computers that would occupy less space and give off less heat than vacuum-tubed-powered computers did. Honeywell (the *Honeywell 400* is shown here) established itself as a major player in the second generation of computers. Burroughs, Univac, NCR, CDC, and Honeywell–IBM's biggest competitors during the 1960s and early 1970s–became known as the BUNCH (the first initial of each name).

The IBM System 360 and the Third Generation of Computers What some computer historians consider the single most important event in the history of computers occurred when IBM announced its *System 360* line of computers on April 7, 1964. The System 360 ushered in the third generation of computers (1964–71). Integrated circuits did for the third-generation of computers what transistors did for the second generation. *Business Week* reported IBM's announcement of its System 360 line of computers, saying that "In the annals of major product changes, it is like Ford's switch from the Model T to the Model A." The System 360s and the third-generation computers of other manufacturers made all previously installed computers obsolete.

The PDP-8 During the 1950s and early 1960s, only the largest companies could afford the six- and seven-digit price tags of mainframe computers. In 1963 Digital Equipment Corporation introduced the *PDP-8* (shown here). It is generally considered the first successful minicomputer. At $18,000, the transistor-based PDP-8 was an instant hit. It confirmed the tremendous demand for small computers for business and scientific applications. By 1971 over 25 firms were manufacturing minicomputers. Digital and Data General Corporation took an early lead in the sale and manufacture of minis.

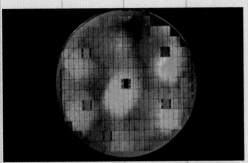

Integrated Circuits and the Fourth Generation of Computers Most computer vendors classify their computers as fourth generation. Some people prefer to pinpoint 1971 as the start of the fourth generation of computers, with the introduction of large-scale integration (more circuits per unit space) of electronic circuitry. The base technology of today's computers is still the integrated circuit. This is not to say that two decades have passed without any significant innovations. In truth, the computer industry has experienced a mind-boggling succession of advances in the further miniaturization of circuitry, data communications, the design of computer hardware and software and input/output devices.

The IBM PC In 1981 IBM tossed its hat into the personal computer ring with the announcement of the *IBM PC*. In the first year, 35,000 were sold. In 1982, 800,000 were sold, and the IBM PC was well on its way to becoming the standard for the micro industry. When software vendors began to orient their products to the IBM PC, many microcomputer manufacturers created and sold clones of the IBM PC. These clones, called *IBM-PC compatibles*, run most or all the software designed for the IBM PC.

The Apple II Not until 1975 and the introduction of the *Altair 8800* personal computer was computing made available to individuals and very small companies. This event has forever changed how society perceives computers. Certainly the most prominent entrepreneurial venture during the early years of personal computers was the *Apple II* computer (shown here). Two young computer enthusiasts, Steven Jobs and Steve Wozniak (then 21 and 26 years of age, respectively), collaborated to create and build their Apple II computer on a makeshift production line in Jobs' garage. Seven years later, Apple Computer earned a spot on the Fortune 500, a list of the 500 largest corporations in the United States.

2

INTERACTING WITH COMPUTERS

OBJECTIVES

To understand the scope of knowledge needed to interact effectively with a personal computer.

To distinguish between the three categories of software: general-purpose, applications, and system software.

To understand the difference between text-based and graphics-based software.

To describe the characteristics and functionality of a graphical user interface (GUI).

To describe various keyboard, mouse, and data entry conventions.

To grasp concepts related to the effective use of computers and software.

2–1   PC MAGIC

The PC has worked its magic on millions of people. Personal computers are everywhere, from kindergartens to corporate boardrooms. You can see them at work, at school, and possibly in your own home. Each passing month brings more power at less expense and an expansion to the seemingly endless array of microcomputer applications. A personal computer can be an electronic version of a scratch pad, a file cabinet, a drawing board, a teacher, a typewriter, a musical instrument, and even a friend. It can help you think logically, improve your spelling, select the right word, expand your memory, organize data, add numbers, and much more.

The relatively low cost and almost unlimited applications for the microcomputer have made it the darling of the computer industry, and, indeed, the entire business/education community. Twenty years ago very few people had heard of a microcomputer. Now the number of microcomputers sold in one month exceeds the total number of operational computers in existence in the United States 20 years ago.

This chapter is intended to give you some insight into the fundamental concepts you will need to know to interact effectively with computers, especially PCs. Although the discussion centers on PCs, the concepts can be applied to workstations and VDTs as well.

2–2   INTERACTING WITH THE SYSTEM

Our Interface with the Computer: Micros, Workstations, and VDTs

The thesaurus lists these synonyms for the word *interact: blend, associate, hobnob, mingle, combine, mix, stir,* and *socialize.* To some extent we do all these, even socialize, when we *interact* with PCs. Most of us will interact directly with a personal computer or a workstation. Or we will interact with a video display terminal (VDT) linked to a mini, a mainframe, or a supercomputer in a remote location. From an end user's perspective, interaction with

Computers are interactive—that is, in their own special way they can communicate with human beings. This capability makes them excellent educational tools. Computers help us learn about physics (shown here) and everything else from auto mechanics to zoology.

workstations is similar to interacting with PCs, the primary difference being the keyboard layout and the point-and-draw devices used. In addition, the look and feel of a modern VDT is very much like that of the PC, except that the actual processing is done on a remote computer.

The terminal, by definition, is part of a computer network. However, both the PC and the workstation can function as stand-alone computers or as part of a network. The concepts associated with computer interaction apply to both circumstances, whether you have total control of a single-user system or are an end user in a computer network.

TAILORING PCs TO THE NEEDS OF MOBILE WORKERS

Thousands of mobile workers could benefit from using a computer—if only the computer were lighter, freed their hands, and didn't tether them to a desk or a power outlet. Now a new generation of wearable computers promises to extend the trend begun by laptop, notebook, and pen-based computers.

Prototypes of wearable computers, long a staple of science fiction, are already being promoted by Japan's NEC Corporation. In an effort to create truly personal computers that meld a computer and its user, NEC designers have divided the PC's components into cable-connected modules that fit into headsets, drape across shoulders, hang around the neck, and fasten around the waist, forearm, or wrist. Lightweight (about two pounds or less), the components would be covered in soft plastic and strapped on with Velcro.

Many of these prototypes combine existing or emerging technologies to create customized PCs for specific types of workers. The TLC (Tender Loving Care) PC for paramedics is a good example. At an accident scene, speech-recognition software would let the paramedic dictate symptoms and vital signs into a slender microphone hanging from a headset. The computer, draped across the medic's shoulders like a shawl, would compare this data to a CD-ROM medical directory in the shoulder unit. The computer would then project possible diagnoses and

suggested treatments onto the headset's goggle-type display. The TLC unit would also improve upon the two-way radio medics now use to communicate with emergency-room doctors. Instead of describing symptoms over a two-way radio, medics could use a track-ball-operated video camera and body sensor strapped to their palm to *show* doctors the patients' condition. The video and additional data would be beamed to the doctors by a satellite link on the medics' back. Headphones would let the medics get feedback and additional advice from the waiting doctors.

Given the industry's ongoing success in miniaturizing electronics and developing more powerful but lightweight batteries, NEC projects the first commercially viable wearable PCs could appear by the late 1990s. However, Grid Systems Corporation, pioneer of the pen-based computer, isn't waiting. It recently introduced the Palmpad, a rugged 2.8-pound computer designed to be worn on a belt, slung over a shoulder, or strapped to a wrist. Perhaps by the twenty-first century, the PC will become as much an essential part of one's wardrobe as an indispensable business tool.

The Future of PCs? *At NEC a handful of engineers and designers are creating what they believe to be the future of PCs— wearable PCs. Their objective is to blend the machine with the body.*

What Do You Need to Know?

To interact effectively with a computer, you need to be knowledgeable in four areas.

1. General software concepts (for example, windows, menus, uploading, and so on)
2. The operation and use of the hardware over which you have control (such as the PC, magnetic disk, and printer)
3. The function and use of the computer's operating system and/or its **graphical user interface,** both of which provide a link between you, the computer system, and the various applications programs (for example, a Lotus 1-2-3 spreadsheet program, an inventory management system)
4. The specific applications programs you are using

The first three areas are prerequisites to the fourth; that is, you will need a working knowledge of software concepts, hardware, and the operating system and/or a **GUI** (graphical user interface) before you can make effective use of Quicken (accounting), Harvard Graphics (presentation graphics), Paradox (database), or any of the thousands of software packages on the market today. We discuss the first two topics in this book. We also discuss concepts associated with operating systems, GUIs, and common applications programs. Tutorials and exercises in supplemental material to this book teach you how to use specific operating systems, GUIs (for example, Microsoft Windows), and general-purpose programs, such as WordPerfect (word processing) and Pagemaker (desktop publishing).

What we need to know to interact with computers is constantly changing. Workers at McKesson Corporation wear their PCs. The wearable PCs weigh 13 ounces, fit over the hand and forearm, contain a small screen and keypad, and can scan bar codes. This receiving clerk can read bar codes and enter data while keeping both hands free to lift and move shipping containers.

2–3   CATEGORIES OF SOFTWARE: KNOWING THE ROOMS IN THE HOUSE

We use the term *software* to refer to programs that direct the activities of the computer system. There are, however, different types of software. If you know what type of software you are using at any given time, you have a better understanding of where you are with respect to other software on your system. It's a lot like being in a big house. If you know where you are and the layout of the house, you can move about the house with ease.

Software falls into three major categories: *general-purpose software, applications software,* and *system software.* Figure 2–1 illustrates examples of and the relationship between the categories of software.

General-Purpose Software

General-purpose software provides the framework for many business, scientific, and personal applications. Spreadsheet, computer-aided design (CAD), and word processing software fall into this category. Most general-purpose software is sold as a package—that is, with software and user-oriented documentation (reference manuals, keyboard templates, and so on). It is then up to the user of the software to create the application. For example, a manager can use spreadsheet software to create *templates* (models) for summarizing sales and maintaining the office's fixed inventory. An aeronautical engineer can use CAD software to design an airplane or an airport.

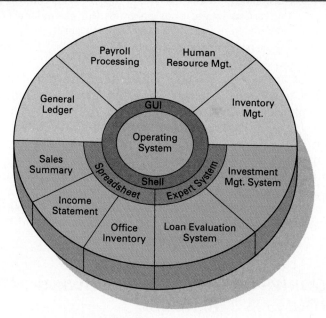

SOFTWARE EXAMPLES		
General-Purpose	Applications	System
Word Processing Spreadsheet Expert System Shell Paint and Draw Desktop Publishing Presentation Graphics Computer-Aided Design Database	Payroll Processing Inventory Mgt. Class Scheduling Human Resource Mgt. Insurance Claims Proc. Utility Billing General Ledger	Operating System Programming Language Compiler/interpreter Database Mgt. System (DBMS) Utility Performance Monitoring Communications Graphical User Interface (GUI)

FIGURE 2–1 Categories of Software *This figure illustrates examples of the various categories of software (top) and the relationship between the categories (bottom).*

Applications Software

Applications software is designed and written to perform specific personal, business, or scientific processing tasks, such as payroll processing, human resource management, or inventory management. Notice that all these applications process data (receipt of materials) and generate information (payroll register) for the user.

System Software

System software is independent of any general-purpose software package or any specific application area. Software in this category controls or in some way supports software in the other two. The operating system and the GUI play a central role in all interaction with the computer. These two important pieces of system software are introduced in this chapter.

The Operating System The nucleus of any computer system is its *operating system* (see Figure 2-1). The operating system monitors and controls all

At this BBC television station, a newsroom automation system controls programming flow, monitors the electronic teleprompter display, and operates studio camera movement through robotics. This newsroom system is a good example of applications software.

input/output and processing activities within a computer system. All hardware and software, including micro productivity software, are under the control of the operating system. Micro and workstation users, in particular, need a working knowledge of their computer's operating system so they can interface their applications programs with the hardware.

The operating system is the first program to be loaded to any general-purpose computer system. Most dedicated computers, such as those that control appliances and electronic games, are controlled by a single program and do not need an operating system.

Popular operating systems for micros include:

- *MS-DOS (Microsoft Corporation).* **MS-DOS** is the operating system used with IBM-compatible personal computers.
- *Macintosh System (Apple Computer, Inc.).* **Macintosh System** is the operating system for the Macintosh line of computers.
- *Operating System/2, or OS/2 (Microsoft/IBM).* **OS/2** is a sophisticated alternative of MS-DOS.
- *UNIX (AT&T).* Originally a mainframe operating system, **UNIX** and its spin-offs, such as **XENIX** and **AIX,** are used frequently with multiuser microcomputers. UNIX is the dominant operating system for workstations.

Although these operating systems accomplish similar functions, what we actually see on the display and the manner in which we interact with them is quite different.

Besides controlling the ongoing operation of microcomputer systems and other types of computer systems, the operating system has two other important functions.

- *Input/output control.* The operating system facilitates the movement of data between peripheral devices, the processor, programs, and the computer's storage.

■ *File and disk management.* The operating system and its file and disk management utility programs enable users to perform such tasks as making backup copies of work disks, erasing disk files that are no longer needed, making inquiries about the number and type of files on a particular disk, and preparing new disks for use. The operating system also handles many file- and disk-oriented tasks that are *transparent* (invisible) to the end user. For example, operating systems keep track of the physical location of disk files so that we, as users, need only refer to them by name (for example, *myfile*) when loading them from disk for processing.

The Graphical User Interface To appreciate the impact and significance of graphical user interfaces (see Figure 2–1), you need to understand what preceded them.

Text-based software. Through the 1980s, the most popular microcomputer operating system, MS-DOS, was strictly *text-based, command-driven* software. That is, we issued commands directly to "DOS" (rhymes with *boss*) by entering them on the keyboard, one character at a time. For example, if you had wished to issue a command to copy a word processing document from one disk to another for your friend, you might have entered "copy c:\myfile a:\yourfile" via the keyboard at the DOS prompt, "C:\>".

C:\> **copy c:\myfile a:\yourfile**

A typical text-based display will display up to 80 characters (A, a, 8, !) or character-sized symbols (♪ ☎ ♥ ®) on each of 25 lines (see Figure 2–2). When using command-driven, text-based software you must be explicit, whether entering a DOS command or an application program command. In the above example, you cannot just enter "copy" or even "copy MYFILE". You must enter the command that tells the micro where to find MYFILE and where to make the copy. If you omit necessary information in a command or the format of the command is incorrect, an error message is displayed and/or an on-screen prompt will request that you reenter the command. Command-driven DOS, in particular, demands strict adherence to command **syntax,** the rules for entering commands, such as word spacing, punctuation, and so on.

FIGURE 2–2 Text-Based Display *This text-based display has 25 lines, each with room for up to 80 characters.*

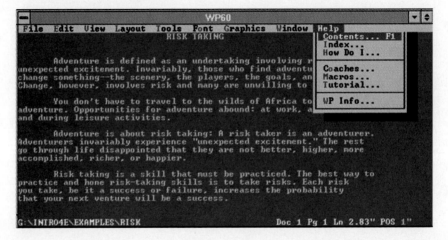

To be an effective user of DOS or any command-driven software, you must memorize its commands and their exact syntax—no easy task.

Graphics-based software.   The trend is away from text-based, command-driven interfaces to a user-friendly, graphics-oriented environment called a *graphical user interface,* or *GUI.* Graphical user interfaces rely on graphics-based software. Graphics-based software permits the integration of text with high-resolution graphic images.

GUIs provide an alternative to the often cryptic command-driven interface. GUI users interact with the operating system and other software packages by using a pointing device and a keyboard to issue commands. Rather than enter a command directly, as in a command-driven interface, the user chooses from options displayed on the screen. The equivalent of a syntax-sensitive operating system command is entered by pointing to and choosing one or more options from menus or by pointing to and choosing a graphics image, called an **icon**. An icon is a graphic rendering that represents a processing activity. For example, the file cabinet icon generally represents processing activities associated with file management. Users choose the "trash can" icon to delete a file from disk storage. Figure 2–3 shows a screen with a variety of symbolic icons.

Graphical user interfaces have effectively eliminated the need for users to memorize and enter cumbersome commands. For example, GUIs permit a file to be copied from one disk to another disk by repositioning the file's icon from one area on the screen to another.

The universal acceptance of GUIs has prompted software entrepreneurs to create GUI alternatives for DOS and popular command-driven software pack-

FIGURE 2–3 Icons   *Each of the icons in this Microsoft Windows display represents an available program. To run a program, simply use the mouse to point to and click on the desired icon.*

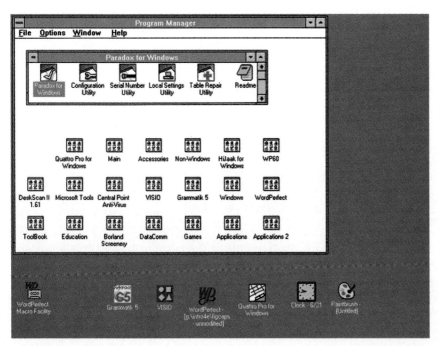

ages. The software that provides a GUI alternative to a command-driven interface is called a **shell**. In effect, a shell is an *optional* layer of user-friendly software between the user and a command-driven interface (see Figure 2–1). Many people prefer using a shell to entering text-based commands.

Transferring information between applications.   One of the most inviting aspects of GUIs is the ability to copy and move information (text, graphics, or a combination) from one application to another. For example, text in a word processing document can be copied into a cell in a spreadsheet. As another example, a block of text from a WordPerfect document can be copied into a paint/draw program's work space. This is done via the **clipboard**. Think of the clipboard as an intermediate holding area in internal storage for information en route to another application.

The procedure for transferring information is as follows.

1. *Mark (highlight) the information in the source application.*
2. *Cut or copy the marked information to the clipboard.* Choosing the *Cut* option causes the marked information to be removed from the source application and placed in the clipboard. The *Copy* option causes the marked information in the source application to be placed on the clipboard, leaving the source application unchanged.
3. *Paste the marked information to the destination application.* The *Paste* option causes the contents of the clipboard to be copied to the cursor position in the destination application. The clipboard contents remain unchanged and can be pasted as often as needed.

The clipboard also can be used to move or copy information within a single application.

The future of user interfaces.   The graphical user interface is still somewhat new, at least to most users. Over the next few years we can expect the integration of other technologies into the interactive process. By the turn of the century, we can expect the next generation of the graphical user interface to become even more user-friendly, permitting voice recognition (voice input) and speech synthesis (voice output).

2–4   COMPUTER OPERATION: GETTING STARTED

Who operates computers? Probably you do. End users routinely do everything from unpacking boxes of hardware to installing and using the software. This is especially true of PCs and workstations.

Installing Hardware and Software

When you purchase a computer system, typically you will receive several boxes containing the various components of the system. Unless it is a portable computer, your system will come in several pieces: a keyboard, a mouse, a monitor, a printer, and a processor unit that houses the magnetic disk drives. Normally you can complete the installation of the hardware simply by linking the pieces of the system with the various types of cables. A computer, however, does nothing without software.

Now you must install the software—first the operating system, then any general-purpose or applications software you intend to run. Software installation is a three-step process for the operating system and all applications software packages.

1. *Make a backup copy.* Seasoned users make duplicates of their vendor-supplied master disks before the initial installation of the software.

2. *Installation.* Normally you would install the operating system, then, if wanted, an optional GUI. Installation involves copying the program and data files from the master disks to the permanently installed hard disk. Frequently you run a program named "install."

3. *Set system information.* An applications software package is designed to fit a variety of computer system configurations; therefore, you must describe your system to the package. The software assumes you have a "typical" PC or workstation. If your system deviates from what is defined as typical in the software package, you will need to revise these **default options** (standard settings) to fit the specifications of your system (for example, type of computer, monitor, keyboard layout, printer, and so on). Typically, you would do this while running the "install" program.

Operating a notebook PC requires some understanding of power management. When operating his PC under battery power, this insurance adjuster will normally elect to conserve power by reducing the contrast on the monitor and choosing an option that spins the hard disk only when it is needed. By using a cellular laptop, he has eliminated the need for intermediate paperwork and the delays associated with communication by mail.

Power Up/Power Down

Booting the Computer System   Computers are similar to copy machines, toasters, and other electrical devices—you must turn them on by applying electrical power. The power-on procedure on almost any computer is straightforward—flip the on/off switch on the processor unit to *on*. Some input/output devices, such as the monitor and the printer, may have separate on/off switches. It is good practice to turn on needed input/output devices before turning on the processor.

When you **power up,** or add electrical power to a computer system, you also **boot** the system. The booting procedure is so named because the computer "pulls itself up by its own bootstraps" (without the assistance of humans). When you boot the system, several significant events take place (see Figure 2–4).

1. A program permanently stored in **read-only memory,** or **ROM** (rhymes with *mom*), is executed. ROM, an integrated circuit, is discussed in Chapter 3, "Inside the Computer." The ROM-based program performs a **system check** to verify that the electronic components are operational and readies the computer for processing. If everything checks out, the program searches for the disk containing the operating system, usually the system's permanently installed disk.

2. Upon finding the operating system, the ROM program loads it from disk storage to **random-access memory,** or **RAM** (rhymes with *ham*). RAM provides temporary storage of data and programs during processing. Once loaded to RAM, the operating system takes control of the system.

3. The operating system executes predefined user instructions, then requests instructions from the user. With a command-driven interface, the user is presented with a **system prompt** (for example, C:\> for MS-DOS), prompting the user to enter a command. With a GUI, the user is asked to make a selection from available options (presented as icons and/or menus).

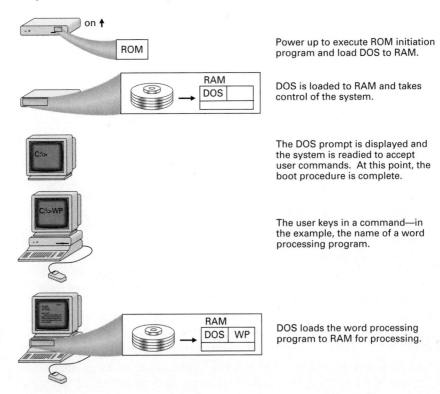

Power up to execute ROM initiation program and load DOS to RAM.

DOS is loaded to RAM and takes control of the system.

The DOS prompt is displayed and the system is readied to accept user commands. At this point, the boot procedure is complete.

The user keys in a command—in the example, the name of a word processing program.

DOS loads the word processing program to RAM for processing.

FIGURE 2–4 The Boot Procedure

The Graceful Exit   Unlike electrical appliances, you do not simply flip the computer switch to *off*. You must **power down** in an orderly manner. This involves a **graceful exit** from all active applications programs before shutting off the power. All applications programs have an exit routine that, when activated, returns you to the GUI, the operating system prompt, or a higher-level applications program. Exit routines perform some administrative processing that, if bypassed, can result in loss of user data and problems during subsequent sessions.

Interacting with Computers from Remote Locations

A video display terminal (VDT) is the hardware that allows you to interact with a computer system, be it a mainframe or a multiuser micro. Microcomputers interact with remote computers by emulating a VDT. With the installation of an optional communications adaptor, a micro has the flexibility to serve as a *stand-alone* computer system or as an *intelligent terminal* for a multiuser micro, a mini, a mainframe, or a supercomputer. When operating in *terminal emulation mode,* micro users can interact with any one of a number of commercial information networks to make airline and hotel reservations, buy consumer goods, send electronic mail, and much more. Or, users can establish a communications link between their micro and their company's mainframe computer. Both the micro and the VDT can transmit and receive data from a remote computer. But, only the micro in terminal mode can process and store the data independently.

To interact with a remote computer, we must establish a link between our computer or terminal and the remote computer. Most VDTs and many small computers are part of established computer networks. In these cases, the link to a larger host computer is permanent, perhaps a coaxial cable. However, if no link exists, the user must dial up the remote computer via the telephone system. In either case, the user must **log-on** to the system. The typical log-on procedure, which helps protect a computer system against unauthorized access and use, involves the following:

1. The user enters a preassigned password. The **password** is simply a character string that typically is assigned by the operating system as a system security tool. A successfully entered password permits limited to full remote access to various databases, applications, and computer networks.

2. The user enters a **personal identification number,** or **PIN**. The PIN, which typically is chosen by the user, provides another level of security and identifies the user.

Once the remote computer validates the password and the PIN, the link is established. At this time, the remote computer normally will prompt the end user to enter a command, or it will present the user with a menu of options.

To terminate a session, the user must **log off** the system. This may be as simple as returning to the main menu and selecting the "log off" option or entering "bye" at the system prompt. Once log off is complete, the user must log-on to begin another session.

2–5   ENTERING COMMANDS AND DATA

Computers Can Be Very Picky

Computers do *exactly* what you tell them to do—no more, no less. If you tell a computer to compute an employee's pay by adding hours worked to rate of pay (PAY=HOURS-WORKED + RATE), then that is what it does. The computer knows only what you tell it, not that you have given it an erroneous command to add rather than multiply. As another example, if you tap the *Delete* key, that is what it does, even if you meant to tap the *Copy* key. Computers can't read your mind. All they can do is interpret and do what you tell them to do.

Generally, the worst that can happen is that you get an error message or inaccurate results. Fortunately, most software packages have built-in safeguards that ask for confirmation before executing a command that might significantly alter or erase your work.

Input and Control: Keyboards and Point-and-Draw Devices

The primary input devices found on all PCs, workstations, and many VDTs are the keyboard and a point-and-draw device. These common devices are discussed in this chapter while other optional input devices are discussed in Chapter 4, "Input/Output Devices."

The Keyboard The *keyboard* is your primary input and control device. You can enter data and issue commands via the keyboard. Figure 2–5 shows the keyboard commonly used by IBM-compatible microcomputers. Besides the standard typewriter keyboard layout, most keyboards have **function keys,** also called **soft keys**. When tapped, these function keys trigger the execution of software, thus the name *soft key*. For example, tapping one function key might call up a displayed list of user options commonly referred to as a **menu**. Function keys are numbered and assigned different functions in different software packages. For example, tapping the Function Key 7, F7, while working with word processing software might cause a document to be printed. HELP (context-sensitive user assistance) may be assigned to F1 (Function Key 1). Software packages usually are distributed with **keyboard templates** that designate which commands are assigned to which function keys. The plastic templates are designed to fit over the keyboard or to be attached with an adhesive.

Most keyboards are equipped with a **numeric key pad** and **cursor-control keys** (see Figure 2–5). The key pad permits rapid numeric data entry. It is normally positioned to the right of the standard alphanumeric keyboard. Space limitations preclude keyboards on portable PCs from having a separate numeric key pad. The cursor-control keys, or "arrow" keys, allow you to move the text cursor *up* (↑) and *down* (↓), usually a line at a time, and *left* (←) and *right* (→), usually a character at a time. The **text cursor** always shows the location of the next keyed-in character on the screen. The text cursor can appear as several shapes depending on the application, but frequently you will encounter an underscore (_), a vertical line (|), or a rectangle (■). To move the text cursor rapidly about the screen, simply hold down the appropriate arrow key.

For many software packages, you can use the arrow keys to view parts of a document or worksheet that extend past the bottom, top, or sides of the

FIGURE 2–5 Microcomputer Keyboard *This is representative of the microcomputer keyboard being configured with the IBM-compatible micros. In the figure, the alphanumeric characters follow the commonly used QWERTY layout. The positioning of the function keys, the cursor-control keys, and the keypad may vary substantially from keyboard to keyboard. On earlier versions of IBM-compatible keyboards, ten function keys were aligned in two columns on the left end.*

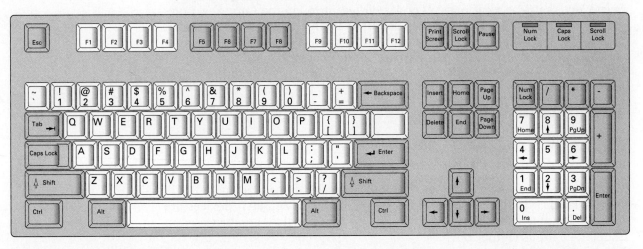

screen. This is known as **scrolling**. Use the up and down arrow keys (↑↓) to *scroll vertically* and the left and right keys (←→) to *scroll horizontally*. For example, if you wish to scroll vertically through a word processing document, move the up or down arrow key to the edge of the current screen and continue to press the key to view more of the document, one line at a time. Figure 2–6 illustrates vertical and horizontal scrolling in a spreadsheet.

In summary, the keyboard provides three basic ways to enter commands:

- *Key in* the command using the alphanumeric portion of the keyboard.
- Tap a *function key.*
- Use the *arrow keys* to select a *menu option* from the displayed menu. (Menus are discussed in detail in the next section.)

Other important keys common to most keyboards are the *Enter, Home, End, Page Up* and *Page Down* (abbreviated as *PgUp* and *PgDn*), *Delete* (*Del*), *Backspace* (*Bksp*), *Insert-typeover toggle* (*Ins*), *Escape* (*Esc*), *Spacebar, Shift, Control* (*Ctrl*), *Alternate* (*Alt*), *Tab, Scroll Lock, Caps Lock, Num Lock,* and *Print Screen* keys (see Figure 2–5).

Enter.   Traditionally the *Enter* key is used to send keyed-in data or a selected command to RAM for processing. For example, when you want to enter data into an electronic spreadsheet, the characters you enter are displayed in an edit area until you tap *Enter*. When you tap *Enter*, the data are displayed in the appropriate area in the spreadsheet. Like most of the special keys, *Enter* has other meanings, depending on the type of software package you are using.

FIGURE 2–6 Scrolling   *When a spreadsheet does not fit on a single screen, you can scroll horizontally (to the right as shown in the figure) and vertically (down in the figure) to view other portions of the spreadsheet.*

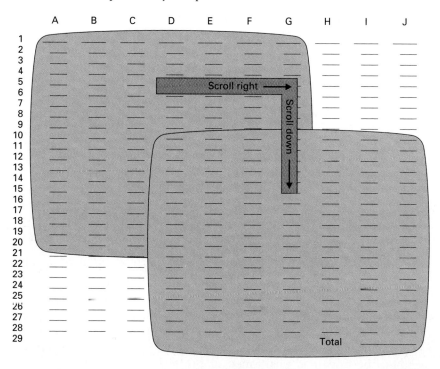

In word processing, for example, you would designate the end of a paragraph by tapping the *Enter* key.

When you highlight a menu option in a software package with an arrow key, you tap *Enter* to select that option. More often than not, *Enter* can be interpreted as "Do."

In graphical user interfaces, the trend is away from using the *Enter* key after each entry. In place of the *Enter* key, the user taps *Tab,* a function key, or a button on the mouse. In a GUI, *Enter* is reserved to signal the system that all user options are set for a particular operation and processing can continue.

Home.   Tapping the *Home* key results in different actions for different packages, but often the cursor is moved to the beginning of a work area (the beginning of the line, screen, or document in word processing; the upper left-hand corner of the spreadsheet; or the first record in a database).

End.   With most software packages, tap *End* to move the cursor to the end of the work area (the end of the line, screen, or document in word processing; the lower right-hand corner of the spreadsheet; or the last record in a database).

Page Up, Page Down.   Tap *Page Up* (*PgUp*) and *Page Down* (*PgDn*) to vertically scroll a page (or screen) at a time to see parts of the document or spreadsheet that extend past the top or bottom of the screen, respectively. *PgUp* and *PgDn* are also used to position the cursor at the previous and next record when using database software.

Delete.   Tap *Delete* (*Del*) to delete the character at the cursor position.

Backspace.   Tap the *Backspace* (*Bksp*) key to move the cursor one position to the left and delete the character in that position.

Insert.   Tap *Ins* to **toggle** (switch) between the two modes of entering data and text—*insert* and *typeover*. When in insert mode, any text entered is *additional* text. When in typeover mode, the character you enter *types over* the character at the cursor position. The term *toggle* is used to describe the action of tapping a single key to alternate between two or more modes of operation (insert and typeover), functions (underline *on* and underline *off*), or operational specifications (for type of database field: character, numeric, date, memo).

Escape.   The *Escape* (*Esc*) key may have many functions, depending on the software package, but in most situations you can tap the *Esc* key to negate the current command or menu and return to the work screen.

Spacebar.   Tap the *Spacebar* at the bottom of the keyboard to key in a space at the cursor position. *Note:* On a computer, a space is recorded internally like any other character, even though it is not displayed or printed.

Shift, Ctrl, Alt.   The *Shift, Ctrl* (*Control*), and *Alt* (*Alternate*) keys are used in conjunction with another key to expand the functionality of the keyboard. Just as you depress the *Shift* key to enter a capital letter or one of the special characters above the numbers, you hold down a *Ctrl* or *Alt* key to give a key new meaning. For example, on some word processing systems you tap *Home* to move the cursor to the beginning of the current line. When you tap *Ctrl* and *Home* together, the cursor is positioned at the beginning of the document.

When used in conjunction with the *Shift, Ctrl,* and *Alt* keys or with combinations of these keys (*Shift+Ctrl, Shift+Alt,* and *Ctrl+Alt*), each key can be assigned several meanings (for example, *F1, Shift+F1, Ctrl+F1, Ctrl+Alt+F1,* and so on).

Tab.   In word processing, the *Tab* key advances the text cursor to the next user-defined tab stop. In most other programs, it advances the text cursor to the next logical area into which data can be entered. For example, a program might position the cursor at the first of three data entry areas. After entering the required data in the first area, sometimes called a **field,** the user taps the *Tab* key to advance to the next area. Tapping the *Tab* key with the text cursor in the last field positions the cursor at the first field again. The *Shift+Tab* combination (hold down *Shift* and tap *Tab*) moves the cursor to the previous field. Typically, you would tap the *Enter* key to enter the data in all fields simultaneously.

Scroll Lock.   Tap the *Scroll Lock* key to toggle the scroll lock feature on and off. When you tap the *Scroll Lock* key to activate the scroll lock feature, the cursor remains fixed and whatever is on the screen scrolls under the cursor. The scroll lock feature is applicable to certain programs only. For example, most spreadsheet programs enable the scroll lock feature to be used.

Caps Lock.   Tap the *Caps Lock* key to toggle the capital letter lock feature on and off. When you tap the *Caps Lock* key to activate the caps-lock feature, all letters entered from the keyboard are entered to the system as capital letters.

Num Lock.   Tap the *Num Lock* key to toggle the number lock feature on and off. When you tap the *Num Lock* key to activate the num lock feature, numbers are entered when you tap the numbered keys on the keypad to the right of the alphanumeric keyboard.

Print Screen.   Tap *Print Screen,* or *Shift+Print Screen* (press and hold the *Shift* key, then tap *Print Screen*) to print what is currently being displayed on the screen.

Point-and-Draw Devices   The hand-held mouse, or something like it, is a must-have item on PCs, workstations, and GUI-based VDTs. The mouse is either attached to the computer by a cable (the mouse's "tail") or linked via a wireless remote connection. The mouse is a small device that, when moved across a desktop, moves the **graphics cursor** accordingly. The graphics cursor, which can be positioned anywhere on the screen, is displayed as a bracket ([), an arrow (➤), a crosshair (+), or a variety of other symbols (for example, ☞). Depending on the application, the text and graphics cursors may be displayed on the screen at the same time. The graphics cursor is used to *point* and *draw.*

All movements of the mouse are reproduced by the graphics cursor on the screen. For example, when a mouse positioned to the right of the keyboard is moved up and away from its user, the graphics cursor moves toward the top right-hand corner of the screen. Use the mouse for quick positioning of the graphics cursor over the desired menu item or an icon. When positioned at a menu item or an icon, the graphics cursor is said to "point" to that item or icon.

Mice and the other point-and-draw devices (discussed in Chapter 4, "Input/Output Devices") have at least two buttons. The mouse normally has a

The mouse is not the only point-and-draw device. This Thumbelina is one of many innovative alternatives to the mouse. The cursor is moved by rolling the thumb over a small trackball. The Thumbelina is used during presentations, in multimedia applications, and with portable computers.

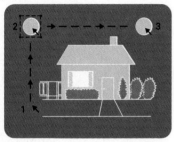

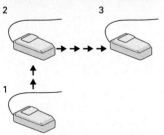

FIGURE 2–7 The Mouse and the Graphics Cursor *In the example, a computer artist moved the sun image from the left to the right side of the screen. The graphics cursor, or pointer, was initially at Position 1 on the display screen. The artist moved the mouse up (toward monitor) to position the pointer over the image to be moved (Position 2). The image, which includes the sun, is temporarily enclosed within a rectangular box. To reposition the sun image to the right of the display (Position 3), the image within the box was dragged (by pressing and holding the mouse's left button) to the desired location. The drag operation was completed when the mouse button was released.*

left and right button (Figure 2–7). You would tap, or **click,** the left button to select a menu item or execute the program represented by an icon. The function of the right button varies between software packages, but often it is used to call up a menu of options. A **double-click,** which is tapping a button twice in rapid succession, gives each button a different meaning. Some software packages permit a **simultaneous click,** or tapping both buttons simultaneously, to give the mouse added functionality.

Press and hold a button to **drag** the graphics cursor across the screen. When using a graphics software program, you drag the graphics cursor across the screen to create the image. When using a word processing program, you highlight a block of text to be deleted by dragging the graphics cursor from the beginning to the end of a block.

Click and drag operations are demonstrated in Figure 2–7 within the context of a graphics software package. In the example, a computer artist uses a mouse to reposition the sun in the drawing.

Levels of Command Interaction

You can interact with software packages, such as spreadsheet and database, at three different levels of sophistication: the *menu level,* the *macro level,* and the *programming level.* These three levels of command interaction are discussed in the following section.

Menus Software that is intended for use by end users is designed such that users issue commands and initiate operations by selecting activities to be performed from a *hierarchy of menus.*

Menu trees. Menu hierarchies are sometimes called **menu trees**. When you select an item from the **main menu,** you are often presented with another menu of activities, and so on. Depending on the items you select, you may progress through as few as one and as many as eight levels of menus before processing is started for the desired activity.

Let's use presentation graphics software to illustrate how you might use a hierarchy of menus. Consider the following main menu.

CREATE CHART	EDIT CHART	GET/SAVE	PRINT CHART	EXIT

Notice that two of the options in the main menu are dimmed. **Dimmed** options, which are usually gray, are disabled or unavailable. The current circumstance dictates whether an option is dimmed. In this example there is no active chart to be edited or printed, so these options are dimmed.

One option on the main menu of a graphics software package might be *Create Chart.*

CREATE CHART	EDIT CHART	GET/SAVE	PRINT CHART	EXIT

If you select this option, you are presented with another menu and an opportunity to choose one of five types of charts.

| BAR | PIE | LINE | **TEXT** | ORGANIZATION |

If you select the *text* option, another menu asks you to choose from three available types of text charts.

| TITLE CHART | SIMPLE LIST | **BULLET LIST** |

If you select the *bullet list* option, you are presented with the bullet list work screen on which you would enter the text for your bullet points.

Menu formats.   Menus are presented in four basic formats.

- *Menu bar.* The main menu is frequently presented as a **menu bar** in the **user interface** portion of the display. The user interface is that portion of the display dedicated to the presentation of user options. It is it normally found around the perimeter of the work area. The menu bar provides a *horizontal list* of menu options, usually at the top of the screen (see Figure 2–8).
- *Pull-down menu.* The result of a menu selection from a menu bar at the top of the screen may be a subordinate menu bar or a **pull-down menu** (see Figure 2–8). The subordinate pull-down menu is "pulled down" from the selected menu bar option and displayed as a *vertical list* of menu options. The entire pull-down menu is shown in a box directly under the selected menu bar option and over whatever is currently on the screen (see Figure 2–8).
- *Pop-up menu.* Like the pull-down menu, the **pop-up menu** is superimposed on the current screen in a window (see Figure 2–9). Pop-up menus usually are displayed by tapping the menu's preassigned hotkey. A **hotkey** typically is a seldom used key combination such as *Ctrl+Esc*.

GRiD Systems Corporation offers a notebook PC that can be converted to a pen-based PC for pen-based interaction and data entry. Here the user selects menu options with a pen.

FIGURE 2–8 Menus   *The WordPerfect for Windows (WPwin) (a word processing program) main menu is presented in a menu bar above the user work area. In the example, the* Layout *option in the bar menu is selected and the pull-down menu is presented. Selecting the* Justification *option results in a pop-out menu of justification options.*

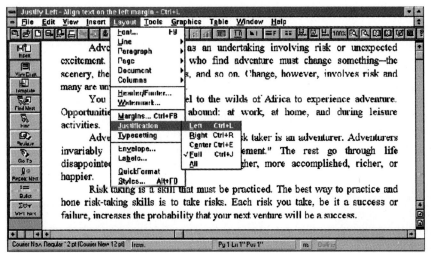

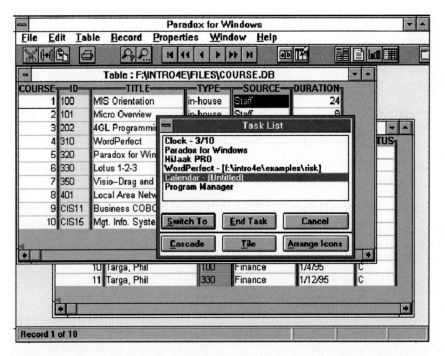

FIGURE 2–9 Pop-up Menu *A hotkey is activated to display this Microsoft Windows pop-up menu.*

■ *Pop-out menu.* The **pop-out menu** is displayed next to the menu option selected in a higher-level pull-down or pop-up menu. The pop-out menu becomes the active menu, but the higher-level menu continues to be displayed (see Figure 2–8).

Selection of menu options. Most software packages provide users with three ways to select an item from a menu.

1. Use the left/right (→←) or up/down (↑↓) arrow keys to highlight the desired menu option and tap *Enter.*
2. Enter the **mnemonic** (pronounced *neh MON ik*) of the desired item. A letter or number within the text of the menu item is noted as its mnemonic, which means memory aid. The mnemonic is usually the first letter in the first word unless there is another option with the same first letter. Examine the underlined mnemonics in the menu bar in Figure 2–10 (File, Edit, View, Layout, Tools, Font, and so on).
3. Use the mouse (or other point-and-draw device) to point to the desired option and click the left button.

Defaults, parameters, and dialog boxes. As you progress through a series of menus, eventually you are asked to enter the specifications for data to be graphed (graphics software), the size of the output paper (word processing software), and so on. Those specifications are presented as parameters. **Parameters** are variables whose values must be defined by the user before the current command can be executed.

As a convenience to the user, many of the parameters are already filled in for common situations. For example, word processing packages set output document size at 8½ by 11 inches. If the user accepts a *default option,* no fur-

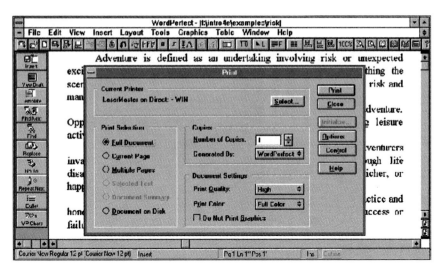

FIGURE 2–10 Dialog Box   *This WordPerfect for Windows (WPwin)* Print *dialog box prompts the user to accept the default options or enter new information.*

ther entry is required for that parameter. Of course, the user can easily revise the default options to fit less common situations. So, to print a document on legal-sized paper, the default paper length of 11 inches would be revised to 14 inches.

Parameters are normally entered and revised in a dialog box. The text in a pop-up **dialog box** gives the user an opportunity to change default options or enter further information. Often the dialog box appears when the user must accept or enter values for parameters before the chosen menu option can be executed.

For example, the parameters in the WPwin (WordPerfect for Windows) *Print* dialog box in Figure 2–10 include the printer to be used, the pages to be printed, and the number of copies to be printed. The default in the example dialog box for the *Number of Copies* parameter is "1."

Menu summary.   All software, whether general-purpose, applications, or system, is designed such that at any given point in a work session, the processing options are either displayed somewhere on the screen or can be displayed by tapping a key or clicking a mouse. So, if you are confused about what to do next or what can be done, the options usually are in front of you.

Macros and Programming   At the menu level of command interaction, you are initiating individual commands, such as *Print, Save,* or *Zoom in.* At the macro and programming levels of interaction, you can string together commands and even introduce logic operations.

A handy feature available with most general-purpose software packages and some applications software is the macro. A **macro** is a sequence of frequently used operations or keystrokes that can be recalled as you need them. You create a macro by recording a sequence of operations or keystrokes and storing them on disk for later recall. To **invoke,** or execute, the macro, you either refer to it by name or enter a keystroke combination that identifies it (for example, ALT+D, CTRL+F4). Spreadsheet users often create macros that can be invoked to generate and print a particular graph.

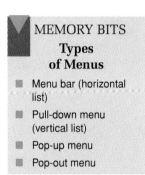

MEMORY BITS
Types of Menus

■ Menu bar (horizontal list)

■ Pull-down menu (vertical list)

■ Pop-up menu

■ Pop-out menu

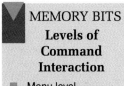

MEMORY BITS

Levels of Command Interaction

■ Menu level

■ Macro level

■ Programming level

Some general-purpose software packages allow users the flexibility to do their own **programming**—that is, to create logical sequences of instructions. For example, a database software program can be written that will retrieve records from a particular database, depending on preset criteria; process the data according to programmed instructions; and print a report. The programming capability enables users to create their own information systems for an endless number of applications, from payroll processing to tennis league scheduling.

2–6 USER-FRIENDLY SOFTWARE

User-friendly software communicates easily understood words, phrases, and icons to the end user, thus simplifying his or her interaction with the computer system. A user-friendly environment helps with **navigation** between the elements of the software package. Navigation refers to movement within and between an application's work areas. A central focus of the design of any modern software package is user-friendliness.

Windows

The **window** has become symbolic of the graphical user interface's user-friendly environment. A window is a rectangular display temporarily superimposed over whatever is currently on the screen. For example, the dialog box in Figure 2–10 is presented in a window. You can "look through" several windows on a single display screen; however, you can manipulate text, data, or graphics in only one window at a time. This is called the **current window**. Generally, each window contains a separate application. Figure 2–11 shows a variety of applications displayed in windows.

Windows can overlap each other on the display screen. For example, in Figure 2–11, you can view several software packages at once. With windows, you can work the way you think and think the way you work. Several projects are at your finger tips, and you can switch between them with relative ease.

You can perform work in one of several windows on a display screen, or you can **zoom** in on a particular window—that is, the window you select expands to fill the entire screen. Tapping a program-specific key combination normally will return the screen to a multiwindow display. A multiwindow display lets you see how a change in one window affects another window. For example, as you change the data in a spreadsheet, you can see how an accompanying pie graph is revised to reflect the new data.

You can even create **window panes**! As you might expect, a window is divided into panes so you can view several parts of the same window subarea at a time. For example, if you are writing a long report in a word processing window, you might wish to write the conclusions of the report in one window pane while viewing other portions of the report in another window pane.

Help Commands

A handy feature available on nearly all modern software packages is the **help command**. When you find yourself in need of a more detailed explanation or instructions on how to proceed, tap the *HELP* key, often assigned to Function

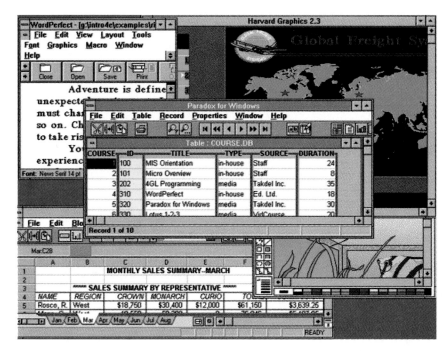

FIGURE 2–11 Viewing Multiple Applications in Windows   *Several popular software packages are shown in windows on the same screen, including spreadsheet, database, word processing, presentation graphics, and paint software.*

Key 1 (F1). In most software packages, the help commands are **context-sensitive;** that is, the explanation relates to what you were doing when you issued the help command. (For example, if you were entering data into a database, the explanation would address how to enter data.) When you are finished reading the help information, the system returns you to your work at the same point you left it. Figure 2–12 shows a pop-up help window for a calendar application.

GUIs in the Micro World

Apple and IBM-compatible micros continue to dominate the marketplace. What we now call user-friendly systems (the use of windows, the mouse, and icons) were first introduced on Apple computers during the early 1980s. Some say Apple computers had an exclusive on user-friendliness until the introduction of Microsoft's Windows, a graphical user interface (GUI) for the IBM-compatible environment.

The Windows Platform   Microsoft's Windows has emerged as the dominant graphical user interface for the IBM-compatible environment. The name Windows describes how the software functions. It runs one or more applications in "windows"—rectangular areas displayed on the screen.

Windows, itself a commercial software package, is more than just another application for micros. It also defines a new **platform,** or standard, for which other applications software packages are developed. Moreover, it offers some

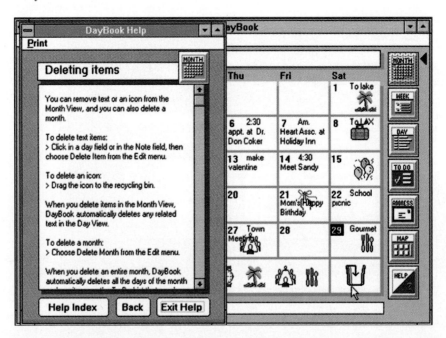

FIGURE 2–12 Help   *A help window is displayed when* Help *is requested within Asymmetric's DayBook calendar program. Help information is available on a variety of topics through the* Help Index.

very inviting solutions to the limitations of MS-DOS, the operating system for IBM-compatible micros.

1. *Windows is user-friendly.* Windows employs a graphical user interface.
2. *Windows enables multiple programs to be run simultaneously.* A user can print out a WordPerfect report while engaged in a Lotus 1-2-3 session. The same user, running under the MS-DOS platform, would need to exit Lotus 1-2-3 and load WordPerfect to print out the report.
3. *Windows enables users to work with large files.* Databases, spreadsheet files, and word processing documents can be as big as available random-access memory will allow. MS-DOS does not permit full and efficient use of available RAM.
4. *Windows permits information to be passed easily between applications via the clipboard.* Use of the clipboard is discussed earlier in Section 2–3.

Although Windows establishes a new platform, virtually all of the thousands of applications software packages created for MS-DOS can run under Windows.

CUA Compliance   All software applications developed specifically to run under Windows must follow Microsoft's **Common User Access,** or **CUA,** standard. These CUA conventions describe the type and style of window, the arrangement and style of menus, the use of the keyboard and mouse, and the format for screen-image display. By following the CUA standard, software developers give all Windows applications a similar *look and feel.* This makes it easier for us, the end users, to learn and use software packages.

IMPORTANT TERMS AND SUMMARY OUTLINE

AIX
applications software
boot
click
clipboard
Common User Access (CUA)
context-sensitive
current window
cursor-control key
default option
dialog box
dimmed
double-click
drag
field
function key
general-purpose software
graceful exit
graphical user interface (GUI)
graphics cursor
help command
hotkey

icon
invoke
keyboard template
log off
log-on
Macintosh System
macro
main menu
menu
menu bar
menu tree
mnemonic
MS-DOS
navigation
numeric key pad
OS/2
parameter
password
personal identification number (PIN)
platform
pop-out menu
pop-up menu

power down
power up
programming
pull-down menu
random-access memory (RAM)
read-only memory (ROM)
scrolling
shell
simultaneous click
soft key
syntax
system check
system prompt
system software
text cursor
toggle
UNIX
user interface
window
window pane
XENIX
zoom

2–1 PC Magic Personal computers are everywhere. The relatively low cost and almost unlimited applications for the microcomputer have made it the darling of the business/education community.

2–2 Interacting with the System The effective user will understand general computer software concepts, how to operate and use the hardware, the operating system and/or a **graphical user interface (GUI)**, and one or more applications programs.

2–3 Categories of Software: Knowing the Rooms in the House Software directs the activities of the computer system. Software falls into three major categories: general-purpose, applications, and system. **General-purpose software** provides the framework for a great number of business, scientific, and personal applications. **Applications software** is designed and written to perform specific personal, business, or scientific processing tasks. **System software** is usually independent of any general-purpose software package or any specific application area.

The operating system, which is system software, monitors and controls all input/output and processing activities within a computer system. The four most popular micro operating systems based on number of installations are **MS-DOS, Macintosh System, OS/2,** and **UNIX** (and spinoffs such as **XENIX** and **AIX**).

Through the 1980s, MS-DOS was a text-based, *command-driven* software in which commands were entered one character at a time. Command-driven software demands strict adherence to command **syntax**. The trend is away from text-based interfaces to a user-friendly, graphics-oriented environment called a graphical user interface (GUI). GUIs are graphics-based software. Graphics-based software permits the integration of text with high-resolution graphic images, called **icons**. The software that provides a GUI alternative to a command-driven interface is called a **shell**. In a GUI, information can be copied or moved between applications via the **clipboard**.

2–4 Computer Operation: Getting Started When you purchase a computer system, you install the software in a three-step process: Make a backup copy; copy files to the permanently installed hard disk; and set system information, revising **default options** (standard settings) as needed.

When you **power up** a computer, you **boot** the system. First, a program in **read-only memory, or ROM,** initializes the system and runs a **system check**. Next, the operating system is loaded to **random-access memory,** takes control of the system, and presents the user with a **system prompt** or a GUI screen full of options. **RAM** provides temporary storage of data and programs during processing.

To **power down** in an orderly manner, **gracefully exit** from all active applications programs prior to shutting off the power.

The user can **log-on** to a remote computer system from a PC or a VDT. A PC has the flexibility to serve as a *stand-alone* computer system or as an *intelligent terminal* for multiuser systems. To log-on the user enters a preassigned **password**. A successfully entered password permits limited to full access to the remote computer's information resources. The user also enters a **personal identification number,** or **PIN**. To terminate a session, the user must **log off** the system.

2–5 Entering Commands and Data When entering a command the user must be explicit.

A keyboard is normally the primary input and control device for a computer. In addition to the standard typewriter keyboard, most keyboards have **function keys,** also called **soft keys**. Tapping a function key might present the user with a **menu,** which is a displayed list of user options. Software packages are usually distributed with **keyboard templates** that designate which commands are assigned to which function keys. Most keyboards are equipped with a **numeric key pad** and **cursor-control keys**. Use the cursor-control keys to position the **text cursor** and for **scrolling**.

Other important keys common to most keyboards are the *Enter, Home, End, Page Up* and *Page Down* (abbreviated as *PgUp* and *PgDn*), *Delete* (*Del*), *Backspace* (*Bksp*), *Insert-typeover* **toggle** (*Ins*), *Escape* (*Esc*), *Spacebar, Shift, Control* (*Ctrl*), *Alternate* (*Alt*), *Tab, Scroll Lock, Caps Lock, Num Lock,* and *Print Screen* keys. In addition to its traditional function, the *Tab* key facilitates movement between data entry areas, sometimes called **fields**. Each keystroke you enter is sent first to an intermediate keystroke buffer.

The hand-held *mouse,* when moved across a desktop, moves the **graphics cursor** accordingly. The graphics cursor is used to *point* and *draw*. Use the mouse, or any of several point-and-draw devices, for quick positioning of the graphics cursor over the desired menu item or icon. Typically, you would **click** the mouse's left button to select a menu item. The **double-click** and **simultaneous click** give the mouse added functionality. You would press and hold a button to **drag** the graphics cursor across the screen.

You can interact with software packages, such as spreadsheet and database, at three different levels of sophistication: the *menu level,* the *macro level,* and the *programming level*. At the menu level you are initiating individual commands. At the macro and programming levels of interaction you can string together commands and even introduce logic operations.

Menu hierarchies are sometimes called **menu trees**. When you select an item from the **main menu,** you are often presented with another menu of activities, and so on. A menu can appear as a **menu bar** in the **user interface** portion of the display, a **pull-down menu,** a **pop-up menu** (via a **hotkey**), or a **pop-out menu**. Menu options that are unavailable or disabled are **dimmed**.

Software packages provide users with three ways to select an item from a menu: Use the left/right or up/down arrow keys; enter the **mnemonic;** or use the mouse to position the graphics cursor at the desired option. Most menus present users with default options in a pop-up **dialog box**. User specifications needed for processing are presented in the form of **parameters**.

A **macro** is a sequence of frequently used operations or keystrokes that can be recalled as you need it. To **invoke** the macro, you refer to it by name or enter the series of keystrokes that identify it. Some software packages permit users to do their own **programming**.

2–6 User-Friendly Software User-friendly software communicates easily understood words, phrases, and icons to the end user, thus simplifying his or her interaction with the computer system. A user-friendly environment facilitates **navigation** between the elements of the software package.

Windows are rectangular displays temporarily superimposed over what is currently on the screen. You can manipulate text or data in only one window at a time, the **current window**. **Zoom** in on a particular window to fill the entire screen. **Window panes** enable users to view several parts of the same window subarea at a time.

The on-line **help command** provides **context-sensitive** explanations or instructions on how to proceed.

Microsoft's Windows software defines a new **platform** for which applications software packages for the IBM-compatible environment are developed. All software applications developed to run under Windows must adhere to Microsoft's **Common User Access,** or **CUA,** standard.

REVIEW EXERCISES

Concepts

1. What is the purpose of soft keys? Of cursor-control keys?
2. Describe the attributes of user-friendly software.
3. Contrast a menu bar with a pull-down menu.
4. Briefly describe two ways you can use a keyboard to enter commands to a software package.

5. During a software session, which key would you commonly press to move to the beginning of the work area? To negate the current command?

6. Name three microcomputer operating systems.

7. How is a pop-out menu displayed?

8. What does "booting the system" mean?

9. What must be accomplished to power down in an orderly manner?

10. Which key is tapped to toggle between insert and typeover modes?

11. The help command is often assigned to which function key?

12. What is software called that provides a graphical user interface alternative to a software package's command-driven interface?

13. When multiple windows are open, the user manipulates text, data, or graphics in which window?

14. Which two cursor-control keys are used to scroll horizontally?

15. Give two examples each of general-purpose, applications, and system software.

16. Describe what is involved in a typical log-on procedure.

Discussion

17. Why would you use the mouse to drag the graphics cursor over text in a word processing document?

18. Most word processing packages have a default document size. What other default options would a word processing package have?

19. What is a macro and how can using macros save time?

20. When would you use the zoom feature of a software package?

SELF-TEST (BY SECTION)

2–1 PCs can help you think logically. (T/F) *GUI*

2–2 Both the operating system and/or a ___*GUI*___ provide a link between the user, the computer system, and the applications programs.

2–3 a. A student registration system is an example of the *application* category of software.

 b. CAD would be considered: (a) a utility program, (b) system software, or (c) general-purpose software?

 c. MS-DOS is a mainframe-based operating system. (T/F)

 d. GUIs are: (a) text-based, (b) graphics-based, or (c) label-based?

2–4 a. A computer user must "kick the system" to load the operating system to RAM prior to processing. (T/F)

 b. A command-driven operating system displays a system *prompt* to signal the user that it is ready to accept a user *command.*

2–5 a. Use the *numeric* *key pad* for rapid numeric data entry.

 b. When interacting with a computer via a keyboard, you must wait until the execution of one command is finished before entering another. (T/F)

 c. Press and hold a mouse button to ___*drag*___ the graphics cursor across the screen.

 d. A sequence of frequently used operations or keystrokes that can be activated by the user is called a: (a) menu, (b) macro, or (c) program?

 e. A mouse can be used to point to a graphic image called an ___*icon*___.

2–6 a. What term refers to movement within and between an application's work areas: (a) routing, (b) navigation, or (c) locomotion?

 b. ___*Zoom*___ in on a particular window to expand it and fill the entire screen.

 c. A standard for which other applications software packages are developed is called a platform. (T/F)

Self-test answers. **2–1** T. **2–2** graphical user interface (GUI). **2–3** **(a)** applications; **(b)** c; **(c)** F; **(d)** b. **2–4** **(a)** F; **(b)** prompt, command. **2–5** **(a)** numeric key pad; **(b)** F; **(c)** drag; **(d)** b; **(e)** icon. **2–6** **(a)** b; **(b)** Zoom; **(c)** T.

3

INSIDE THE COMPUTER

OBJECTIVES

To describe how data are stored in a computer system.

To demonstrate the relationships between bits, bytes, characters, and encoding systems.

To understand the translation of alphanumeric data into a format for internal computer representation.

To explain and illustrate the principles of computer operations.

To identify and describe the relationships between the internal components of a computer.

To distinguish processors by their word length, speed, and memory capacity.

3–1   DATA STORAGE: DATA IN THE COMPUTER

The three most basic questions encountered during one's computer learning adventure are:

1. What is a computer?
2. What does it do?
3. How does it do it?

Chapters 1 and 2 address the first two questions. By now you should have a good idea of what a computer is and what it does. This chapter deals with the third question as we peek inside the computer to learn how it works.

The first step in learning what happens inside a computer is learning how data are stored. In Chapter 1 we learned that *data,* not *information,* are stored in a computer system. *Data are the raw material from which information is derived,* and *information is data that have been collected and manipulated into a meaningful form.* To manipulate data within a computer system, we must have a way to store and retrieve this raw material.

It is easy to understand data storage in a manual system. For example, when a customer's address changes, we pull the customer's manila folder from the file cabinet, erase the old address, and write in the new one. We can see and easily interpret data that are kept manually. We cannot see or easily interpret data stored in a computer. Data are represented and stored in a computer system to take advantage of the physical characteristics of electronics and computer hardware, not human beings.

Data are stored *temporarily* during processing in a section of the computer system called random-access memory (RAM). RAM was introduced and discussed briefly in Chapter 2, "Interacting with Computers." RAM is also referred to as **primary storage.** Data are stored *permanently* on **secondary storage** devices such as magnetic tape and disk drives. We discuss primary storage (RAM) in detail later in this chapter. Secondary storage is covered in Chapter 5, "Data Storage and Organization." In this chapter we focus on the details of how data are represented electronically in a computer system and on the internal workings of a computer.

Programs and data are stored temporarily in these solid-state RAM chips (primary storage) during processing. Permanent storage can be on magnetic disk or optical laser disk (secondary storage). This optical laser disk contains the operating system and graphical user interface software for Sun Microsystems' workstations.

3–2   A BIT ABOUT THE BIT

The computer's seemingly endless potential is, in fact, based on only two electronic states—*on* and *off.* The physical characteristics of the computer make it possible to combine these two electronic states to represent letters, numbers, and even colors. An "on" or "off" electronic state is represented by a **bit.** (*Bit* is short for *binary digit.*) The presence or absence of a bit is referred to as *on-bit* and *off-bit,* respectively. In the **binary** numbering system (base 2) and in written text, the on-bit is a 1 and the off-bit is a 0.

An eight-bit encoding system, with its 256 unique bit configurations, is more than adequate to represent all the alphanumeric characters used in the English language. The Japanese, however, need a 16-bit encoding system to represent their 50,000 Kanji characters.

The vacuum tubes, transistors, and integrated circuits that characterize the generations of computers all enable them to distinguish between on and off and, therefore, to use binary logic.

Physically, these states are achieved in a variety of ways. In primary storage the two electronic states are represented by the direction of current flow. Another approach is to turn the circuit itself on or off. In secondary storage the two states are made possible by the magnetic arrangement of the surface coating on magnetic tapes and disks (see Chapter 5, "Data Storage and Organization").

Bits may be fine for computers, but human beings are more comfortable with letters, decimal numbers (the base-10 numerals 0 through 9), and colors. Therefore, the letters, decimal numbers, and colors that we input to a computer system while doing word processing, graphics, and other applications must be translated into 1s and 0s for processing and storage. The computer translates the bits back into letters, decimal numbers, and colors for output on monitors, printers, and so on. This translation is performed so we can recognize and understand the output. It is made possible by encoding systems.

3–3 ENCODING SYSTEMS: COMBINING BITS TO FORM BYTES

Computers do not speak to one another in English, Spanish, or French. They have their own languages, which are better suited to electronic communication. In these languages, bits are combined according to an **encoding system** to represent letters (**alpha** characters), numbers (**numeric** characters), and special characters (such as *, $, +, and &). For example, in the seven-bit **ASCII** encoding system (*American Standard Code for Information Interchange*—pronounced *AS key*), a *B* and a 3 are represented by 1000010 and 0110011, respectively. There is also an eight-bit version of ASCII called **ASCII-8.**

Letters, numbers, and special characters are collectively referred to as **alphanumeric** characters. Alphanumeric characters are *encoded* into a bit configuration on input so that the computer can interpret them. When you press the letter *B* on a PC keyboard, the *B* is transmitted to the processor as a coded string of binary digits (for example, 1000010 in ASCII). The characters are *decoded* on output so we can interpret them. For example, a monitor's device controller will interpret an ASCII 0110011 as a 3 and display a 3 on the screen. This coding, based on a particular encoding system, equates a unique series of bits and no-bits with a specific character. Just as the words *mother* and *father* are arbitrary English-language character strings that refer to our parents, 1011010 is an arbitrary ASCII code that refers to the letter *Z*. The combination of bits used to represent a character is called a **byte** (pronounced *bite*). Figure 3–1 shows the binary value (the actual bit configuration) and the decimal equivalent of commonly used characters in ASCII.

The seven-bit ASCII code can represent up to 128 characters (2^7). Although the English language has considerably fewer than 128 *printable* characters, the extra bit configurations are needed to represent a variety of common and not-so-common special characters (such as - [hyphen]; @ [at]; | [a broken vertical bar]; and ˜ [tilde]) and to signal a variety of activities to the computer (such as ringing a bell or telling the computer to accept a piece of datum).

Character	ASCII Code Binary Value	Decimal Value
A	100 0001	65
B	100 0010	66
C	100 0011	67
D	100 0100	68
E	100 0101	69
F	100 0110	70
G	100 0111	71
H	100 1000	72
I	100 1001	73
J	100 1010	74
K	100 1011	75
L	100 1100	76
M	100 1101	77
N	100 1110	78
O	100 1111	79
P	101 0000	80
Q	101 0001	81
R	101 0010	82
S	101 0011	83
T	101 0100	84
U	101 0101	85
V	101 0110	86
W	101 0111	87
X	101 1000	88
Y	101 1001	89
Z	101 1010	90
a	110 0001	97
b	110 0010	98
c	110 0011	99
d	110 0100	100
e	110 0101	101
f	110 0110	102
g	110 0111	103
h	110 1000	104
i	110 1001	105
j	110 1010	106
k	110 1011	107
l	110 1100	108
m	110 1101	109
n	110 1110	110
o	110 1111	111
p	111 0000	112
q	111 0001	113
r	111 0010	114
s	111 0011	115
t	111 0100	116
u	111 0101	117
v	111 0110	118
w	111 0111	119
x	111 1000	120
y	111 1001	121
z	111 1010	122

Character	ASCII Code Binary Value	Decimal Value
0	011 0000	48
1	011 0001	49
2	011 0010	50
3	011 0011	51
4	011 0100	52
5	011 0101	53
6	011 0110	54
7	011 0111	55
8	011 1000	56
9	011 1001	57
Space	010 0000	32
.	010 1110	46
<	011 1100	60
(	010 1000	40
+	010 1011	43
&	010 0110	38
!	010 0001	33
$	010 0100	36
*	010 1010	42
)	010 1001	41
;	011 1011	59
,	010 1100	44
%	010 0101	37
–	101 1111	95
>	011 1110	62
?	011 1111	63
:	011 1010	58
#	010 0011	35
@	100 0000	64
'	010 0111	39
=	011 1101	61
"	010 0010	34
½	1010 1011	171
¼	1010 1100	172
▪	1011 0010	178
■	1101 1011	219
▬	1101 1100	220
▮	1101 1101	221
▮	1101 1110	222
▬	1101 1111	223
√	1111 1011	251
n	1111 1100	252
2	1111 1101	253
▪	1111 1110	254
(blank)	1111 1111	255

FIGURE 3–1 ASCII Codes   *This figure contains the binary and decimal values for commonly used ASCII characters.*

ASCII is a seven-bit code, but the microcomputer byte can store eight bits. There are 256 (2^8) possible bit configurations in an eight-bit byte. Hardware and software vendors use the extra 128 bit configurations to represent control characters or noncharacter images to complement their hardware or software product. For example, the IBM-PC version of extended ASCII contains the characters of many foreign languages (such as *ä* [umlaut] and *é* [acute]) and a wide variety of graphic images that can be combined on a text screen to produce larger images (for example, the box around a window on a display screen).

Various encoding systems are used to represent colors inside a computer. A 4-bit code can represent up to 16 colors. Very high resolution monitors that can display more than 16 million different colors need 24-bit codes.

3–4 COMPONENTS OF A COMPUTER SYSTEM: A CLOSER LOOK AT THE PROCESSOR AND RAM

Let's review. We have learned that all computers have similar capabilities and perform essentially the same functions, although some might be faster than others. We have also learned that a computer system has input, output, storage, and processing components; that the *processor* is the "intelligence" of a computer system; and that a single computer system may have several processors. We have discussed how data are represented inside a computer system in electronic states called *bits*. We are now ready to expose the inner workings of the nucleus of the computer system—the processor.

Literally hundreds of different types of computers are marketed by scores of manufacturers. The complexity of each type may vary considerably, but in the end each processor, sometimes called the **central processing unit** or **CPU**, has only two fundamental sections: the *control unit* and the *arithmetic and logic unit. Random-access memory (RAM)* also plays an integral part in the internal operation of a processor. These three—random-access memory (same as primary storage), the control unit, and the arithmetic and logic unit—work together. Let's look at their functions and the relationships between them.

RAM: Random-Access Storage

The Technology Unlike magnetic secondary storage devices, such as tape and disk, *RAM* (primary storage) has no moving parts. With no mechanical movement, data can be accessed from RAM at electronic speeds, or close to the speed of light. Most of today's computers use CMOS (*C*omplementary *M*etal-*O*xide *S*emiconductor) technology for RAM. A state-of-the-art CMOS memory chip about one-eighth the size of a postage stamp can store about 4,000,000 bits, or more than 400,000 characters of data!

There is one major problem with semiconductor storage: It is **volatile memory.** That is, when the electrical current is turned off or interrupted, the data are lost. Researchers are working to perfect a RAM technology that will retain its contents after an electrical interruption. Several **nonvolatile memory** technologies, such as **bubble memory,** have emerged, but none has exhibited the qualities necessary for widespread application. However, bubble memory is superior to CMOS for use in certain computers because it is highly reliable, it is not susceptible to environmental fluctuations, and it can operate on battery power for a considerable length of time. These qualities make bubble memory well-suited for use with industrial robots and in portable computers.

Function RAM provides the processor with *temporary* storage for programs and data. *All programs and data must be transferred to RAM from an input device (such as a keyboard) or from secondary storage (such as a disk) before*

In the first generation of computers (1951–1959), each bit was represented by a vacuum tube about the size of a small light bulb. Today computers use chips, like this one, that can store millions of bits.

CMOS is magnified 5000 times so we can see its physical structure.

Nonvolatile bubble memory is frequently the memory of choice for computer-controlled machine tools that must operate in harsh environments.

programs can be executed and data can be processed. RAM space is always at a premium; therefore, after a program has been executed, the storage space it occupied is reallocated to another program awaiting execution.

Figure 3–2 illustrates how all input/output (I/O) is "read to" or "written from" RAM. In the figure, an inquiry (input) is made on a VDT. The inquiry, in the form of a message, is routed to RAM over a channel. The **channel** is a pathway over which signals are transmitted between devices in a computer system. The message is interpreted, and the processor initiates action to retrieve the appropriate program and data from secondary storage. The program and data are "loaded," or moved, to RAM from secondary storage. This is a **nondestructive read** process. That is, the program and data that are read reside in both RAM (temporarily) and secondary storage (permanently). The data are manipulated according to program instructions, and a report is written from RAM to a printer.

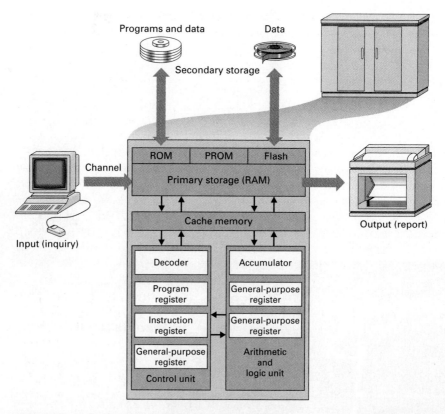

FIGURE 3–2 Interaction between Primary Storage and Computer System Components   *All programs and data must be transferred from an input device or from secondary storage before programs can be executed and data can be processed. During processing, instructions and data are passed between the various types of internal memories, the control unit, and the arithmetic and logic unit. Output is transferred to the printer from primary storage.*

A program instruction or a piece of datum is stored in a specific RAM location called an **address.** Addresses permit program instructions and data to be located, accessed, and processed. The content of each address is constantly changing as different programs are executed and new data are processed.

RAM, ROM, and PROM   A special type of RAM, called *read-only memory* (*ROM*), cannot be altered by the programmer. ROM (rhymes with *mom*), a nonvolatile technology, is introduced briefly in Chapter 2, "Interacting with Computers." The contents of ROM are "hard-wired" (designed into the logic of the memory chip) by the manufacturer and can be "read only." When you turn on a microcomputer system, a program in ROM automatically readies the computer system for use. Then the ROM program produces the initial display-screen prompt.

A variation of ROM is **programmable read-only memory (PROM)**. PROM is ROM into which you, the user, can load "read-only" programs and data. Some microcomputer software packages, such as electronic spreadsheets, are available as PROM units as well as on interchangeable disks. Generally, once a program is loaded to PROM, it is seldom, if ever, changed. **Flash memory** is a type of PROM that can be altered easily by the end user. Flash memory is a feature of many new I/O and storage devices. The intelligence of these devices can be upgraded by simply downloading new software from a vendor-supplied disk to flash memory. Upgrades to early input/output and storage devices required the user to replace the old circuit board or chip with a new one.

Cache Memory   Programs and data are loaded to RAM from secondary storage because the time required to access a program instruction or piece of datum from RAM is significantly less than from secondary storage. Thousands of instructions or pieces of data can be accessed from RAM in the time it would take to access a single piece of datum from disk storage. RAM is essentially a high-speed holding area for data and programs. In fact, *nothing really happens in a computer system until the program instructions and data are moved from RAM to the processor.* This transfer of instructions and data to the processor can be time-consuming, even at microsecond speeds. To facilitate an even faster transfer of instructions and data to the processor, some computers are designed with **cache memory** (see Figure 3–2). Cache memory is employed by computer designers to increase computer system throughput. **Throughput** refers to the rate at which work can be performed by a computer system.

Like RAM, cache is a high-speed holding area for program instructions and data. However, cache memory uses a technology that is about 10 times faster than RAM and about 100 times more expensive. With only a fraction of the capacity of RAM, cache memory holds only those instructions and data that are *likely* to be needed next by the processor.

The Control Unit

Just as the processor is the nucleus of a computer system, the **control unit** is the nucleus of the processor. If you will recall from an earlier discussion, the control unit and the arithmetic and logic unit are the two fundamental sections of a processor. The control unit has three primary functions:

1. To read and interpret program instructions
2. To direct the operation of internal processor components
3. To control the flow of programs and data in and out of RAM

A program must first be loaded to RAM before it can be executed. During execution, the first in a sequence of program instructions is moved from RAM to the control unit, where it is decoded and interpreted by the **decoder.** The control unit then directs other processor components to carry out the operations necessary to execute the instruction.

The control unit contains high-speed working storage areas called **registers** that

Modern technology has taken away some of the romance associated with the computer mystique. Today's computers don't have hundreds of multi-colored blinking lights and swirling tapes. The processing component of this supercomputer has only one switch—on/off.

can store no more than a few bytes (see Figure 3–2). Registers handle instructions and data at a speed about 10 times faster than that of cache memory and are used for a variety of processing functions. One register, called the **instruction register,** contains the instruction being executed. Other general-purpose registers store data needed for immediate processing. Registers also store status information. For example, the **program register** contains the RAM address of the next instruction to be executed. Registers facilitate the movement of data and instructions between RAM, the control unit, and the arithmetic and logic unit.

The Arithmetic and Logic Unit

The **arithmetic and logic unit** performs all computations (addition, subtraction, multiplication, and division) and all logic operations (comparisons). Examples of *computations* include the payroll deduction for Social Security, the day-end inventory, and the balance on a bank statement. A *logic* operation compares two pieces of datum. Then, based on the result of the comparison, the program "branches" to one of several alternative sets of program instructions. Let's use an inventory system to illustrate the logic operation. At the end of each day the inventory level of each item in stock is compared to a reorder point. For each comparison indicating an inventory level that falls below (<) the reorder point, a sequence of program instructions is executed that produces a purchase order. For each comparison indicating an inventory level at or above (= or >) the reorder point, another sequence of instructions is executed.

The arithmetic and logic unit also does alphabetic comparisons. For example, when comparing Smyth and Smith, Smyth is evaluated as being greater alphabetically, so it is positioned after Smith.

The design architecture of IBM-PC–compatible computers and the IBM PS/2 (shown here) is based on the Intel line of microprocessors. All components needed to build an IBM-PC–compatible computer are readily available on the open market. Literally hundreds of companies purchase the individual components and assemble and sell PCs for sale. The most successful companies enhance the fundamental design architecture to give the user added throughput and flexibility.

The Machine Cycle

You have probably heard of computer programming languages such as COBOL, BASIC, and RPG. There are dozens of programming languages in common usage. However, in the end, COBOL, BASIC, RPG, and the other languages are translated into the only language that a computer understands—its own **machine language.** Machine-language instructions are represented inside the computer as strings of binary digits, up to 64 digits in length.

Every machine language has a predefined format for each type of instruction. The relative position within the instruction designates whether a sequence of characters is an **operation code,** an **operand,** or irrelevant. The typical machine language will have from 50 to 200 separate operation codes. The operation code, or **op-code,** is that portion of the fundamental computer instruction that designates the operation to be performed (add, compare, retrieve data from RAM, and so on). The operand is that portion of the instruction that designates data or refers to one or more addresses in RAM in which data can be found or placed. The op-code determines whether the operand contains data, addresses, or both. The following example illustrates the format of typical machine-language instructions. In this example, the AC op-code tells the computer to add the amount stored at RAM address 11011101 to whatever is in the accumulator.

OP-CODE	OPERAND
AC (*a*dd to a*c*cumulator)	11011101 (a RAM address)

Every computer has a **machine cycle.** The following actions take place during the machine cycle (see Figure 3–3):

■ *Fetch instruction.* The next machine-language instruction to be executed (op-code and operand) is retrieved, or "fetched," from RAM or cache memory and loaded to the instruction register in the control unit (see Figure 3–2).

■ *Decode instruction.* The instruction is decoded and interpreted.

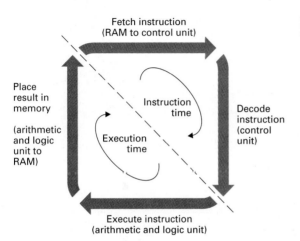

Fetch instruction
(RAM to control unit)

Place result in memory

(arithmetic and logic unit to RAM)

Instruction time

Execution time

Decode instruction (control unit)

Execute instruction
(arithmetic and logic unit)

FIGURE 3–3
The Machine Cycle

■ *Execute instruction.* Using whatever processor resources are needed (primarily the arithmetic and logic unit), the instruction is executed.

■ *Place result in memory.* The results are placed in the appropriate memory position (usually RAM or a register in the arithmetic and logic unit called the **accumulator**). See Figure 3–2.

The speed of a processor is sometimes measured by how long it takes to complete a machine cycle. The timed interval that comprises the machine cycle is the total of the **instruction time,** or **I-time,** and the **execution time,** or **E-time** (see Figure 3–3). The I-time is made up of the first two activities of the machine cycle—fetch and decode the instruction. The E-time comprises the last two activities of the machine cycle—execute the instruction and store the results.

3–5   DESCRIBING THE PROCESSOR: DISTINGUISHING CHARACTERISTICS

People are people, and computers are computers, but how do we distinguish one from another? We describe people in terms of height, build, age, and so on. We describe computers or processors in terms of *word length, speed,* and the *capacity* of their associated RAM. For example, a computer might be described as a 32-bit, 66-MHz, 16-MB micro. Let's see what this means.

Word Length

Just as the brain sends and receives signals through the central nervous system, the processor sends and receives electrical signals through a common electrical **bus.** The bus is the path through which the processor sends/receives data and commands to/from primary and secondary storage and all **peripheral devices** (keyboard, printer, magnetic disk, and so on). A **word** is the number of bits that are handled as a unit within a particular computer system's bus or during internal processing.

Fifteen years ago, a computer's word size applied both to transmissions through the electrical bus and to all internal processing. This is no longer the case. In some of today's computers, one word size defines the bus's **data path** and another word size defines internal processing capacity. Internal processing involves the movement of data and commands between registers, the control unit, and the arithmetic and logic unit. Many popular micros have 32-bit internal processing but only a 16-bit data path through the bus. For certain input/output-oriented applications, a 32-bit computer with a 16-bit data path may not realize the throughput of a full 32-bit computer.

The word length of modern microcomputers is normally 32 bits (four 8-bit bytes). Early micros had word lengths of 8 bits (one byte) and 16 bits (two bytes). High-end micros, workstations, minis, and mainframes have anywhere from 32-bit to 64-bit word lengths. Supercomputers have 64-bit (eight-byte) words.

Processor Speed

A tractor can go 12 miles per hour (mph), a minivan can go 90 mph, and a drag racer can go 220 mph. These speeds, however, provide little insight into the relative capabilities of these vehicles. What good is a 220-mph tractor or a 12-mph minivan? The same is true of computers. Generally, micros are measured in *MHz;* workstations, minis, and mainframes are measured in *MIPS;* and supercomputers in *FLOPS.*

Megahertz: MHz   A *crystal oscillator* paces the execution of instructions within the processor of a microcomputer. A micro's processor speed is rated by its frequency of oscillation, or the number of clock cycles per second. Most personal computers are rated between 5 and 100 **megahertz,** or **MHz** (millions of clock cycles). The elapsed time for one clock cycle is 1/frequency (1 divided by the frequency). For example, the time it takes to complete one cycle on a 50-MHz processor is 1/50,000,000, or 0.00000002 seconds, or 20 nanoseconds. Normally several clock cycles are required to fetch, decode, and execute a single program instruction. The shorter the clock cycle, the faster the processor.

To properly evaluate the processing capability of a micro, you must consider both the processor speed and the word length. A 32-bit micro with a 66-MHz processor has more processing capability than a 16-bit micro with a 66-MHz processor.

MIPS   The processing speed of today's workstations, minis, and mainframes is often measured in **MIPS,** or *m*illions of *i*nstructions *p*er *s*econd. These computers operate in the 20 to 1000 MIPS range. A 100-MIPS computer can execute 100 million instructions per second. Now that computers are performing at 1000 MIPS, look for BIPS (*b*illions of *i*nstructions *p*er *s*econd) to emerge as a measure of speed on high-end mainframe computers.

Many retail establishments are installing kiosks to better assist their customers. This kiosk gives customers an interactive, multimedia-based introduction to the latest fashion trends. The microcomputer behind this kiosk is based on the Intel 80486 chip. It has a processor speed of 66 MHz, a RAM capacity of 32 MB, and a word length of 32 bits.

THE COMPUTER ON A CHIP

The invention of the light bulb in 1879 symbolized the beginning of electronics. Electronics evolved into the use of vacuum tubes, then transistors, and now integrated circuits. Today's microminiaturization of electronic circuitry is continuing to have a profound effect on the way we live and work.

Current technology permits the placement of hundreds of thousands of transistors and electronic switches on a single chip. Chips already fit into wristwatches and credit cards, but electrical and computer engineers want them even smaller. In electronics, smaller is better. The ENIAC, the first full-scale digital electronic computer, weighed 50 tons and occupied an entire room. Today a complete computer is fabricated within a single piece of silicon the size of a child's fingernail.

Chip designers think in terms of nanoseconds (one billionth of a second) and microns (one millionth of a meter). They want to pack as many circuit elements as they can into the structure of a chip. High-density packing reduces the time required for an electrical signal to travel from one circuit element to the next—resulting in faster computers.

Chips are designed and manufactured to perform a particular function. One chip might be a microprocessor for a personal computer. Another might be primary storage. Another might be the logic for a talking vending machine.

The fabrication of integrated circuits involves a multistep process using various photochemical etching and metallurgical techniques. This complex and interesting process is illustrated here with photos, from silicon to the finished product. The process is presented in four steps: *design, fabrication, testing,* and *packaging.*

Design

Using CAD for Chip Design *Chip designers use computer-aided design (CAD) systems to create the logic for individual circuits. A chip contains from one to thirty layers of circuits. In this multilayer circuit design, each layer is color-coded so the designer can distinguish between the various layers.*

Creating a Mask *Each circuit layer is transformed into a mask, or reticle, a glass or quartz plate with an opaque material (such as chrome) formed to create the pattern. The number of layers depends on the complexity of the chip's logic.*

Fabrication

Creating Silicon Ingots *Molten silicon is spun into cylindrical ingots. Because silicon, the second most abundant substance, is used in the fabrication of integrated circuits, chips are sometimes referred to as "intelligent grains of sand."*

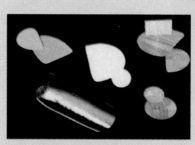

Cutting the Silicon Wafers *The ingot is shaped and prepared prior to being cut into silicon wafers. Once the wafers are cut, they are polished to a perfect finish.*

Coating the Wafers *Silicon wafers that eventually will contain several hundred chips are placed in an oxygen furnace at 1200 degrees Celsius. In the furnace the wafer is coated with other minerals to create the physical properties needed to produce transistors and electronic switches on the surface of the wafer.*

Etching the Wafer

A photoresist is deposited onto the wafer surface creating a film-like substance to accept the patterned image. The mask is  placed over the wafer and both are exposed to ultraviolet light. In this way the circuit pattern is transferred onto the wafer. The photoresist is developed, washing away the unwanted resist and leaving the exact image of the transferred pattern. Plasma (superhot gases) technology is used to etch the circuit pattern permanently into the wafer. This is one of several techniques used in the etching process. The wafer is returned to the furnace and given another coating on which to etch another circuit layer. The procedure is repeated for each circuit layer until the wafer is complete.*

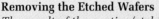

Removing the Etched Wafers

The result of the coating/etching process is a silicon wafer that contains from 100 to 400 integrated circuits.

Drilling the Wafers

It takes only a second for this instrument to drill 1440 tiny holes in a wafer. The holes enable the interconnection of the layers of circuits. Each layer must be perfectly aligned (within a millionth of a meter) with the others.

Testing

Testing the Chips *The chips are tested while they are still part of the wafer. Each integrated circuit on the wafer is powered up and given a series of tests. Fine needles make the connection for these computer-controlled tests. The precision demands are so great that as*  *many as half the chips are found to be defective. A drop of ink is deposited on defective chips.*

Packaging

Dicing the Wafers *A diamond saw separates the wafer into individual chips in a process called dicing.*

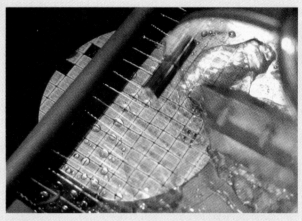

Packaging the Chips *The chips are packaged in protective ceramic or metal carriers. The carriers have standard-sized electrical pin connectors that allow the chip to be plugged conveniently into circuit boards. Because the pins tend to corrode, the pin connectors are the most vulnerable part of a computer system. To avoid corrosion and a bad connection, the pins on some carriers are made of gold.*

Installing the Finished Chips

The completed circuit boards are installed in computers and thousands of other computer-controlled devices.

77

FLOPS   Supercomputer speed is measured in **FLOPS** (rhymes with *plops*)—*fl*oating point *o*perations *p*er *s*econd. Supercomputer applications, which are often scientific, frequently involve floating point operations. Floating point operations accommodate very small or very large numbers. State-of-the-art supercomputers operate in the 30 to 100 **GFLOPS** range. GFLOPS (gigaflops) refers to a billion FLOPS.

Capacity of RAM

The capacity of RAM is stated in terms of the number of bytes it can store. As we learned in this chapter, a byte, or eight bits, is roughly equivalent to a character (such as *A, 1, &*).

Memory capacity for most computers is stated in terms of **megabytes (MB)**, a convenient designation for 1,048,576 (2^{20}) bytes. Memory capacities of modern micros range from 4 MB to 32 MB. Memory capacities of early micros were measured in **kilobytes (KB)**, which is 1024 (2^{10}) bytes of storage.

Some high-end mainframes and supercomputers have more than 1000 MB of RAM. Their RAM capacities are stated as **gigabytes (GB)**, about one billion bytes. It's only a matter of time before we state RAM in terms of **terabytes (TB)**, about one trillion bytes. GB and TB are frequently used in reference to high-capacity secondary storage. Occasionally you will see memory capacities of individual chips stated in terms of **kilobits (Kb)** and **megabits (Mb)**.

Now if anyone ever asks you what a 32-bit, 66-MHz, 16-MB micro is, you've got the answer! This describes the processor of what is emerging as the entry-level PC in the work place.

Differences in Processor Personality

Word length, speed, and *RAM capacity* are the primary descriptors of processors. However, computers, like people, have their own "personalities." That is, two similarly described computers might possess attributes that give one more capability than the other. For example, one 32-bit, 66-MHz, 16-MB PC might permit the connection of three peripheral devices and another six peripheral devices. Or, one might be configured with an accelerator to speed up processing of numeric data. Just remember when you buy a PC that the basic descriptors tell most but not all of the story.

3–6   INSIDE THE PC

Now that you have had an opportunity to see what happens inside computers in general, let's take a closer look inside a personal computer.

Microprocessors: Computer on a Chip

What is smaller than a postage stamp and found in wristwatches, sewing machines, and CD players? The answer: a **microprocessor.** The microprocessor is a small processor that embodies all elements of its larger mainframe cousins: registers, control unit, arithmetic and logic unit, cache memory, and so on (see Section 3–4). Microprocessors play a very important role in our lives. You probably have a dozen or more of them at home and may not know it. They are used in telephones, ovens, televisions, thermostats, greeting cards, automobiles, and, of course, personal computers.

The microprocessor is a product of the microminiaturization of electronic circuitry; it is literally a "computer on a chip." **Chip** refers to any self-contained integrated circuit. The size of chips, which are about 30 thousandths of an inch thick, vary in area from fingernail size (about ¼-inch square) to postage-stamp size (about 1-inch square). These relatively inexpensive microprocessors have been integrated into thousands of mechanical and electronic devices—even elevators, band saws, and ski-boot bindings. In a few years virtually everything mechanical or electronic will incorporate microprocessor technology into its design.

The System Board

In a personal computer, the microprocessor, the electronic circuitry for handling input/output signals from the peripheral devices (keyboard, printer, and so on), and the memory chips are mounted on a single circuit board called a **system board,** or **motherboard.** Before being attached to the system board, the microprocessor and other chips are mounted onto a **carrier.** Carriers have standard-sized pin connectors that allow the chips to be attached to the system board.

The system board, the "guts" of a microcomputer, is what distinguishes one microcomputer from another. The central component of the system board, the microprocessor, is generally not made by the manufacturers of micros. It is made by companies, such as Motorola and Intel, that specialize in the development and manufacture of microprocessors.

Motorola Microprocessors   Motorola manufactures the 68000, or 68K, family of microprocessors. The family includes the 68000, 68020, 68030, 68040, and 68060 microprocessors. Most of Apple's Macintosh-series micros use Motorola 68K chips: the Motorola 68000 in earlier models, the Motorola 68020 in the Macintosh II, and the Motorola 68030 and 68040 chips in recent models. The 68060 is popular with high-performance workstations.

Some people say that electric automobiles are the wave of the future. Microprocessors in the electric motors help optimize the use of stored energy and the delivery of power to the drive train.

Some industry observers are predicting that Motorola's new PowerPC line of microprocessors may emerge as a new industry standard—time will tell. They say this because the PowerPC is a product of an alliance between three of the computer industry's most powerful players: Motorola, Apple, and IBM. The PowerPC family includes the PowerPC 601, the PowerPC 603, the PowerPC 604, and the PowerPC 620. The first three are designed for use in PCs, including those manufac-

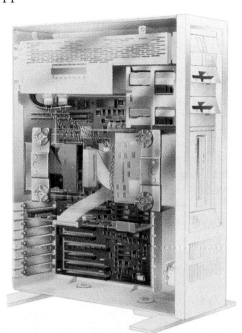

The system board on this tower PC is based on the high performance Intel 486 microprocessor. The chip packs 1.2 million transistors in a 0.414-inch by 0.619-inch die.

tured by Apple and IBM. The PowerPC 620 is designed for use with every-thing from high-end workstations to supercomputers. The PowerPC provides users with tremendous flexibility in that it can run all major industry-standard operating system platforms, including IBM's OS/2 and AIX, Apple's Macintosh System, and Microsoft's Windows.

Intel Microprocessors   The system board for the original IBM PC, the IBM PC/XT, and most of the IBM-PC compatibles manufactured through 1984, used the Intel 8088 microprocessor chip. The Intel 8088 chip is a slower version of the Intel 8086, which was developed in 1979. At the time of the introduction of the IBM PC (1981), the Intel 8086 was thought to be too advanced for the emerging PC market. Ironically, the more powerful Intel 8086 chip was not used in micros until the introduction of the low-end models of the IBM PS/2 series in 1987. The 8086 is considered the base technology for all microprocessors used in IBM-PC–compatible and PS/2 series computers.

The IBM PC/AT (Advanced Technology), which was introduced in 1984, employed an Intel 80286 microprocessor. As much as six times faster than the 8088, the 80286 provided a substantial increase in PC performance. High-end IBM-PC–compatible micros and PS/2s use the more advanced Intel 80386 and 80486 chips. When someone talks about a "286," "386," or "486" machine, he or she is referring to a micro that uses an Intel 80286, 80386, or 80486 chip. Successor Intel microprocessors to the 486 fall in the Pentium family of microprocessors. The performance of the initial Pentium chip is expected to be double that of the 486. The Pentium chip is being designed to better accommodate multimedia applications that involve sound and motion video.

Summary   After the microprocessor and other chips have been mounted on the system board, it is simply inserted in the slot designed for the system board. Once installed in the slot, the system board is linked to the bus and, therefore, anything else that is connected to the bus (see Figure 3–4). Remember, the bus is the path through which the processor communicates with memory components and peripheral devices.

Configuring a Microcomputer System

Normally, computer professionals are called upon to select, configure, and install the hardware associated with minicomputers and mainframe computers. But for micros, the user typically selects, configures, and installs his or her own system; therefore, it is important that you know what makes up a microcomputer system and how it fits together.

A Typical Microcomputer Configuration   The computer and its peripheral devices are called the computer system **configuration.** The configuration of a microcomputer can vary. Generally, the minimal micro configuration consists of the following:

1. A microcomputer
2. A keyboard and a point-and-draw device for input
3. A monitor for *soft-copy* (temporary) output

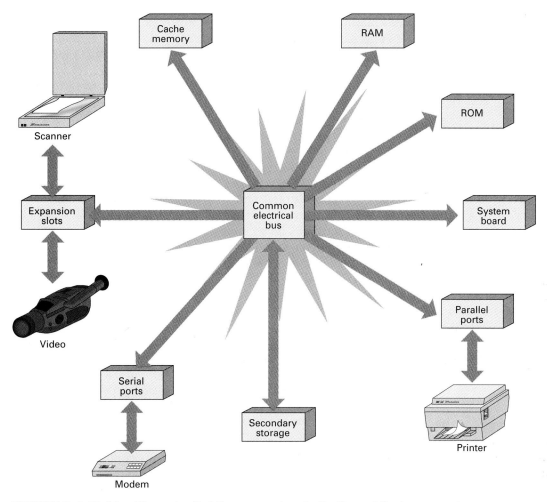

FIGURE 3–4 Linking Elements of a Microcomputer via the Bus   *All microcomputer components are linked via a common electrical bus. The bus is the path through which the processor (on the system board) communicates with memory components and peripheral devices.*

   4. A printer for *hard-copy* (printed) output
   5. Two magnetic disk drives for permanent data and program storage (one for a permanently installed disk; one to accommodate interchangeable disks)

In desktop and tower microcomputer systems, these components are purchased as separate physical units and then linked together. Portable PCs may include all but the printer in a single unit. A few portable PCs even include the printer. Virtually all micros, even pocket PCs, give users the flexibility to configure the system with a variety of peripheral devices and are said to have an **open architecture.** We use the term *architecture* to refer to a computer system's design. A component stereo system provides a good analogy with which to illustrate the concept of open architecture. In a stereo system, the tuner is the central component to which equalizers, tape decks, compact disk players, speakers, and so on can be attached. An open-architecture microcomputer system is configured by linking any of a wide variety of peripheral devices to the processor component via the bus.

Linking Micro Components   An open architecture, also called a **bus architecture,** is possible because all micro components are linked via a common electrical bus. Figure 3–4 illustrates how RAM, ROM, cache memory, storage devices, and other elements of a PC interact with the system board through the bus. In short, the bus is the vehicle by which the processor communicates with its peripherals and vice versa. The processor, RAM, ROM, cache memory, and disk storage devices usually are enclosed in the same physical unit as the system board and bus; therefore, they are connected directly to the bus—that is, without cables.

In an open architecture, external input/output devices (such as a printer and other devices external to the processor cabinet) and some storage devices come with a cable and a multipin connector. To link a device to the PC, you plug its connector into a receptacle in much the same way you plug a lamp cord into an electrical outlet. The receptacle, called a **port,** provides a direct link to the micro's common electrical bus.

External peripheral devices are linked to the processor via cables through either a **serial port** or a **parallel port** (see Figure 3–4).

- *Serial ports.* Serial ports facilitate the *serial transmission* of data, *one bit at a time.* The bit is the basic unit of data for computers. Serial ports provide an interface for modems and low-speed printers. A **modem** permits communication with remote computers via a telephone-line link. The standard for micro serial ports is the 9-pin or 25-pin (male or female) **RS-232C connector.**

- *Parallel ports.* Parallel ports facilitate the *parallel transmission* of data; that is, several bits are transmitted simultaneously. Parallel ports use the same 25-pin RS-232C connector or the 36-pin **Centronics connector.** Parallel ports provide the interface for such devices as high-speed printers, magnetic tape backup units, and other computers.

Expansion Slots and Add-on Boards   The processing components of most micros are sold with several empty **expansion slots** so you can purchase and plug in optional capabilities in the form of **add-on boards.** The expansion slots provide direct connections to the common electrical bus. These slots enable a micro owner to enhance the functionality of a basic micro configuration with a wide variety of special-function *add-on boards,* also called **add-on cards.** These "add-ons" contain the electronic circuitry for a wide variety of computer-related functions. The number of available expansion slots varies from computer to computer. Some of the more popular add-on boards are listed below.

- *RAM.* RAM add-ons expand the capacity of random-access memory, usually in increments of 1 MB.
- *Color and graphics adapter.* These adapters permit interfacing with video monitors that have graphics and/or color capabilities. The VGA (video graphics array) board enables the interfacing of high-resolution monitors with the processor.
- *Fax modem.* The **fax modem** performs the same function as a regular modem plus it has an added capability—it enables a PC to emulate a **facsimile** or **fax** machine. Fax machines transfer images of documents via telephone lines to another location. Modems are discussed further in Chapter 6, "Data Communications and Networking."
- *Serial port.* Installation of this board provides access to the bus via another serial port. Most micros are sold with at least one serial and one parallel port.

When installed in a PC's expansion slot, this video graphics add-on card enhances the monitor's resolution to enable CAD and desktop publishing applications.

- *Parallel port.* Installation of this board provides access to the bus via another parallel port.

- *Video capture.* This card enables full-motion color video with audio to be captured and stored on disk. Once on disk storage, video information can be integrated with text, graphics, and other forms of presentation (see Figure 3–4).

- *Peripheral device interface.* Some peripheral devices, such as scanners (devices that capture images on hard-copy documents), very high resolution printers, plotters (devices that provide precision plots of graphs), and external magnetic disk drives are sold with an interface card, as well as a cable. To install one of these devices you will need to insert its interface card into an empty expansion slot, then connect its cable to the interface card (see Figure 3–4). Devices with interface cards do not require the use of one of the PC's serial or parallel ports.

- *Accelerator.* The accelerator board gives the user the flexibility to upgrade a micro's processor. In effect, the higher speed processor on the accelerator board replaces the existing processor.

- *Network interface.* The network interface card (NIC) facilitates and controls the exchange of data between the micros in a PC *network* (several micros linked together). Each PC in a network must be equipped with an NIC. The cables that link the PCs are physically connected to the NICs.

- *Sound.* The sound card is becoming very popular and may well become part of the *minimal PC configuration* within a few years. The sound card enables two basic functions. First, it enables sounds to be captured and stored on disk. Second, it enables sounds to be played through external speakers. The sound card adds realism to computer games with stereo music and sound effects. It allows us to insert verbal notes within our word processing documents. The sound card gives us the capability to ask associated software to read portions of our on-screen displays to us.

Most of the add-on boards are *multifunction:* They include two or more of these capabilities. For example, one popular **multifunction add-on board** comes with a serial port and a fax modem.

Expansion slots are at a premium. To make the most efficient use of these slots, circuit-board manufacturers have created **half-size expansion boards** that fit in a "short slot" (half an expansion slot). Judicious use of these half-size boards can effectively double the number of expansion slots available for a given microcomputer.

Notebook PCs, because of their compact size, have fewer expansion slots than desktop PCs. For this reason, some notebook PCs are designed so that add-on cards can be easily installed and removed. For example, the same expansion slot could be used for a network interface card or a fax modem card as needed.

PC Cards: PCMCIA Technology   The **PCMCIA card,** sometimes called **PC card,** emerged a few years ago as a credit-card–sized memory module. The Personal Computer Memory Card International Association (PCMCIA) was established in 1989 to create standards for the manufacture of PC cards.

Since the PC card's introduction, entrepreneurs have expanded its functional horizons far past simple supplementary memory. Virtually all PDAs (personal digital assistants) and most portable computers are being equipped with a PCMCIA-compliant interface. The interface is an external slot that permits easy connection of any PC card to the computer's bus. Besides offering supplementary nonvolatile memory, PC cards offer many capabilities embodied in add-on boards, including fax modems, network interface adapters, hard disks, and sound. PC cards even offer some capabilities that are not available on add-on boards. For example, one PC card comes in the form of a Mobile

GPS (global positioning system). The Mobile GPS card can be used to pinpoint the latitude and longitude of the user within 80 feet, anywhere on or near earth. The PC card is especially handy for the portable environment because the user can insert capabilities as they are needed. PDAs and notebook PCs do not have enough space to accommodate the same permanent variety of add-on capabilities as their desktop cousins do.

IMPORTANT TERMS AND SUMMARY OUTLINE

accumulator
add-on board/card
address
alpha
alphanumeric
arithmetic and logic unit
ASCII
ASCII-8
binary
bit
bubble memory
bus
bus architecture
byte
cache memory
carrier
central processing unit (CPU)
Centronics connector
channel
chip
configuration
control unit
data path
decoder

encoding system
execution time (E-time)
expansion slot
facsimile (fax)
fax modem
flash memory
FLOPS
GFLOPS
gigabyte (GB)
half-size expansion board
instruction register
instruction time (I-time)
kilobit (Kb)
kilobyte (KB)
machine cycle
machine language
megabit (Mb)
megabyte (MB)
megahertz (MHz)
microprocessor
MIPS
modem
motherboard
multifunction add-on board

nondestructive read
nonvolatile memory
numeric
open architecture
operand
operation code (op-code)
parallel port
PC card
PCMCIA card
peripheral device
port
primary storage
program register
programmable read-only memory
(PROM)
register
RS-232C connector
secondary storage
serial port
system board
terabyte (TB)
throughput
volatile memory
word

3–1   Data Storage: Data in the Computer Data, not information, are stored in a computer system. Data are stored temporarily during processing in **primary storage** (RAM) and permanently on **secondary storage** devices, such as magnetic tape and disk drives.

3–2   A Bit About the Bit The two electronic states of the computer—on and off—are represented by a **bit,** short for *bi*nary dig*it.* These electronic states are compatible with the **binary** numbering system. Letters and decimal numbers are translated into bits for storage and processing on computer systems.

3–3   Encoding Systems: Combining Bits to Form Bytes **Alphanumeric** (**alpha** and **numeric**) characters are represented in computer storage by combining strings of bits to form unique bit configurations for each character.

Characters are translated into these bit configurations, also called **bytes,** according to a particular coding scheme, called an **encoding system.** Popular encoding systems include **ASCII** and **ASCII-8.**

3–4   Components of a Computer System: A Closer Look at the Processor and RAM The processor is the "intelligence" of a computer system. A processor, which is also called the **central processing unit** or **CPU,** has only two fundamental sections, the **control unit** and the **arithmetic and logic unit,** which work together with RAM to execute programs. The control unit reads and interprets instructions and directs the arithmetic and logic unit to perform computation and logic operations.

RAM, or random-access memory, provides the processor with temporary storage for programs and data.

Input/output (I/O) is "read to" or "written from" RAM over a **channel.** In RAM, datum is stored at a specific **address.** Most of today's computers use CMOS technology for RAM. CMOS is **volatile memory;** that is, the data are lost when the electrical current is turned off or interrupted. In contrast, **bubble memory** provides **nonvolatile memory.** All input/output, including programs, must enter and exit RAM. Programs are loaded to RAM from secondary storage in a **nondestructive read** process. Other variations of internal storage are ROM, **programmable read-only memory** or **PROM,** and **flash memory.**

Some computers employ **cache memory** to increase **throughput** (the rate at which work can be performed by a computer system). Like RAM, cache is a high-speed holding area for program instructions and data. However, cache memory holds only those instructions and data likely to be needed next by the processor. During execution, instructions and data are passed between very high-speed **registers** (for example, the **instruction register,** the **program register,** and the **accumulator**) in the control unit and the arithmetic and logic unit.

Every **machine language** has a predefined format for each type of instruction. Each instruction has an **operation code (op-code)** and an **operand.** During one **machine cycle,** an instruction is "fetched" from RAM, decoded by the **decoder** in the control unit, executed, and the results are placed in memory. The machine-cycle time is the total of the **instruction time (I-time)** and the **execution time (E-time).**

3–5   Describing the Processor: Distinguishing Characteristics A processor is described in terms of its word length, speed, and RAM capacity.

A **word** is the number of bits that are handled as a unit within a particular computer system's common electrical bus or during internal processing. The **bus** is the path through which the processor sends/receives data and commands to/from storage and **peripheral devices.** In some of today's computers, one word size defines the bus's **data path** and another word size defines internal processing capacity.

Microcomputer speed is measured in **megahertz (MHz).** Workstation, mini, and mainframe speed is measured in **MIPS.** Supercomputer speed is measured in **FLOPS** and **GFLOPS.**

Memory capacity is measured in **kilobytes (KB), megabytes (MB), gigabytes (GB),** and **terabytes (TB).** Chip capacity is sometimes stated in **kilobits (Kb)** and **megabits (Mb).**

3–6   Inside the PC The **microprocessor,** a product of the microminiaturization of electronic circuitry, is literally a "computer on a chip." **Chip** refers to any self-contained integrated circuit. In a microcomputer, the microprocessor, the electronic circuitry for handling input/output signals from the peripheral devices, and the memory chips are mounted on a single circuit board called a **system board,** or **motherboard.** Before being attached to the system board, the microprocessor and other chips are mounted onto a **carrier.**

The computer and its peripheral devices are called the computer system **configuration.** A typical micro configuration would be a computer, a keyboard, a monitor, a printer, and two magnetic disk drives. Micro users have the flexibility to configure their systems with a variety of peripheral devices because of the systems' **open architecture,** or **bus architecture.** A **port** provides a direct link to the micro's bus. **Modems,** which permit communication with remote computers via a telephone-line link, and other external peripheral devices are interfaced with the processor through either a **serial port** or a **parallel port.** The standard for micro serial ports is the **RS-232C connector.** The RS-232C and **Centronics connectors** are used with parallel ports.

The processing components of most micros are sold with several empty **expansion slots** so you can purchase and plug in optional capabilities in the form of **add-on boards** (also **add-on cards**). Popular add-on boards include RAM, color and graphics adapter, **fax modem** (enables emulation of a **facsimile** or **fax** machine), serial port, parallel port, video capture, peripheral device interface, accelerator, network interface, and sound. Most are **multifunction add-on boards. Half-size expansion boards** fit in a "short slot."

The **PCMCIA card,** sometimes called **PC card,** provides a variety of interchangeable add-on capabilities in the form of credit-card–sized modules. The capabilities include supplementary nonvolatile memory, fax modems, network interface adapters, hard disks, sound, and more. The PC card is especially handy for the portable environment.

REVIEW EXERCISES

Concepts

1. Distinguish between RAM, ROM, and PROM.
2. How many ASCII-8 bytes can be stored in a 32-bit word?

3. Which two functions are performed by the arithmetic and logic unit?
4. List examples of alpha, numeric, and alphanumeric characters.

5. Write your first name as an ASCII bit configuration.
6. What are the functions of the control unit?
7. We describe computers in terms of what three characteristics?
8. What is the basic difference between CMOS technology and nonvolatile technology, such as bubble memory?
9. For a given computer, which type of memory would have the greatest capacity to store data and programs: cache or RAM? RAM or registers? registers or cache?
10. Name three types of registers.
11. Which portion of the fundamental computer instruction designates the operation to be performed?
12. What do the *I* in *I-time* and the *E* in *E-time* stand for?
13. What is the relationship between a microprocessor, a motherboard, and a microcomputer?
14. List five functional enhancements that can be added to a microcomputer by inserting one or more optional add-on boards into expansion slots.
15. Why are some microcomputers sold with empty expansion slots?

Discussion

16. *KB* is used to represent 1024 bytes of storage. Would it have been much easier to let *KB* represent 1000 bytes? Explain.
17. Compute the time it takes to complete one cycle on a 66-MHz processor in both seconds and nanoseconds.
18. List at least 10 products that are smaller than a breadbox and use microprocessors. Select one and describe the function of its microprocessor.
19. What options would you like to have on your own personal micro that are not included in a minimum configuration? Why?

SELF-TEST (BY SECTION)

3–1 Data are stored permanently on secondary storage devices, such as magnetic tape. (T/F)

3–2 **a.** *Bit* is the singular of *byte.* (T/F)
  b. The base of the binary number system is: (a) 2, (b) 8, or (c) 16?

3–3 The combination of bits used to represent a character is called a ____byte____.

3–4 **a.** Data are loaded from secondary storage to RAM in a nondestructive read process. (T/F)
  b. The _control unit_ is that part of the processor that reads and interprets program instructions.
  c. The arithmetic and logic unit controls the flow of programs and data in and out of main memory. (T/F)
  d. Put the following memories in order based on speed: cache, registers, and RAM. _cache ram reg_
  e. The timed interval that comprises the machine cycle is the total of the ____instruction____ time and the _execution_ time.

3–5 **a.** The word length of most microcomputers is 64 bits. (T/F)
  b. *MIPS* is an acronym for "millions of instructions per second." (T/F)
  c. _FLOPS_ is a common measure of super-computer processor speed.

3–6 **a.** The processing component of a motherboard is a _microprocessor_.
  b. The computer and its peripheral devices are called the computer system _configuration_.
  c. The RS-232C connector provides the interface to a port. (T/F)
  d. In an open architecture, all PC components are linked via a common electrical _bus_.

Self-test answers. **3–1** T. **3–2 (a)** F; **(b)** a. **3–3** byte. **3–4 (a)** T; **(b)** control unit; **(c)** F; **(d)** from the slowest to the fastest memory: RAM, cache, registers; **(e)** instruction, execution. **3–5 (a)** F; **(b)** T; **(c)** FLOPS or GFLOPS. **3–6 (a)** microprocessor; **(b)** configuration; **(c)** T; **(d)** bus.

4

INPUT/OUTPUT DEVICES

OBJECTIVES

To explain alternative approaches to and devices for data entry.

To describe the operation and application of common output devices.

To describe the use and characteristics of the different types of terminals.

4–1   I/O DEVICES: OUR INTERFACE WITH THE COMPUTER

Data are created in many places and in many ways. Before data can be processed and stored, they must be translated into a form the computer can interpret. For this, we need *input* devices. Once the data have been processed, they must be translated back into a form *we* can understand. For this, we need *output* devices. These input/output (I/O) devices, or peripheral devices, enable communication between us and the computer.

Just about everyone routinely communicates directly or indirectly with a computer via I/O devices. This includes people who have never sat in front of a personal computer or video display terminal. For example, have you ever been hungry and short of cash? It's lunch time and you have only 47 cents in your pocket. No problem. Just stop at an automatic teller machine (ATM) and ask for some "lunch money." The ATM's keyboard (input) and monitor (output) enable you to hold an interactive conversation with the bank's computer. The ATM's printer (output) provides you with a hard copy of your transactions when you leave.

In this chapter we discuss commonly used input and output devices. Also, we discuss terminals with I/O capabilities.

Most of today's jobs require some interaction with computers, including those in the military. These soldiers at a Defense Department command and control center are in constant communication with one another and their computers.

4–2   TRADITIONAL INPUT DEVICES

The Keyboard

Alphanumeric Keyboards   All PCs, workstations, and VDTs have a keyboard, the mainstay device for user input to the computer system. One of the most widely used keyboard layouts is the 101-key keyboard with the traditional *QWERTY* key layout, 12 function keys, a key pad, a variety of special-function keys, and dedicated cursor-control keys. We discuss this keyboard and its important keys in Chapter 2, "Interacting with Computers" (see Figure 2–5). PC, workstation, and VDT keyboards vary considerably in appearance. Portable computers have a simple QWERTY keyboard with a minimum number of function keys. Desktop computers are frequently configured with a 124-key PC keyboard that includes an extended set of function keys and extra unlabeled keys that can be programmed to perform user-defined keystroke sequences (macros) when tapped.

Special-Function Keyboards   Some keyboards are designed for specific applications. For example, the cash-register-like terminals at most fast-food restaurants have special-purpose keyboards. Rather than key in the name and price of an order of French fries, attendants need only press the key marked "French fries" to record the sale. These keyboards help shop supervisors, airline ticket agents, retail sales clerks, and many others interact more quickly with their computer systems.

The keyboard remains the primary vehicle for on-line data entry. Here, classified ad personnel at the Daily Camera in Boulder, Colorado, take ad orders for 12 Denver-area newspapers.

Point-and-Draw Devices

The Mouse   The keyboard is too cumbersome for some applications, especially those that rely on a graphical user interface (GUI) or require the user to point or draw. The effectiveness of GUIs depends on the user's ability to make a rapid selection from a screen full of graphic icons or menus. In these instances the mouse can position the pointer (graphics cursor) over an icon quickly and efficiently. Computer artists use mice to create images. Engineers use them to "draw" lines that connect points on a graph. We discuss the operation of the mouse in Chapter 2, "Interacting with Computers."

Other Point-and-Draw Devices   The mouse is the most popular point-and-draw device. However, a variety of devices are available that move the graphics cursor to point and draw, each with its advantages and disadvantages. The *joystick, track ball,* and *digitizer tablet and pen* are also input devices that move the graphics cursor to point or draw.

Video arcade wizards are no doubt familiar with the joystick and track ball. The **joystick** is a vertical stick that moves the graphics cursor in the direction the stick is pushed. The **track ball** is a ball inset in a small external box or adjacent to and in the same unit as the keyboard. Track balls are often configured with portable computers and workstations. The ball is "rolled" with the fingers to move the graphics cursor. Some people find it helpful to think of a track ball as an upside-down mouse with a bigger ball on the bottom. Many laptop PCs include a track ball below or to the side of the keyboard.

There are two mice in this photo. Both move freely about the desktop. Both have tails. But only one eats cheese.

The **digitizer tablet and pen** are a pen and a pressure-sensitive tablet with the same X–Y coordinates as the screen. Some digitizing tablets also use a *crosshair* device instead of a pen. The movement of the pen or crosshair is reproduced simultaneously on the display screen. When configured with a laptop or a desktop PC, the digitizer tablet and pen enables the PC to perform pen-based computing applications, such as entering handwritten data to the system.

Summary   The relatively inexpensive mouse remains popular, but its disadvantages, namely its lack of precision and desk space requirements, are encouraging users to seek alternatives. In response, a number of companies are trying to build a better mouse. For example, several innovative devices allow the hand to remain stationary, permitting precision cursor manipulation with the fingers. They have innovative names like Felix, Gulliver, MousePen, and Thumbelina.

Look for rapid changes in point-and-draw technology in the next few years. Already a growing number of manufacturers of point-and-draw devices are going wireless; that is, they are eliminating the cable that attaches the device to the processor and replacing it with a wireless alternative.

The Handwriter for Windows point-and-draw tool is as easy to use as a pen and paper. A cordless pen and an ultra-thin tablet provide the familiarity of a pen and paper. The tablet's 10-foot cord lets the user point, write, and draw in almost any position from lying down to standing.

4–3   SOURCE-DATA AUTOMATION: GETTING CLOSER TO THE ACTION

Trends in Data Entry

The trend in data entry has been toward decreasing the number of transcription steps. This is accomplished by entering the data as close to the source as possible. For example, in most sales departments, salespeople key in orders directly to the system. In many accounting departments, bookkeepers and accountants record and enter financial transactions into the system from their VDT keyboards. However, whenever possible, the need for key entry transcription of data can be eliminated altogether. This is known as **source-data automation**.

Until recently, data entry has been synonymous with *keystrokes*. The keystroke will continue to be the basic mode of data entry for the foreseeable future, but the need for key-driven data entry has been eliminated in many applications. For example, you have probably noticed the preprinted **bar codes** on grocery products. At supermarket checkout counters these bar codes have eliminated the need for most key entry. Checkers need only pass the product over the *laser scanner*. The price is entered and the shelf inventory is updated as well.

Data entry is an area in which enormous potential exists for increases in productivity. The technology of data entry devices is constantly changing. New and improved methods of transcribing raw data are being invented and put on the market each month. These data entry methods and associated devices are discussed next.

Optical Character Recognition

Optical character recognition (OCR) is a way to encode (write) certain data in machine-readable format on the original source document. For example, the

International Standard Book Number (ISBN) on the back cover of this book is printed in machine-readable OCR. This eliminates the need for publishers and bookstore clerks to key these data manually. OCR equipment consists of a family of devices that encode and read OCR data.

OCR Scanners OCR characters are identified by light-sensitive devices called **OCR scanners**. There are two types of scanners, *contact* and *laser*. Both bounce a beam of light off an image, then measure the reflected light to determine the value of the image. Hand-held contact scanners make contact as they are brushed over the printed matter to be read. Laser-based scanners are more versatile and can read data passed near the scanning area. Scanners of both technologies can recognize printed characters and various types of codes.

OCR devices can "learn" to read almost any typeface, including the one used for this book! The "learning" takes place when the structure of the character set is described to the OCR device. Special OCR devices can even read hand-printed letters if they are recorded on a standard form and written according to specific rules.

OCR scanners can be classified into the following six categories:

- *Hand-held label scanners.* These devices read data on price tags, shipping labels, inventory part numbers, book ISBNs, and the like. Hand-held label scanners, sometimes called **wand scanners,** use either contact or laser technology. You have probably seen both types used in various retail stores. Wand scanners also are used to read package labels in shipping and receiving and in inventory management.
- *Stationary label scanners.* These devices, which rely exclusively on laser technology, are used in the same types of applications as wand scanners. Stationary scanners are common in grocery stores and many high-volume discount stores.

Supermarket checkout systems are now an established cost-saving technology. The automated systems use stationary laser scanners to read the bar codes that identify each item. Price and product descriptions are retrieved from a database and recorded on the sales slip. Also, the store's inventory is updated after each sale.

- ■ *Page scanners.* These devices scan and interpret the alphanumeric characters on regular printed pages. People use page scanners to translate printed hard copy to machine-readable format. For applications that demand this type of translation, page scanners can minimize or eliminate the need for key entry.
- ■ *Document scanners.* Document scanners are capable of scanning documents of varying sizes (for example, utility-bill invoice stubs and sales slips from credit-card transactions).
- ■ *Continuous-form scanners.* These devices read data printed on continuous forms, such as cash register tapes.
- ■ *Optical mark scanners.* Optical mark scanners scan preprinted forms, such as multiple-choice test answer forms. The position of the "sense mark" indicates a particular response or character.

Bar Codes Stationary scanners, such as those in supermarkets, use lasers to interpret the bar codes printed on products. Bar codes represent alphanumeric data by varying the width and combination of adjacent vertical lines. Just as there are a variety of internal bit encoding systems, there are a variety of bar-coding systems (see Figure 4–1). One of the most visible of these systems is the Universal Product Code (UPC). The UPC, originally used for supermarket items, is now being printed on other consumer goods. The advantage of bar codes over characters is that the position or orientation of the code being read is not as critical to the scanner. In a supermarket, for example, the data can be recorded even if a bottle of ketchup is rolled over the laser scanner.

Applications of Optical Scanners Source-data automation has resulted in the use of optical scanners for a variety of applications. One of the more innovative uses of stationary scanners is along toll roads. Drivers who frequently use a particular toll road pay tolls in advance and receive labels for their cars. Stationary scanners along the toll road read the labels as cars pass at highway speeds. The electronic toll booths transmit the data directly to a central computer system. At the central site, the drivers' accounts are debited the amount of the toll.

FIGURE 4–1 Various Codes That Can Be Interpreted by OCR Scanners

In an electric utility company's billing system, invoices are generated from the customer master file and the electricity usage file. Data on the invoice are printed in a format that can be read by an OCR document scanner. Therefore, no data entry is required when the customer returns the OCR-readable invoice stub with the payment.

Image Scanners

In recent years, source-data automation has expanded to allow the direct entry of graphic information, as well as text-based information, via scanners. An **image scanner** uses laser technology to scan and **digitize** an image. That is, the hard-copy image is translated into an electronic format that can be interpreted by and stored on computers. The digitized image is then stored on disk. The image to be scanned can be handwritten notes, a photograph, a drawing, an insurance form—anything that can be digitized. Once an image has been digitized and entered to the computer system, it can be retrieved, displayed, altered, merged with text, stored, sent via data communications to one or several remote computers, and even faxed. This application, known as **image processing,** is experiencing rapid growth. As a result, image scanners may become a must-have peripheral in most offices.

Clerks in retail stores use wand scanners to expedite the recording of sales. The possibility of entering erroneous data is significantly less with a wand scanner than with a keyboard.

Image scanners are of two types: *page* and *hand.* Either can be gray scale (the image is presented in shades of gray) or color. (Gray scale is discussed later in this chapter.) The *page image scanner* works like a desktop duplicating machine. That is, the image to be scanned is placed face down on the scanning surface, covered, then scanned. The result is a high-resolution digitized image. The *hand image scanner* is rolled manually over the image to be scanned. Because it must be guided across the image by the human hand, the resolution of a hand image scanner is not as high. Hand image scanners, about five inches in width, are appropriate for capturing small images or portions of large images.

If you purchase optional hardware and software, you can turn your image scanner into an OCR page scanner. That is, the image scanner can read and interpret the characters from most printed material, such as a printed letter or a page from this book.

Relatively inexpensive image scanners have given rise to a variety of image processing applications. On the left an attorney is using a page scanner to scan passages from pertinent cases into storage. On the right an author of education software is using a hand scanner to enter graphic images that will be integrated into the software.

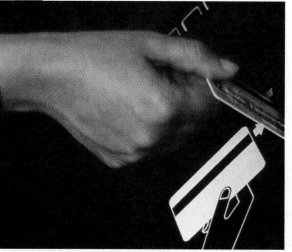

The magnetic stripe on the back of your credit card opens the door to many applications. Not only can you obtain instant cash from automatic teller machines all over the world, but you can purchase a growing number of products and services by simply inserting your card in a badge reader. For example, thousands of gasoline service stations are now totally self-service, including self-pay.

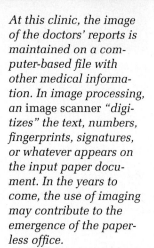

At this clinic, the image of the doctors' reports is maintained on a computer-based file with other medical information. In image processing, an image scanner "digitizes" the text, numbers, fingerprints, signatures, or whatever appears on the input paper document. In the years to come, the use of imaging may contribute to the emergence of the paperless office.

Magnetic Stripes and Smart Cards

The magnetic stripes on the back of charge cards and badges offer another means of data entry at the source. The magnetic stripes are encoded with data appropriate for the application. For example, your account number and privacy code are encoded on a card for automatic teller machines.

Magnetic stripes contain much more data per unit of space than do printed characters or bar codes. Moreover, because they cannot be read visually, they are perfect for storing confidential data, such as a privacy code. Employee cards and security badges often contain authorization data for access to physically secured areas, such as the computer center. To gain access, an employee inserts a card or badge into a **badge reader**. This device reads and checks the authorization code before permitting the individual to enter a secured area. When badge readers are linked to a central computer, a chronological log of people entering or leaving secured areas can be maintained.

The enhanced version of cards with a magnetic stripe is called the **smart card**. The smart card, similar in appearance to other cards, contains a microprocessor that retains certain security and personal data in its memory at all times. Because the smart card can hold more information, has some processing capability, and is almost impossible to duplicate, smart cards may soon replace cards with magnetic stripes.

Voice Data Entry

Speech-recognition systems can be used to enter limited kinds and quantities of data. Successful speech-recognition systems are limited to accepting words and tasks within a relatively small domain. Despite its limitations, speech recognition has a number of applications. Salespeople in the field can enter an order simply by calling the computer and stating the customer number, item number, and quantity. Quality-control personnel who must use their hands call out defects as they are detected. Baggage handlers at airports simply state the three-letter destination identifier ("L-A-X" for Los Angeles International) and luggage is routed to the appropriate conveyer system. Physicians in the operating room can request certain information about a patient while operating. A computer-based *audio-response unit* or a *speech synthesizer* makes the conversation two-way.

TO TALK WITH A COMPUTER

Ever since "thinking machines" first captured the public imagination, users have dreamed of conversing with a computer—a feat immortalized in science-fiction tales from *2001: A Space Odyssey* to *Star Trek*. Today, advances in both *voice response* and *speech recognition* are helping to keep the dream alive.

Voice Response: An Accomplished Fact Voice response takes two forms: digitized recordings of a human voice and speech synthesis, which combines digitized phonemes to "speak" words and phrases. A *phoneme* is the smallest unit of recognizable speech.

The most prevalent application of voice response is probably directory assistance. Callers give their requests to human operators, who initiate a database search and sometimes verify the entry desired, perhaps by confirming an address. From there, the system's audio unit takes over. A digitized recording—"The number is . . ."—is followed by a synthesized reading of the number, followed by a second recording, "If you need further assistance, . . ."

Microcomputer systems are also gaining a voice, thanks to speech-synthesizing utilities like Monologue for Windows, which will read aloud any words or numbers users highlight within Windows applications.

Speech Recognition: A Still Emerging Technology Building a talking computer is simple compared to the challenge of creating a computer that obeys spoken commands. First, the computer has to be equipped with artificial ears, in the form of a microphone and sound board that converts the audio signals of the human voice into digital signals the computer can process. Second, the computer must be equipped with software that can decipher speech. This is an enormous programming challenge, given the vagaries of human speech.

■ *Assembly-line work.* General Motors and a number of other major organizations are using speech-recognition software to simplify quality control, safety reporting, and inventory recording.

■ *Computer control for the disabled.* Thousands of disabled workers are using speech-recognition systems to perform such traditional applications as word processing, spreadsheets, and database management.

■ *Telephone service.* Telephone companies, such as Sprint and AT&T, have voice-recognition systems that automate the processing of most collect and third-party-billing calls. The new system would combine digitized recordings ("This is a collect call from . . .") and sophisticated speech-recognition software that uses "word spotting" to filter out room noise and irrelevant words, "hearing" only key words such as *yes, no,* or *operator.* (The word *operator* would summon a human operator.)

These companies are also using speech-recognition systems to validate calling-card users, who are identified by their "voice prints." Because voice prints are as unique as fingerprints, this eliminates calling-card fraud. Another application allows no-hands dialing of car phones.

■ *Office work.* Securities traders are using speech-recognition systems to issue buy and sell orders. Another system under development would let law-enforcement officers dictate, rather than type, arrest reports. And at a major newspaper chain, copy editors are experimenting with a speech-recognition system that lets them work with spoken, not written, commands.

The sophistication of speech recognition is growing with each new application. Perhaps by the twenty-first century we will realize the dream of conversing with the computer in continuous language without unnatural pauses or limited vocabulary.

Quick Reports
Speech-recognition technology allows emergency-room physicians to prepare complete reports rapidly using spoken key words and phrases.

This USA Today *entertainment editor speaks, rather than types, her articles and editorial remarks into this PC. The voice-recognition software automatically converts her spoken words into text, and the text is displayed on the monitor's screen. This technology allows* USA *staffers with repetitive strain injury and other debilitating conditions to resume productive careers.*

The four steps in Figure 4–2 illustrate how speech recognition works.

1. *Say the word.* When you speak into a microphone, each sound is broken down into its various frequencies.
2. *Digitize the word.* The sounds in each frequency are digitized so they can be manipulated by the computer.
3. *Match the word.* The digitized version of the word is matched against similarly formed *templates* in the computer's electronic dictionary. The digitized template is a form that can be stored and interpreted by computers (in 1s and 0s).
4. *Display the word or perform the command.* When a match is found, the word (*Move* in Figure 4–2) is displayed on a VDT or the appropriate command is performed (for example, move the marked text). In some cases, the word is repeated by a speech synthesizer for confirmation. If no match is found, the speaker is asked to repeat the word.

In speech recognition, the creation of the database is called *training.* Most speech-recognition systems are *speaker-dependent;* that is, they respond to the speech of a particular individual. Therefore, a database of words must be created for each person using the system. To create this database, each person using the system must repeat—as many as 20 times—each word to be interpreted by the system. This training is necessary because we seldom say a word the same way each time. Even if we say a word twice in succession, it will probably have a different inflection or nasal quality.

FIGURE 4–2 Speech Recognition
The sound waves created by the spoken word Move *are digitized by the computer. The digitized template is matched against templates of other words in the electronic dictionary. When the computer finds a match, it displays a written version of the word.*

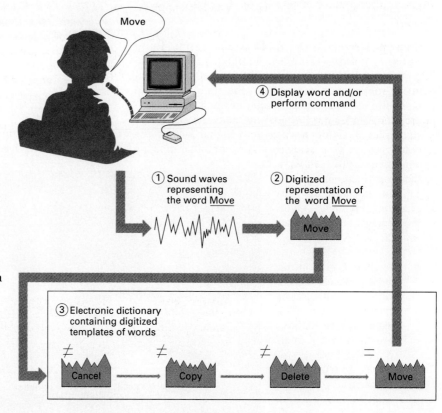

State-of-the-art *speaker-independent* systems have a limited vocabulary: perhaps *yes, no,* and the 10 numeric digits. Although the vocabulary is limited, speaker-independent systems do not require training and can be used by anyone. However, they do require a very large database to accommodate anyone's voice pattern.

Vision-Input Systems

The simulation of human senses, especially vision, is extremely complex. A computer does not actually see and interpret an image the way a human being does. A camera is needed to give computers "eyesight." To create the database, a vision system, via a camera, digitizes the images of all objects to be identified, then stores the digitized form of each image in the database. When the system is placed in operation, the camera enters the image into a digitizer. The system then compares the digitized image to be interpreted to the prerecorded digitized images in the computer's database, much like a speech-recognition system does with voice input. The computer identifies the image by matching the structure of the input image with those images in the database. This process is illustrated by the digital vision-inspection system shown in Figure 4–3.

As you can imagine, **vision-input systems** are best-suited to very specialized tasks in which only a few images will be encountered. These tasks are usually simple, monotonous ones, such as inspection. For example, in Figure 4–3 a digital vision-inspection system on an assembly line rejects those parts that do not meet certain quality-control specifications. The vision system performs rudimentary gauging inspections, and then signals the computer to take appropriate action.

Hand-Held Data Entry Devices

The typical *hand-held data entry device,* which is actually a small computer, would have:

FIGURE 4–3 Digital Vision-Inspection System   *In this digital vision-inspection system, the system examines parts for defects. If the digitized image of the part does not match a standard digital image, the defective part is placed in a reject bin.*

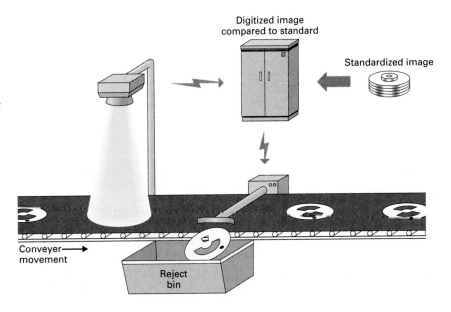

Digitized image compared to standard

Standardized image

Conveyer→ movement

Reject bin

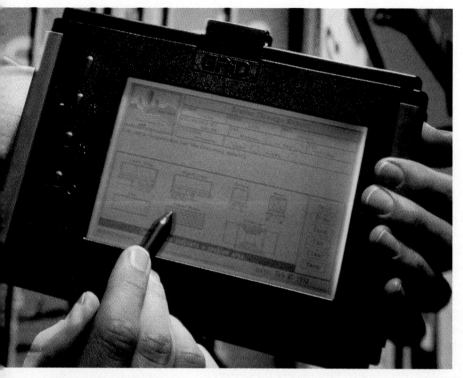

■ A limited keyboard
■ A calculator-like display
■ Some kind of storage capability for the data, usually solid-state non-volatile random-access memory
■ A scanning device, capable of optical character recognition

After the data have been entered, the portable data entry device is linked with a central computer and data are *uploaded* (transmitted from the data entry device to a central computer) for processing.

Stock clerks in department stores routinely use hand-held devices to collect and enter reorder data. As clerks visually check the inventory level, they identify the items that need to be restocked. They first scan the price tag (which identifies the item), then enter the number to be ordered on the keyboard.

This hand-held GRiD PalmPAD enables the entry of both text and graphic data. This insurance adjuster is using the pen-based computer to file a report on an 18-wheeler truck accident.

Hand-held pen-based PCs and PDAs (personal digital assistants) frequently are used as data entry devices. Pen-based computing and PDAs are introduced in Chapter 1, "The World of Computers." Pen-based PCs have pressure-sensitive writing pads that recognize hand-printed alphanumeric characters. Also, they permit the entering of graphic information. For example, police use pen-based PCs to document accidents, including recording the handwritten signatures of the participants.

4–4   OUTPUT DEVICES: COMPUTERS COMMUNICATE WITH US

Output devices translate bits and bytes into a form we can understand. The most common "output only" devices are discussed in this section. These include monitors, printers, desktop film recorders, screen image projectors, and voice-response units.

Monitors

Alphanumeric and graphic output are displayed on the televisionlike monitor. Monitors are defined by three attributes.

■ *Size* (diagonal dimension of the display screen)
■ *Resolution* (detail of the display)
■ *Monochrome or color*

Size   Display screens vary in size from 5 to 30 inches (diagonal dimension). The monitor size for newly purchased desktop PCs has inched up from 9 inches to 15 inches over the past 10 years and is moving toward 17 inches. Output on a monitor is *soft copy*. This means it is temporary and available to the end user only until another display is requested (as opposed to the permanent *hard-copy* output of printers).

Resolution   Monitors vary in their quality of output, or **resolution**. Resolution refers to the number of addressable points on the screen—the number of points to which light can be directed under program control. These points are sometimes called **pixels,** short for *picture elements.* Each pixel can be assigned a shade of gray or a color. A low-resolution monitor has about 64,000 (320 by 200) addressable points. A monitor used primarily for computer graphics and computer-aided design may have more than 16 million addressable points. The high-resolution monitors project extremely clear images that look almost like photographs.

PC displays are in either **text mode** or **graphics mode**. MS-DOS–based programs operate in text mode, generally with 25 rows of up to 80 characters in length. Some monitors permit characters to be displayed with greater density (for example, 43 rows of up to 132 characters). All software applications developed to run under Microsoft's Windows, graphical user interfaces (GUIs), draw programs, and design programs operate in graphics mode. The

Monitors are designed to accomplish a particular function. Top: *An engineer at E-Systems needs a large high-resolution monitor for computer-aided design (CAD) applications.* Right: *Notebook PCs are equipped with lightweight flat-panel color or monochrome monitors to enhance portability.*

trend in software development is toward the exclusive use of the graphics mode, even in word processing and spreadsheet software.

Monochrome Monitors Monitors are either monochrome or color. Monochrome monitors display images in a single color, usually white, green, blue, red, or amber. A monochrome monitor can, however, display shades of one color. The industry uses the term **gray scales** to refer to the number of shades of a color that can be shown on a monochrome monitor's screen. Monochrome monitors are popular on low-end portable PCs. Relatively few new desktop PCs are configured with monochrome displays.

Color Monitors Color monitors add another dimension to the display. Their use of colors can focus attention on different aspects of the output. For example, an engineer designing pipelines for an oil refinery can use colors to highlight such things as the direction and type of fluid flow, the size of the pipes, and so on.

Most color monitors mix red, green, and blue to achieve a spectrum of colors, and are called **RGB monitors**. Several color video display standards have evolved since the introduction of the IBM PC in 1981. Each is implemented by installing an add-on board and connecting it to the appropriate monitor. The four most popular monitors are listed here.

- *CGA.* The initial *color graphics adapter* standard was low resolution (320 by 200 pixels).
- *EGA.* The *enhanced graphics adapter* provided higher resolution (640 by 350) and greater variety in the selection of colors (from 4 to 16).
- *VGA.* The *video graphics array* standard provides a slightly improved resolution to 640 by 480 and uses up to 256 colors.
- *Super VGA.* The Super VGA provides resolutions from 800 by 600 to 1280 by 1024.

All four—CGA, EGA, VGA, and Super VGA—are in widespread use today. Add-on graphics boards and monitors are available that enable very high resolution; however, these can be more expensive than the PC.

Flat-Panel Monitors Some space-saving monitors are flat. Most **flat-panel monitors** are used in conjunction with laptop PCs. Flat-panel monitors use three basic types of technology: *LCD* (liquid crystal display), the technology commonly used in digital wristwatches; *gas plasma;* and *EL* (electroluminescent). Each has its advantages. For example, LCD displays use relatively little power and EL displays provide a wider viewing angle. Up until the late 1980s all flat-panel monitors were monochrome. With the recent introduction of color LCD monitors, portable-PC buyers now have a choice.

Touch-Screen Monitors **Touch-screen monitors** permit input as well as output. Touch-sensitive screens enable users to choose from available options simply by touching the desired icon or menu item with their finger. Interactive touch-screen systems are installed in shopping centers, zoos, airports, grocery stores, post offices, and many other public locations. Within a few years the information you need will be at your finger tips wherever you go.

We are born with an ability to point and touch. Educators realize this and are beginning to use touch-screen technology in the classroom to teach everything from reading to geography.

Truckers have joined the ranks of knowledge workers. At J. B. Hunt Transport, headquartered in Lowell, Arkansas, drivers keep a fleet of 7000 eighteen wheelers rolling while on-board computers do the reporting. Each truck is equipped with a user-friendly computer in the cab and a small satellite dish on top of the cab. The on-board computers are configured with touch screen monitors. Transmissions from the truck's computer are picked up by a commercial communications satellite. The on-board computers enable fleet managers to be in direct communication with drivers. They can alter delivery schedules, give directions, or let drivers know of family emergencies.

Printers

Printers produce hard-copy output, such as management reports, cash register receipts, memos, payroll checks, and program listings. Generally classified as **serial printers, line printers,** or **page printers,** printers are rated by their print speed. Print speeds are measured in *characters per second* (*cps*) for serial printers, in *lines per minute* (*lpm*) for line printers, and in *pages per minute* (*ppm*) for page printers. The print-speed ranges for the three types of printers are 40–450 cps, 1000–5000 lpm, and 4–800 ppm. The maximum speed for PC page printers is about 22 ppm. These speeds are based on text output. Speeds for outputs that contain graphic images as well as text are much less. For example, some printers may take several minutes to produce a single page of graphics output.

Printers are further categorized as *impact* or *nonimpact.*

- **Impact printers** use some type of hammer or hammers to hit the ribbon and the paper, much as a typewriter does.
- **Nonimpact printers** use chemicals, lasers, and heat to form the images on the paper. All page printers are nonimpact printers.

Virtually all types of printers have the capability of printing graphs and charts and offer considerable flexibility in the size and style of print. Printers also can print in portrait or landscape format. **Portrait** and **landscape** refer to the orientation of the print on the page. Portrait format is like the page of this book—the lines run parallel to the shorter sides of the page. In contrast, landscape output runs parallel to the longer sides of the page. Landscape is frequently the orientation of choice for spreadsheet outputs with many columns.

Impact Printers   Generally, serial and line printers are impact printers that rely on *dot-matrix* technology.

Serial dot-matrix printers.   The serial **dot-matrix printer** forms images *one character at a time* as the print head moves across the paper. Virtually all serial printers are *bidirectional;* that is, they print whether the print head is moving left to right or right to left.

The dot-matrix printer arranges printed dots to form characters and all kinds of images in much the same way as lights display time and temperature on bank signs. One or several vertical columns of small print hammers, referred to as *pins,* are contained in a rectangular print head. The hammers are activated independently to form a dotted character image as the print head moves horizontally across the paper. The characters in Figure 4–4 are formed by a 9-pin print head within a matrix that is 7 dots high and 5 dots wide (7 × 5). The number of dots within the matrix varies from one printer to the next.

Most dot-matrix printers can accommodate both *single-sheet paper* and *continuous-form paper,* sometimes called fan-fold paper. If your output is mostly single sheet (for example, letters and envelopes), you may need to purchase an *automatic sheet feeder.* The *tractor-feed* that handles fan-fold paper is standard with most serial printers.

The quality of the printed output is directly proportional to the density of the dots in the matrix. The 18-pin and 24-pin dot-matrix printers form characters that appear solid, and they can be used for business letters as well as for routine data processing output. Figure 4–5 illustrates how the dots can be

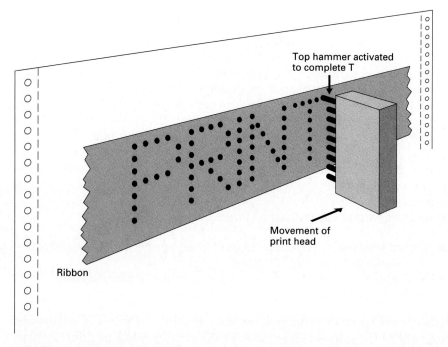

Top hammer activated
to complete T

Movement of
print head

Ribbon

FIGURE 4–4 Dot-Matrix–Printer Character Formation *Each character is formed in a 7 × 5 matrix as the 9-pin print head moves across the paper. The two bottom pins are used for lowercase letters that extend below the line (for example, g and p).*

overlapped with an 18-pin print head to create a *near-letter-quality* (*NLQ*) appearance. These printers are called *dual-mode* because of their dual-function capabilities (draft and NLQ).

Dot-matrix printers are further categorized as *monochrome* and *color*. The monochrome printer prints in the color of the ribbon, usually black. Color dot-matrix printers can select and print any of the colors on a multicolored ribbon (usually bands of black, yellow, red, and blue), or the printer can mix these colors via multiple passes and overstrikes to create the appearance of other colors in the rainbow. As you might imagine, you have to wait a little longer for a color graph than you would for a monochrome graph.

Depending on the model, dot-matrix printers can print a variety of sizes and types of characters (even old English and script characters), graphics, and bar codes.

Line dot-matrix printers. Dot-matrix line printers are impact printers that print *one line of dots at a time*. Needlelike hammers are lined up across the width of the paper. Like serial matrix printers, the characters are formed in rectangular dot configurations as the paper passes the line of print hammers. Line printers are used primarily in the mini/mainframe processing environments as workhorses to generate large volumes of output (for example, shipping labels and utility bills).

Dot-matrix summary. As long as people have a need to print on multipart forms, there will be a need for impact dot-matrix printers. Impact printers, as opposed to nonimpact printers, touch the paper and can produce carbon

FIGURE 4–5 Near-Letter-Quality Dot-Matrix Character Formation *The 18-pin print head permits dots to overlap to increase the density and, therefore, the quality of the image.*

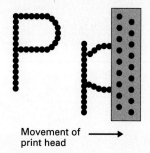

Movement of
print head

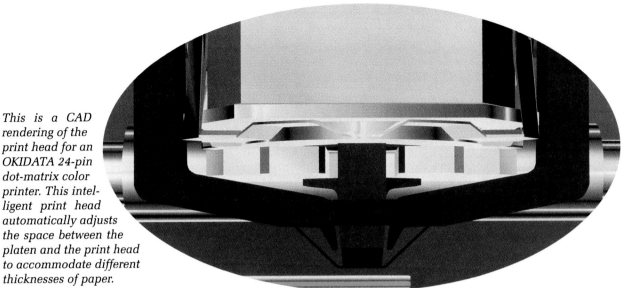

This is a CAD rendering of the print head for an OKIDATA 24-pin dot-matrix color printer. This intelligent print head automatically adjusts the space between the platen and the print head to accommodate different thicknesses of paper.

copies along with the original. The other advantage of dot-matrix printers over the other types of printers is cost. However, this advantage is fading as the cost of high-speed, high-resolution page printers approaches that of dot-matrix printers.

Page Printers   Page printers are of the nonimpact type and use a variety of technologies to achieve high-speed hard-copy output by printing *a page at a time*. Most page printers employ laser and ink-jet technology; however, other technologies are used. These include thermal wax transfer, LED (light-emitting diode), and LCS (liquid crystal shutter), solid ink, and dye sublimation. The operation of a laser-based page printer is illustrated in Figure 4–6. Ink-

FIGURE 4–6 Desktop Page Printer Operation   *The enclosure of a desktop page printer is removed to expose its inner workings. (a) Prior to printing, an electrostatic charge is applied to a drum. Then laser beam paths to the drum are altered by a spinning multisided mirror. The reflected beams selectively remove the electrostatic charge from the drum. (b) Toner is deposited on those portions of the drum that were affected by the laser beams. The drum is rotated and the toner is fused to the paper to create the image.*

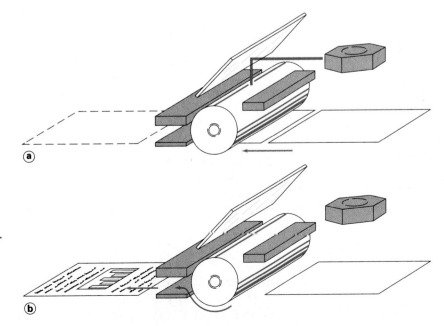

jet–based page printers employ several independently controlled injection chambers to squirt ink droplets on the paper. The droplets, which dry instantly as dots, form the images. The majority of page printers print shades of gray; however, color page printers are becoming increasingly popular as their price continues to drop.

Desktop page printers.   Until the mid-1980s, virtually all printers configured with microcomputers were serial printers. Now economically priced desktop page printers are becoming the standard for office microcomputer systems. These printers, capable of print speeds up to 22 pages per minute, have redefined the hard-copy output potential of micros. Automatic sheet feeders, which hold from 100 to 400 blank pages, are standard equipment on desktop page printers. Most page printers print on a standard 8½- by 11-inch paper; however, some models can print on paper up to 17 by 22 inches.

All desktop page printers are capable of producing *letter-quality* (*LQ*) text and graphics. Some can produce *near-typeset-quality* (*NTQ*) text and graphics as well. The resolution (quality of output) of the typical letter-quality desktop page printer is *300 dpi* (dots per inch). High-end desktop page printers, which are sometimes called *desktop typesetters,* are capable of at least 1000 dpi. The dpi qualifier refers to the number of dots that can be printed per linear inch, horizontally or vertically. That is, a 300-dpi printer is capable of printing 90,000 (300 times 300) dots per square inch.

Commercial typesetting quality is a minimum of 1200 dpi and is usually in excess of 2000 dpi. Desktop page printers are also quiet (an important consideration in an office setting). The emergence of desktop page printers has fueled the explosion of *desktop publishing* (discussed in detail in Chapter 7, "Word Processing and Desktop Publishing Software").

Mainframe-based page printers.   Operating at peak capacity during an 8-hour shift, the fastest page printer can produce almost a quarter of a million

This portable ink-jet page printer is about half the size of a notebook PC and weighs only four pounds. The emergence of letter-quality portable printers means that we can now carry both soft- and hard-copy capability with us wherever we go.

A single desktop page printer (on the left) can service the hard-copy output needs of all the people in this graphics arts department. If the printer is being used, the print requests of other people are stored in a queue on disk or in RAM until the printer becomes available. On the right is a desktop film recorder that can capture graphic images directly onto 35-mm slides.

pages—that's 50 miles of output. This enormous output capability is normally directed to people outside an organization. For example, large banks use page printers to produce statements for checking and savings accounts; insurance companies print policies on page printers; and electric utility companies use them to bill their customers.

Very high-speed laser printers used in the mainframe environment have the capability of superimposing preprinted forms on continuous-feed stock paper. This eliminates a company's need to purchase expensive preprinted forms.

The hydra printer.   Traditionally, businesses have purchased separate machines to handle these paper-related tasks: computer-based printing, facsimile (fax), scanning, and copying. The considerable overlap in the technologies used in these machines has enabled manufacturers to create all-in-one multi-function printers called **hydra printers**. Hydra printers are relatively new, but they may well be the wave of the future, especially for desktop page printers.

Printer Summary   Hundreds of printers are produced by dozens of manufacturers. There is a printer manufactured to meet the hard-copy output requirements of any individual or company, and almost any combination of features can be obtained. You can specify its size (some weigh less than a pound), speed, quality of output, color requirements, flexibility requirements, and even noise level. Micro printers sell for as little as a good pair of shoes or for as much as an automobile.

Presentation Graphics: Desktop Film Recorders and Screen Image Projectors

Business people have found that sophisticated and colorful graphics add an aura of professionalism to any report or presentation. This demand for *presentation graphics* has created a need for corresponding output devices. Computer-generated graphic images can be recreated on paper and transparency acetates with printers. Graphic images also can be captured on 35-mm slides, displayed on a monitor or projected onto a large screen.

Desktop film recorders reproduce a high-resolution graphic image on 35-mm film in either black and white or color. Some models allow users to process and mount their own slides. Others require outside processing. **Screen image projectors** project the graphic or text image onto a large screen, similar to the way television programs are projected onto a large TV screen. Another type of screen image projector is used in conjunction with an ordinary overhead projector. The light from the overhead projector is directed through an LCD panel and the image is shown on a large screen.

Voice-Response Units

If you have ever called directory assistance, you probably have heard something like: "The number is five-seven-five-six-one-three one." You may have driven a car that advised you to "fasten your seat belt." These are examples of talking machines that use output from voice-response units. There are two types of **voice-response units:** One uses a *reproduction* of a human voice and other sounds, and the other uses a **speech synthesizer**. Like monitors, voice-response units provide temporary, soft-copy output.

Dot-matrix and page printers are capable of page-size graphics, but for larger outputs that require perfectly proportioned graphic output, plotters are used. On this drum plotter, the paper and a drawing pen move concurrently to produce the image. The plot is an architect's rendering of the floor plan for an office building.

Screen image projectors fill this room with information. The people in this computerized control room help to operate the OxyMar vinyl chloride monomer complex near Corpus Christi, Texas. For output, each operator has a couple of monitors plus three large common displays.

This PC-based system can read novels, newspapers, or any printed matter to visually impaired people. An image scanner's output is automatically converted into computer signals which, in turn, are converted into full-word English speech using a speech synthesizer.

The first type of voice-response unit selects output from user-recorded words, phrases, music, alarms, or anything you might record on audiotape, just as a printer would select characters. In these recorded voice-response units, the actual analog recordings of sounds are converted into digital data, then permanently stored on disk or in a memory chip. When output occurs, a particular sound is converted back into analog before being routed to a speaker. Chips are mass-produced for specific applications, such as output for automatic teller machines, microwave ovens, smoke detectors, elevators, alarm clocks, automobile warning systems, video games, and vending machines, to mention only a few. When sounds are stored on disk, the user has the flexibility to update them to meet changing application needs.

Speech synthesizers, which convert raw data into electronically produced speech, are more popular in the microcomputer environment. To produce speech, these devices combine sounds resembling the *phonemes* (basic sound units) that make up speech. A speech synthesizer is capable of producing at least 64 unique sounds. The existing technology produces synthesized speech with only limited vocal inflections and phrasing, however. Even with its limitations, the number of speech synthesizer applications is growing. For example, a visually impaired person can use the speech synthesizer to translate printed words into spoken words. Translation systems offer one of the most interesting applications for speech synthesizers and speech-recognition devices. Researchers are making progress toward enabling conversations between people speaking different languages. A prototype system has already demonstrated that three people, each speaking a different language (English, German, and Japanese), can carry on a computer-aided conversation.

4–5   TERMINALS: INPUT AND OUTPUT

The Tube and the Telephone

Terminals enable interaction with a remote computer system in a wide variety of applications. The two most popular general-purpose terminals are the *video display terminal* (*VDT*) and the *telephone*. VDTs, or *terminals,* were first introduced in Chapter 1. The VDT is affectionately known as "the tube," short for **cathode-ray tube**. A VDT's primary input mechanism is usually a *keyboard,* and the output is usually displayed on a *monitor*. Terminals come in all shapes and sizes and have a variety of input/output capabilities.

Dumb Terminals   Most terminals are dumb; that is, they have little or no intelligence. The terminals you see in a hospital or an airport are dumb terminals. These terminals only display text and must be linked to a multiuser processor, such as a mini or mainframe computer.

So much has been written and said about the personal computer that we sometimes forget that millions of knowledge workers work on VDTs. At this company, VDTs provide the link to enterprise-wide mainframe-based information systems.

X Terminals   **X terminals** have processing capabilities and RAM comparable to some micros and workstations; however, they are not designed for stand-alone operation. The X terminal's processing capability enables the user to interact via a graphical user interface (GUI). All X terminals are configured with some type of point-and-draw device, such as a mouse, to permit efficient interaction with the GUI.

Dumb terminals support only text I/O within a single application. In contrast, the X terminal user can work with several applications at a time, any of which can display high-resolution graphics. Each application is displayed in its own window. Some X terminals can even run applications on different computers at the same time.

Telephone Terminals   The telephone's widespread availability is causing greater use of it as a terminal. You can enter alphanumeric data on the touch-tone key pad of a telephone or by speaking into the receiver (voice input). You would then receive computer-generated voice output. Salespeople use telephones as terminals for entering orders and inquiries about the availability of certain products into their company's mainframe computer.

Although the telephone, with its touch-tone key pad and computer-generated voice output, is the terminal with which we are most familiar, the VDT and the microcomputer remain the most commonly used general-purpose terminals. From our past discussions (Chapter 2, "Interacting with Computers"), we know that a microcomputer can serve as a stand-alone computer or as a terminal linked to a mainframe.

Special-Function Terminals

The number and variety of special-function terminals is growing rapidly. Special-function terminals are designed for a specific application, such as convenience banking. You probably are familiar with the *automatic teller machine* (*ATM*) and its input/output capabilities (see Figure 4–7). A badge reader (magnetic stripe) and a key pad enable input to the system. A monitor and a printer (for printing transaction receipts) provide output. Some ATMs use voice response as a backup to the monitor to alert people when to perform certain actions (for example, take their receipts).

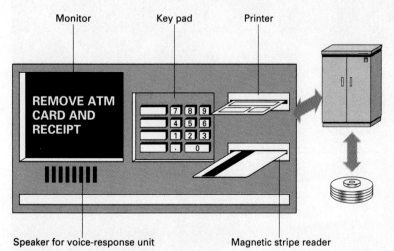

Monitor   Key pad   Printer

REMOVE ATM CARD AND RECEIPT

Speaker for voice-response unit

Magnetic stripe reader

FIGURE 4–7 Terminals for Banking Customers: Automatic Teller Machines
The widely used automatic teller machine (ATM) supports a variety of input/output methods. The magnetic stripe on the ATM card contains identification and security information that, when read, is sent to the bank's computer system. The ATM responds with instructions via its monitor. The customer enters an identification number and data via a key pad. In the figure, the computer processes the customer's request, then provides instructions for the customer via the monitor and verbally with a voice-response unit.

Terminals are being created to meet a variety of needs. Cashiers at fast-food restaurants tap keys that identify the item purchased, such as large fries or junior burger. This expedites both the payment and food preparation process. As the clerk enters the order, it is displayed simultaneously in the kitchen.

Another widely used special-function terminal is the *point-of-sale* (*POS*) terminal. At a minimum, POS terminals in retail establishments have a key pad for input and at least one small monitor. Some have other input devices, such as a badge reader for credit cards and a wand scanner to read price and inventory data. Many grocery stores have POS terminals with voice-response units that verbally confirm the price on each item.

IMPORTANT TERMS AND SUMMARY OUTLINE

badge reader	impact printer	serial printer
bar code	joystick	smart card
cathode-ray tube	landscape	source-data automation
desktop film recorder	line printer	speech synthesizer
digitize	nonimpact printer	speech-recognition system
digitizer tablet and pen	OCR scanner	text mode
dot-matrix printer	optical character recognition (OCR)	touch-screen monitor
flat-panel monitor	page printer	track ball
graphics mode	pixel	vision-input system
gray scales	portrait	voice-response unit
hydra printer	resolution	wand scanner
image processing	RGB monitor	X terminal
image scanner	screen image projector	

4–1 I/O Devices: Our Interface with the Computer A variety of input/output peripheral devices provide the interface between us and the computer system.

4–2 Traditional Input Devices All PCs, workstations, and VDTs are configured with a keyboard. The QWERTY 101-key version is popular with PCs. Some special-function keyboards are designed for specific applications. The mouse, which is now standard on most PCs, is one of several devices that move the graphics cursor to point and draw. The **joystick, track ball,** and **digitizer tablet and pen** are also input devices that move the graphics cursor. Companies always are trying to build a better mouse, so the variety of point-and-draw devices continues to expand.

4–3 Source-Data Automation: Getting Closer to the Action The trend in data entry has been toward **source-data automation,** where the need for the key entry transcription of data is eliminated altogether.

Optical character recognition (OCR) reduces the need for manual data entry by encoding certain data in machine-readable format. **OCR scanners** (hand-held label or **wand,** stationary label, page, document, continuous-form, and optical mark) recognize printed characters and certain coded symbols, such as **bar codes.**

An **image scanner** enables **digitized** images of photos, drawings, and other images to be stored on magnetic disk. **Image processing** enables digitized images to be entered to the computer system, and then retrieved, displayed, altered, merged with text, stored, and sent via data communications to one or several remote locations.

Magnetic stripes and **smart cards** provide input to **badge readers. Speech-recognition systems** can be used to enter limited kinds and quantities of data. They do this by comparing digitized representations of words to similarly formed templates in the computer's electronic dictionary. **Vision-input systems** are best-suited for tasks that involve only a few images. Hand-held data entry devices may or may not be linked to the central computer during data collection activities.

4–4 Output Devices: Computers Communicate with Us Output devices translate data stored in binary into a form that can be interpreted by the end user. A soft copy of alphanumeric and graphic output is displayed on a monitor. The three attributes of monitors are size (diagonal dimension 5 to 30 inches), color (monochrome or color), and **resolution.** A monochrome monitor can display shades of one color, called **gray scales.** A monitor's resolution is determined by the number of **pixels** it has.

Several **RGB monitor** standards have evolved since the introduction of the IBM PC in 1981: CGA, EGA, VGA, and Super VGA. PC displays are in either **text mode** or **graphics mode.**

Space-saving monochrome and color **flat-panel monitors** use LCD, gas plasma, and EL technologies. **Touch-screen monitors** permit input as well as output.

Generally, printers are classified as **serial printers, line printers,** or **page printers** with speeds from 40 characters per second to 800 pages per minute and are either impact or nonimpact. Printers can print in **portrait** and **landscape.**

The impact serial **dot-matrix printer** forms images one character at a time as the print head moves across the paper. Dot-matrix line printers are **impact printers** that print one line at a time. Page printers, which are **nonimpact printers,** use a variety of technologies to achieve high-speed hard-copy output by printing a page at a time. **Hydra printers** handle several paper-related tasks: computer-based printing, facsimile (fax), scanning, and copying.

Desktop film recorders reproduce a high-resolution graphic image on 35-mm film in either black and white or color. **Screen image projectors** project the graphic image onto a large screen. **Voice-response units** provide recorded or synthesized voice output (via **speech synthesizers**).

4–5 Terminals: Input and Output Terminals enable interaction with a remote computer system. The VDT is often called "the tube," short for **cathode-ray tube.** Terminals come in all shapes and sizes and have a variety of input/output capabilities.

Terminals with little or no intelligence are called *dumb terminals.* **X terminals** with processing capabilities enable the user to interact via a graphical user interface.

A variety of special-function terminals, such as automatic teller machines and point-of-sale terminals, are designed for a specific application.

REVIEW EXERCISES

Concepts

1. What is meant when someone says that speech-recognition devices are "speaker-dependent"?

2. List devices, other than key-driven, that are used to input data into a computer system.

3. What is the relationship between a joystick and a graphics cursor?

4. What output device reproduces high-resolution graphic images on 35-mm film?

5. Name a device other than a monitor that produces soft-copy output.

6. Which kind of printer can produce near-typeset-quality output?

7. Which type of OCR scanner is designed to read documents of varying sizes?

8. What are two modes of an IBM-PC display?

9. List the following in order of increasing resolution: VGA, CGA, and EGA.

10. Identify all input and output methods used by an automatic teller machine.

11. What is a smart card?

12. Give two applications for bar codes.

Discussion

13. Describe the input/output characteristics of a terminal that would be used by engineers for computer-aided design.

14. Some department stores use hand-held label scanners and others use stationary label scanners to interpret the bar codes printed on the price tags of merchandise. What advantages does one scanner have over the other?

15. What input/output capabilities are available at your college or place of work?

16. Compare today's vision-input systems with those portrayed in such films as *2001* and *2010*. Do you believe we will have a comparable vision technology by the year 2001?

SELF-TEST (BY SECTION)

4–1 a. Input devices translate data into a form that can be interpreted by a computer. (T/F)

   b. The primary function of I/O peripherals is to facilitate computer-to-computer data transmission. (T/F)

4–2 a. Only those keyboards configured with VDTs have function keys. (T/F)

   b. Which of the following is not a point-and-draw device: (a) joystick, (b) document scanner, or (c) mouse?

4–3 a. Optical character recognition is a means of source-data automation. (T/F)

   b. In speech recognition, words are _digitized_ and matched against similarly formed _templates_ in the computer's electronic dictionary.

   c. Vision-input systems are best-suited to generalized tasks in which a wide variety of images will be encountered. (T/F)

   d. The Universal Product Code (UPC) was originally used by which industry: (a) supermarket, (b) hardware, or (c) mail-order merchandising?

4–4 a. The quality of output on a monitor is determined by its _resolution_

   b. Most flat-panel monitors are used in conjunction with desktop PCs. (T/F)

   c. Ink-jet page printers are classified as nonimpact printers. (T/F)

   d. Dot-matrix printing technology is available in serial and line printers. (T/F)

   e. What type of printers are becoming the standard for office microcomputer systems: (a) desktop page printers, (b) serial dot-matrix printers, or (c) hydra printers?

   f. _Speech syn_ convert raw data into electronically produced speech.

4–5 Which terminal permits system interaction via a GUI: (a) dumb terminal, (b) X terminal, or (c) text-based terminal?

Self-test answers. **4–1 (a)** T; **(b)** F. **4–2 (a)** F; **(b)** b. **4–3 (a)** T; **(b)** digitized, templates; **(c)** F; **(d)** a. **4–4 (a)** resolution; **(b)** F; **(c)** T; **(d)** T; **(e)** a; **(f)** Speech synthesizers. **4–5** b.

5

DATA STORAGE AND ORGANIZATION

OBJECTIVES

To distinguish between primary and secondary storage.

To describe and illustrate the relationships between the levels of the hierarchy of data organization.

To describe how data are stored, retrieved, and manipulated in computer systems.

To demonstrate an understanding of the fundamental principles of sequential processing and random processing.

To distinguish between secondary storage devices and secondary storage media.

To describe the principles of operation, methods of data storage, and use of magnetic disk and magnetic tape drives.

To discuss the applications and use of optical laser disk storage.

5–1   SECONDARY STORAGE: PERMANENT DATA STORAGE

Did you ever stop to think what happens behind the scene when you

- Request a telephone number through directory assistance?
- Draw money from your checking account at an ATM?
- Check out at a supermarket?

Needed information, such as telephone numbers, account balances, and item prices are retrieved from rapidly rotating disk storage media and loaded to random-access memory (RAM) for processing. Untold terabytes (trillions of characters) of data representing thousands of applications are stored *permanently* for periodic retrieval in **secondary storage,** such as magnetic disk. Interaction with secondary storage takes place in milliseconds. As soon as the directory assistance operator keys in the desired name, the full name and number are retrieved from disk storage and displayed. Moments later, a digitized version of voice recordings of numbers is accessed from disk storage and played in response to the caller's request.

Within a computer system, programs and data are stored in both *primary storage* and in *secondary storage* (see Figure 5–1). Programs and data are retrieved from secondary storage and stored *temporarily* in high-speed primary storage (RAM) for processing. RAM is discussed in detail in Chapter 3, "Inside the Computer."

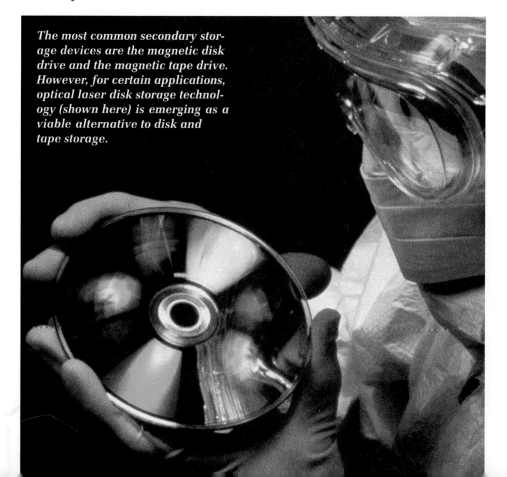

The most common secondary storage devices are the magnetic disk drive and the magnetic tape drive. However, for certain applications, optical laser disk storage technology (shown here) is emerging as a viable alternative to disk and tape storage.

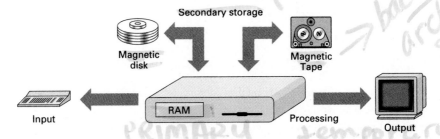

FIGURE 5–1 Primary and Secondary Storage *Programs and data are stored permanently in secondary storage and temporarily in primary storage (RAM).*

Over the years, manufacturers have developed a variety of devices and media for the permanent storage of data and programs. Today the various types of **magnetic disk drives** and their respective storage media are the state of the art for permanent storage of programs and data. **Magnetic tape drives** complement magnetic disk storage by providing inexpensive *backup* capability and *archival* storage. We will discuss these as well as the potential and applications of **optical laser disk** technology, a rapidly emerging alternative to magnetic disk and magnetic tape storage. The terminology, principles, operation, and trade-offs of these secondary storage devices are covered in the context of data organization.

5–2 THE HIERARCHY OF DATA ORGANIZATION: BITS TO DATABASES

The six levels of the *hierarchy of data organization* are illustrated in Figure 5–2. They are *bit, character, field, record, file,* and *database.* You are already familiar with several levels of the hierarchy. Bits and characters are discussed in some detail in Chapter 3, "Inside the Computer." Records and files are introduced in Chapter 1, "The World of Computers."

FIGURE 5–2 The Hierarchy of Data Organization

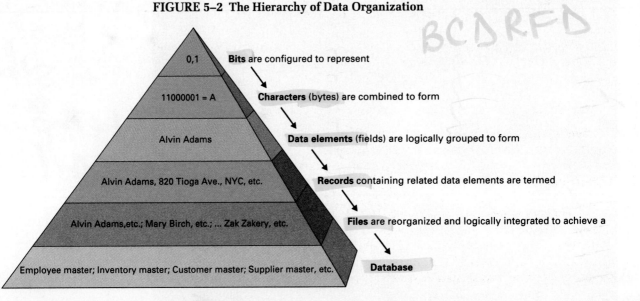

At the Olympic Games in Barcelona, Spain, a vast network of computers and terminals kept officials and the media up-to-the-minute on every competition at every venue. The database included background information on thousands of athletes.

Each information system has a hierarchy of data organization, and each succeeding level in the hierarchy is the result of combining the elements of the preceding level (see Figure 5–2). Data are logically combined in this fashion until a database is achieved. Bits—the first level—are handled automatically, without action on the part of either the programmer or the end user. The other five levels are important design considerations for any information processing activity. The following paragraphs explain each level of the hierarchy and how it relates to the succeeding level.

Bits and Characters

In a computer system, a *character* (*A*, *B*, *C*, 1, 2, and so on) is represented by a group of *bits* that are configured according to an encoding system, such as ASCII. Whereas the bit is the basic unit of primary and secondary storage, the character is the basic unit for human perception. When we enter a program instruction on a PC or a terminal, each character is automatically encoded into a bit configuration. The bit configurations are decoded on output so we can read and understand the output. In terms of data storage, a character is usually the same as a *byte*. (See Chapter 3 for more on bits, bytes, and encoding systems.)

Fields

The **field** is the lowest level *logical* unit in the data hierarchy. For example, a single character (such as *A*) has little meaning out of context. But when characters are combined to form a name (for example, *Alicia* or *Alvin*), they form a logical unit. A field is best described by example: social security number, first name, street address, marital status. These are all fields.

An address is not one, but four fields: street address, city, state, and ZIP code. If we treated the entire address as one field, it would be cumbersome to print because the street address is normally placed on a separate line from the city, state, and ZIP code. Because name-and-address files are often sorted by ZIP code, it is also a good idea to store the ZIP code as a separate field.

Fields	Data Items
Employee/social security number	445447279
Last name	SMITH
First name	ALVIN
Middle initial	E
Department (coded)	ACT
Sex (coded)	M
Marital status (coded)	S
Salary (per week)	800.00

FIGURE 5–3 A Portion of an Employee Record
The fields listed are commonly found in employee records. Data items appear next to each field.

When it is stored in secondary storage, a field is allocated a certain number of character positions. The number of these positions is called the *field length*. The field length of a telephone area code is three. The field length of a telephone number is seven.

Whereas the field is the general (or generic) reference, the specific content of a field is called the **data item**. For example, a social security number is a field, but the actual number, *445487279,* is a data item. A street address is a field, but *1701 El Camino* and *134 East Himes Street* are data items.

Records

A *record* is a description of an event (a sale, a hotel reservation) or an item (for example, a customer, a part). Related fields describing an event or item are logically grouped to form a record. For example, Figure 5–3 contains a partial list of fields for a typical employee record. It also shows the data items for an *occurrence* of a particular employee record (Alvin E. Smith): "Department," "Sex," and "Marital status" are *coded* for ease of data entry and to save storage space.

In general, the record is the lowest level logical unit that can be accessed from a file. For instance, if the personnel manager needs to know only the marital status of Alvin E. Smith, he will have to retrieve Smith's entire record from secondary storage and transmit it to primary storage for processing.

Files

A **file** is a collection of related records. The employee file contains a record for each employee. An inventory file contains a record for each inventory item. The accounts receivable file contains a record for each customer. In processing involving traditional, or **flat files**, files are sorted, merged, and processed by a **key field**. For example, in an employee file the key might be "social security number," and in an inventory file the key might be "part number." A file is said to be a *flat file* when it does not point to or physically link with another file.

The term *file* is also used to refer to a named area on a secondary storage device that contains a *program, textual material* (such as a letter), or even an *image*.

Databases

The **database** is the integrated data resource for a computer-based information system. In essence, a database is a collection of files that are in some way logically related to one another. In a database, the data are integrated and related so that data redundancy is minimized. For example, if records are kept in a traditional file environment at a university and a student moves, his or her address must be changed in all files that maintain address data (registrar, financial aid, health services, and so on). In an integrated database, student-address data are stored only once and are made available to all departments. Therefore, only one update is needed.

Data management encompasses the storage, retrieval, and manipulation of data. Your present or future employer will probably use both the traditional file-oriented and the database approaches to data management. Many existing information systems were designed using traditional approaches to data man-

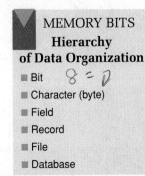

MEMORY BITS
Hierarchy of Data Organization
- Bit   8 = 🗩
- Character (byte)
- Field
- Record
- File
- Database

agement, but the trend now is to use the database approach to develop new information systems. The integrated database environment offers three important advantages over the flat-file approach.

- *Greater access to information.* Most organizations have accumulated a wealth of data, but translating these data into meaningful information has, at times, proved difficult, especially with the exclusive use of traditional files. The structure of an integrated database provides enormous flexibility in the type of reports that can be generated and the type of on-line inquiries that can be made.
- *Better control.* A database management system allows data to be centralized for improved security. Also, by centralizing data, advanced *data structures* can be used to control data redundancy. The term *data structures* refers to the manner in which the fields and records are related to one another.
- *More efficient software development.* The programming task is simplified with a database management system because data are more readily available.

5–3 DATA STORAGE CONCEPTS

On-Line versus Off-Line

As we discussed earlier, the four fundamental components of a computer system are input, processing, storage, and output. In a computer system, the input, output, and data storage components receive data from and transmit data to the processor. These hardware components are said to be **on-line** to the processor. Hardware devices that are not accessible to nor under the control of a processor are said to be **off-line.** A peripheral device that is connected to the processor, but not turned on, is considered off-line. The concepts of on-line and off-line also apply to data and, therefore, files and databases. Data are said to be *on-line* if they can be accessed and manipulated by the processor. All other machine-readable (can be read by a computer) data are *off-line.*

On-line and off-line are important data storage concepts. Consider the payroll example in Figure 5–4. In an *off-line* operation, all supervisors complete the weekly time sheets. The time sheets are then collected and *batched* for input to the computer system. When transactions are grouped together for processing, it is called **batch processing.**

Crude-oil traders at Phillips Petroleum Company keep close watch on oil prices for future trading operations. They do this by being on-line to a complex system of computer-based networks that provide up-to-the-minute information on oil prices. The on-line information system allows traders both to "hedge," or protect, against future price changes and to gain insights about oil-market trends.

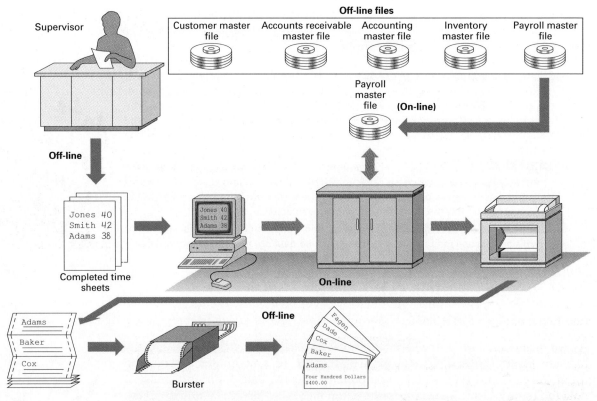

FIGURE 5–4 On-Line and Off-Line Operations *Those processing activities, hardware, and files that are not controlled by or accessible to the computer are referred to as off-line.*

Before the data can be entered and the payroll checks printed, the payroll master file must be placed on-line, if it is not already. To do this, it is retrieved manually from a library of interchangeable disks and loaded to a storage component called a disk drive. Once loaded, the payroll master file is on-line. The process is analogous to selecting the compact disk you wish to play and mounting it on the CD player. (Many computer-based files and databases are stored on permanently installed fixed disks. These files and databases are on-line whenever the computer system is operational.)

In Figure 5–4 an operator at a terminal enters the data on the time sheets directly into the computer system in an *on-line* operation. Employee data, such as name, social security number, pay rate, and deductions, are retrieved from the payroll master file and combined with the number of hours worked to produce the payroll checks. The payroll checks are produced on a printer, which is an output device.

The payroll checks are printed on continuous preprinted forms and they must be separated before distribution to the employees. In an *off-line* operation, a machine called a *burster* separates and stacks the payroll checks.

Data Entry Concepts

Source Data   Most data do not exist in a form that can be "read" by the computer. In the example of Figure 5–4, the supervisor records manually the

Companies are beginning to make their information resources available to customers. This means that the system must be designed for people who may or may not be comfortable with computers. This retailer has installed a system that helps customers with their gift-buying decisions. Customers describe the person(s) for whom a gift is intended by entering sex, age, and lifestyle information. They also indicate how much they are willing to spend and they identify the occasion (birthday, wedding, anniversary, and so on). The system responds with gift ideas.

hours worked by the staff on the time sheet. Before the payroll checks can be computed and printed, the data on these time sheets must be *transcribed* (converted) into a *machine-readable format* that can be interpreted by a computer. This is done in an *on-line* operation by someone at a terminal. The time sheet is the *source document* and, as you might expect, the data on the time sheet are the **source data.**

Not all source data have to be transcribed. For example, the numbers printed at the bottom of your bank checks are your individual account number and bank number. They are already machine-readable, so they can be read directly by an input device. Other approaches to *source-data automation* are discussed in Chapter 4, "Input/Output Devices."

Approaches to Data Entry   The term *data entry* describes the process of entering data into an information system. Information systems are designed to provide users with display-screen prompts to make on-line data entry easier. The display on the operator's screen, for example, may be the image of the source document (such as a time sheet). A **prompt** is a brief message to the operator that describes what should be entered (for example, "INPUT HOURS WORKED _____").

Data can be entered on a terminal or PC in the following ways:

- *Batch processing.* In batch processing, transactions are grouped, or batched, and entered consecutively, one after the other.
- *Transaction-oriented processing.* In **transaction-oriented processing,** transactions are recorded and entered to the system as they occur.

To illustrate the difference between batch and transaction-oriented processing, consider the order-processing system for Bravo International (see Figure 5–5). The system accepts orders by both mail and phone. The orders received by mail are accumulated, or batched, for data entry—usually at night. There are no handwritten source documents for phone orders; people taking the phone orders interact with the computer via terminals and enter the order data on-line while talking with the customer.

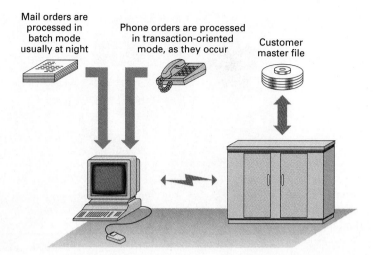

Mail orders are processed in batch mode usually at night

Phone orders are processed in transaction-oriented mode, as they occur

Customer master file

FIGURE 5–5 Batch and Transaction-Oriented Processing   *The typical order entry system accepts orders by mail and by phone.*

On-Line Data Entry   Most data entered into mainframe computer systems or into PC-based networks is done on-line. This is true for both batch and trans-action-oriented processing. In a mainframe environment, terminal operators enter data *directly* into the central computer system for processing as shown in Figure 5–5. In a PC-based network, PC users interact directly with the central database. The primary advantage of transaction-oriented data entry is that records on the database are updated immediately, as the transaction occurs. With batch data entry, records are batched periodically. In a transaction-oriented environment, the database remains continuously up-to-date and can be queried at any time. In the example of Figure 5–5, a salesperson can check the availability of an item and tell the customer when to expect delivery.

Sequential and Direct Access: New Terms for Old Concepts

An important consideration in both the design of an information system and the purchase of a computer system is the way that data are accessed. Magnetic tape can be used for *sequential access* only. Magnetic disks have *random-* or *direct-access* capabilities as well as sequential-access capabilities. You are quite familiar with these concepts, but you may not realize it. Operationally, the magnetic tape is the same as the one in home and automobile audiotape decks. The magnetic disk can be compared to a compact disk (CD).

Suppose you have Paul Simons' CD, *The Rhythm of the Saints.* The first four songs on this CD are: (1) "The Obvious Child," (2) "Can't Run But," (3) "The Coast," and (4) "Proof." Now suppose you also have this CD on a tape cassette. To play the third song on the cassette, "The Coast," you would have to wind the tape forward and search for it sequentially. To play "The Coast" on the CD, all you would have to do is select track number 3. This simple

THE PROMISE OF VIRTUAL REALITY

Virtual reality is moving from computer fantasy to computer fact. *Virtual reality* (VR) combines computer graphics with special hardware to immerse users in *cyberspace,* an artificial three-dimensional world. Instead of passively viewing data or graphics on a screen, users can move about, handle "virtual" representations of data and objects, and get visual, aural, and tactile feedback. In the world of computers, the term *virtual* refers to an environment that is *simulated by hardware and software.*

Dressing for Cyberspace

To enter cyberspace, users must don special hardware.

- *Headpiece.* The goggles-like headpiece blocks out visual sensations from the real world and substitutes images presented on *two small video screens*—one for each eye, creating a three-dimensional effect. The headpiece also contains *motion,* or *balance sensors;* move your head and the computer will shift the view presented on the video screens.

- *Headphones.* Headphones block out room noise and substitute three-dimensional *holophononic* sounds.

- *Data glove.* The ensemble is completed by a data glove outlined with *fiber-optic sensors* and cables. The glove can be used, like a floating mouse, to "gesture" a command or to grasp and move virtual objects about.

Each piece of hardware is tethered to a power pack and to one or more powerful computers via two-way data transfer cables that record the user's movements and provide real-time feedback.

The Quest for Commercial Applications

Virtual reality was born in the late 1960s, when the U.S. Air Force began experimenting with flight simulators. From there, the technology was picked up by NASA. Today, NASA and a number of universities and corporations are either developing or using virtual reality systems for the following applications:

- *Architecture and computer-aided design.* Architects already have access to a number of commercial VR systems that let them conduct electronic "walk-throughs" of proposed buildings.

- *Exploration of hostile environments.* NASA is using raw data to create a VR version of an Antarctic lake bottom that will let researchers study life forms beneath the rigid waters without risk. Researchers are proposing similar systems for exploring the sun and for examining nuclear reactor cores.

- *Sales.* In the spring of 1991, a Japanese department store opened a "virtual kitchen" for planning custom-designed remodeling projects. After store personnel input a kitchen's existing layout and measurements, customers don the VR gear and play around with different appliances and arrangements—usually a half-hour process. Two weeks later, the store delivers the custom-designed kitchen. All hardware and software used in this high-tech application are made in the United States.

- *Education and training.* In addition to the flight and tank simulators used by the military, researchers are looking into VR systems that could be used to train firefighters and rookie police officers.

- *Entertainment.* Virtual reality arcades featuring space travel games are now appearing in the United States and Europe. In addition, a joint venture has been formed to build a series of test theaters that would use VR to let users "walk among" the on-screen actors.

Already experts are predicting that virtual reality will emerge as the user interface of the future. In the near future, perhaps by the year 2000, you will be literally immersed in your work, not merely viewing it.

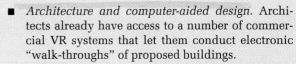

It's Almost Real *Virtual reality lets you walk into an imaginary home and meet people who do not exist in real life.*

analogy demonstrates the two fundamental methods of storing and accessing data—*random* and *sequential.*

Magnetic disk drives are secondary storage devices that provide a computer system with **random-** *and* **sequential-processing** capabilities. In random processing, the desired programs and data are accessed *directly* from the storage medium. In sequential processing, the computer system must search the storage medium to find the desired programs or data. Magnetic tapes have only sequential-processing capabilities. Today's on-line information systems demand immediate and direct access to information; therefore, virtually all files and databases are maintained on media that permit random processing, primarily magnetic disk.

5–4 MAGNETIC DISKS: ROTATING STORAGE MEDIA

Hardware and Storage Media

Because of its random- and sequential-processing capabilities, magnetic disk storage is the overwhelming choice of computer users, whether on micros, workstations, or supercomputers. A variety of magnetic disk drives (the hardware device) and magnetic disks (the media) are manufactured for different business requirements. There are two fundamental types of magnetic disks: interchangeable and fixed.

- **Interchangeable magnetic disks** can be stored off-line and loaded to the magnetic disk drives as they are needed.
- **Fixed magnetic disks,** also called *hard disks,* are permanently installed, or fixed. The trend in magnetic storage media is to fixed disks. All fixed disks are rigid and are usually made of aluminum with a surface coating of easily magnetized elements, such as iron, cobalt, chromium, and nickel.

In the past, interchangeable disks containing certain files and programs were taken from the shelf and loaded to the disk drives as needed. This is still true today but to a much lesser extent. Today's integrated software and databases require all data and programs to be on-line at all times.

The different types of interchangeable magnetic disks and fixed disks are shown in the accompanying photographs. As you can see, magnetic disk drives are available in a wide variety of shapes and storage capacities. The type used would depend on the volume of data you have and the frequency with which those data are accessed. Disk drives are sometimes called **direct-access storage devices,** or **DASDs** (*DAZ deez*).

Magnetic Disks: The Microcomputer Environment

Microcomputer Disk Media Virtually all micros sold today are configured with at least one hard disk drive and one interchangeable disk drive. Having two disks increases system flexibility and throughput. The interchangeable disk drive provides a vehicle for the distribution of data and software, a means for backup and archival storage, and, of course, on-line storage. The

The trend in disk storage is toward permanently installed storage media. Fixed disks are manufactured in rooms that are 1000 times cleaner than hospital operating rooms.

high-capacity hard-disk storage has made it possible for today's micro user to enjoy the convenience of having all data and software readily accessible at all times.

The diskette. Two types of PC disk drives are in widespread use. These disk drives accommodate interchangeable magnetic disks called **diskettes.**

■ *51/4-inch diskette.* The 5¼-inch diskette is a thin, flexible disk that is permanently enclosed in a soft, 5¼-inch-square jacket. Because the magnetic-coated mylar diskette and its jacket are flexible like a page in this book, the diskette is also called a **floppy disk.**

Early 5¼-inch diskettes recorded data on only one side of the disk. These were *single-sided* (SS) diskettes. Today all common-usage diskettes are *double-sided* and are labeled "DS" or simply "2." Similarly, the technological evolution of the early diskettes is classified as *double-density* (DD), as opposed to *single-density*. **Disk density** refers to the number of bits that can be stored per unit of area on the disk-face surface.

The *360-KB DS/DD* (double-sided, double-density) 5¼-inch diskette dominated during the 1980s and is still the only diskette that can be used on many PCs. However, the new 5¼-inch disk drives support both the popular 360-KB diskette and the *1.2-MB DS/HD* (double-sided, high-density) diskette. A 1.2-MB diskette has about three times the storage capacity of a 360-KB diskette.

■ *3½-inch diskette.* The 3½-inch diskette is enclosed in a rigid plastic jacket. Like its 5¼-inch cousin, the 3½-inch diskette comes in two capacities, the 720-KB DS/DD and the 1.44-MB DS/HD diskettes. The diskette is slowly displacing the 5¼-inch diskette because of its durability, convenient size, and higher capacity.

Diskette technology continues to evolve. Some PC disk drives are able to store 2.88 MB on 3½-inch diskettes. The **floptical disk drive** uses optical technology to read and write to 20-MB diskettes as well as the standard 3½-inch diskettes. These, however, are not in widespread use.

Winchester disk. The microcomputer hard disk is called the **Winchester disk.** The Winchester disk got its nickname from the 30-30 Winchester rifle. Early disk drives had two 30-MB disks—thus the nickname "Winchester." The storage capacity of these 1- to 5¼-inch hard disks ranges from about 30 MB (megabytes) to 3 GB (gigabytes). One 3-GB hard disk can store as much data as

The most recent addition to the world of interchangeable floppies is the 21-MB 3½-inch floptical. It looks similar to the billions of 3½-inch diskettes already in use, but it has over 14 times the capacity. This drive reads and writes to the floptical disk as well as the traditional 720-KB and 1.44-MB diskettes. Floptical drives, like this Iomega drive, use the same magnetic recording of conventional floppy drives; however, they use an optical tracking system that allows precision positioning of the read/write head. The precision movement of the head enables more tracks and, thus, a greater storage capacity.

As PCs downsize, so must disk drives. This multiplatter 1.3-inch Winchester disk, which has a capacity of 80 MB, is designed for use in notebook PCs, palmtop PCs, and other mobile computing devices.

3600 revolutions per minute

(megabytes) to 3 GB (gigabytes). One 3-GB hard disk can store as much data as two thousand 3½-inch high-density diskettes.

A Winchester hard disk contains several disk platters stacked on a single rotating spindle. Data are stored on all *recording surfaces.* For a disk with four platters, there are eight recording surfaces on which data can be stored (see Figure 5–6). The disks spin continuously at a high speed (usually 3600 revolutions per minute) within a sealed enclosure. The enclosure keeps the disk-face surfaces free from contaminants, such as dust and cigarette smoke. This contaminant-free environment allows Winchester disks to have greater density of data storage than the interchangeable diskettes. In contrast to a Winchester disk, a diskette is set in motion only when a command is issued to read from or write to the disk. An indicator light near the disk drive is illuminated only when the diskette is spinning.

The rotational movement of a magnetic disk passes all data under or over a **read/write head,** thereby making all data available for access on each revolution of the disk (see Figure 5–6). A fixed disk will have at least one read/write head for each recording surface. The heads are mounted on **access arms** that move together and literally float on a cushion of air over (or under) the spinning recording surfaces. The tolerance is so close that a particle of smoke from a cigarette will not fit between these "flying" heads and the recording surface!

Winchester disks normally are permanently installed in the same physical unit as the processor and diskette drives. There are, however, *interchangeable hard disks* on the market. These interchangeable Winchester modules are inserted and removed in a manner that is similar to the way you insert and remove tapes on a VCR. Only a small percentage of PCs are configured to accept interchangeable Winchester disks.

FIGURE 5–6 Fixed Hard Disk with Four Platters and Eight Recording Surfaces   *A cylinder refers to similarly numbered concentric tracks on the disk-face surfaces. In the illustration, the read/write heads are positioned over Cylinder 0012. At this position, the data on any one of the eight tracks numbered 0012 are accessible to the computer on each revolution of the disk. The read/write heads must be moved to access data on other cylinders.*

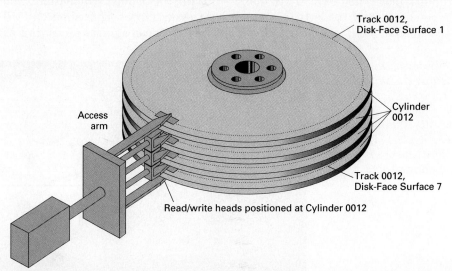

Micro Disk Organization   The way in which data and programs are stored and accessed is similar for both hard and interchangeable disks. The disk-storage medium has a thin film coating of one of the easily magnetized elements (cobalt, for example). The thin film coating on the disk can be magnetized electronically by the read/write head to represent the absence or presence of a bit (0 or 1).

Data are stored in concentric **tracks** by magnetizing the surface to represent bit configurations (see Figure 5–7). Bits are recorded using *serial representation.* The number of tracks varies greatly between disks, from as few as 40 on some diskettes to several thousand on high-capacity Winchester disks. The spacing of tracks is measured in **tracks per inch,** or **TPI.** The 3½-inch diskettes are rated at 135 TPI. The TPI for Winchester disks can be in the thousands.

The *track density* (TPI) tells only part of the story. The *recording density* tells the rest. Recording density, which is measured in *bits per inch,* refers to the number of bits (1s and 0s) that can be stored per inch of track. Both the 720-KB and 1.44-MB diskettes have a track density of 135 TPI, but the recording density of the high-density disk is twice that of the double-density disk.

Microcomputer disks use **sector organization** to store and retrieve data. In sector organization, the recording surface is divided into pie-shaped **sectors.** The number of sectors depends on the density of the disk. The surface of the diskette in Figure 5–7 is logically divided into 15 sectors. Typically, the storage capacity of each sector on a particular track is 512 bytes, regardless of the number of sectors per track. Each sector is assigned a unique number; therefore, the *sector number* and *track number* are all that are needed for a **disk address** on a particular disk-face surface. The disk address represents the physi-

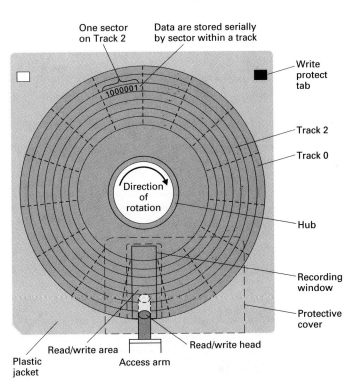

FIGURE 5–7 Cutaway of a 3½-Inch Diskette   *The access arm on this 3½-inch disk drive is positioned at a particular track (Track 2 in the example). Data are read or written serially in tracks within a given sector.*

One sector on Track 2

Data are stored serially by sector within a track

1000001

Write protect tab

Track 2

Track 0

Direction of rotation

Hub

Recording window

Protective cover

Read/write area

Read/write head

Plastic jacket

Access arm

cal location of a particular set of data or a program. To read from or write to a disk, an access arm containing the read/write head is moved, under program control, to the appropriate *track* (see Figures 5–6 and 5–7). When the sector containing the desired data passes under or over the read/write head, the data are read or written.

Each of the high-density disk-face surfaces of a Winchester disk may have several thousand tracks, numbered consecutively from outside to inside. A particular **cylinder** refers to every track with the same number on all recording surfaces (see Figure 5–6). When reading from or writing to a Winchester disk, all access arms are moved to the appropriate *cylinder*. For example, each recording surface has a track numbered 0012, so the disk has a cylinder numbered 0012. If the data to be accessed are on Recording Surface 01, Track 0012, then the access arms and the read/write heads for all eight recording surfaces are moved to Cylinder 0012.

In Figure 5–7 the access arm is positioned over Cylinder 0012. In this position, data on any of the sectors on the tracks in Cylinder 0012 can be accessed without further movement of the access arm. If data on Surface 5, Track 0145 are to be read, the access arm must be positioned over Cylinder 0145 until the desired record passes under the read/write head.

Fortunately, software automatically monitors the location, or address, of our files and programs. We need only enter someone's name to retrieve his or her personnel record. The computer system locates the record and loads it to primary storage for processing. Although the addressing schemes vary considerably between disks, the address normally will include the *cylinder (or track)*, the *recording surface*, and the *sector number*.

Disk Access Time   **Access time** is the interval between the instant a computer makes a request for transfer of data from a disk-storage device to RAM and the instant this operation is completed. The access of data from RAM is performed at electronic speeds—approximately the speed of light. But the access of data from disk storage depends on mechanical apparatus. Any mechanical movement significantly increases the access time. The access time for hard disks is significantly less than for floppy disks because the hard disk is in continuous motion.

The *seek time,* the largest portion of the total access time, consists of how long it takes the mechanical access arm to move the read/write head to the desired track or cylinder. Some Winchester disk drives have two sets of access arms, one for reading and writing on the inside tracks and another for the outside tracks. Two independent sets of access arms significantly reduce the average seek time because they have a shorter distance to move and one can move while the other is reading or writing.

The *rotational delay time* is the time it takes for the appropriate data to be positioned under the read/write head. On the average, it would be half the time it takes for one revolution of the disk, or about 8 milliseconds for a hard disk spinning at 3600 rpm. The rotational delay time for a diskette spinning at 400 rpm is 75 milliseconds, almost 10 times that of a hard disk. The *transmission time,* or the time it takes to transmit the data to primary storage, is negligible. The average access time for most hard-disk drives is less than 20 milliseconds—still very slow when compared with the microsecond-to-nanosecond internal processing speeds of computers.

MEMORY BITS
**Disk Access
Time** =

■ Seek time +
■ Rotational delay time +
■ Transmission time

Disk Caching   The **data transfer rate** is the rate at which data are read from (or written to) secondary storage to (from) RAM. Even though the data transfer rate from magnetic disk to RAM may be millions of bytes per second, the rate of transfer between one part of RAM to another is much faster. **Disk caching** (pronounced *cashing*) enhances system performance by placing programs and data that are likely to be called into RAM for processing from a disk into an area of RAM that simulates disk storage. When an application program issues a call for the data or programs in the disk cache area, called the **RAM disk,** the request is serviced directly from RAM rather than magnetic disk. Data or programs in the RAM disk eventually must be transferred to a disk for permanent storage. All state-of-the-art PCs come with software that takes full advantage of the potential of RAM disks.

Backup: Better Safe Than Sorry   Safeguarding the content of your disks may be more important than safeguarding hardware. The first commandment in computing, at any level, is

𝕭𝖆𝖈𝖐 𝖀𝖕 𝖄𝖔𝖚𝖗 𝕱𝖎𝖑𝖊𝖘

If data and program on your disk files are destroyed, it may be impossible for them to be re-created within a reasonable period of time. If, on the other hand, the hardware is destroyed, it can be replaced fairly quickly. The impact of losing critical software or files makes *backup* a major concern.

When you create a document, a spreadsheet, or a graph and you wish to recall it at a later time, you *store* the file on disk. You can, of course, store many files on a single disk. If the disk is in some way destroyed (scratched, demagnetized, and so on) or lost, you have lost your files unless you have a backup disk. To minimize the possibility of losing valuable files, you should periodically back up (make a copy of) the files on your work disks.

The frequency with which a work disk is backed up depends on its *volatility,* or how often you update the files on the disk. If you spend time every day working with files on a work disk, you should back it up each day. Others are backed up no more often than they are used. Because some updating will occur between backup runs, the re-creation of lost files means that subsequent updates and changes must be redone from the point of the last backup.

Figure 5–8 illustrates the backup procedure for working files on an interchangeable disk that is used daily. The procedure is the same whether your working files are on an interchangeable or a permanently installed disk. Two *generations* of backup are maintained on backup Disks A and B. After each day's processing, the contents of the work disk are copied (or dumped) alternately to Disk A or B. In this manner, one backup is always current within a day's processing. If the work disk and the

This highly magnified area of a magnetic disk-face surface shows elongated information bits recorded serially along eight of the disk's 1774 concentric tracks. One square inch of this disk's surface can hold 22 million bits of information.

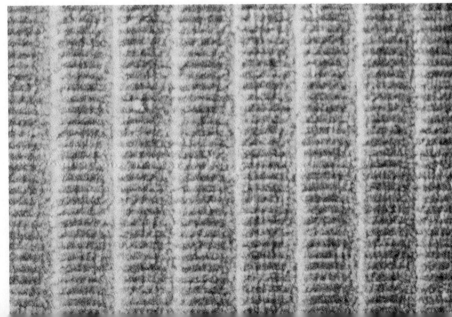

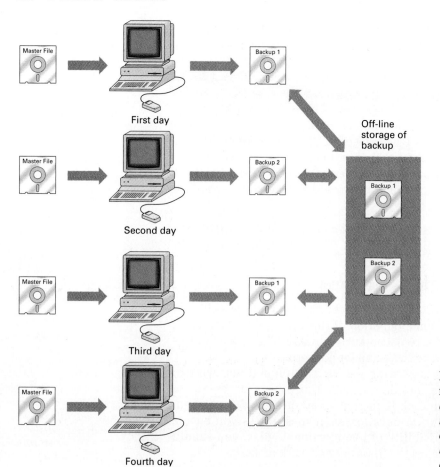

First day

Second day

Third day

Fourth day

Off-line storage of backup

Backup 1

Backup 2

FIGURE 5–8 Backup Procedure for User Files *The interchangeable disk containing user files is backed up alternately to Disk A or B at the end of each day so that one backup file is always current within one day's processing.*

most recent backup are accidentally destroyed, a third backup is current within two days' processing. Disks A and B are alternated as the most current backup.

At one time or another, just about everyone who routinely works with computers has experienced the trauma of losing work for which there was no backup. It is no fun seeing several days (or weeks) of work disappear, but it does emphasize the point that it is well worth the effort to make backup copies of your work.

Care of Interchangeable Diskettes A blank interchangeable disk, costing about a dollar, has a very modest value. But once you begin to use the disk, its value, at least to you, increases greatly. Its value includes the many hours you have spent entering data, preparing spreadsheets, or writing programs. Such a valuable piece of property should be handled with care. The following are a few guidelines for handling interchangeable disks.

Do

- *Do* label each disk using a felt-tipped pen on the label.
- *Do* cover the *write-protect notch* on all important 5¼-inch disks intended for read-only use, such as the program disks for micro software packages. On the 3½-inch disks, slide the *write-protect tab* to its open position.

- ■ *Do* store 5¼-inch disks in their jackets so the exposed surface is covered.
- ■ *Do* store 5¼-inch disks vertically or, if stored flat, place no more than 10 in a stack.
- ■ *Do* store disks at temperatures between 50 and 125 degrees Fahrenheit.
- ■ *Do* keep a backup of disks containing important data and programs.
- ■ *Do* remove disks from disk drives before you turn off the computer.

Don't

- ■ *Don't* fold, spindle, or mutilate disks.
- ■ *Don't* force a disk into the disk drive. It should slip in with little or no resistance.
- ■ *Don't* touch the disk surface.
- ■ *Don't* place disks near a magnetic field, such as magnetic paper-clip holders, tape demagnetizers, or electric motors.
- ■ *Don't* expose disks to direct sunlight for a prolonged period.
- ■ *Don't* insert or remove a disk from a disk drive if the "drive active" light is on.

Magnetic Disks: The Mainframe Environment

Mainframe Disk Media Direct-access storage devices (DASDs) are the prerequisite for all information systems where the data must be on-line and accessed directly. An airline reservation system provides a good mainframe-oriented example of this need. Direct-access capability is required to retrieve the record for any flight at any time from any reservations office. The data must be current, or flights may be overbooked or underbooked. Because of the random nature of the reservations data, sequential-only magnetic tape cannot be used as a storage medium for this or any other system that requires random processing. File and database organization for random processing, also called **direct-access processing,** is covered in Section 5–5.

This mainframe computer center collects massive amounts of data which are stored on the hard disk drives in the foreground. The computer system, which supports government applications, reads or writes up to a billion bytes per second to the hard disks.

The demand for on-line systems during the past decade has caused the virtual disappearance of interchangeable disk storage media in the mainframe environment. The once popular **disk cartridge** and **disk pack** have been replaced with permanently installed high-density fixed disks. The current technology enables a single disk drive, which might include 4 platters (see Figure 5–6), to store more than 20 gigabytes of data.

Minis, mainframes, and supercomputers use a wide variety of fixed-disk media. The differences are primarily the size of the platter (1 inch to 14 inches in diameter), the number of platters per disk drive, and the density at which data are recorded.

Mainframe Disk Organization The way data are organized on mainframe disk systems is similar to that on microcomputer disk systems. That is, the read/write heads are positioned over/under the track containing the desired data or software (see Figure 5–6). The data are read from or written to the appropriate sector as it passes over/under the read/write head.

5–5 RANDOM, OR DIRECT-ACCESS, PROCESSING: PICK AND CHOOSE

A **direct-access file,** or **random file,** is a collection of records that can be processed randomly (in any order). Only the value of the record's key field is needed in order to retrieve or update a record in random processing. More often than not, magnetic disks are the storage medium for random processing.

You can access records on a direct-access file by more than one key. For example, a salesperson inquiring about the availability of a particular product could inquire by *product number* and, if the product number is not known, by *product name.* The file, however, must be created with the intent of having multiple keys.

Federal Express couriers and handlers use the SuperTracker (left), a hand-held OCR data collection device, to track the progress of packages from source to destination. Package status information, such as pickup or delivery times, is transmitted directly to the company's centralized database through the DADS (Digitally Assisted Dispatch System) units in the courier vans and sorting facilities. These customer service agents (right) access the up-to-the-minute database for package status information when responding to customer inquiries.

Inventory master file (sorted by part number)

	Part no.	Price	No. used to date	No. in stock
One record →	2	25	40	200
	4	1.40	100 (106)*	100 (94)
	8	.80	500	450
	•	•	•	•
	•	•	•	•
	•	•	•	•
	20	4.60	60 (72)	14 (2)
	21	2.20	50	18

*[ ] reflects updated values

FIGURE 5–9 Inventory Master and Transaction Files *Both files are sorted by part number. The numbers in parentheses ( ) reflect the inventory master file after the update. Figure 5–10 illustrates the update process for random processing.*

Transaction file (sorted by part number)

Part no.	No. used to date
4	6
20	12

Random-Access Methods

The procedures and mechanics of the way a particular record is accessed directly are, for the most part, transparent (not a concern) to users and even to programmers. These methods may involve index files, mathematical algorithms, and other concepts that are beyond the scope of this book.

Principles of Random Processing

Figure 5–9 lists the contents of an inventory *master file,* which is the permanent source of inventory data, and a *transaction file,* which reflects the daily inventory activity. In Figure 5–10, the inventory master file of Figure 5–9 is updated from an *on-line* terminal to illustrate the principles of random processing. The following activities take place during the update:

FIGURE 5–10 Random Processing *An inventory master file is updated using random processing and magnetic disks. Processing steps are discussed in the text.*

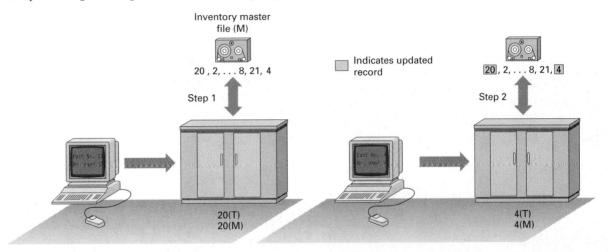

FIGURE 5–11 Backup Procedure for Random Processing

■ *Step 1.* The first transaction (for Part Number 20) is entered into primary storage from an on-line terminal. The computer issues a read for the record of Part Number 20 on the inventory master file. The record is retrieved and transmitted to primary storage for processing. The record is updated and written back to the *same* location on the master file. The updated record is simply written over the old record.

■ *Step 2.* A second transaction (for Part Number 4) is entered into primary storage. The computer issues a read for the record of Part Number 4 on the inventory master file. The record is retrieved and transmitted to primary storage for processing. The record is then updated.

Because only two updates are to be made to the inventory master file, processing is complete. Random processing requires a special run to provide backup to the inventory master file. In the backup activity illustrated in Figure 5–11, the master file is "dumped" from disk to tape at frequent intervals, usually daily. If the inventory master file is destroyed, it can be re-created by dumping the backup file (on magnetic tape) to disk (the reverse of Figure 5–11). Magnetic tape is discussed in the next section.

5–6 MAGNETIC TAPE: RIBBONS OF DATA

Magnetic Tape and PCs: The Data Cartridge

This Iomega tape backup unit plugs directly into a PC's parallel port. This handy feature for laptop PC users can store up to 250 MB of data on a single tape. This tape backup unit is also extremely reliable. The unit's MTBF (mean time before failure) is 30,000 hours of continuous use and its data reliability is less than one error in 100,000,000,000,000 bits.

During the 1950s and 1960s, the foundation of many information systems was *sequential processing* using *magnetic tape.* Today, however, magnetic tape storage is used primarily as a backup medium for magnetic disk storage (see Figure 5–11). A magnetic tape medium, such as the **magnetic tape cartridge,** can be loaded conveniently to a tape drive (the hardware device) for processing. Once loaded to a tape drive, the magnetic tape is on-line; that is, the data and programs on the tape are accessible to the computer system. Also, data and programs can be loaded to the tape. When processing is complete, the tape is removed for off-line storage until it is needed again for processing.

The magnetic tape cartridge, which is also called a **data cartridge,** is self-contained and is inserted into and removed from the tape drive in much the same way you would load or remove a videotape from a VCR. Like the videotape, the supply and the take-up reels are encased in a plastic shell.

Principles of Operation

The mechanical operation of a magnetic tape drive is similar to that of an audiocassette tape deck. The tape, a thin polyester ribbon coated with a magnetic material on one side, passes under a *read/write head,* and the data are either

1. Read and transmitted to primary storage, or
2. Transmitted from primary storage and written to the tape.

Magnetic tape media come in several widths up to ½ inch and many different lengths, some over 2000 feet. Because the majority of us, as PC users, will use magnetic tape cartridges designed for use with PCs, our discussion of tape devices and media will focus on magnetic tape in the PC environment.

The tape format describes the characteristics of the tape. One of the most popular PC tape cartridge formats is the *QIC-80 minicartridge.* The minicartridge tape drive normally is housed in the same physical unit as the processor and disk drives. The QIC-80 (*QIC* stands for *quarter-inch cartridge*) minicartridge is designed to hold 80 MB of data. However, the actual amount of data a given tape cartridge can store depends on the precision of the magnetic tape drive. For example, several popular tape drives enable up to 125 MB to be stored on a QIC-80 minicartridge. With **data compression,** a feature available with most tape drives, the same tape can store up to 250 MB. Larger data cartridges, which require a larger tape drive, can store several gigabytes (billion bytes).

The ¼-inch tape cartridges used with PCs record data in a continuous stream. Drives for ¼-inch tape cartridges, often called **tape backup units (TBUs),** store data in a **serpentine** manner (Figure 5–12). Data are recorded using **serial representation;** that is, the bits are aligned in a row, one after another, in tracks. The tracks run the length of the tape (see Figure 5–12). A tape cartridge can be formatted to have from 4 to 60 tracks, depending on the precision of the tape drive. The read/write head reads or writes data to one, two, or four tracks at a time. Figure 5–12 illustrates how data are written two tracks at a time. In the figure, data are written serially on the top two tracks for the entire length of the tape or until the data are exhausted. The tape is reversed, the read/write head is positioned over the next two tracks, and writing continues in a similar manner. If more backup capacity is needed, the computer operator is informed. A clean tape is inserted and writing continues.

A tape drive is rated by its *storage capacity* and its *data transfer rate.* You might recall that the data transfer rate is the rate at which data are read from (or written to) secondary storage to (from) RAM. A tape backup unit that uses the QIC-80 data cartridge has a capacity of 80 MB to 250 MB (with data compression) and a data transfer rate of about 1 MB per second.

FIGURE 5–12 Cross-Section of a Magnetic Tape *Data are recorded serially on this eight-track tape in a serpentine manner, two tracks at a time.*

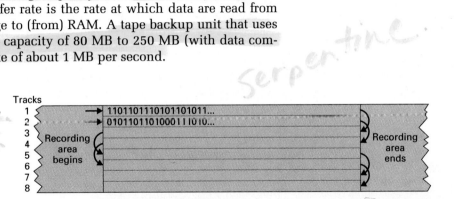

Significant advances are being made in tape cartridge technology each year. Magnetic tape cartridges, half the size of this book, are capable of storing up to 4 gigabytes on a single cartridge. Four gigabytes sounds like ample storage for just about anything, but this is not the case. For example, six high-capacity tape cartridges would be required to store just the names and addresses of all the people living in the United States.

5–7   OPTICAL LASER DISKS: HIGH-DENSITY STORAGE

Some industry analysts have predicted that *optical laser disk* technology eventually may make magnetic disk and tape storage obsolete. With this technology, the read/write head used in magnetic storage is replaced by two lasers. One laser beam writes to the recording surface by scoring microscopic pits in the disk, and another laser reads the data from the light-sensitive recording surface. A light beam is easily deflected to the desired place on the optical disk, so a mechanical access arm is not needed.

Optical laser disks are becoming a very inviting option for users. They are less sensitive to environmental fluctuations, and they provide more direct-access storage at a cost that is much less per megabyte of storage than the magnetic disk alternative. Optical laser disk technology is still emerging and has yet to stabilize. At present there are three main categories of optical laser disks: *CD-ROM, WORM disks,* and *rewritable optical disks.*

CD-ROM

Introduced in 1980 for stereo buffs, the extraordinarily successful CD, or compact disk, is an optical laser disk designed to enhance the reproduction of recorded music. To make a CD recording, the analog sounds of music are translated into their digital equivalents and stored on a 4.72-inch optical laser disk. Seventy-four minutes of music can be recorded on each disk in digital format in 2 billion digital bits. (A bit is represented by the presence or absence of a pit on the optical disk.) With its tremendous storage capacity per square inch, computer industry entrepreneurs immediately recognized the potential of optical laser disk technology. In effect, anything that can be digitized can be stored on optical laser disk: data, text, voice, still pictures, music, graphics, and motion video.

CD-ROM, a spinoff of audio CD technology, stands for *compact disk–read-only memory*. The name implies its application. CD-ROM disks are created at a mastering facility, just as audio CDs are created at a recording studio. The master copy is duplicated, or "pressed," at the factory and the copies are distributed with their prerecorded contents (for example, the complete works of Shakespeare or the first 30 minutes of *Gone with the Wind*). Once inserted into the CD-ROM disk drive, the text, video images, and so on can be read into primary storage for processing or display. However, the data on the disk are fixed—they cannot be altered. This is in contrast, of course, to the read/write capability of magnetic disks.

The capacity of a single CD-ROM is more than 550 MB—about that of 400 DS/HD 3½-inch diskettes. To put the density of CD-ROM into perspective, the words in every book ever written could be stored on a hypothetical CD-ROM that is seven feet in diameter.

A single CD-ROM disk can hold the equivalent of 13,000 images, 250,000 pages of text, or 1500 floppy disks. This tremendous storage capacity has opened the door to a variety of multimedia applications. This CD-ROM gives you an opportunity to relive Columbus's journey of discovery. The CD-ROM gives the user instant random access to images, motion video, animation, sound, or text.

The introduction of *multidisk player/changers* enables ready access to vast amounts of on-line data. Like a compact-disk audio player/changer, a desired CD-ROM disk is loaded to the CD-ROM disk drive under program control. These player/changers, sometimes called *jukeboxes,* can hold from 6 to more than 100 disks.

The tremendous amount of low-cost direct-access storage made possible by optical laser disks has opened the door to many new applications. Currently, most of the estimated 20,000 commercially produced CD-ROM disks contain reference material. This number is growing rapidly every year. The following is a sampling of available CD-ROM disks.

- *The New Groliers Multimedia Encyclopedia* (including text, thousands of stills, motion video sequences, and sounds)
- *The Oxford English Dictionary*
- *Microsoft Bookshelf* (dictionary, thesaurus, almanac, atlas, book of facts, and more)
- The 1990 U.S. Census (county level)
- The text of 450 titles (including *Moby Dick,* the *King James version of the Bible, Beowolf, The Odyssey,* and many more)
- Multilingual dictionaries (one disk contains translation dictionaries for 12 languages)
- Scientific writings for the Apple Macintosh
- *The Daily Oklahoman* newspaper (1981–1986)
- *Cinemania* (19,000 movie reviews from 1914 to 1991, actor biographies, movie stills, and more)
- *Great Cities of the World* (narratives, facts, photos, hotel and transportation information)

This is the Sony Multimedia Player, perhaps a preview of how we will work with reference material in the future. The CD-ROM player, which is not a laptop PC, is designed specifically to enable the playing of and interaction with a CD-ROM disk. Salespeople, managers, educators, maintenance personnel, and others can use the player to have ready access to the information they need to do their jobs better. Companies can combine pictures, graphics, audio, video, and text in the form of brochures, catalogs, sales presentations, technical manuals, or whatever is needed to improve personnel productivity.

- *Space Quest IV* (space adventure game)
- Sound effects
- The Animals (multimedia zoo with 225 animals)
- World Atlas (thousands of maps and graphs, flags, audio of anthems, and more)
- *Desert Storm: The War in the Persian Gulf* (chronological multimedia presentation)

The cost of commercially produced CD-ROMs varies considerably from as little as $30 to several thousand dollars.

CD-ROM is the backbone of multimedia applications. **Multimedia** applications involve the integration of text, sound, graphics, motion video, and animation. Multimedia is discussed in detail in Chapter 10, "Graphics, Multimedia, Communications, and Other PC Applications."

WORM Disks

Write once, read many optical laser disks, or **WORM disks,** are used by end user companies to store their own proprietary information. Once the data have been written to the medium, they can only be read, not updated or changed.

Typically, WORM applications involve image processing or archival storage. A single mainframe-based 200-gigabyte (GB) WORM disk can store more than 3 million digitized images the size of this page. A good example of an image processing application is an "electronic catalog." The retailer digitizes images of items for sale and stores these images for ready access on WORM disks. A customer can peruse a retailer's electronic catalog on a VDT, or perhaps a PC, and see the item while reading about it. And, with a few keystrokes the customer can order the item as well. The Library of Congress is using WORM technology to help alleviate a serious shelf-space problem. The pages of many books can be digitized and stored on a single WORM disk.

The WORM disk cartridge, which has a data storage life in excess of 30 years, provides an alternative to magnetic tape for archival storage. For example, one real estate company maintains a permanent record (digitized image) of all completed hard-copy transactions (contracts, deeds, and so on) on a PC-based WORM disk. A few WORM disk cartridges take up a lot less space than a bunch of file cabinets. The PC version of a WORM disk cartridge has a capacity of 200 MB.

The IBM PS/2 Rewritable Optical Drive uses 3½-inch interchangeable optical cartridges that store up to 127 MB each. The optical cartridge stores the equivalent of eighty-eight 1.44-MB diskettes. Optical cartridge applications include distribution of databases to branch offices, multimedia presentations, distribution of PC software, hard disk backup, and archival storage.

Rewritable Optical Disks

Rewritable optical disks use magneto-optical technology to integrate optical and magnetic disk technology to enable read- *and*-write storage. The 5¼-inch rewritable disk cartridges can store up to 1 GB. However, the technology must be improved before the optical disks can be considered as a direct alternative to magnetic media. At present, rewritable optical disk drives are more expensive and less reliable than magnetic media. In addition, the disk access times for rewritable optical disks are slow relative to magnetic media. For these reasons, most traditional information systems continue to rely on magnetic disks.

Rewritable optical disks are beginning to find their niche. Applications that call for large volumes of storage with relatively little update activity are made to order for rewritable optical disks. Also, applications that require hardware to operate in harsh environments may be candidates for rewritable optical disks. Optical disks can function with a wide range of temperatures, from below freezing to 100 degrees Farenheit. Magnetic storage media may malfunction when operating in extreme temperatures. As optical laser disk technology matures to offer reliable, cost-effective read/write operation, it eventually may dominate secondary storage in the future as magnetic disks and tape do today.

*I*MPORTANT TERMS AND SUMMARY OUTLINE

access arm	diskette	random file
access time	field	random processing
batch processing	file	read/write head
CD-ROM	fixed magnetic disk	rewritable optical disks
cylinder	flat file	secondary storage
data cartridge	floppy disk	sector
data compression	floptical disk drive	sector organization
data item	interchangeable magnetic disk	sequential processing
data transfer rate	key field	serial representation
database	magnetic disk drive	serpentine
direct-access file	magnetic tape cartridge	source data
direct-access processing	magnetic tape drive	tape backup unit (TBU)
direct-access storage device (DASD)	multimedia	track
disk address	off-line	tracks per inch (TPI)
disk caching	on-line	transaction-oriented processing
disk cartridge	optical laser disk	Winchester disk
disk density	prompt	WORM disks
disk pack	RAM disk	

5–1 Secondary Storage: Permanent Data Storage Data and programs are stored in **secondary storage** for permanent storage. **Magnetic disk drives** and **magnetic tape drives** are the primary devices for secondary storage. **Optical laser disk** technology is emerging as an alternative to magnetic disks and magnetic tapes.

5–2 The Hierarchy of Data Organization: Bits to Databases The six levels of the hierarchy of data organization are bit, character (or byte), **field**, record, **file**, and **database.** The first level is transparent to the programmer and end user, but the other five are integral to the design of any information processing activity. A string of bits is combined to form a character. Characters are combined to represent the content of fields—**data items.** Related fields are combined to form records. Records with the same data elements combine to form a file. In traditional **flat-file** processing, files are sorted, merged, and processed by a **key field.**

The database is the company's data resource for all information systems. The integrated database environ-

ment offers greater access to information, better control, and more efficient software development.

5–3 Data Storage Concepts In a computer system, the input, output, and data storage components that receive data from and transmit data to the processor are said to be **on-line.** Hardware devices, including data storage media, that are not accessible to nor under the control of a processor are said to be **off-line. Source data** on source documents must be transcribed into a machine-readable format before they can be interpreted by a computer. Data entry describes the process of entering data into an information system. Information systems are designed to provide users with display-screen **prompts** to make on-line data entry easier.

When transactions are grouped together for processing, it is called **batch processing.** In **transaction-oriented processing,** transactions are recorded and entered as they occur.

Data are retrieved and manipulated either sequentially or randomly. Magnetic disk drives enable **random-**

and **sequential-processing** capabilities. Magnetic tapes have only sequential-processing capabilities.

5-4 Magnetic Disks: Rotating Storage Media **Direct-access storage devices** (**DASDs**), such as magnetic disk, permit random processing of records.

In the microcomputer environment, the two most popular types of **interchangeable magnetic disks** are the 5¼-inch and 3½-inch **diskettes** (or **floppy disks**). The microcomputer **fixed magnetic disk** is called the **Winchester disk.** The multifunction **floptical disk drive** provides high-volume storage capacity on interchangeable diskettes.

In **sector organization,** the recording surface is divided into pie-shaped **sectors,** and each sector is assigned a number. Data are stored via serial representation in **tracks** on each recording surface. The spacing of tracks is measured in **tracks per inch,** or **TPI.** A particular **cylinder** refers to every track with the same number on all recording surfaces. **Disk density** refers to the number of bits that can be stored per unit of area on the disk-face surface. A particular set of data stored on a disk is assigned a **disk address** that designates its physical location (disk-face surface, track, sector). An **access arm** with one or more **read/write heads** is moved to the appropriate track to retrieve the data.

The **access time** for a magnetic disk is the sum of the seek time, the rotational delay time, and the transmission time.

The **data transfer rate** is the rate at which data are read from (or written to) secondary storage to (from) RAM. **Disk caching** enhances system performance by placing programs and data that are likely to be called into RAM for processing from a disk into an area of RAM that simulates disk storage, called the **RAM disk.** The data transfer rate within RAM is considerably less than between secondary storage and RAM.

Safeguarding software and your data may be more important than safeguarding hardware. The impact of losing critical software or files makes backup a major concern. The frequency with which a work disk is backed up depends on its volatility. It is common practice to maintain two generations of backup.

Apply the dictates of common sense to the care of diskettes: Avoid excessive dust, avoid extremes in temperature and humidity, and don't fold, spindle, or mutilate the disks.

In the mainframe environment, DASDs are the prerequisite for virtually all information systems that demand **direct-access processing.** The once popular **disk cartridge** and the **disk pack** have been replaced with permanently installed high-density fixed disks. Mainframe disks are organized like PC disks.

5-5 Random, or Direct-Access, Processing: Pick and Choose A **direct-access file,** or **random file,** is a collection of records that can be processed in any order. In random processing, the unsorted transaction file is run against a random master file. Only the records needed to complete the transaction are retrieved from secondary storage.

5-6 Magnetic Tape: Ribbons of Data A **magnetic tape cartridge,** which is also called a **data cartridge,** is loaded to a tape drive, where data are read or written as the tape is passed under a read/write head. The physical nature of the magnetic tape results in data being stored and accessed sequentially.

Magnetic tape media come in several widths up to ½ inch and many different lengths. One of the most popular PC tape cartridge formats is the *QIC-80 minicartridge.* With the **data compression** feature active, a tape's storage capacity increases.

Drives for ¼-inch tape cartridges, often called **tape backup units** (**TBUs**), store data in a **serpentine** manner. Data are recorded in tracks using **serial representation.**

A tape drive is rated by its *storage capacity* and its *data transfer rate.*

5-7 Optical Laser Disks: High-Density Storage Optical laser disk storage is capable of storing vast amounts of data. The three main categories of optical laser disks are **CD-ROM, WORM disk,** and **rewritable optical disk.** Most of the commercially produced read-only CD-ROM disks contain reference material or support **multimedia** applications involving the integration of text, sound, graphics, motion video, and animation. The write once, read many (WORM) optical laser disks are used by end user companies to store their own proprietary information. WORM applications usually involve image processing or archival storage. The rewritable optical disks offer the promise that optical laser disks will become commercially viable as a read-and-write storage technology.

REVIEW EXERCISES

Concepts

1. What are other names for diskette and direct processing?

2. CD-ROM is a spinoff of what technology?

3. A program issues a "read" command for data to be retrieved from a magnetic tape. Describe the resulting movement of the data.

4. What are the three main categories of optical laser disks?

5. What is the nickname of the hard disk used with microcomputers?

6. What are the six levels of the hierarchy of data organization?

7. What is the lowest level logical unit in the hierarchy of data organization?

8. Name two possible key fields for a personnel file. Name two for an inventory file.

9. How many megabytes are there in a gigabyte?

10. A 20-sectored disk contains 8 recording surfaces and 1000 cylinders. Each sector of a disk-face surface can store 512 bytes of data. What is the storage capacity of 8 such disks?

11. What is the width of the magnetic tape in the QIC-80 minicartridge?

12. List two titles available on CD-ROM.

Discussion

13. A floppy disk does not move until a read or write command is issued. Once it is issued, the floppy begins to spin. It stops spinning after the command is executed. Why is a disk pack not set in motion in the same manner? Why is a floppy not made to spin continuously?

14. Every Friday night a company makes backup copies of all master files and programs. Why is this necessary? The company has both tape and disk drives. Which storage medium would you suggest for the backup? Why?

15. Describe the potential impact of optical laser disk technology on public and university libraries. On home libraries.

SELF-TEST (BY SECTION)

5–1 Data are retrieved from temporary secondary storage and stored permanently in RAM. (T/F)

5–2 a. The specific value of a field is called the _data item_.

b. Flat files are sorted, merged, and processed by what kind of field: (a) solution field, (b) key field, or (c) central field?

5–3 a. A burster separates and stacks the payroll checks in an _off-line_ (on-line or off-line) operation.

b. In transaction-oriented processing, transactions are recorded and entered to the system as they occur. (T/F)

5–4 a. Magnetic disks have both _random_- and _sequent_-access capabilities.

b. In a disk drive, the read/write heads are mounted on an access arm. (T/F)

c. Fixed disks can be removed and stored off-line. (T/F)

d. The standard sizes for magnetic diskettes are _3½_ inch and _5¼_ inch.

e. What percentage of the data on a magnetic disk is available to the system with each complete revolution of the disk: (a) 10%, (b) 50%, or (c) 100%?

f. The _disk address_ denotes the physical location of a particular set of data or a program on a magnetic disk.

g. The frequency with which a work disk is backed up depends on its volatility. (T/F)

5–5 An inventory transaction file is the permanent source of inventory data for an organization. (T/F)

5–6 a. When activated, which tape backup unit feature results in increased capacity on the data cartridge: (a) data compression, (b) data reduction, or (c) tape stretching?

b. Streamer tape drives store data in a _serpen_ manner.

5–7 a. _optical laser disk_ storage technology uses laser beams to write to the recording surface.

b. CD-ROM is read-only. (T/F)

c. Disks that use magneto-optical technology are: (a) rewritable, (b) read-only, or (c) write only.

Self-test answers. **5–1** F. **5–2 (a)** data item; **(b)** b. **5–3 (a)** off-line; **(b)** T. **5–4** random, sequential; **(b)** T; **(c)** F; **(d)** 5¼, 3½; **(e)** c; **(f)** disk address; **(g)** T. **5–5** F. **5–6 (a)** a; **(b)** serpentine. **5–7 (a)** Optical laser disk; **(b)** T; **(c)** a.

6

DATA COMMUNICATIONS AND NETWORKING

OBJECTIVES

To describe the concept of connectivity.

To demonstrate an understanding of data communications terminology and applications.

To detail the function and operation of data communications hardware.

To describe alternatives and sources of data transmission services.

To illustrate the various kinds of network topologies.

To describe a local area network and its associated hardware and software.

6–1 DATA COMMUNICATIONS: LINKING THE WORLD

Today, workers at all levels are knowledge workers. Their scope of responsibility continues to expand, as does their need for ready access to information. In the present competitive environment, we cannot rely solely on verbal communication for information transfer. Corporate presidents cannot wait until the Monday morning staff meeting to find out whether production is meeting demand. Field sales representatives can no longer afford to play telephone tag with headquarters personnel to get answers for impatient customers. The president, the field rep, and millions of knowledge workers now rely on *computer networks* to retrieve and share information quickly. Of course, we will continue to interact with our co-workers. Computer networks simply enhance the efficiency and effectiveness of that interaction. The computer network, first introduced in Chapter 1, "The World of Computers," is the integration of computer systems, terminals, and communication links. Computer networks and related technology are the focus of this chapter.

Connectivity: Tying It All Together

In the 1960s computers numbered in the tens of thousands. Today computers number in the tens of millions! Information is everywhere. The challenge of the next decade is to make this information more accessible to more people. To do this, the business and computer communities are seeking ways to interface, or connect, a diverse set of hardware, software, and databases. In so doing, they are attempting to achieve some degree of **connectivity**. Connectivity is necessary to facilitate the electronic communication between companies, end user computing, and the free flow of information within an enterprise.

■ Connectivity means that a marketing manager can use a microcomputer to access information in a database on the finance department's minicomputer.

This is the nerve center of EDSNET, Electronic Data-Systems Corporation's global communications system. EDSNET facilitates data, voice, and video communication between a quarter of a million sites on five continents. Here in Plano, Texas, (near Dallas) more than 100 operators manage the system. Operators view 12-by-16-foot screens to keep abreast of system activity. Fourteen smaller screens provide detailed information for troubleshooting situations, and 13 clocks display times from around the world.

■ Connectivity means that a network of microcomputers can route output to the same laser printer.

■ Connectivity means that a manufacturing company's mainframe computer can communicate with the mainframe computers of its suppliers.

To the user, the ideal implementation of connectivity would be to make all corporate computer and information resources accessible from his or her PC or terminal. This ideal is called **total connectivity**. Realistically, industry analysts are predicting that total connectivity is still a decade or more away. Nevertheless, users are expecting, even demanding, that their companies strive for total connectivity.

Data communications is, very simply, the collection and distribution of the electronic representation of information from and to remote facilities. The information can appear in a variety of formats: data, text, voice, still pictures, graphics, and video. The raw information must be *digitized* before transmission. (For example, data and text might be translated into their corresponding ASCII codes.) Ultimately, all forms of information are sent over the transmission media as a series of binary bits (1s and 0s). Information is transmitted from computers to terminals and other computers over land via fiber optic cable, through the air by satellites, and under the sea through coaxial cable. The technical aspects of data communications are discussed later in this chapter.

The Beginning of an Era: Cooperative Processing

This is the era of **cooperative processing**. Information is the password to success in today's business environment. To get meaningful, accurate, and timely information, businesses must cooperate internally and externally to take full advantage of what is available. To promote internal cooperation, businesses are setting up *intracompany networking* (see Figure 6–1). For example, information maintained in the personnel department is readily accessible to people throughout the company on a *need-to-know* basis. At the individual level, managers or knowledge workers create microcomputer-based systems and databases to help them do their jobs.

Companies have recognized that they must cooperate with one another to compete effectively in a world market. They cooperate via *intercompany networking* (Figure 6–1) or, more specifically, via **electronic data interchange** (EDI). EDI uses computers and data communications to transmit data electronically between companies. Invoices, orders, and many other intercompany transactions, including the exchange of information, can be transmitted from the computer of one company to the computer of another. For example, at major retail chains, such as Walmart, over 90% of all orders are processed directly between computers via EDI. Figure 6–2 contrasts traditional interactions between a customer and supplier company with interactions via EDI.

This office is one of eight regional customer support centers, each of which is part of a computer network. The terminals and PCs at this office are linked to a local minicomputer that is connected via a high-speed communications line to the company's headquarters in Boise, Idaho. The regional minis also are used for local processing.

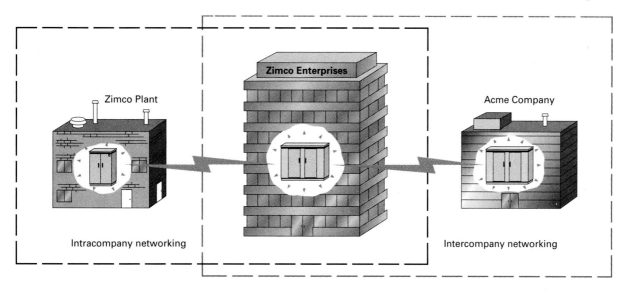

FIGURE 6–1   Intracompany and Intercompany Networking

The phenomenal growth of the use of micros in the home is causing companies to expand their information system capabilities to allow linkages with home and portable PCs. This form of cooperative processing increases system efficiency while lowering costs. For example, in more than 100 banks, ser-

FIGURE 6–2   Interactions between Customer and Supplier   *In the figure, the traditional interactions between a customer company and a supplier company are contrasted with similar interactions via electronic data interchange (EDI).*

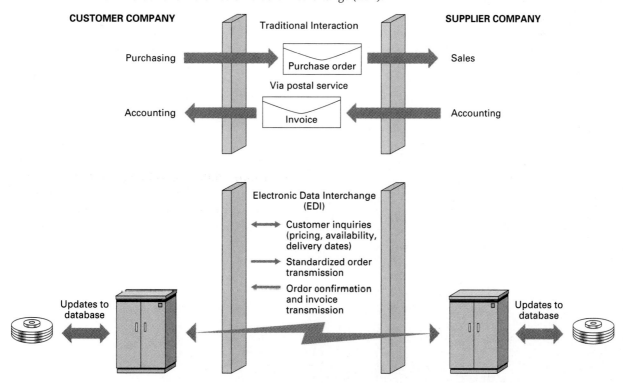

vices have been extended to home micro owners in the form of home banking systems. Subscribers to a home banking service use their personal computers as terminals linked to the bank's mainframe computer system to pay bills, transfer funds, and ask about account status.

6–2   DATA COMMUNICATIONS HARDWARE

Data communications hardware is used to transmit data between terminals (including PCs that emulate terminals) and computers and between computers. These primary hardware components include the modem, the down-line processor, and the front-end processor. The integration of these devices with terminals and computer systems is illustrated in Figure 6–3 and discussed in the paragraphs that follow.

The Modem

If you have a micro, you can establish a communications link between your microcomputer and any remote computer system in the world. However, to do this you must have ready access to a telephone line and your micro must be equipped with a *modem*. Most new PCs and many existing PCs are configured with modems.

Telephone lines were designed to carry *analog signals* for voice communication, not the binary *digital signals* (1s and 0s) needed for computer-based data communication. The **modem** (*mo*dulator-*dem*odulator) converts micro-

FIGURE 6–3 Hardware Components in Data Communications   *Devices that handle the movement of data in a computer network are the modem, the down-line processor, the front-end processor, and the host processor.*

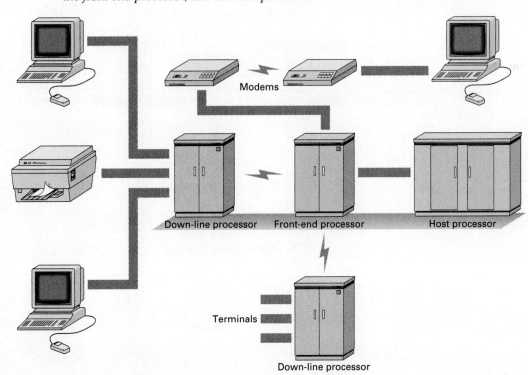

Modems

Down-line processor   Front-end processor   Host processor

Terminals

Down-line processor

to-computer and terminal-to-computer electrical *digital* signals into *analog* signals so that the data can be transmitted over telephone lines (see Figure 6–4). The digital electrical signals are modulated to make sounds similar to those you hear on a touch-tone telephone. Upon reaching their destination, these analog signals are demodulated by another modem into computer-compatible electrical signals for processing. The procedure is reversed for computer-to-terminal or computer-to-micro communication. A modem is always required when you dial up the computer on a telephone line. The modulation-demodulation process is not needed when a micro or a terminal is linked directly to a network by a transmission medium such as a coaxial cable.

The modem is a must-have piece of hardware for any application that requires the use of a telephone line for data communications. Many PC owners use their modems to take advantage of commercial information network services, such as CompuServe, GEnie, or Prodigy. These companies offer a variety of information services, such as up-to-the-minute sports, home shopping, financial information, entertainment, special-interest bulletin boards, and much more. (See Chapter 1, "The World of Computers," for more on information network services.)

The fax machine offers another means of communication. A newsletter containing up-to-the-minute oil-pricing information (shown here) is broadcast (sent) to subscribers via fax. You do not have to have a fax to enjoy the benefits of fax communication. Many PC users routinely use their fax modems to send and receive faxes. When you send a fax on a PC, you simply route page(s) to the fax modem rather than a printer. To receive a fax via PC, you enable your fax modem software.

Internal and External Modems   There are two types of modems for micros and terminals: *internal* and *external*. Most micros and terminals have internal modems; that is, the modem is on an optional add-on circuit board that is simply plugged permanently into an empty expansion slot in the micro's processor unit or the terminal's housing. Laptops with PCMCIA-compliant interfaces use modems on interchangeable PC cards. The external modem is a separate component, as illustrated in Figure 6–4, and is connected via a serial interface port (see Chapter 2, "Interacting with Computers"). To make the connection with a telephone line and either type of modem, you simply plug the telephone line into the modem just as you would when connecting the line to a telephone.

Fax Modems   The *fax modem* performs the same function as a regular modem. Also, it has an added capability—it enables a PC to simulate a *facsimile* or *fax* machine. The fax modem was mentioned first in Chapter 2 with add-on boards. Fax machines transfer images of hard-copy documents via telephone lines to another location. The process is similar to using a copying machine except that the original is inserted in a fax machine at one location and a hard copy is produced on a fax machine at another location. PCs configured with a fax modem (an add-on board or a PC card) can fax text and images directly from an electronic file to a remote facsimile machine or to another similarly equipped micro.

FIGURE 6–4 The Modulation-Demodulation Process   *Electrical digital signals are modulated into analog signals for transmission over telephone lines and then demodulated for processing at the destination.*

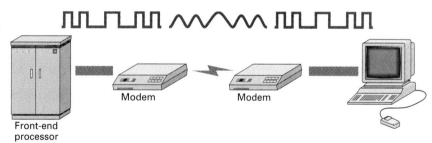

Front-end
processor

Modem

Modem

BEAT THE TRAFFIC BY TELECOMMUTING

Traditionally, people get up in the morning, get dressed, and fight through rush-hour traffic to go to the office because that is where the work is. However, for many knowledge workers, work is really at a micro or terminal, whether at the office or at home. More and more employees are beginning to question the wisdom of going to the office in the traditional sense. Many would prefer to telecommute and work in the more comfortable surroundings of a home or studio. Telecommuting is "commuting" to work via a data communications link between home and office.

In theory, millions of people could telecommute to work at least a few days a week. People whose jobs involve telephone communication and/or considerable interaction with a computer system are perfect candidates (such as those who process insurance claims, those in the financial services, salespersons, and programmers). Already thousands of self-employed consultants, writers, and others telecommute to their clients. More and more managers who need a few hours, or perhaps a few days, of uninterrupted time have found telecommuting to be the solution.

Telecommuting and the accompanying flexible work hours have emerged as an important "perk" of employment. The company that does not offer current and prospective employees the opportunity to telecommute may be at a disadvantage in recruiting quality workers.

The trend is definitely toward an increased level of telecommuting, especially with the proliferation of facsimile (fax) machines and sophisticated telephone systems that include voice mail and call forwarding. In effect, a knowledge worker's home office could function much like his or her "at work" office. In some cases, the at work office could be eliminated.

Telecommuting may never catch on as a general alternative to working in the office, but for some applications it has proved to be a boon to productivity. As a personnel director observed: "With the elimination of travel time, coffee breaks, idle conversations, and numerous office distractions, we have found that conscientious, self-motivated employees can be more productive at home when working on certain projects."

Working at Home
The familiar surroundings of home inspire some people to do their best work. Others, however, are more comfortable working in a traditional office setting.

Special-Function Processors

In Figure 6–3, the **host processor,** or central computer, is responsible for overall control of the computer system and for the execution of applications, such as a hotel reservation system. To improve the efficiency of a computer system, the *processing load* is sometimes *distributed* among several other special-function processors. The two communications-related processors in the computer system of Figure 6–3, the front-end processor and the down-line processor, are under the control of and subordinate to the host. In Figure 6–3, the host processor is a mainframe; however, the host could just as well be a micro, a workstation, a mini, or a supercomputer, depending on the size and complexity of the network.

The Front-End Processor   The terminal or computer sending a **message** is the *source.* The terminal or computer receiving the message is the *destination.* The **front-end processor** establishes the link between the source and destination in a process called **handshaking.** The front-end processor relieves the host processor of communications-related processing duties. These duties include the transmission of data to and from remote terminals and other computers. In this way, the host can concentrate on overall system control and the execution of applications software.

If you think of messages as mail to be delivered to various points in a computer network, the front-end processor is the post office. Each computer system and terminal/PC in a computer network is assigned a **network address.** The front-end processor uses these addresses to route messages to their destinations. The content of a message could be a prompt to the user, a user inquiry, a program instruction, an "electronic memo," or any type of information that can be transmitted electronically—even the image of a handwritten report.

The Down-Line Processor   The **down-line processor,** also called a **multiplexer,** is an extension of the front-end processor. Its name is derived from its physical location relative to the host processor. It is located "down-line"—at or near a remote site. The down-line processor collects data from several low-speed devices, such as terminals and serial printers. It then "concentrates" the data—sending the data over a single communications channel (see Figure 6–5)

FIGURE 6–5 "Concentrating" Data for Remote Transmission   *The down-line processor "concentrates" the data from several low-speed devices for transmission over a single high-speed line. At the host site, the front-end processor separates the data for processing. Data received from a front-end processor are interpreted by the down-line processor and routed to the appropriate device.*

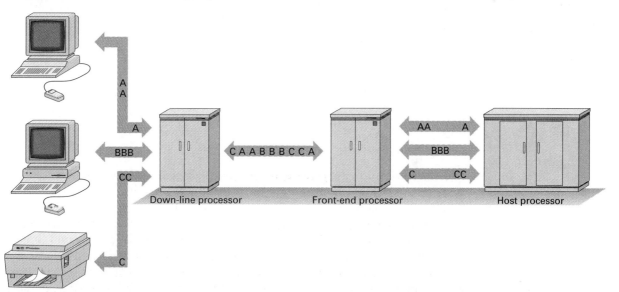

MEMORY BITS
**Hardware
for Data
Communications**
■ Modem
■ Down-line processor
■ Front-end processor
■ Router

to the front-end processor. The down-line processor also receives and distributes host output to the appropriate remote terminals.

The down-line processor is an economic necessity when several low-speed terminals are at one remote site. One high-speed line connecting the down-line processor to the host is considerably less expensive than several low-speed lines connecting each terminal to the host. An airline reservation counter might have 10 terminals. Each terminal is connected to a common down-line processor, which in turn is connected to a central host computer. An airline might have one or several down-line processors at a given airport, depending on the volume of passenger traffic.

A microcomputer can be made to emulate the function of a down-line processor. This often occurs when a network of micros is linked to a mainframe computer.

Routers: Bridging the Gap

Computer networks are everywhere: in banks, in law offices, and even in the classroom. In keeping with the trend toward greater connectivity, computer networks are being interconnected to give users access to a greater variety of applications and to more information. For example, one company linked its several PC-based networks to the company's enterprise-wide mainframe network. This enabled end users on all networks to share information and resources.

Communications protocols are rules established to govern the way data are transmitted in a computer network. Because networks use a variety of communications protocols and operating systems, incompatible networks cannot "talk" directly to one another. The primary hardware/software technology used to help alleviate the problems of linking incompatible computer networks is the **router**. Routers help to bridge the gap between incompatible networks. Upon receiving a message, the router performs the necessary protocol conversion and routes the message to its destination.

Organizations that are set up to interconnect computer networks do so over a **backbone**. The backbone is composed of a system of routers and the associated transmission media (for example, fiber optic cable) that link the computers in an organization.

6–3   THE DATA COMMUNICATIONS CHANNEL: DATA HIGHWAYS

Transmission Media

A **communications channel** is the facility through which electronic signals are transmitted between locations in a computer network. Data, text, digitized images, and digitized sounds are transmitted as combinations of bits (0s and 1s). A *channel's capacity* is rated by the number of bits it can transmit per second. A regular telephone line can transmit up to 9600 **bits per second (bps)**, or 9.6 K bps (thousands of bits per second). Under normal circumstances, a 9.6 K-bps line would fill the screen of a typical video monitor with text in one or two seconds.

In practice, the word **baud** is often used interchangeably with *bits per second*. Technically speaking, however, it is quite different. But if someone says *baud* when talking about computer-based communications, that person probably means bits per second.

Data rates of 1540 K bps are available through common carriers such as American Telephone & Telegraph (AT&T). The channel may comprise one or a combination of the transmission media discussed next.

Telephone Lines   The same transmission facilities we use for voice communication via telephones can also be used to transmit data. This capability is provided by communications companies throughout the country and the world.

Coaxial Cable   **Coaxial cable** contains electrical wire and is constructed to permit high-speed data transmission with a minimum of signal distortion. If you have ever hooked up a television, you probably are familiar with coaxial cable. Coaxial cable is laid along the ocean floor for intercontinental voice and data transmission. It is also used to connect terminals and computers in a "local" area (from a few feet to a few miles).

Fiber Optic Cable   Very thin transparent fibers have been developed that will eventually replace the twisted-pair copper wire traditionally used in the telephone system. These hairlike **fiber optic cables** carry data faster and are lighter and less expensive than their copper-wire counterparts. Twisted-pair wire and coaxial cable carry data as electrical signals. Fiber optic cable carries data as laser-generated light beams.

The differences between the data transmission rates of copper wire and fiber optic cable are tremendous. In the time it takes to transmit a single page of *Webster's Unabridged Dictionary* over twisted-pair copper wire (about 6 seconds), the entire dictionary could be transmitted over a single fiber optic cable.

Another of the many advantages of fiber optic cable is its contribution to data security. It is much more difficult for a computer criminal to intercept a signal sent over fiber optic cable (via a beam of light) than it is over copper wire (an electrical signal).

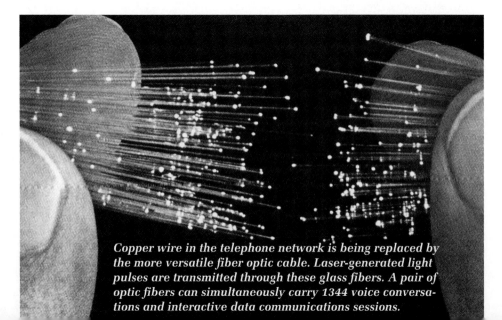

Copper wire in the telephone network is being replaced by the more versatile fiber optic cable. Laser-generated light pulses are transmitted through these glass fibers. A pair of optic fibers can simultaneously carry 1344 voice conversations and interactive data communications sessions.

Microwave repeater stations, such as this one on top of a corporate headquarters building, relay signals to transceivers or other repeater stations. This microwave station enables communication between the headquarters building and a plant 15 miles away.

Microwave   Communications channels do not have to be wires or fibers. Data can also be transmitted via **microwave radio signals**. Transmission of these signals is *line-of-sight;* that is, the radio signal travels in a direct line from one repeater station to the next until it reaches its destination. Because of the curvature of the earth, microwave repeater stations are placed on the tops of mountains and towers, usually about 30 miles apart.

Satellites have made it possible to reduce the line-of-sight limitation. Satellites are routinely launched into orbit for the sole purpose of relaying data communications signals to and from earth stations. A satellite, which is essentially a repeater station, is launched and set in a **geosynchronous orbit** 22,300 miles above the earth. A geosynchronous orbit permits the communications satellite to maintain a fixed position relative to the earth's surface. Each satellite can receive and retransmit signals to slightly less than half of the earth's surface; therefore, three satellites are required to cover the earth effectively (see Figure 6–6). The main advantage of satellites is that data can be transmitted from one location to any number of other locations anywhere on (or near) our planet.

Wireless Transceivers   Perhaps the greatest challenge and one of the biggest expenses in a computer network is the installation of the physical links between its components. The *wireless transceiver* provides an alternative when the expense of running a permanent physical line (twisted-pair wire, coaxial

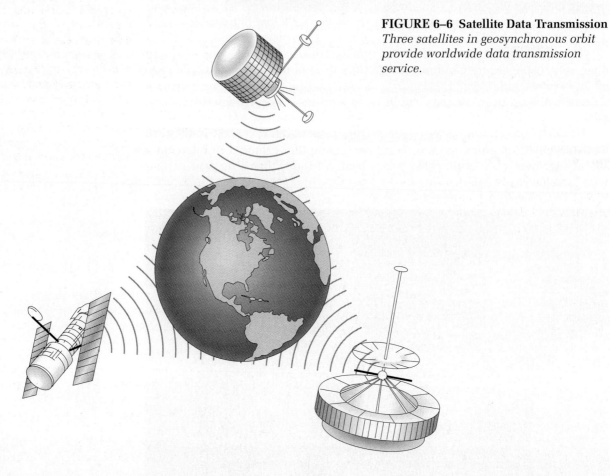

FIGURE 6–6 Satellite Data Transmission
Three satellites in geosynchronous orbit provide worldwide data transmission service.

cable, and fiber optic cable) is prohibitive. Two wireless transceivers, each smaller than this book, replace a physical line between source and destination (micro and mainframe, terminal and down-line processor, and so on). The source transmits digital signals via a physical link to a nearby transceiver, which, in turn, retransmits the signals over radio waves to another transceiver. Transceivers provide users with tremendous flexibility in the location of PCs and terminals in a network; however, the flexibility advantage is offset by the transceivers' limited channel capacity. Also, the number of terminals/PCs that can be linked via transceivers is limited by the frequencies allotted for this purpose.

Common Carriers

It is impractical, not to mention illegal, for companies to string their own coaxial cables between two locations, such as Philadelphia and New York City. It is also impractical for them to set their own satellites in orbit. Therefore, companies turn to **common carriers** for data communications, such as AT&T, MCI, Western Union, and GTE, to provide communications channels. Organizations pay communications common carriers for *dedicated* or *dial-up* (via a telephone) access to a data communications channel between any two points in their computer networks. Common carriers are regulated by the Federal Communications Commission (FCC).

Computers and data communications have turned our world into a "global village." This data communications satellite has just been placed into geosynchronous orbit about the earth at 174 degrees west longitude. In satellite communications, data are transmitted first to an earth station where giant antennae route signals to another earth station via a communications satellite. The signals are then transmitted to their destination over another type of communications channel.

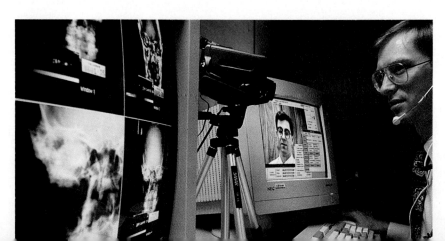

One of the services offered by common carriers is the facilitation of conferencing via telecommunications, or teleconferencing. This doctor in Charleston, South Carolina, saved the cost and time of a cross-country flight by teleconferencing with his colleague in Portland, Oregon. The doctors can see and talk with each other and pass information back and forth via computer and facsimile machines.

151

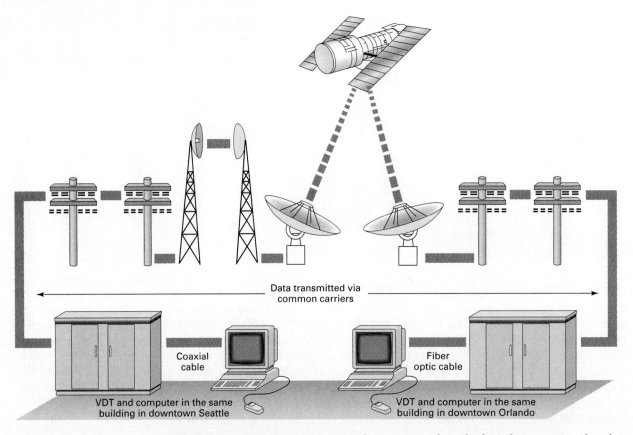

Data transmitted via common carriers

Coaxial cable

Fiber optic cable

VDT and computer in the same building in downtown Seattle

VDT and computer in the same building in downtown Orlando

FIGURE 6–7 Data Transmission Path *It's more the rule than the exception that data are carried over several transmission media between source and destination.*

Data Transmission in Practice

A communications channel from Computer A in Seattle, Washington, to Computer B in Orlando, Florida (see Figure 6–7), usually would consist of several different transmission media. The connection between Computer A and a terminal in the same building is probably coaxial cable. The Seattle company might use a common carrier company such as AT&T to transmit the data. AT&T would then send the data through a combination of transmission facilities that might include copper wire, fiber optic cable, and microwave radio signals.

6–4 NETWORKS: LINKING COMPUTERS AND PEOPLE

Each time you use the telephone, you use the world's largest computer network—the telephone system. A telephone is an endpoint, or a **node,** connected to a network of computers that routes your voice signals to any one of the 500 million telephones (other nodes) in the world. In a computer network the node can be a terminal, a computer, or any destination/source device (for example, a printer or an automatic teller machine). Computer networks are configured to meet the specific requirements of an organization. Some have 5 nodes; others have 10,000 nodes. This section addresses the various approaches used to link nodes within an organization into a computer network.

Network Topologies

The basic computer **network topologies**—star, ring, and bus—are illustrated in Figure 6–8. A network topology is a description of the possible physical con-

FIGURE 6–8 Network Topologies   *(a) star (b) ring (c) bus*

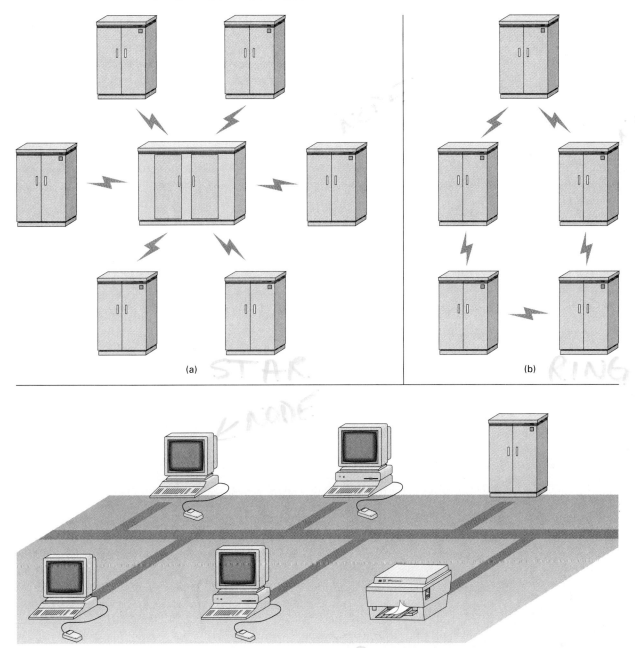

(a)

(b)

(c)

Many insurance companies say that they are quick to process claims, but some are more effective than others. This insurance claims adjuster brings a cellular laptop to the site of an accident or a natural disaster. His laptop is configured with a modem. When the modem is used in conjunction with the cellular phone link, the laptop can transmit voice, data, and images over communications links to a LAN at his company's home office. He also carries a video camera. While writing up the claim, he transmits selected videos, frame by frame, to the company's home office. Normally, electronic approval for issuing a check is sent to him via his laptop. He then issues a check on the spot to the policyholder.

nections within a network. The topology is the configuration of the hardware and shows which pairs of nodes can communicate.

Star Topology   The **star topology** involves a centralized host computer connected to several other computer systems that are usually smaller than the host. The smaller computer systems communicate with one another through the host and usually share the host computer's database. The host could be anything from a PC to a supercomputer. Both the central computer and the remote computer systems are connected to terminals (micros or VDTs). Any terminal can communicate with any other terminal in the network. Banks usually have a large home-office computer system with a star network of minicomputer systems in the branch banks.

Ring Topology   The **ring topology** involves computer systems approximately the same size, with no one computer system as the focal point of the network. When one system routes a message to another system, it is passed around the ring until it reaches its destination address.

Bus Topology   The **bus topology** permits the connection of terminals, peripheral devices, and microcomputers along a central cable called a **transmission medium**. It is easy to add devices or delete them from the network. Bus topologies are most appropriate when the linked devices are physically close to one another. (See the discussion of local area networks that follows.)

Topology Summary   A pure form of any of these three basic topologies is seldom found in practice. Most computer networks are *hybrids*—combinations of these topologies.

Client/Server Computing: Downsizing

Through the 1980s, processing activity within a computer network was accomplished by a centralized host processor (usually a mainframe computer) and a few subordinate processors (for example, the front-end processor). The economies of scale were applicable and shared use of a centralized host offered the greatest return for the hardware/software dollar. This is no longer true. PCs and workstations offer more computing capacity per dollar than mainframe computers. This reversal of hardware economics has caused information technology professionals to rethink the way they design computer networks.

The trend in the design of computer networks is toward client/server computing. In **client/server computing,** processing capabilities are distributed throughout the network. The *client,* which is typically a PC or a workstation, requests processing or another type of service from the *server.* The server computer, which can be anything from a PC to a supercomputer, performs the processing requested by the client. Both, however, do processing. Client and server share processing duties to optimize application efficiency. The client performs processing associated with the user interface and applications processing that can be done locally (for example, spreadsheet and word processing). The server performs processing tasks in support of its clients. For example, the server might accomplish those tasks associated with storage and retrieval of a centralized database.

In the client/server environment, users at client PCs frequently request that data be **downloaded** (server-to-client) from the server to their PCs for processing. Upon completion of processing, user data may be **uploaded** from a client PC to the server.

Over 70% of all PCs are linked to at least one computer network and most workstations are networked. In a client/server environment, clients often have the flexibility to interact with more than one server. The trend toward client/server computing has resulted in companies downsizing their computers. **Downsizing** was coined to describe the trend toward increased reliance on smaller computers for *personal* and *enterprise-wide* processing tasks.

This company is moving toward a client/server computing environment. Minicomputers at regional offices, such as this one, do most of the on-line processing; however, these client systems are linked to and use the database on the corporate mainframe (server).

6–5 LOCAL AREA NETWORKS

WANs and LANs

A **WAN,** or **wide area network,** connects nodes in widely dispersed geographic areas, such as cities, states, and even countries. The WAN will normally depend on the transmission services of a common carrier to transmit signals between nodes in the network. In contrast, the **local area network (LAN),** or **local net,** connects nodes in close proximity, such as in a suite of offices or a building. The local net, including all data communications channels, is owned by the organization using it. Because of the proximity of nodes in local nets, a company can install its own communications channels (such as coaxial cable, fiber optic cable, or wireless transceivers); therefore, LANs do not need common carriers. When we refer to WANs and LANs, we refer to all hardware, software, and communications channels associated with them.

The focus of this section is the LAN. A LAN allows the movement of data (including text, voice, and graphic images) between computers and I/O devices. Strictly speaking, any type of computer can be incorporated within a LAN, but, in practice, microcomputers provide the foundation for local area networks. Micros in a typical LAN are linked to each other and share resources such as printers and disk storage. The distance separating devices in the local net may vary from a few feet to a few miles. As few as two and as many as several hundred micros can be linked on a single local area network.

The ability to share valuable resources is the main reason companies are incorporating more PCs into local area networks. In a few years, most corporate-based PCs will be part of a LAN. In a LAN, data, applications software, links to mainframes, communications capabilities (for example, modems), CD-ROM databases (for example, an on line national telephone directory), add-on boards (for example, fax modem boards), and other resources can be shared among users of the system. LANs make good business sense because available resources can be shared. For example, the cost of a LAN-based spreadsheet is far less than the cost of a spreadsheet for each PC in the LAN. Also, in a nor-

The knowledge workers at this shuttle tracking station are linked with one another by a LAN and with other tracking stations by a wide area network (WAN).

mal office setting, a single page printer can service the printing needs of up to 10 micro users.

Like computers, automobiles, and just about everything else, local nets can be built at various levels of sophistication. At the most basic level, they permit the interconnection of PCs in a department so that users can send messages to one another and share files and printers. The more sophisticated local nets permit the interconnection of mainframes, micros, and the gamut of peripheral devices throughout a large but geographically constrained area, such as a cluster of buildings.

In the near future you will be able to plug a terminal into a communications channel just as you would plug a telephone line into a telephone jack. This type of data communications capability is being installed in the new "smart" office buildings and even in some hotel rooms.

Local nets are often integrated into "long-haul" networks (WANs). For example, a bank will link home-office teller terminals to the central computer via a local net. But for long-haul data communications, the bank's branch offices must rely on common carriers.

LAN Hardware

As we mentioned before, most LANs link micros in the local area. The three basic hardware components in a PC-based LAN are the network interface cards, or NICs; the cables that connect the nodes in the network; and the servers.

These network interface cards are placed in PC expansion slots to enable PCs to become nodes on a token-ring LAN.

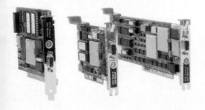

Network Interface Cards The **network interface card** (**NIC**), which we described briefly in Chapter 3, "Inside the Computer," is a PC add-on card or PCMCIA card that facilitates and controls the exchange of data between the micros in a LAN. Each PC in a LAN must be equipped with an NIC. The cables that link the PCs are physically connected to the NICs. Whether as an add-on card or a PCMCIA card, the NIC is connected directly to the PC's bus.

The transfer of data and programs between nodes is controlled by the access method embedded in the network interface card's ROM. The two most popular access methods are *token-ring* and *Ethernet*.

Token-ring access method.   In a token-ring network, an electronic *token* travels around a ring of nodes (ring network topology) in the form of a *header* (see Figure 6–9). The header contains control signals, including one specifying whether the token is "free" or carrying a message. A sender node captures a free token as it travels from node to node, changes it to "busy," and adds the message. The resulting *message frame* travels around the ring to the addressee's NIC, which copies the message and returns the message frame to the sender. The sender's NIC removes the message frame from the ring and circulates a new free token.

Ethernet access method.   The Ethernet access method, which employs the *CSMA/CD* (Carrier Sense Multiple Access/Collision Detection), is based on the bus network topology. To gain access to the network, a node with a message to be sent automatically requests network service from the network software. The request might result in a "line busy" signal. In this case the node waits a fraction of a second and tries again, and again, until the line is free. Upon assuming control of the line, the node sends the message and then relinquishes control of the line to another node.

Cables   Three kinds of cables are connected to the network interface cards: twisted-pair cable (the same four-wire cables used to connect telephones in a home), coaxial cable, and fiber optic cable. In wireless transmission, the cable runs from the transceiver to the NIC.

Servers   In a LAN, a *server* is a component that can be shared by users on the LAN. The three most popular servers are the **file server,** the **print server,** and the **communications server**. These server functions may reside in a single micro or may be distributed among the micros that make up the LAN. When the server functions are consolidated, the server micro usually is *dedicated* to servicing the LAN and, therefore, is not used for applications.

Until recently, you would purchase a traditional single-user micro and make it a dedicated server. This continues to be an option with small to medium-sized LANs, but not in large LANs with 100 or more users. Now, micro vendors manufacture powerful micros designed specifically as network servers. These micros can comfortably handle hundreds of micros on a single LAN.

The *file server* normally is a dedicated micro with a high-capacity disk for storing the data and programs shared by the network users. For example, the master client file, word processing software, spreadsheet software, and so on would be stored on the server disk. When a user wants to begin a spreadsheet session, the spreadsheet software is downloaded from the file server to the user's RAM.

The *print server* typically is housed in the same dedicated micro as the file server. The print server handles user print jobs and controls at least one printer. If needed, the server *spools* print jobs; that is, it saves print jobs to disk until the requested printer is available, then routes the print file to the printer.

A network within a network? Yes, the Home Shopping Network operators rely on a local area network to enter orders.

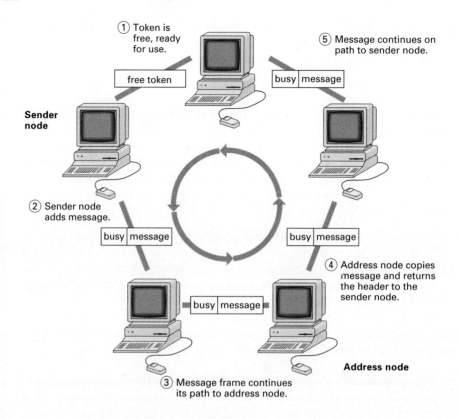

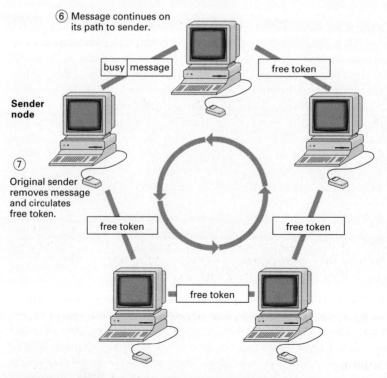

FIGURE 6–9 The Token-Ring Local Area Network

The *communications server* provides communication links external to the LAN—that is, links to other networks. To accomplish this service, the communications server controls one or more modems.

LAN Software

Network Operating Systems   **LAN operating systems,** the nucleus of a local net, come in two formats: *peer-to-peer* and *dedicated server.* In both cases, the LAN operating system is actually several pieces of software. Each processing component in the LAN has a piece of the LAN operating system resident in its RAM. The pieces interact with one another to enable the nodes to share resources and communication.

The individual user in a LAN might appear to be interacting with an operating system, such as MS-DOS or OS/2. However, the RAM-resident LAN software *redirects* certain requests to the appropriate LAN component. For example, a print request would be redirected to the print server.

In a **peer-to-peer LAN,** all PCs are peers, or equals. Any PC can be a client to another peer PC or any PC can share its resources with its peers. Peer-to-peer LANs are less sophisticated than those that have one or more dedicated servers. Because they are relatively easy to install and maintain, peer-to-peer LANs are popular when small numbers of PCs are involved (for example, from 2 to 20). Two popular peer-to-peer LAN operating systems are Microsoft's *Windows for Workgroups* and Artisoft's *LANtastic.*

In *LANs with dedicated servers,* the controlling software resides in the file server's RAM. LANs with dedicated servers can link hundreds of PCs in a LAN while providing a level of system security that is not possible in a peer-to-peer LAN. Two popular LAN operating systems are Novell's *NetWare* and Microsoft's *LAN Manager.*

Applications Software for LANs   LAN-based PCs can run all applications that stand-alone PCs can run plus those that involve electronic interaction with groups of people.

Shared applications software.   LANs enable the sharing of general-purpose software, such as WordPerfect (word processing) and Excel (spreadsheet). The PCs on the LAN with a dedicated central server interact with a file server to load various applications programs. When a LAN-based PC is booted, software that enables the use of the network interface card, communication with the file server, and interaction with the operating system is loaded from the PC's hard disk to RAM. Depending on how the LAN system administrator configured the LAN, you may see a graphical user interface that lists software options or you may see a prompt from the operating system. When you select a software package, it is downloaded from the LAN's file server to your PC's RAM for processing. You can then work with shared files on the file server or with your own local files (those stored on your PC).

Groupware.   LANs have opened the door to applications that are not possible in the one-person, one-computer environment. For example, users linked together via a LAN can send electronic mail to one another. Scheduling meetings with other users on the LAN is a snap. This type of software is called groupware. *Groupware,* which was introduced in Chapter 1, "The World of Computers," is software whose application is designed to benefit a group of people. Local area networks and groupware provide the foundation for *workgroup computing,* also introduced in Chapter 1. The breadth of workgroup computing encompasses any application that involves groups of people linked by a computer network. Several workgroup computing applications follow.

- *Electronic mail (E-mail).* E-mail enables people on a LAN to route messages to one another's electronic mailbox. E-mail can be sent over the network to individuals or to groups of people (for example, all department heads).
- *Calendar and scheduling.* Each person on a LAN maintains an on-line calendar on which the times for all meetings, appointments, events, and so on can be blocked out. The existence of an up-to-date calendar database enables the automatic scheduling of meetings. Scheduling software automatically checks appropriate users' electronic calendars for possible meeting times, schedules the meeting, and informs the participants via electronic mail.
- *Brainstorming and problem solving.* A LAN enables collaborative brainstorming and problem solving. People on a LAN can work together on a master document to come up with ideas and solve problems. Each person's input to the collaborative effort is seen immediately by all other participants.
- *Setting priorities.* Groupware is available that enables LAN users to establish priorities for projects through collective reasoning. Groups of people can use this software to work toward a consensus opinion on priorities.
- *Electronic conferencing.* Conferencing groupware lets LAN users meet electronically. Users exchange information anonymously with fellow participants via a LAN. Electronic conferencing encourages input that may be lost in face-to-face meetings. For example, introverts are less likely to express their opinions in meetings. Also, subordinates are much more candid when remarks are anonymous.
- *Policy/procedure library.* Rapidly changing policies and procedures are placed on-line to eliminate the need to constantly update many hard-copy manuals. All updates are made only once, to the on-line library.
- *Electronic messaging.* Electronic messaging may be the next generation of E-mail. **Electronic messaging** associates the message with one or more work-

Throughout this public relations office, employees routinely schedule meetings, brainstorm, set priorities, and gather input from colleagues using groupware.

group applications. For example, suppose your manager sends a "to-do" message to you via electronic messaging. The manager receives confirmation when you read the message. The to-do activities are linked automatically to both on-line calendars (yours and your manager's). The manager is informed when you complete the to-do activity. Should you not complete the activity by the due date, both parties are informed automatically of the situation.

■ *Electronic forms.* Electronic-forms groupware lets LAN users create forms for gathering information from other LAN users. For example, if you want feedback on a new procedure, you would design a form and ask LAN users (via E-mail) to complete the on-line form. Data are gathered and automatically assimilated in a format that is compatible with spreadsheet and database software.

Networks on the fly.   The number and variety of workgroup computing applications can only increase. Already notebook PC users are creating networks on the fly. That is, they bring their computers to the meeting and attach them to a common cable to create a peer-to-peer LAN. In effect, we have progressed from the *portable computer* to the *portable network*. Once part of a LAN, users can enjoy the advantages of groupware.

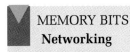

MEMORY BITS
Networking

■ Network topologies
  Star
  Ring
  Bus
■ Client/server computing
■ Local area network
  Also called LAN or local net
  Components: NICs, cables, and servers

IMPORTANT TERMS AND SUMMARY OUTLINE

backbone
baud
bits per second (bps)
bus topology
client/server computing
coaxial cable
common carrier
communications channel
communications protocols
communications server
connectivity
cooperative processing
data communications
down-line processor
downloaded

downsizing
electronic data interchange (EDI)
electronic messaging
fiber optic cable
file server
front-end processor
geosynchronous orbit
handshaking
host processor
LAN operating system
local area network (LAN, local net)
message
microwave radio signal
modem
multiplexer

network address
network interface card (NIC)
network topology
node
peer-to-peer LAN
print server
ring topology
router
star topology
total connectivity
transmission medium
uploaded
wide area network (WAN)

6–1 Data Communications: Linking the World Connectivity facilitates the electronic communication between companies, end user computing, and the free flow of information within an enterprise. The ideal implementation of connectivity is referred to as **total connectivity**. Modern businesses use **data communications** to transmit data and information at high speeds from one location to the next. Data communications makes an information system more accessible to the people who use it. The integration of computer systems via data communications is referred to as a computer network.

This is the era of **cooperative processing**. To obtain meaningful, accurate, and timely information, businesses have decided that they must cooperate internally and externally to take full advantage of available information. To promote internal cooperation, businesses are promoting intracompany networking. An application of intercompany networking is **electronic data interchange (EDI)**.

6–2 Data Communications Hardware The data communications hardware used to facilitate the transmission of data from one remote location to another includes **modems, down-line processors** (also called **multiplexers**), **front-end processors,** and **routers**. Modems modulate and demodulate signals so that data can be transmitted over telephone lines. The fax modem acts as a modem and enables a PC to simulate a facsimile machine.

To improve the overall efficiency of a **host processor,** the processing load is distributed among several other special-function processors. The down-line processor collects data from a number of devices, then "concentrates" the data—sending the data over a single communications channel to the front-end processor. The front-end processor establishes the link between the source and destination in a process called **handshaking,** then sends a **message** to a **network address**. The front-end processor relieves the host processor of communications-related tasks.

Different computer networks use different **communications protocols,** the rules established to govern the way data are transmitted within a computer network. The primary hardware/software technology used to enable the interconnection of incompatible computer networks is the router. A **backbone** is composed of one or more routers and the associated transmission media.

6–3 The Data Communications Channel: Data Highways A **communications channel** is the facility through which electronic signals are transmitted between locations in a computer network. A channel's capacity is rated by the number of bits it can transmit per second (**bits per second** or **bps**). In practice, the word **baud** is often used interchangeably with *bits per second;* in reality, they are quite different.

A channel may be composed of one or more of the following transmission media: telephone lines, **coaxial cable, fiber optic cable, microwave radio signals,** and wireless transceivers. Satellites are essentially microwave repeater stations that maintain a **geosynchronous orbit** around the earth.

Common carriers provide communications channels to the public, and lines can be arranged to suit the application.

6–4 Networks: Linking Computers and People Computer systems are linked together to form a computer network. In a computer network the **node** can be a terminal, a computer, or any other destination/source device. The basic patterns for configuring computer systems within a computer network are **star topology, ring topology,** and **bus topology**. The bus topology permits the connection of nodes along a **transmission medium**. In practice, most networks are actually hybrids of these **network topologies.**

In **client/server computing,** processing is distributed throughout the network. The *client* computer requests processing or some other type of service from the *server* computer. Data can be **downloaded** from the server to the client or **uploaded** from the client to the server.

The trend toward client/server computing has resulted in companies **downsizing** their computers.

6–5 Local Area Networks A **wide area network (WAN)** connects nodes in widely dispersed geographic areas and typically uses a common carrier. A **local area network (LAN),** or **local net,** connects nodes in close proximity and does not involve a common carrier.

The three basic hardware components in a PC-based LAN are the **network interface cards (NICs)**; the cables that connect the nodes in the network; and the servers. The physical transfer of data and programs between LAN nodes is controlled by the access method embedded in the network interface card's ROM, usually the *token-ring* or *Ethernet* access method.

A server is a LAN component that can be shared by users on the LAN. The three most popular servers are the **file server,** the **print server,** and the **communications server.**

The **LAN operating system** is actually several pieces of software, a part of which resides in each LAN component's RAM. In a **peer-to-peer LAN,** all PCs are equals. Any PC can share its resources with its peers. In LANs with dedicated servers, the controlling software resides in the file server's RAM.

LANs and *groupware* provide the foundation for *workgroup computing*. The breadth of workgroup computing encompasses any application that involves groups of people linked by a computer network. Workgroup computing applications include electronic mail, calendar and scheduling, brainstorming and problem solving, **electronic messaging,** and others.

REVIEW EXERCISES

Concepts

1. Would EDI be more closely associated with inter-company networking or intracompany networking?

2. What is meant by *geosynchronous orbit,* and how does it relate to data transmission via satellite?

3. What is the unit of measure for the capacity of a data communications channel?

4. Expand the following acronyms: WAN, bps, VAN, and EDI.

5. What is the purpose of a multiplexer?

6. What is the relationship between a communications channel and a computer network?

7. What term describes the trend toward increased reliance on smaller computers?

8. What term refers to the degree to which hardware devices can be functionally linked to one another?

9. What device converts digital signals into analog signals for transmission over telephone lines? Why is it necessary?

10. Why is it not advisable to increase the distance between microwave relay stations to 200 miles?

11. What is the ideal implementation of connectivity called?

12. Name two subordinate processors that might be configured with a host processor to improve the overall efficiency of the computer system.

13. Name the three basic computer network topologies.

14. Name two popular LAN access methods. Which one passes a token from node to node?

15. Name three types of LAN servers.

16. Give two examples of groupware.

17. Briefly describe the function of a router.

Discussion

18. What is the relationship between EDI, electronic funds transfer (EFT), and connectivity?

19. Describe how information can be made readily accessible to many people in a company, but only on a need-to-know basis.

20. The five PCs in the purchasing department of a large consumer-goods manufacturer are used primarily for word processing and database applications. What would be the benefits and burdens associated with connecting the PCs in a local area network?

21. The mere fact that a system uses data communications poses a threat to security. Why?

SELF-TEST (BY SECTION)

6–1 a. A company has either total connectivity or no connectivity. (T/F) F

b. The integration of computer systems, terminals, and communication links is referred to as a _computer network_.

c. Using computers and data communications to transmit data electronically between companies is called: (a) EDI, (b) DIE, or (c) DEI.

6–2 a. The modem converts computer-to-terminal electrical _digital_ (digital or analog) signals to _analog_ (digital or analog) signals so that the data can be transmitted over telephone lines.

b. The terminal sending a message is the source and the computer receiving the message is the destination. (T/F) T

c. Another name for a front-end processor is a multiplexer. (T/F) F

d. _ROUTERS_ facilitate the interconnection of dissimilar networks.

6–3 a. It is more difficult for a computer criminal to tap into a fiber optic cable than a copper telephone line. (T/F) T

b. A 9600-bits-per-second channel is the same as a: (a) 9.6-kps line, (b) 9.6 K-bps line, or (c) dual 4800X2 K-bps line.

c. The wireless transceiver replaces the physical link between the source and the destination in a network. (T/F) T

6–4 a. An endpoint in a network of computers is called a _node_.

b. The central cable called a transmission medium is most closely associated with which network topology: (a) ring, (b) star, or (c) bus?

c. The trend in the design of computer networks is toward: (a) distributed transmission, (b) client/server computing, or (c) CANs?

6–5 a. A LAN is designed for "long-haul" data communications. (T/F) F

b. Which of the following is not a popular LAN access method: (a) token-ring, (b) Ethernet, or (c) parity checking? C

c. In a LAN with a dedicated server, the LAN operating system resides entirely in the server processor's RAM. (T/F) F

Self-test answers. **6–1 (a)** F; **(b)** computer network; **(c)** a. **6–2 (a)** digital, analog; **(b)** T; **(c)** F; **(d)** routers. **6–3 (a)** T; **(b)** b; **(c)** T. **6–4 (a)** node; **(b)** c; **(c)** b. **6–5 (a)** F; **(b)** c; **(c)** F.

PART III
SOFTWARE

7

WORD PROCESSING AND DESKTOP PUBLISHING SOFTWARE

OBJECTIVES

To describe the function and applications of word processing software.

To understand word processing concepts.

To identify and describe add-on capabilities of word processing software packages.

To describe the function and applications of desktop publishing software.

To understand desktop publishing concepts.

7–1   WORD PROCESSING

At work, at home, at school, and even during leisure activities we spend much of our time writing. At work we send memos and write procedures manuals. At home we keep to-do lists and prepare party announcements. At school we write reports and essays. During leisure time, we keep diaries and write letters to our family and friends. These are just a few of the myriad of day-to-day writing activities that can be made easier and more professional through judicious use of word processing software and desktop publishing software. This section addresses word processing software.

Word processing is using the computer to enter, store, manipulate, and print text in letters, reports, books, and so on. Today's sophisticated *word processing software* packages do much more than text-oriented word processing. For example, most packages let you integrate images with text and some let you integrate audio, such as voice annotations, within your on-screen word processing document. Once you have used word processing software, you will probably wonder (like a million others before you) how in the world you ever survived without it!

Word processing has virtually eliminated the need for opaque correction fluid and the need to rekey revised letters and reports. Revising a hard copy is often time-consuming and cumbersome, but revising the same text and images in an electronic format can be quick and easy. You simply make corrections and revisions on the computer before the document is displayed or printed in final form.

Concepts

Creating a Document   When you begin a word processing session, the word processing software presents you with a blank work area that dominates the screen, a menu bar with user options, and some status information (for example, cursor position: page 1, line 1, position 1). At this point you have two options: You can *create an original document* or you can *recall an existing document from disk storage.* The term *document* is a generic reference to currently keyed-in text or stored text (perhaps a report or an outline). To create an origi-

Having word processing skills is like having money in the bank for this and millions of other college students. This student uses her skills to write reports, compose short stories, organize class notes, write letters home, and for many other applications.

nal document, such as a report, you simply begin entering text from the keyboard and occasionally enter commands that enhance the appearance of the document when it is printed (spacing, italics, and so on). If you wish to work with the document later, you will need to save it to disk storage for later recall. When you recall a document from disk storage, you can *edit* (revise) it, then save the revised version of the document to disk storage. Once you are satisfied with the content and appearance of the document, you can print it.

Formatting a document.   Before you begin keying in the text of a word processing document, you may need to *format* the document to meet your application needs. You do this by specifying what you wish the general appearance of the document to be when it is printed. However, if you are satisfied with the software's preset format specifications, you can begin keying in text right away. Typically, the preset format, or *default settings,* fit most word processing applications. For example, the size of the output document is set at letter size (8½ by 11 inches); the left, right, top, and bottom margins are set at 1 inch; tabs are set every ½ inch; and line spacing is set at 6 lines per inch. If you want to print your document on legal-size paper, you would need to reset the size of the output document to 8½ by 14 inches. If you are preparing a newsletter, you might wish to specify a double-column format. Generally, you can change format specifications as often as needed. Text is printed according to the most recent specification in the running text of the document. For example, if you specify a double-column format beginning with the fourth page, the fourth and all subsequent pages until the next column format change have a double-column format when printed.

Entering text.   Text is entered in either **typeover mode** or **insert mode.** On most word processing systems you *toggle,* or switch, between typeover and insert modes by tapping the *Insert* (or INS) key.

Let's use the draft copy of a memo written by B. J. McCue (see Figure 7–1), the national sales manager for BrassCo Enterprises (a manufacturer of quality brass products) to illustrate the two modes of data entry. When in typeover mode, the character you enter *types over* the character at the cursor position. For example, in the last sentence of the memo, B. J. began with *The* and real-

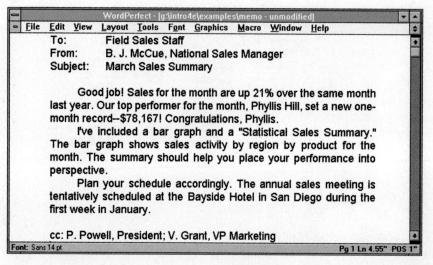

FIGURE 7–1 A Word Processing Memorandum *This first-draft memo is revised for illustrative purposes in Figures 7–2, 7–4 through 7–7, and 7–13. The word processing software used in the examples is WPwin (WordPerfect for Windows).*

ized that *Our* is a better word. To make the correction in typeover mode, B. J. positioned the cursor at the *T* and typed *O-u-r*, thereby replacing *The* with *Our.* When in insert mode, any text entered is *additional* text.

B. J. forgot to enter the full name of the hotel (Bayside Hotel and Marina) in the last sentence of Figure 7–1. To complete the name, B. J. selected the insert mode, placed the cursor at the *i* in the word *in* (after *Bayside Hotel*), and entered *and Marina* followed by a space (see Figure 7–2).

On most word processing packages, text that extends past the defined margins is automatically *wrapped* to the next line. That is, the words that extend past the right margin are automatically moved down to the next line, and so on, to the end of the paragraph. Consider this modified version of the first two sentences of this book.

> *We are in the midst of a revolution that is changing our way of life. The cornerstone of this revolution, the computer, is transforming the way we communicate, do business, and learn.*

Notice that the remaining lines are wrapped when the word *technological* is inserted in the first line.

> *We are in the midst of a technological revolution that is changing our way of life. The cornerstone of this revolution, the computer, is transforming the way we communicate, do business, and learn.*

When you enter text in insert mode, the computer manipulates the text so it wraps around. This type of text movement is called **word wrap.** In Figures 7–1 and 7–2, notice how the words *during the* (in the last sentence) are wrapped to the next line when *and Marina* is inserted. When you enter text in typeover mode, the cursor automatically moves to the next line when you reach the right-hand margin.

Word processing permits **full-screen editing.** In other words, you can move the text cursor to any position in the document to insert or type over text. You can browse through a multiscreen document by *scrolling* a line at a time, a screen at a time, or a page (the text that corresponds to a printed page) at a time. You can edit (revise) any part of any screen.

FIGURE 7–2 Typeover and Insert Mode *This memo is the result of two revisions of the first sentence of the last paragraph. The* is replaced with Our *in typeover mode. The phrase* and Marina *and a space are added in insert mode. Notice how the text wraps around to make room for the additional words.*

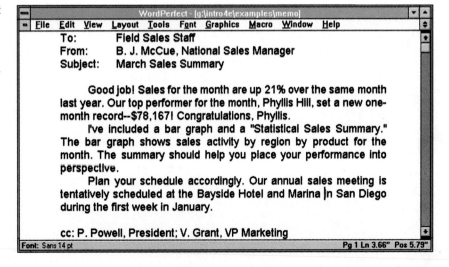

Most jobs requires a fair amount of writing and/or drawing. This is true for architects, teachers, lawyers, insurance agents, executives, and it is true for this geologist at Kerr-McGee. In the photo he is writing up the findings of a recent geological survey.

When you enter text, *tap the ENTER key only when you wish to begin a new line of text.* In the memo of Figure 7–1, B. J. tapped ENTER after each of the three information lines, after each paragraph in the body of the memo, and after the "copy to" (cc) line. B. J. also tapped ENTER to insert each of the blank lines. The TAB key was tapped at the beginning of each paragraph to indent the first line of the paragraph.

What you see is what you get. Most modern word processing packages are considered **WYSIWYG** (pronounced *WIZ e wig*), short for "What you see is what you get." What you see on the screen is essentially what the document will look like when it is printed—the type of font, font size, graphics, and all (see Figure 7–3). The **font** refers to the style, appearance, and size of print. Fonts are described in more detail in the section on desktop publishing. Full WYSIWYG word processing packages employ high-resolution graphics. However, the WYSIWYG label is slightly misleading when applied to text-based packages. What you see on the screen while editing your document is not what the document will look like when printed. To see a WYSIWYG display, you must activate the *preview* feature. This option lets you see what the document will look like when it is printed, but you cannot edit the WYSIWYG display.

Features Common to Word Processing Software Packages More than a hundred word processing packages are in use today, all of which have the features discussed in this section.

Block operations. *Block* operations are among the handiest word processing features. With this feature you can select a block of text (for example, a word, a sentence, a paragraph, a section of a report, or as much adjoining text as you need), then copy or move it to another portion of the document. You also have the option to delete a block of text. This feature enables the electronic equivalent of a "cut-and-paste job." In fact, the block commands are usually called *copy, delete, cut,* and *paste.*

To copy or move text in a document, you first must copy or cut the selected text to a temporary storage area in RAM. In the Windows-based word processing software, this storage area is called the *clipboard*. Think of the clipboard as an intermediate holding area for a block of text that is en route to

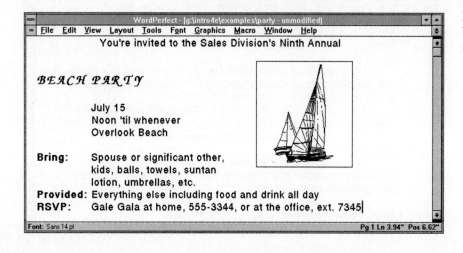

FIGURE 7–3 A WYSIWYG Word Processing Display: Text and Graphics

another part of the current document or to another document. Depending on the word processing package, you can work with up to seven documents at a time, copying and moving text among them as needed.

The procedure for copying or moving a block is as follows.

1. *Mark the block.* On most word processing packages, use the mouse to point to the start of the block in question, then drag the graphics cursor to the end of the block to highlight it.

2. *Cut or copy the marked text to the clipboard.* Choosing the *cut* option causes the highlighted text to be removed from the document and placed in the clipboard. The *copy* option causes the highlighted text to be placed in the clipboard, leaving the source document unchanged.

3. Switch to the destination document and place the cursor at the desired insertion point.

4. *Paste (insert) the marked text.* Choosing the *paste* option causes the contents of the clipboard to be copied to the cursor position in the destination document. The clipboard contents remain unchanged and can be pasted as often as needed.

The following example demonstrates the procedure for marking and moving a block of text. After reading over the memo to the field staff (Figure 7–2), B. J. decided to edit the memo to make it more readable. B. J. moved the first sentence in the last paragraph to the end of the memo. To perform this operation, B. J. marked the beginning (*P* in *Plan*) and end (the position following the period at the end of that sentence) of the block. On most word processing systems, the portions of text marked for a block operation are usually displayed in **reverse video** (see Figure 7–4a). To complete the operation (see Figure 7–4b), B. J. selected the *cut* option to remove the block from the memo and placed it in the clipboard. Then, B. J. positioned the cursor at the destination location (after a space following the end of the paragraph), and issued the *paste* option to complete the move operation. Notice that the text in the last paragraph is wrapped to accommodate the block move.

FIGURE 7–4 Marking and Moving Text *(a) The first sentence of the last paragraph of the memo is marked to be moved. (b) The marked sentence is moved to the end of the paragraph.*

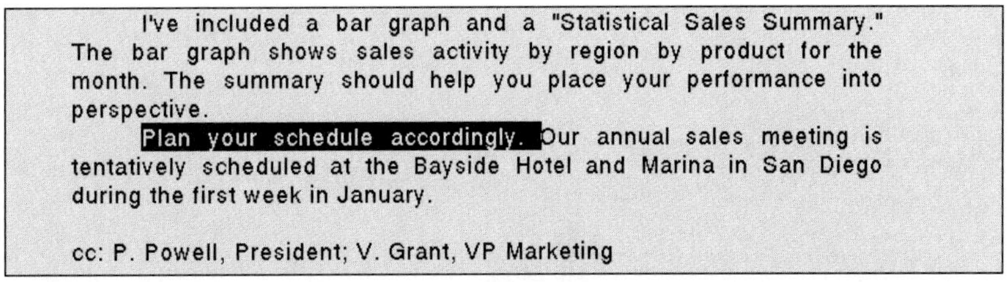

I've included a bar graph and a "Statistical Sales Summary." The bar graph shows sales activity by region by product for the month. The summary should help you place your performance into perspective.
    Plan your schedule accordingly. Our annual sales meeting is tentatively scheduled at the Bayside Hotel and Marina in San Diego during the first week in January.

cc: P. Powell, President; V. Grant, VP Marketing

(a)

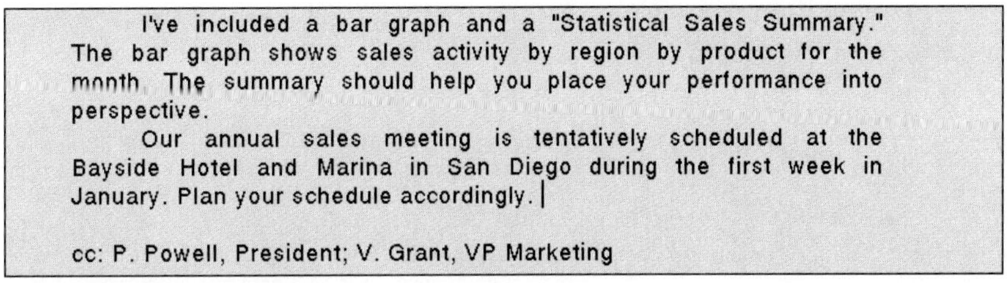

I've included a bar graph and a "Statistical Sales Summary." The bar graph shows sales activity by region by product for the month. The summary should help you place your performance into perspective.
    Our annual sales meeting is tentatively scheduled at the Bayside Hotel and Marina in San Diego during the first week in January. Plan your schedule accordingly.

cc: P. Powell, President; V. Grant, VP Marketing

(b)

To delete a block of text, mark the block in the same manner, then select the *delete* option. The meeting at the Bayside Hotel and Marina was confirmed while B. J. was composing the memo in Figure 7–1. To reflect the confirmation, B. J. used the block-delete command to drop the phrase *tentatively scheduled,* then inserted the word *set.* This operation is illustrated in sequence in Figure 7–5.

The search features. While looking over the memo, B. J. McCue decided that it would read better if all generic references to *the month* were replaced by the name of the month, *March.* The necessary revisions in the memo can be made by using any of several word processing features. One option is to use the *search,* or *find,* feature. This feature allows B. J. to search the entire document and identify all occurrences of a particular character string. For example, if B. J. wanted to search for all occurrences of *the month* in the memo, the manager simply would initiate the search command and type in the desired *search string—the month,* in this example. Immediately, the cursor is positioned at the first occurrence of the character string *the month* so B. J. can easily edit the text to reflect the specific month. From there, other occurrences of *the month* can be located by tapping the appropriate search key.

An alternative to changing each occurrence of *the month* to *March* involves using the *search-and-replace* feature. This feature enables *selective* replacement of *the month* with *March.* Issuing the *global search-and-replace* command causes *all* occurrences of *the month* to be replaced with *March.*

I've included a bar graph and a "Statistical Sales Summary." The bar graph shows sales activity by region by product for the month. The summary should help you place your performance into perspective.
    Our annual sales meeting is **tentatively scheduled** at the Bayside Hotel and Marina in San Diego during the first week in January. Plan your schedule accordingly.

cc: P. Powell, President; V. Grant, VP Marketing

(a)

FIGURE 7–5 Marking and Deleting Text *(a) The phrase* tentatively scheduled *in the first sentence of the last paragraph is marked to be deleted. (b) The phrase is deleted. (c) The word* set *is inserted at the cursor position.*

I've included a bar graph and a "Statistical Sales Summary." The bar graph shows sales activity by region by product for the month. The summary should help you place your performance into perspective.
    Our annual sales meeting is | at the Bayside Hotel and Marina in San Diego during the first week in January. Plan your schedule accordingly.

cc: P. Powell, President; V. Grant, VP Marketing

(b)

I've included a bar graph and a "Statistical Sales Summary." The bar graph shows sales activity by region by product for the month. The summary should help you place your performance into perspective.
    Our annual sales meeting is set| at the Bayside Hotel and Marina in San Diego during the first week in January. Plan your schedule accordingly.

cc: P. Powell, President; V. Grant, VP Marketing

(c)

Opting for the global search-and-replace command, B. J. replaced all three occurrences of *the month* with *March* (see Figure 7–6).

Features that enhance appearance and readability.   B. J. used several other valuable word processing features to enhance the appearance and readability of the memo before distributing it to the field sales staff. First, the manager decided to enter the current date at the top of the memo and use the automatic *centering* feature to position it at the center of the page. On many word processing systems, centering a particular line is as easy as moving the text cursor to the desired line and tapping the *center* function key. The rest is automatic (see Figure 7–7).

Word processing provides the facility to *boldface* and/or *underline* parts of the text for emphasis. In the memo, B. J. decided to highlight the remarkable 21% increase in sales by requesting that it be printed in boldface type (see Figure 7–7c). To do so, the manager marked *21%* and issued the boldface command. To make the point that sales representatives should plan now for the January meeting, B. J. followed a similar procedure to make sure the last sentence is underlined on output (see Figure 7–7c).

Text-based word processing packages highlight boldface and underlined words by displaying them in different colors (Figure 7–7b). Sometimes text that is to be printed in boldface type or underlined on output is displayed in reverse video.

To enhance the appearance of a document, some people like to *justify* (align) text on the left or the right margin, or on both margins, like the print in newspapers and in this book. Word processing software can produce "clean" margins on both sides by adding small spaces between characters and words in a line as it is output. The right and left margins of the memo in Figure 7–7c

FIGURE 7–6 Search and Replace   *(a) The memo contains three occurrences of the string* the month. *(b) The search-and-replace command is used to replace all occurrences of* the month *with* March.

At USA Today, *word processing skills are critical. Here several of the 425* USA Today *reporters, editors, and researchers are writing and editing copy at their computer terminals. Their late-breaking stories are entered directly into a central computer system. The system processes the copy and sends it to phototypesetters. Within minutes the stories are transmitted via satellite to 33 print sites across the United States. A couple of hours later, you can pick up a copy of* USA Today *and read the stories.*

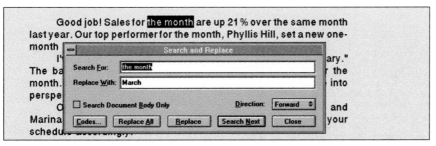

Good job! Sales for the month are up 21% over the same month last year. Our top performer for the month, Phyllis Hill, set a new one-month

| Search and Replace |
| Search For: the month |
| Replace With: March |
| ☐ Search Document Body Only   Direction: Forward ⬦ |
| Codes... Replace All Replace Search Next Close |

(a)

Good job! Sales for March are up 21% over the same month last year. Our top performer for March, Phyllis Hill, set a new one-month record--$78,167! Congratulations, Phyllis.
  I've included a bar graph and a "Statistical Sales Summary." The bar graph shows sales activity by region by product for March. The summary should help you place your performance into perspective.
  Our annual sales meeting is set at the Bayside Hotel and Marina in San Diego during the first week in January. Plan your schedule accordingly.

(b)

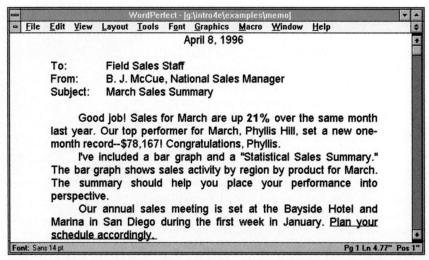

(a)

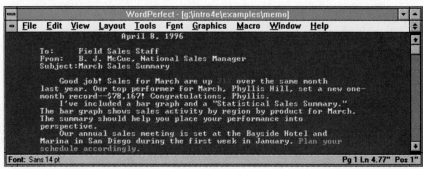

(b)

April 8, 1996

To: Field Sales Staff
From: B. J. McCue, National Sales Manager
Subject: March Sales Summary

Good job! Sales for March are up **21%** over the same month
last year. Our top performer for March, Phyllis Hill, set a new one-
month record--$78,167! Congratulations, Phyllis.
I've included a bar graph and a "Statistical Sales Summary."
The bar graph shows sales activity by region by product for March.
The summary should help you place your performance into
perspective.
Our annual sales meeting is set at the Bayside Hotel and
Marina in San Diego during the first week in January. <u>Plan your
schedule accordingly</u>.

cc: P. Powell, President; V. Grant, VP Marketing

(c)

FIGURE 7–7 Center, Boldface, and Underline *The date is centered at the top of the memo. (a) In a WYSIWYG display, text is shown as boldface and under-lined. (b) On a color monitor, text to be in printed in boldface type or underlined is displayed in different colors. (c) The memo is printed on a desktop page printer.*

are justified. However, B. J. prefers the more traditional *ragged right* margin on personal letters. The first paragraph in Figure 7–8 is printed as ragged right.

In creating the memo of Figure 7–7, B. J. used many but not all the word processing features available to enhance its appearance and readability. Figure 7–8 illustrates other features. Users can *indent* a block of text, cause *header* and *footer labels* to be printed on each page, and request that pages be num-

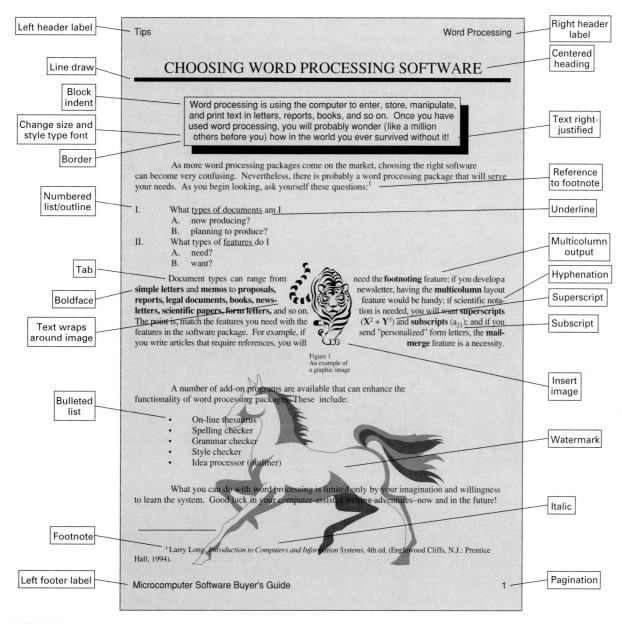

Left header label

Line draw

Block indent

Change size and style type font

Border

Numbered list/outline

Tab

Boldface

Text wraps around image

Bulleted list

Footnote

Left footer label

Right header label

Centered heading

Text right-justified

Reference to footnote

Underline

Multicolumn output

Hyphenation

Superscript

Subscript

Insert image

Watermark

Italic

Pagination

FIGURE 7–8 Features Overview   *Many of the more common capabilities of word processing software are illustrated in this printout.*

bered (*pagination* feature). On long reports, B. J. usually repeats the report title at the top of each page (header label) and numbers each page at the bottom (pagination).

The example in Figure 7–8 also illustrates hyphenation, footnotes, numbered list/outline, bulleted list, line draw, border, superscripts and subscripts, the insertion of an image into the running text, the insertion of watermark image behind the printed document text, the use of a multicolumn format, and other features.

- *Hyphenation.* The *hyphenation* feature automatically breaks and hyphenates words to create a smoother appearing right margin.

- *Footnoting.* One of the most tedious typing chores, *footnoting,* is done automatically. Footnote spacing is resolved electronically before anything is printed.

- *Numbered list and outline.* The *numbered list* and *outline* features enable descriptive items to be presented in a numbered list or in outline format (shown in Figure 7–8). The numbers and/or letters are inserted automatically by the word processing program.

- *Bulleted list.* The *bulleted list* is created in a similar manner to the numbered list.

- *Line draw and border.* Users can create special effects with the *line-draw* and *border* features. The line-draw feature lets you include vertical and horizontal lines of varying widths. The border feature lets you enclose a paragraph, a page, or whatever you want to enclose with a variety of decorative borders.

- *Superscripts and subscripts. Superscripts* and *subscripts,* which place characters above or below the center of a line, respectively, are common in technical writing.

- *Integration of images.* One popular feature of the more sophisticated word processing programs is the ability to *insert images* into the running text. In Figure 7–8, notice how the text follows the contour of the image.

- *Watermarks.* The watermark feature lets you add a drawing, a company logo, headline-sized text (such as DRAFT or CONFIDENTIAL), or any image behind the printed document text.

- *Multicolumn format.* All or part of the running text can be formatted as *multicolumn* (see Figure 7–8). The multicolumn option, which is two or more columns of text, is used frequently in newsletters.

Depending on the type of software and printer you have, you can even mix the size and style of fonts in a single document. In Figure 7–8, the heading, headers, footer, quotation, and figure caption are printed in a different size and style of type than the rest of the document. The heading is a larger type font and the others are in a smaller type font. Fonts are discussed in more detail in the section on desktop publishing.

Some word processing software contains sophisticated features for writers and people who are charged with the preparation of long, involved documents (strategic plans, annual reports, procedures manuals, and so on). A simple command creates a *table of contents,* much like the "Contents" section in the front matter of this book, with page references for chapters and various levels of headings. An alphabetical *index of key words* can be compiled that lists the page numbers for each occurrence of user-designated words.

The *table* feature, found in the more advanced word processing packages, speeds up the tabular presentation of data. The user sets up a table format by entering the number of rows and columns desired. Once data have been entered into the table, spreadsheet type functions can be performed. For example, Figure 7–9 illustrates a table designed to list and summarize fixed-asset inventory in a home office. The totals in the last row are automatically calculated by formulas inserted in the cells containing the totals.

The more sophisticated word processing packages provide users with the capability of doing *desktop publishing.* We discuss desktop publishing in detail later in this chapter.

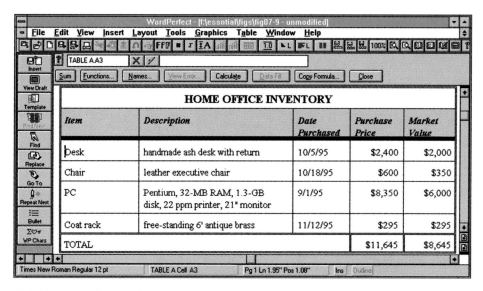

FIGURE 7–9 The Word Processing Table Feature   *To create the table shown in this figure, you would tell the software to generate a table with seven rows and five columns. Then you would eliminate unneeded cells (the top row has only one cell). You can enhance the appearance of the table by choosing a mix of line styles (single, double, solid, and so on) and by shading cells (second row). Finally, you would enter text, data, and formulas (totals in bottom row) in the cells. The formulas in the* totals row sum the amounts in the *purchase price and* market value *columns.*

Printing a document.   To print a document, ready the printer and select the print option on the main menu. Some word processing systems present you with other print options. For example, you may choose to print in draft mode (low resolution with no graphics) or graphics mode; you also could be given the option of printing specific pages or the whole document.

File features.   Certainly a very important feature of a word processing package is the ability to store a document on disk for later recall. The stored version of a document is referred to as a *document file.* The *file* feature permits you to save, retrieve, and delete a document file. At a minimum, most word processing systems provide users with the save-, retrieve-, and delete-file options. No matter which option you choose, the system asks you to identify the file (document). You then enter an arbitrary name that in some way identifies the document (for example, MEMO).

B. J. McCue "saved" the memo in Figure 7–7 (stored it on disk) under the file name MEMO. Because the memo is stored in electronic format on disk, B. J. can retrieve and edit it to report the sales results for another month.

Add-on Capabilities   A number of programs are designed to enhance the function of word processing programs. Often these add-on capabilities are bundled with the word processing package. Those that are not can be purchased separately.

On-line thesaurus.   Have you ever been in the middle of writing a letter or memo and been unable to put your finger on the right word? Some word processing packages have an **on-line thesaurus**! Suppose you have just written: *The Grand Canyon certainly is beautiful.* But *beautiful* is not quite the right word. Your electronic thesaurus is always ready with suggestions: *pretty, gor-*

geous, exquisite, angelic, stunning, ravishing, divine, and so on. The Word-Perfect for Windows thesaurus dialog box is shown in Figure 7–10.

Spelling checker. If spelling is a problem, then word processing can be the answer. Once you have entered the text and formatted the document, you can call on the **spelling checker** capability. The spelling checker checks every word in the text against an **electronic dictionary** (usually from 75,000 to 150,000 words) and alerts you if a word is not in the dictionary. Upon finding an unidentified word, the spell function normally will give you several options:

1. You can correct the spelling.
2. You can ignore the word and continue scanning the text. Normally you do this when a word is spelled correctly but is not in the dictionary (for example, a company name such as BrassCo).
3. You can ask for possible spellings. The spell function then gives you a list of words of similar spellings from which to choose. For example, assume that B. J. left out the *o* in *month.* Upon finding the nonword *mnth,* the spelling checker might suggest the following alternatives: *math, month, moth, myth,* and *nth.*
4. You can add the word to the dictionary and continue scanning.

Grammar and style checkers. Grammar and style checkers are the electronic version of a copy editor. A **grammar checker** highlights grammatical concerns and deviations from conventions (see Figure 7–11). For example, it highlights split infinitives, phrases with redundant words (*very highest*), misuse of capital letters (*JOhn or MarY*), subject and verb mismatches (*they was*), double words (*and*), and punctuation errors. When applied to the memo in

FIGURE 7–10 The Thesaurus Feature *The WordPerfect for Windows thesaurus feature helps you find the right word. In the example, the user requested synonyms for the word* failure. *The user extended the search by requesting synonyms for the word* flop.

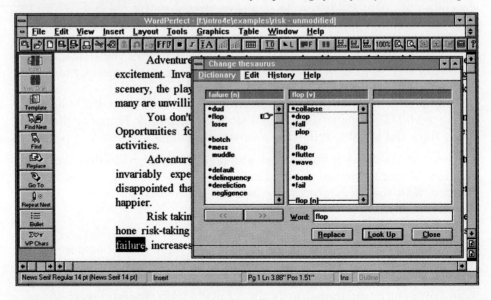

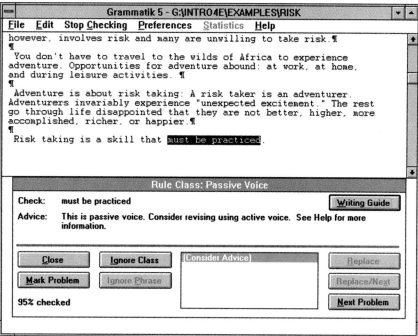

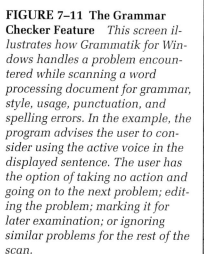

FIGURE 7–11 The Grammar Checker Feature *This screen illustrates how Grammatik for Windows handles a problem encountered while scanning a word processing document for grammar, style, usage, punctuation, and spelling errors. In the example, the program advises the user to consider using the active voice in the displayed sentence. The user has the option of taking no action and going on to the next problem; editing the problem; marking it for later examination; or ignoring similar problems for the rest of the scan.*

Figure 7–7, the grammar checker noted the incomplete sentence at the end of the first paragraph ("Congratulations, Phyllis"). A **style checker** alerts users to such writing concerns as sexist words or phrases (*chairman*), long or complex sentence structures, clichés (for example, *the bottom line*), and sentences written in the passive (*The letter was written by Sherry*) rather than the active voice (*Sherry wrote the letter*).

Idea processor.   Like word processing software, an **idea processor** permits the manipulation of text, but with a different twist. It deals with brief explanations of items—for example: ideas, points, notes, and so on. Idea processors can organize these brief items into an outline format. Referred to by some as an electronic version of the yellow note pad, the idea processor lets you focus your attention on the thought process by letting the computer help document your ideas.

Document-conversion programs.   Although a handful of word processing packages dominates the marketplace, about 30 are commonly used. It is not unusual for people within a company to use half a dozen incompatible word processing packages and, of course, these people frequently need to share text in their word processing documents. There are two ways to do this.

1. *Create an ASCII file.* When you save a word processing document, you save all the text in the file *plus* the hidden control characters that end paragraphs, start and end boldface, cause page breaks, and so on. These control characters are unique to each word processing package; therefore, one package cannot read a file produced by another. However, all word processing packages can read **ASCII files.** An ASCII file is a generic text file stripped of program-specific control characters. One way to pass text from one word processing

THE VALUE OF PC ADD-INS

Frustration! Imagine how much better your writing could be if your word processing program checked grammar, as well as spelling. Or, imagine how much time you could save if your presentation graphics program stored files in a variety of graphics formats. Add-in programs promise to help when you can do almost everything you need to . . . but not quite! Add-in software in some way enhances the functionality of a major PC software package, such as WordPerfect or Lotus 1-2-3, or it provides you with other ways to use the package. Add-ins may be supplied with the basic applications software or, as is normally the case, marketed by another company.

Add-ins evolve from need. Once a PC software package has been on the market for a while, the vendor or software entrepreneurs create ingenious solutions to problems users are having.

- Microsoft's *Windows* enables the viewing of multiple applications on a single screen; however, only parts of the applications are shown in each window. *WideAngle,* an add–in, compresses the individual application such that up to nine applications can be shown in their entirety on a single screen.

- Most presentation graphics packages are accompanied by a variety of clip art (prepackaged electronic images). Several companies offer supplemental extensive arrays of clip art that are electronically pre-indexed for fast identification and retrieval. For example, you could call up images that relate to a particular season, holiday, geographic location, business scenario, and so on.

- *Perfect Exchange,* an add-in for WordPerfect, converts documents between WordPerfect and 55 word processor, spreadsheet, and database formats. This gives offices which use several packages the flexibility to exchange text without losing markings such as boldface and underline.

- *PC-Translator,* an add-in for word processors, helps international businesses translate technical manuals, business letters, purchase orders, invoices, and so on to English.

- Several companies market rhymer add-ins to help writers, educators, language teachers, songwriters, and others find just the right word.

package to another is to create a generic ASCII file with one and read it with another. Of course, when you do this, you lose everything (tabs, underlines, and so on) except the text in the transfer.

2. *Use a document-conversion program.* **Document-conversion programs** help solve the dilemma created when several word processing packages are used within one company. This add-on converts documents generated on one word processing package into a format consistent with another. For example, document-conversion programs enable a Microsoft Word user to convert files to WordPerfect files—control characters and all. The more sophisticated word processing packages come with this feature.

Putting Word Processing to Work

You can create just about any type of text-based document with word processing: letters, reports, books, articles, forms, memos, tables, and so on. This section summarizes applications of word processing software.

Mail Merge   The features of some word processing packages go beyond the generation of text documents, however. For example, some word processing systems provide the capability of merging parts of a database with the text of a

- An add-in called *Compare and Contrast* helps you keep tabs on spreadsheets by comparing two spreadsheets cell by cell and informing you of any differences.
- *R & R Report Writer* turns your raw data into useful information by creating reports that relate, analyze, summarize, and handsomely present the data in spreadsheets and data bases.

If you and others have an add-in–type problem, there is a good chance that someone has a product on the market or, if not, is planning to create one in the near future.

The Alarm Clock *Many add-ins come in the form of useful macros written in an application's macro language. For example,* 60 Macros for WordPerfect 6.0 for Windows *works with WPwin to help users do many useful tasks such as preparing four-fold greeting cards, a graphics catalog, calendars, an address book, an alarm clock (shown here), and many more. To execute a particular macro, the user simply "plays" the macro within the application. In the example, at 10:00 A.M. a tone will sound and a message will appear reminding the user of a meeting.*

document. Figure 7–12 illustrates an example of this **mail-merge** application. In the example, BrassCo Enterprises announced the enhanced version of its Curio, one of its hottest selling items. Each regional sales manager sent a "personal" letter to every one of the thousands of BrassCo customers in his or her region. Using word processing, a secretary enters the text of the letter once, stores it on the disk, then simply merges the customer name-and-address file (also stored on the disk) with the letter. The letters then can be printed with the proper addresses and salutations. Figure 7–12 illustrates how the Curio announcement letter is merged with the customer name-and-address file to produce a "personalized" letter.

Boilerplate   The mail-merge example is a good illustration of the use of **boilerplate.** Boilerplate is existing text that can be customized for a variety of word processing applications. One beauty of word processing is that you can accumulate text on disk storage that eventually will help you meet other word processing needs. You can even *buy* boilerplate (i.e., text for business letters).

The legal profession offers some of the best examples of the use of boilerplate. Simple wills, uncontested divorces, individual bankruptcies, real estate

FIGURE 7–12 Merging Data with Word Processing *The names and addresses from a customer master file are retrieved from secondary storage and are merged with the text of a letter. In the actual letter, the appropriate data items are inserted for *First Name*, *Company*, *Address*, *City*, and so on. In this way, a "personalized" letter can be sent to each customer.*

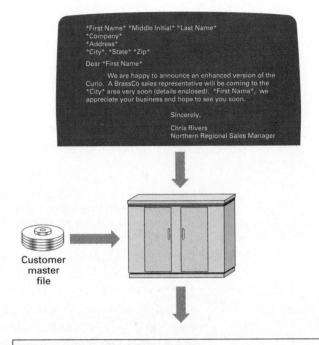

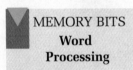

Customer
master
file

BrassCo Enterprises   PO Box 723, Becker, MN 55308

Marty E. Chambers
Chambers Specialty Shop
115 Vista Drive
Ames, IA 50010

Dear Marty:

We are happy to announce an enhanced version of the Curio. A BrassCo sales representative will be coming to the Ames area very soon (details enclosed). Marty, we appreciate your business and hope to see you soon.

Sincerely,

Chris Rivers

Chris Rivers
Nothern Regional Sales Manager

Enclosure

MEMORY BITS
Word Processing

Entering text
■ Typeover mode
■ Insert mode

Block operations on marked text
■ Copy block (*copy* then *paste*)
■ Move block (*cut* then *paste*)
■ Delete block (*delete*)

Search or find
■ Search only
■ Selective search and replace
■ Global search and replace

Add-ons
■ On-line thesaurus
■ Spelling checker
■ Grammar and style checkers
■ Idea processor
■ Document-conversion program

---

transfers, and other straightforward legal documents may be as much as 95% boilerplate. Even more-complex legal documents may be as much as 80% boilerplate. Once the appropriate boilerplate has been merged into a document, the lawyer edits the document to add transition sentences and the variables, such as the names of the litigants. Besides the obvious improvement in productivity, lawyers can be relatively confident that their documents are accurate and complete. The use of boilerplate is common in all areas of business, education, government, and personal endeavor.

Integration of Text and Graphics Most state-of-the-art word processing packages allow the integration of text and graphic images. For example, the text in Figure 7–13 refers to a "bar graph" and a "Statistical Sales Summary." Figure 7–13 shows how the memo, the bar graph (produced with spreadsheet software), and the sales summary (from a spreadsheet file) can be integrated into a single word processing document.

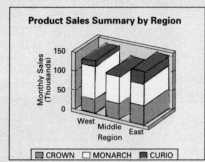

April 8, 1996

To: Field Sales Staff
From: B. J. McCue, National Sales Manager
Subject: March Sales Summary

        Good job! Sales for March are up **21%** over the same month last year. Our top performer for March, Phyllis Hill, set a new one-month record--$78,167! Congratulations, Phyllis.
        I've included a bar graph and a "Statistical Sales Summary." The bar graph shows sales activity by region by product for March. The summary should help you place your performance into perspective.
        Our annual sales meeting is set at the Bayside Hotel and Marina in San Diego during the first week in January. Plan your schedule accordingly.

cc: P. Powell, President; V. Grant, VP Marketing

Product Sales Summary by Region

Figure 1 Region/Product Graph

STATISTICAL SALES SUMMARY BY REPRESENTATIVE				
SALES BY REP.	*CROWN*	*MONARCH*	*CURIO*	*TOTAL*
LOW	$15,570	$24,660	$0	$48,305
AVG.	$21,551	$36,069	$7,250	$64,869
HIGH	$28,067	$58,388	$25,440	$78,167
RANGE	$12,497	$33,728	$25,440	$29,862

Figure 2 Sales Stats

FIGURE 7–13 Integrating Text with Graphics *The bar graph and the "Statistical Sales Summary" referred to in the memo of Figure 7–7 are combined in the same word processing document and printed on a desktop page printer. The bar graph and summary were produced using spreadsheet software.*

Summary

Word processing is the perfect example of how automation can be used to increase productivity and foster creativity. It reduces the effort you must devote to the routine aspects of writing so you can focus your attention on its creative aspects. Most word processing users will agree that their writing styles have improved. The finished product is less verbose, better organized, without spelling errors, and, of course, more visually appealing.

7–2   DESKTOP PUBLISHING

The ultimate extension of word processing is *desktop publishing,* sometimes abbreviated as **DTP.** Desktop publishing refers to the capability of producing *near-typeset-quality camera copy* from the confines of a desktop. Desktop publishing software can help you produce camera-ready copy for every conceivable type of printed matter, from graduation certificates to catalogs. This concept is changing the way companies, government agencies, and individuals approach printing newsletters, brochures, business cards, user manuals, pamphlets, restaurant menus, periodicals, greeting cards, and thousands of other items.

Desktop publishing software certainly has captured the business community's attention. Not only can users bypass the expense of professional typesetting and page layout, they also can drastically reduce the time needed to prepare a camera-ready document. Here, designers are discussing the layout for a quarterly stockholder report.

Concepts

Traditionally, drafts of documents to be professionally printed are delivered to commercial typographers to be typeset. The typeset text is physically pasted together with photos, artwork, ruled lines, and so on to achieve the final layout. Desktop publishing eliminates the typesetting and pasteup process for those documents that require only near-typeset-quality (for example, those documents produced by desktop page printers with resolutions [quality of output] of 300 to 1000 dots per inch [dpi]). In practice, near-typeset-quality copy is acceptable for most printed documents. Relatively few need to be prepared using the expensive commercial phototypesetting process (which uses 1200 dpi or greater). The output of the desktop publishing process is called *camera-ready copy.* The camera-ready copy is reproduced by a variety of means, from duplicating machines to commercial offset printing.

The Components of Desktop Publishing The components required for desktop publishing include

- Document-composition software
- Microcomputer
- Desktop page printer
- Image scanner
- Typefaces and fonts
- Clip art

Document-composition software. The document-composition software enables users to design and make up the page or pages of a document. When people talk of desktop publishing software, they are actually talking about document-composition software. Popular DTP packages include Microsoft's *Publisher,* Xerox's *Ventura Publisher,* Quark's *QuarkXPress,* and Aldus Corporation's *PageMaker.*

Microcomputer.   Of all of the microcomputer productivity tools, DTP is the most technologically demanding. A high-end microcomputer is a prerequisite for effective desktop publishing. The typical micro used for DTP will be fast and will be configured with a high-resolution *monitor,* a *mouse,* plenty of RAM, and a high-capacity *hard disk.*

Desktop page printer.   The overwhelming majority of desktop page printers configured with DTP systems are laser printers that print at 300 dpi. However, affordable desktop page printers with 1000 dpi resolution are available.

Image scanner.   Image scanners (see Chapter 4, "Input/Output Devices"), found on high-end DTP systems, are used to digitize images, such as photographs. Image scanners re-create an electronic version of text or an image (photograph or line drawing) that can be manipulated and reproduced under computer control.

Typefaces and fonts.   Most DTP-produced documents use a variety of **typefaces.** A typeface refers to a set of characters that are of the same type style (Helvetica, Courier, Swiss Light, Park Avenue, Dutch Roman, and so on). A *font* is described by its typeface, its height in points (8, 10, 14, 24, and so on; 72 points to the inch), and its presentation attribute (light, roman [or normal], medium, bold, italic, bold italic, extra bold, and so on). A variety of typefaces and *point* sizes are illustrated in Figure 7–14.

Each font (such as 24-*point* Helvetica Bold) *is* stored on disk or in ROM (read-only memory). When needed to print a document, the **soft font** for a particular font is retrieved from disk storage and downloaded to the printer's memory. A **resident font** is accessed directly from the printer's built-in ROM. Some printers have removable ROM cartridges, each of which contains a variety of fonts. The cartridges must be inserted manually in the printer when the fonts are needed for a print job. People engaged in DTP typically will have a minimum of a dozen soft and/or resident fonts available for use. The more sophisticated user will have access to hundreds of fonts.

The latest round of high-speed micros has made it possible to generate fonts as they are needed. To do this, they use **scalable typefaces** stored in outline format. The outline is essentially a template, described in mathematical terms, from which fonts of any point size can be created. These scalable type-

The image scanner is one of the six components required for desktop publishing. Relatively inexpensive hand image scanners have made it possible for the casual PC user to get into desktop publishing.

Literally tens of thousands of pieces of clip art can be purchased from third-party vendors to supplement those distributed with desktop publishing software. These are representative.

Typefaces fall into three categories:

Serif: those that have short crosslines projecting from the ends of the strokes.

Sans Serif: those without serifs.

Decorative: those used for headlines and special effects.

The lowercase *x* sits on the baseline and defines the x-height. That portion of a character that is below the baseline is the descender (as in *g*, *p* and *y*) and that which is above the x-height is the ascender (as in *d*, *f*, and *h*).

A typeface's style is defined in terms of

Weight: light, medium, **heavy** or **bold** (with extra and ultra prefixes).

Slant: *italic (for serif typefaces); oblique (for sans serif typefaces)*.

Proportion: condensed, regular, or extended.

Typeface families (those typefaces with similar shapes) are usually named for their designers (Frederick Goudy, Oswald Cooper) or their function (Bookman). Examples of the Claude Garamond family are illustrated below.

Garamond Book   ***Garamond Bold Italic***
Garamond Book Italic   Garamond Book Condensed
Garamond Bold   *Garamond Book Condensed Italic*

A font refers to a particular typeface size and style. All previous fonts in this illustration are 12 point (72 points to an inch). Other fonts follow.

Opti Jefferson: 4 point (4 point) and *8 point*.

Gill Sans: 24 point and

36 point.

Klang: *72 point*.

Bitmapped fonts, which are made up of pixels, require a separate character set file for each point size. Outline fonts of any size (and orientation) for a particular typeface are generated from a single typeface file.

FIGURE 7–14
Typeface Tutorial

faces provide the user with tremendous flexibility in font selection. For example, you might elect to print your first-level headings in 20-point Goudy (bold) and your second-level headings in 16-point Goudy (bold). These two fonts are generated by the processor from the Goudy (bold) scalable typeface, then downloaded to the printer's memory.

Clip art. No DTP environment would be complete without a healthy supply of **clip art.** Clip art refers to prepackaged electronic images stored on disk to be used as needed. The tiger and horse in Figure 7–8 are clip art. Clip art items could be a clock, a rose, two people talking, a hamburger, or just about anything you can imagine.

Desktop Publishing Files Typically, a DTP-produced document, such as a newsletter, consists of several files. A long report or a book may be made up of hundreds of files. During the document-composition process, each file is assigned to a rectangular **frame.** A frame holds the text or an image of a particular file. Each page is a frame. There also can be frames within a frame (for example, figures and photos on a page).

A DTP document will involve one or more text files, perhaps one or more picture files, a style-sheet file, and a print file.

- ■ *Text files.* The *text files* are created by a word processing program, such as WordPerfect. Although DTP software provides the facility to create and edit text, it is much easier to do these tasks with a word processing program.
- ■ *Picture files. Picture files* are made up of clip art, line art, scanned-in graphics and photos, and renderings of screen displays (for example, the summary at the bottom of Figure 7–13).
- ■ *Style-sheet file.* In the traditional approach to publishing, the designer of a print job (a book or a restaurant menu) creates a style sheet that provides the information needed by the typesetter (for example, typeface size and attributes for first-level headings). In DTP, the user creates a *style-sheet file* that tells the document-composition software what to do with the text. To create the style-sheet file, the user must go into the document and *tag* each paragraph with the appropriate typographical attributes (such as typeface and size).
- ■ *Print file.* The *print file* contains all the information needed to combine the text and picture files with the style sheet and print the document.

The Document-Composition Process The document-composition process involves integrating graphics, photos, text, and other elements into a visually appealing *document layout.* With DTP, you can produce finished, professional-looking documents in four steps (see Figure 7–15).

1. *Prepare text and graphics.* Use your word processing software to create and edit the text of your document. For illustrations you can use clip art, computer-created graphics (such as a pie graph), or scanned images (photos).

2. *Create the style sheet.* Define the document format (for example, margins and number of columns) and text attributes. Once a style-sheet file for a particular job is created, it can be applied to similar text files (for example, monthly newsletters).

3. *Combine text and picture files.* Create and position needed frames, then insert text and picture files to fit your needs. The DTP display is WYSIWYG—that is, "What you see is what you get" when the document is

As you gain experience in desktop publishing, the vision of what you wish to produce demands greater sophistication. Desktop publishers rely on a variety of supplemental software packages to meet these demands. For example, they routinely use image editors, such as Micrografx® Picture Publisher (shown here). An image editor lets you add special effects to photos that you include in your documents. With Picture Publisher you can paint over the picture, blur portions of the picture, touch up a picture, change colors, and much more.

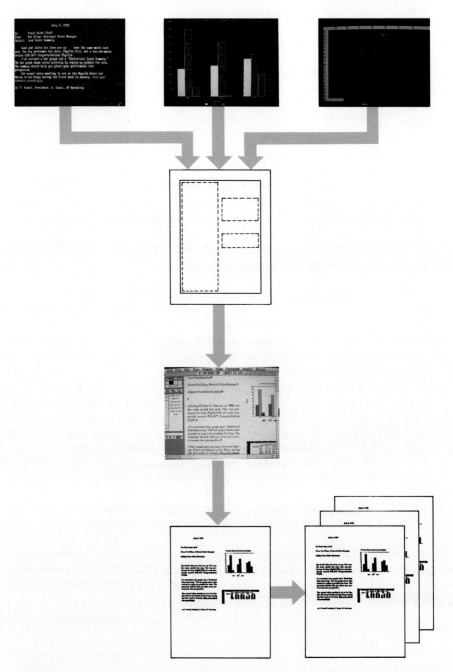

FIGURE 7–15 Preparing a Document with Desktop Publishing Software *Desktop publishing software combines text prepared using word processing software with images from a variety of sources and loads each into prepositioned frames. The graph and spreadsheet frames appear within the larger frame of the word processing text. The style sheet combines the elements, and the document is printed. The camera-ready copy document is reproduced in multiples.*

printed. If what you see is not what you want, then you can use the mouse to reposition frames containing text and graphics to the desired locations.

4. *Print the document.* Once the WYSIWYG display shows what you want, use a desktop page printer to produce the finished camera-ready copy.

Desktop Publishing and Word Processing

Traditionally, users have combined the text manipulation capabilities of word processing software with the document-composition capabilities of DTP software to produce camera copy for reproduction. Word processing-generated text provides input to the document-composition process. This distinction may begin to blur soon. Already state-of-the-art word processing programs, such as Microsoft Word and WordPerfect, provide users with sophisticated DTP capabilities. Word processing users routinely produce camera-ready copy for everything from letterheads to books—all without the aid of DTP software.

By now you are probably thinking, "If word processing software does it all, why do we need DTP software?" At this time, word processing software doesn't do it all. DTP software offers a full range of sophisticated capabilities that are not available with word processing software. For example, suppose the last sentence of a paragraph was, "The binary digits are 0 and 1." and "1." ended up alone on the last line. With DTP software, you can force the "1." onto the previous line. You can't do that with word processing software. In general, DTP software provides users with tremendous flexibility in formatting documents. The document-composition capabilities of word processing software are typically more cumbersome and time-consuming than similar DTP capabilities.

It is inevitable that future generations of high-end word processing software will incorporate more document-composition capabilities. In time, word processing software will be all that is needed for most jobs that require camera-ready copy. On the other hand, vendors of desktop publishing software plan to incorporate advanced text-manipulation capabilities, thereby eliminating the need for word processing–generated text. Look for the differences between the two to diminish over the next few years.

*I*MPORTANT TERMS AND SUMMARY OUTLINE

ASCII file
boilerplate
clip art
document-conversion program
DTP
electronic dictionary
font
frame

full-screen editing
grammar checker
idea processor
insert mode
mail-merge
on-line thesaurus
resident font
reverse video

scalable typeface
soft font
spelling checker
style checker
typeface
typeover mode
word wrap
WYSIWYG

7–1 Word Processing Word processing is using the computer to enter, store, manipulate, and print text in letters, reports, books, and so on. Today's sophisticated word processing packages do much more than text processing, such as the integration of images with text.

When you format a document, you are specifying the size of the page to be printed and how you want the document to look when it is printed. To enter and edit text, you toggle between **typeover mode** and **insert mode. Word wrap** occurs when text that extends past the defined margins automatically wraps around to the next line. Word processing permits **full-screen editing.** Most word processing packages are considered **WYSIWYG,** short for "What you see is what you get." Some are **WYSIWYG-MOL.**

The block-move, the block-copy, and the block-delete commands are known collectively as block operations, the electronic equivalent of "cut and paste." The portions of text marked for a block operation are usually displayed in **reverse video.** The search, or find, feature permits the user to search the entire word processing document and identify all occurrences of a particular character string. The search-and-replace feature enables selective replacement of a search string with a user-defined string.

Word processing has several features that enable users to enhance the appearance and readability of their documents. These include left and/or right justification, automatic centering, boldface, underlining, indentation, header and footer labels, pagination, hyphenation, footnotes, numbered list/outline format, bulleted-list format, line draw and border, superscripts and subscripts, the insertion of an image into the running text, a variety of **fonts,** watermarks, multicolumn text, and tables.

Some word processing packages enable the automatic generation of a table of contents and an alphabetical index of key words; have a table feature that expedites the presentation of tabular data; and enable rudimentary desktop publishing.

All word processing packages allow users to save, retrieve, and delete files that contain word processing documents. The print function transforms your electronic document into a hard-copy document.

Several add-on programs are designed to enhance the functionality of word processing programs. An **online thesaurus** is always ready with synonyms for any word in a document. The **spelling checker** program checks every word in the text against an **electronic dictionary** and alerts the user when a word is not in the dictionary. A **grammar checker** highlights grammatical concerns and deviations from conventions. A **style checker** alerts users to such writing concerns as sexist words and hackneyed clichés. **Idea processors** can be used to organize single-line items into an outline format.

There are two ways to pass documents between different types of word processing programs—via **ASCII files** and the use of **document-conversion programs.**

Any kind of text-based document can be created with word processing software. **Boilerplate** is existing text that can in some way be customized so it can be used in a variety of word processing applications (for example, **mail merge**). Most state-of-the-art word processing packages enable the integration of text and graphic images.

7–2 Desktop Publishing Desktop publishing (**DTP**) refers to the capability of producing near-typeset-quality camera copy from the confines of a desktop. The components required for desktop publishing include document-composition software, a high-end microcomputer, a desktop page printer, an image scanner, **typefaces** and fonts, and **clip art.**

Most DTP-produced documents use a variety of typefaces, all of which fall in one of two categories—serif and sans serif. **Soft fonts** are retrieved from disk storage and downloaded to the printer's memory as needed. A **resident font** is accessed directly from the printer's built-in ROM. **Scalable typefaces** give users the flexibility to scale them to any point size.

Typically, a DTP-produced document consists of several (often many) files. During the document-composition process, each file is assigned to a rectangular **frame.** A frame holds the text or an image of a particular file.

A DTP document will involve one or more text files, perhaps one or more picture files, a style-sheet file, and a print file. Text files are created by a word processing program. Picture files are made up of clip art and other images. The style-sheet file tells the document-composition software what to do with the text. The print file contains all the information needed to combine the text and picture files with the style sheet and print the document.

The document-composition process involves integrating graphics, photos, text, and other elements into a visually appealing layout. The steps are (1) prepare text and graphics; (2) create the style sheet; (3) combine text and picture files in frames; and (4) print the document.

REVIEW EXERCISES

Concepts

1. What is the function of word processing software?
2. What must be specified when formatting a document?
3. What is meant when a document is formatted to be justified on the right and on the left?
4. Text is entered in either of which two modes? Which mode would you select to change *the table*

to *the long table*? Which mode would you select to change *pick the choose* to *pick and choose*?

5. What causes text to wrap around?

6. Give an example of when you might issue a global search-and-replace command.

7. When running the spelling checker, what options does the system present when it encounters an unidentified word?

8. What productivity software package has the capability of producing near-typeset-quality copy for printing jobs?

9. Name two software components and two hardware components of a desktop publishing system.

10. What is the shape of a desktop publishing frame?

11. What term is used to refer to prepackaged electronic images?

12. Which DTP file tells the document-composition software what do with the text?

Discussion

13. Customer-service representatives at BrassCo Enterprises spend almost 70% of their day interacting directly with customers. Approximately one hour each day is spent preparing courtesy follow-up letters, primarily to enhance good will between BrassCo and its customers. Do you think the "personalized" letters are a worthwhile effort? Why or why not?

14. Describe the relationship between word processing, electronic images, and desktop publishing software.

15. With the advent of desktop publishing, the number of printed items bearing the company logo has increased dramatically. Many companies require that all such documents be approved by a central DTP review board prior to distribution. What concerns prompted these managers to establish the review board?

SELF-TEST (BY SECTION)

7–1 a. Preset format specifications are referred to as _defaults_.

b. To add a word in the middle of an existing sentence in a word processing document, you would use the insert mode. (T/F)

c. Which word processing feature enables the automatic numbering of pages of a document: (a) pagination, (b) page breaking, or (c) footers?

d. The word processing feature that automatically breaks long words that fall at the end of a line is called _hyphenation_.

e. An on-line thesaurus can be used to suggest synonyms for a word in a word processing document. (T/F)

7–2 a. The type of printer normally associated with desktop publishing is the daisy-wheel printer. (T/F)

b. The output of the desktop publishing process is _camera-ready_ copy.

c. What device re-creates a black-and-white version of an image in an electronic format: (a) image scanner, (b) image-reduction aid, or (c) vision-entry device?

d. The height of a 36-point typeface is: (a) ¼ inch, (b) ½ inch, or (c) 1 inch?

e. Fontware is that component of the document-composition software that enables WYSIWYG display of DTP documents. (T/F)

Self-test answers.   **7–1 (a)** default settings; **(b)** T; **(c)** a; **(d)** hyphenation; **(e)** T. **7–2 (a)** F; **(b)** camera-ready; **(c)** a; **(d)** b; **(e)** F.

8

DATA MANAGEMENT SOFTWARE

OBJECTIVES

To describe the function and applications of spreadsheet software.

To discuss common spreadsheet concepts.

To describe how presentation graphics can be created from spreadsheet data.

To describe the function and applications of database software.

To discuss common database software concepts.

To describe the concepts associated with programming and programs.

8–1 DATA MANAGEMENT IN PRACTICE

Our upbringing prepared us better for word processing software than it did for data management software, the focus of this chapter. Just as you need to learn sentence structure and grammar to be an effective user of word processing software, you need to learn fundamental data management principles to be an effective user of spreadsheet and database software. These principles, which are new to most people taking this course, include the terms and concepts associated with the hierarchy of data organization (Section 5–2 in Chapter 5, "Data Storage and Organization"). The concepts presented in Chapter 5 and in this chapter should give you the background knowledge you need to feel comfortable with applying data management software in practice.

8–2 SPREADSHEET: THE MAGIC MATRIX

The name *spreadsheet* aptly describes this software's fundamental application. The spreadsheet has been a common business tool for centuries. Before computers, the ledger (a book of spreadsheets) was the accountant's primary tool for keeping a record of financial transactions. A professor's grade book is also set up in spreadsheet format.

Spreadsheet software is simply an electronic alternative to thousands of traditionally manual tasks. We are no longer confined to using pencils, erasers, and hand calculators to deal with rows and columns of data. Think of anything that has rows and columns of data and you have identified an application for spreadsheet software: income (profit-and-loss) statements, personnel profiles, demographic data, and budget summaries, just to mention a few. Because spreadsheets parallel so many of our manual tasks, they are enjoying widespread acceptance.

All commercially available spreadsheet packages enable you to manipulate rows and columns of data. However, the *user interface,* or the manner in which you enter data and commands, differs from one package to the next. The conceptual coverage that follows is generic: It applies to all spreadsheets. The examples in the figures are from Quattro Pro for Windows (a Borland International product).

Concepts

B. J. McCue, the national sales manager for BrassCo Enterprises, a manufacturer of an upscale line of brass coat hanger products (the Crown, the Monarch, and the Curio), uses spreadsheet software to compile a monthly sales summary. We will use B. J.'s March sales summary shown in Figure 8–1 to demonstrate spreadsheet concepts. B. J. uses a monthly sales **template** each month. The template, simply a spreadsheet model, contains the layout

This corporate planner in Los Angeles is discussing the results displayed in a spreadsheet with a plant manager in Houston. They are networked via a communications link that permits them to view both the spreadsheet and one another.

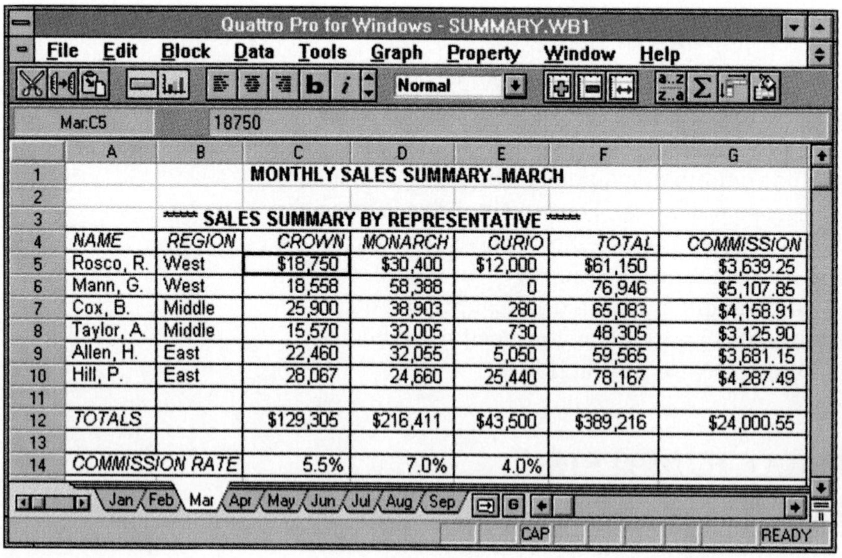

	A	B	C	D	E	F	G
1			MONTHLY SALES SUMMARY--MARCH				
2							
3		***** SALES SUMMARY BY REPRESENTATIVE *****					
4	NAME	REGION	CROWN	MONARCH	CURIO	TOTAL	COMMISSION
5	Rosco, R.	West	$18,750	$30,400	$12,000	$61,150	$3,639.25
6	Mann, G.	West	18,558	58,388	0	76,946	$5,107.85
7	Cox, B.	Middle	25,900	38,903	280	65,083	$4,158.91
8	Taylor, A.	Middle	15,570	32,005	730	48,305	$3,125.90
9	Allen, H.	East	22,460	32,055	5,050	59,565	$3,681.15
10	Hill, P.	East	28,067	24,660	25,440	78,167	$4,287.49
11							
12	TOTALS		$129,305	$216,411	$43,500	$389,216	$24,000.55
13							
14	COMMISSION RATE		5.5%	7.0%	4.0%		

FIGURE 8–1 A Monthly Sales Summary Spreadsheet Template *This spreadsheet template is the basis for the explanation and demonstration of spreadsheet concepts.*

and formulas needed to produce the summary in Figure 8–1. B. J. entered only the data for the current month (March in the example) and the spreadsheet template did all the needed calculations. For example, B. J. entered the *sales amounts* for each salesperson and the spreadsheet software calculated the *totals* and the *commission.*

Viewing Data in a Spreadsheet Scrolling through a spreadsheet is much like looking through a magnifying glass as you move it around a newspaper page. You scroll left and right (horizontal scrolling) and/or up and down (vertical scrolling) to see different portions of a large spreadsheet. In Figure 8–1, the entire sales summary can be displayed on a single screen. However, if five more products or twenty more salespeople were added, B. J. would scroll horizontally and vertically to view the entire spreadsheet. Scrolling is discussed and illustrated in Chapter 2, "Interacting with Computers."

Organization Spreadsheets are organized in a *tabular structure* with *rows* and *columns.* The intersection of a particular row and column designates a **cell**. As you can see in Figure 8–1, the rows are *numbered* and the columns are *lettered.* Single letters identify the first 26 columns; double letters are used after that (A, B, . . . Z; AA, AB, . . . AZ; BA, BB, . . . BZ). The number of rows or columns available to you depends on the size of your micro's RAM (random-access memory). Most spreadsheets permit hundreds of columns and thousands of rows.

Data are entered and stored in a cell at the intersection of a column and a row. During operations, data are referred to by their **cell address**. A cell address identifies the location of a cell in the spreadsheet by its column and row, with the column designator first. For example, in the monthly sales summary of Figure 8–1, C4 is the address of the column heading for product Crown, and D5 is the address of the total amount of Monarch sales for R. Rosco ($30,400).

In the spreadsheet work area (the rows and columns), a movable highlighted area "points" to the *current cell.* The current cell is highlighted with either a dark border around the current cell or a different color. This high-lighted area, called the **pointer,** can be moved around the spreadsheet with the arrow keys (→ ←↑↓) to any cell address, or it can be repositioned by pointing and clicking with the mouse. To add or edit (revise) an entry at a particular cell, the pointer must be positioned at that cell. The address and content of the current cell (the location of the pointer) are displayed in the user-interface portion of the spreadsheet, the area above and/or below the spreadsheet work area (above in Figure 8–1). Specifically, the information for a particular cell (Cell C5 in Figure 8–1) is displayed in a *cell status line.* The content, or resulting value (for example, from a formula), of each cell is shown in the spreadsheet work area. Notice in Figure 8–1 that when the pointer is positioned at C5, the actual numeric value (18750) is displayed as the cell contents in the user interface, and an optional *formatted* version ($18,750) is displayed in C5.

Cell Entries   To make an entry in the spreadsheet, simply move the pointer to the appropriate cell, and key in the data. To *edit* (revise) or replace an existing entry, you also move the pointer to the appropriate cell. However, you key in the new or revised entry in the cell status line of the user-interface panel (see Figure 8–1). Once you have completed work on a particular entry, press the ENTER key or an arrow key to insert the entry in the actual spreadsheet.

Spreadsheet packages allow the user to vary the column width to improve readability. Column widths can be adjusted in terms of characters or inches. The width for Column A in Figure 8–1 is set at 11 characters; the width for Column B is set at 7 characters.

Ranges   Many spreadsheet operations ask you to designate one or more **ranges** of cells. The four types of ranges are highlighted in Figure 8–2:

■ *Cell range.* A single cell (Example range is G12.)
■ *Column range.* All or part of a column of adjacent cells (Example range is A5..A10.)

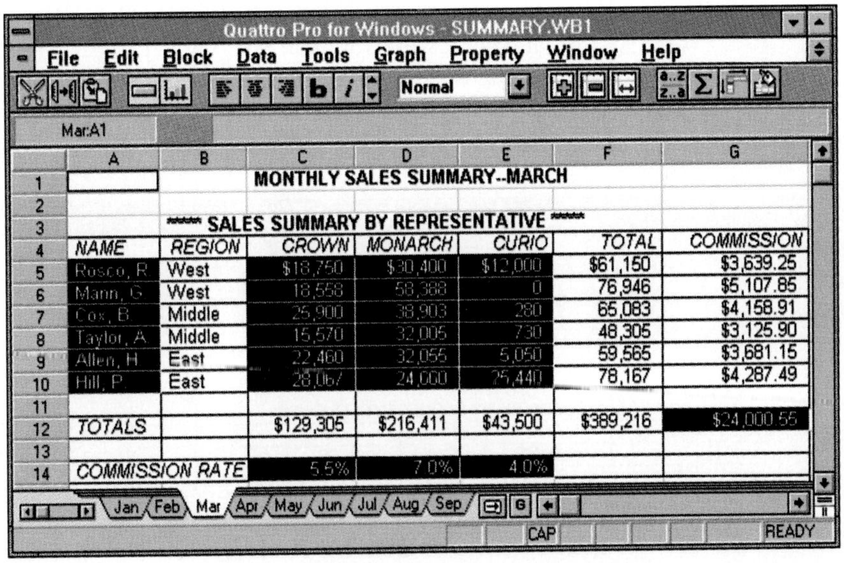

FIGURE 8–2 Spreadsheet Ranges
The highlighted cells in this spreadsheet display illustrate the four types of ranges: cell (G12), column (A5..A10), row (C14..E14), and block (C5..E10).

- *Row range.* All or part of a row of adjacent cells (Example range is C14..E14.)
- *Block range.* A rectangular group of cells (Example range is C5..E10.)

A particular range is indicated by the addresses of the endpoint cells separated by two periods. (Some spreadsheet packages use only one period or a colon, for example: C5.E10 or C5:E10.) Any cell can comprise a single-cell range. The range for the commission percentages in Figure 8–2 is C14..E14, and the range for the row labels (salespeople's names) is A5..A10. The range of sales amounts for the three products is indicated by any two opposite-corner cell addresses (for example, C5..E10 or E5..C10).

When you want to copy, move, or erase part of the spreadsheet, you must first define the range you wish to copy, move, or erase.

Types of Cell Entries   An entry to a cell is classified as either a *label* entry, a *numeric* entry, a *formula* entry, or a *date/time* entry. We will discuss the first three because these are present in just about every spreadsheet template.

Label entries.   A label entry is a word, a phrase, or any string of alphanumeric text (spaces included) that occupies a particular cell. Whenever you begin an entry with a letter, the spreadsheet software automatically assumes that you are entering a label. In Figure 8–1, "NAME" in Cell A4 is a label entry, as is "COMMISSION" in G4 and "MONTHLY SALES SUMMARY— MARCH" in C1. Notice that the label in C1 extends across Columns C, D, and E. This is possible when the adjacent cells (D1 and E1) are blank. If an entry were made in D1, only the first eleven positions (the width of Column C) of the entry in Cell C1 would be visible on the spreadsheet (that is, "MONTHLY S"). Unless otherwise specified, label entries are left-justified and numeric entries are right-justified (lined up on the right edge of the column). However, you can specify that any entry is left- or right-justified or centered in the column. In Figure 8–1, headings for Columns A and B are left-justified and the remainder is right-justified.

Numeric and formula entries.   In Figure 8–1, the dollar sales values in the range C5..E10 are *numeric*. The dollar sales values in the ranges F5..G10 and C12..G12 are results of *formulas*. Cell F5 contains a formula, but it is the numeric result (for example, $61,150 in Figure 8–3) that is displayed in the spreadsheet work area. With the pointer positioned at F5, the formula appears in the cell contents line in the user-interface panel. The actual numeric value appears in the spreadsheet work area (see Figure 8–3). The formula value in

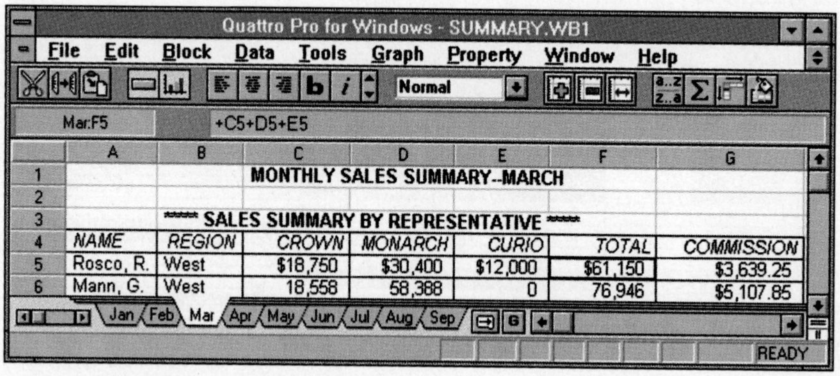

FIGURE 8–3 Spreadsheet Formulas   *The actual content of F5 is the formula in the user-interface panel in the upper left-hand part of the screen. The result of the formula appears in the spreadsheet at F5.*

F5 computes the total sales made by the salesperson in Row 5 for all three products (that is, total sales is +C5+D5+E5).

Spreadsheet formulas use standard notation for **arithmetic operators:** + (add), − (subtract), * (multiply), / (divide), $\wedge$ (raise to a power, or exponentiation). The formula in F5 (user-interface portion of Figure 8–3) computes the total sales for R. Rosco. The range F6..F10 contains similar formulas that apply to their respective rows (+C6+D6+E6, +C7+D7+E7, and so on). For example, the formula in F6 computes the total sales for G. Mann. You might look ahead at Figure 8–8, which will be discussed later, to get an idea of what formulas are needed to generate the monthly sales summary template spreadsheet shown in Figure 8–1.

Spreadsheet Formulas   This section expands on the use and application of formulas—the essence of spreadsheet operations. A formula enables the spreadsheet software to perform numeric and/or string calculations and/or logic operations that result in a numeric value (for example, 18750) or an alphanumeric character string (for example, *ABOVE QUOTA* or *BELOW QUOTA*).

Relative and absolute cell addressing.   The formulas in the range G5..G10 (see Figure 8–4 and look ahead at Figure 8–8) compute the commission for the salespeople based on the commission rates listed in Row 14. The commission rates vary from month to month. The percentages in Row 14 reflect the rates for March. The commission for R. Rosco is computed by the following formula.

G5	+$C$14*C5+$D$14*D5+$E$14*E5

The distinction between the way the sales amounts and the commission-rate variables are represented in the formula highlights an important concept in spreadsheets, that of **relative cell addressing and absolute cell addressing**. The dollar signs ($), which preface both the column and row in an absolute

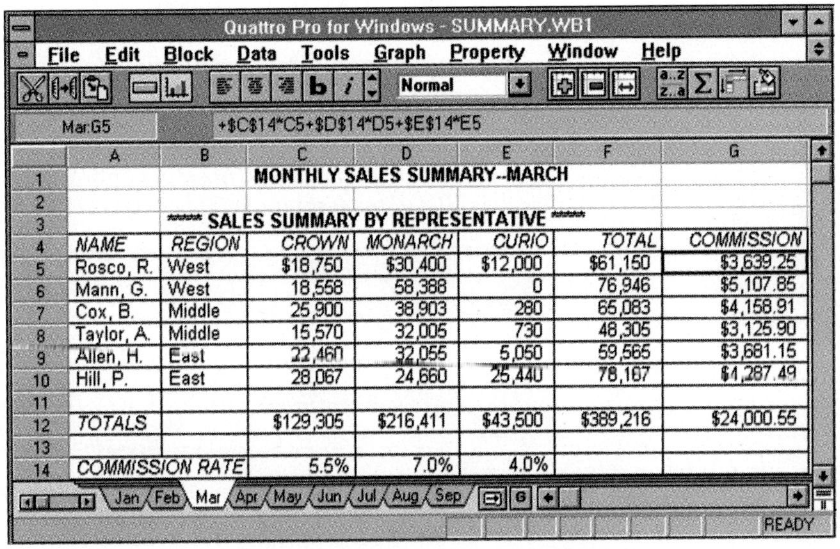

FIGURE 8–4 Spreadsheet Formulas with Relative and Absolute Cell Addresses   *Each of the commission computation formulas in the range G5..G10 has the same multipliers—the commission rates in the range C14..E14. Because the relative positions between the commission formulas in G5..G10 and the commission rates in C14..E14 vary from row to row, the commission rates are entered as absolute cell addresses.*

cell address ($C$14), distinguish it from a relative cell address (C5). *The relative cell address is based on its position relative to the cell containing the formula.* If the contents of a cell containing a formula are copied to another cell, the relative cell addresses in the copied formula are revised to reflect the new position, but the absolute cell addresses are unchanged. In the same manner, relative cell addresses in a formula are updated if a row or column is inserted into the template, but any absolute cell addresses in the formula remain the same.

The two types of cell addressing are illustrated in the spreadsheet in Figure 8–5. Suppose the formula B3*$E$1 is in Cell A1. B3 is a relative cell address that is one column to the right of and two rows down from A1. If this formula is copied to C2, the formula in C2 is D4*$E$1. Notice that D4 has the same *relative position* to the formula in Cell C2 as B3 has to the formula in Cell A1—one column to the right and two rows down. The *absolute cell address* ($E$1) remains the same as the original (A1) and the copied (C2) formulas. As you gain experience in building spreadsheet templates, you can experiment with making part of the address absolute. For example, $E1 locks the column and E$1 locks the row.

Copying formulas. In creating the spreadsheet template for the monthly sales summary, B. J. McCue entered only one formula to compute salesperson commission—the one in G5 (see Figure 8–4). Then spreadsheet commands were selected that *copied,* or *replicated,* the formula into each cell in the range G6..G10. Notice in the following copied formulas for G. Mann and B. Cox (rows 6 and 7) how the absolute addresses ($C$14, $D$14, and $E$14) remained the same in each formula and the relative addresses were revised to reflect the applicable row.

G6	+$C$14*C6+$D$14*D6+$E$14*E6
G7	+$C$14*C7+$D$14*D7+$E$14*E7

The formula in G6 (above) applies to the sales data in the cells next to G. Mann, not R. Rosco (as in the formula in G5). The same is true of other formulas in the range G5..G10.

Creating spreadsheet formulas. A formula may include one or all of the following: *arithmetic operations, functions, string operations,* and *logic opera-*

FIGURE 8–5 Relative and Absolute Cell Addressing   *When the formula in A1 is copied to C2, the formula in C2 becomes D4*$E$1.*

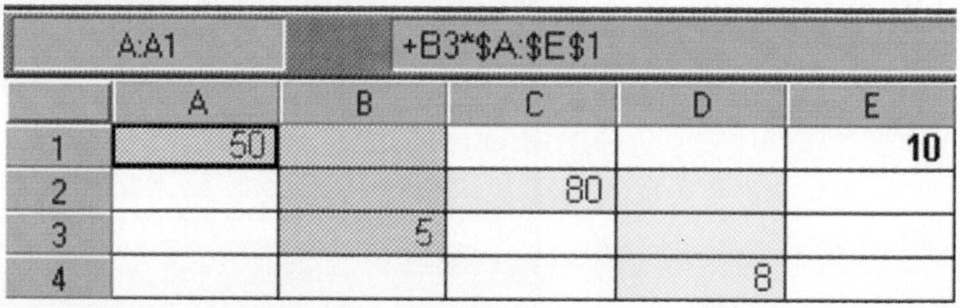

A:A1		+B3*$A:$E$1			
	A	B	C	D	E
1	50				10
2			80		
3		5			
4				8	

tions. The first two are discussed here in more detail. String operations (for example, joining, or *concatenating,* character strings) and logic operations [formulas that involve relational operators, such as < (less than) and > (greater than), and logic operators, such as *AND* and *OR*] are beyond the scope of this presentation.

When you design the spreadsheet, keep in mind where you want to place the formulas and what you want them to accomplish. Because *formulas are based on relative position,* you will need a knowledge of the layout and organization of the data in the spreadsheet. When you define a formula, you must first decide what you wish to achieve (for example, to calculate total sales for the first salesperson). Then select a cell location for the formula (for example, F5), and create the formula by connecting relative cell addresses, absolute cell addresses, and/or numbers with operators, as appropriate. In many instances, you will copy the formula to other locations. For example, in Figure 8–4, F5 (total for a salesperson) was copied to each cell in F6..F10.

Spreadsheet applications begin with a blank screen and an idea. The spreadsheet you create is a product of skill and imagination. What you get from a spreadsheet depends on how effectively you use formulas.

Arithmetic operations. Formulas containing arithmetic operators are resolved according to a hierarchy of operations. That is, when more than one operator is included in a single formula, the spreadsheet software uses a set of rules to determine which operation to do first, second, and so on. In the hierarchy of operations illustrated in Figure 8–6, exponentiation has the highest priority, followed by multiplication-division and addition-subtraction. In the case of a tie (for example, * and /, or + and −), the formula is evaluated *from left to right. Parentheses,* however, override the priority rules. Expressions placed in parentheses have priority. When several parentheses exist, the expression within the innermost parentheses is evaluated first.

The steps in the evaluation of the formula that results in the value in G5 ($3639.25) of Figure 8–4 are shown below:

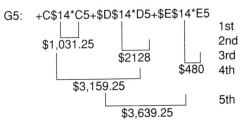

Following the hierarchy of operations, the three multiplications are performed first (leftmost first). The products are then added to arrive at the result in G5.

FIGURE 8–6 Hierarchy of Operations

The Hierarchy of Operations	
OPERATION	**OPERATOR**
Exponentiation	^
Multiplication-Division	* /
Addition-Subtraction	+ -

B. J. McCue's monthly sales summary template also includes a "Sales Summary by Region" in Rows 16 through 20 (see Figure 8–7). All the formulas in the spreadsheet of Figure 8–7 are listed in Figure 8–8.

Functions. Spreadsheets offer users a variety of predefined operations called **functions**. These functions can be used to create formulas that perform mathematical, logical, statistical, financial, and character-string operations on spreadsheet data. To use a function, simply enter the desired function name (for example, SUM for "Compute the sum") and enter the **argument**. Most spreadsheet programs require the user to prefix the function with a symbol such as @. The argument, which is placed in parentheses, identifies the data to be operated on. The argument can be one or several numbers, character strings, or ranges that represent data.

In the spreadsheet of Figure 8–7, the "TOTALS" for each column (C12..G12) are determined by adding the amounts in the respective columns. For example, the total sales amount for the Crown is determined with the following formula:

C12	+C5+C6+C7+C8+C9+C10

The total sales for the Crown also can be computed with a function and its argument:

C12	@SUM(C5..C10)

Quattro Pro for Windows - SUMMARY.WB1

File Edit Block Data Tools Graph Property Window Help

Mar:C1 — 'MONTHLY SALES SUMMARY–MARCH

	A	B	C	D	E	F	G
1			MONTHLY SALES SUMMARY--MARCH				
2							
3			**** SALES SUMMARY BY REPRESENTATIVE ****				
4	NAME	REGION	CROWN	MONARCH	CURIO	TOTAL	COMMISSION
5	Rosco, R.	West	$18,750	$30,400	$12,000	$61,150	$3,639.25
6	Mann, G.	West	18,558	58,388	0	76,946	$5,107.85
7	Cox, B.	Middle	25,900	38,903	280	65,083	$4,158.91
8	Taylor, A.	Middle	15,570	32,005	730	48,305	$3,125.90
9	Allen, H.	East	22,460	32,055	5,050	59,565	$3,681.15
10	Hill, P.	East	28,067	24,660	25,440	78,167	$4,287.49
11							
12	TOTALS		$129,305	$216,411	$43,500	$389,216	$24,000.55
13							
14	COMMISSION RATE		5.5%	7.0%	4.0%		
15							
16			**** SALES SUMMARY BY REGION ****				
17		REGION	CROWN	MONARCH	CURIO	TOTAL	
18		West	$37,308	$88,788	$12,000	$138,096	
19		Middle	$41,470	$70,908	$1,010	$113,388	
20		East	$50,527	$56,715	$30,490	$137,732	

Jan / Feb \ Mar / Apr / May / Jun / Jul / Aug /

READY

FIGURE 8–7 Expanding an Existing Template *The "Sales Summary by Region" portion of the template is extrapolated from the data in the "Sales Summary by Representative" portion.*

A	A	B	C	D	E	F	G
1			MONTHLY SALES SUMMARY--MARCH				
2							
3			*****SALES SUMMARY BY REPRESENTATIVE*****				
4	NAME	REGION	CROWN	MONARCH	CURIO	TOTAL	COMMISSION
5	Rosco, R.	West	$18,750	$30,400	$12,000	+C5+D5+E5	+$C$14*C5+$D$14*D5+$E$14*E5
6	Mann, G.	West	18,558	58,388	0	+C6+D6+E6	+$C$14*C6+$D$14*D6+$E$14*E6
7	Cox, B.	Middle	25,900	38,903	280	+C7+D7+E7	+$C$14*C7+$D$14*D7+$E$14*E7
8	Taylor, A.	Middle	15,570	32,005	730	+C8+D8+E8	+$C$14*C8+$D$14*D8+$E$14*E8
9	Allen, H.	East	22,460	32,055	5,050	+C9+D9+E9	+$C$14*C9+$D$14*D9+$E$14*E9
10	Hill, P.	East	28,067	24,660	25,440	+C10+D10+E10	+$C$14*C10+$D$14*D10+$E$14*E10
11							
12	TOTALS		@SUM(C5..C10)	@SUM(D5..D10)	@SUM(E5..E10)	@SUM(F5..F10)	@SUM(G5..G10)
13							
14	COMMISSION RATE		5.5%	7.0%	4.0%		
15							
16			*****SALES SUMMARY BY REGION*****				
17		REGION	CROWN	MONARCH	CURIO	TOTAL	
18		West	+C5+C6	+D5+D6	+E5+E6	+C18+D18+E18	
19		Middle	+C7+C8	+D7+D8	+E7+E8	+C19+D19+E19	
20		East	+C9+C10	+D9+D10	+E9+E10	+C20+D20+E20	

FIGURE 8–8 Actual Content of Formula Cells   *This figure illustrates the actual content of the cells in Figure 8–7 that contain formulas. In an actual spreadsheet display, the formulas would be resolved when displayed (F5 would appear as $61,150).*

The use of predefined functions can save much time. For example, what if the range to be added were C5..C100? Other spreadsheet functions include trigonometric functions, square roots, comparisons of values, manipulations of strings of data, computation of net present value and internal rate of return, and a variety of techniques for statistical analysis.

B. J. McCue has included a "Statistical Sales Summary" in Rows 22 through 27 of the spreadsheet template (see Figure 8–9). The summary uses three common statistical functions: low or minimum (@MIN), average (@AVG), and high or maximum (@MAX). For example, @MIN(C5..C10), the statistical function in C24 of Figure 8–9, determines the minimum sales amount for the Crown. The actual formulas in Rows 22 through 27 are shown in Figure 8–10. Vendors of spreadsheet software create slightly different names for their functions.

FIGURE 8–9 Spreadsheet Functions   *The "Statistical Sales Summary" portion of the template is extrapolated from the data in the "Sales Summary by Representative" portion (see Figure 8–7). The statistical summary employs the minimum (@MIN), average (@AVG), and maximum (@MAX) functions (see Figure 8–10).*

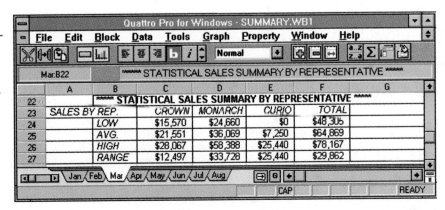

A	A	B	C	D	E	F
22			*****STATISTICAL SALES SUMMARY BY REPRESENTATIVE*****			
23	SALES BY REP.		CROWN	MONARCH	CURIO	TOTAL
24		LOW	@MIN(C5..C10)	@MIN(D5..D10)	@MIN(E5..E10)	@MIN(F5..F10)
25		AVG.	@AVG(C5..C10)	@AVG(D5..D10)	@AVG(E5..E10)	@AVG(F5..F10)
26		HIGH	@MAX(C5..C10)	@MAX(D5..D10)	@MAX(E5..E10)	@MAX(F5..F10)
27		RANGE	+C26-C24	+D26-D24	+E26-E24	+F26-F24

FIGURE 8–10 Actual Content of Formula Cells *This figure illustrates the actual content of the cells in Figure 8–9 that contain formulas.*

Formatting Data for Readability The appearance of data in the spreadsheet of Figures 8–7 and 8–9 has been modified to enhance readability. For example, the value .055 was entered as the rate of commission for the Crown in C14 (Figure 8–7), but it appears in the spreadsheet display as a percent (5.5%). This is because the range C14..E14 was *formatted* so the values are automatically displayed as percentages with one decimal place rather than as decimals.

All currency amounts in the spreadsheet template of Figure 8–7 were entered without commas or dollar signs. The currency amounts are formatted so that commas and a dollar sign (first row and totals) are inserted. For example, in Figure 8–7 the value for R. Rosco's Crown sales was entered as 18750 in C5, which is formatted for currency. Notice that it is displayed as $18,750.

Numeric data can be defined so they are displayed with a fixed number of places to the right of the decimal point. In Figure 8–7, the format of the sales data in the range C5..C10 is currency with the number of decimal places fixed at zero (for example, $18,750). Numbers with more decimal digits than specified in the format are rounded when displayed. The amounts in the "COMMISSION" column of the spreadsheet of Figure 8–7 are formatted to be displayed as currency with two decimal places (for example, $3,639.25).

Putting Spreadsheet Software to Work

The possibilities of what B. J. McCue, you, and others can do with spreadsheet software and micros are endless. Find any set of numbers and you have identified a potential application for spreadsheet software.

Spreadsheet Templates The spreadsheet in Figures 8–7 and 8–9 is a *template,* or a model, for B. J. McCue's monthly sales summary. All B. J. has to do is enter the sales data for the current month in the range C5..E10. All other data are calculated with formulas.

Most spreadsheet applications eventually take the form of a spreadsheet template. Once created, the template becomes the basis for handling a certain type of data (for example, monthly sales data).

Spreadsheet templates are modified easily. For example, any of these modifications of Figures 8–7 and 8–9 would require only a few minutes.

- Add another column to accommodate a new product.
- Delete a row to accommodate one less salesperson.
- Compute the standard deviation for Crown sales data.
- Change the rate of commission for the Crown from 5.5% to 6.0%.
- Sort the sales summary portion (A5..G10) alphabetically by name.
- Sort the sales summary portion (A5..G10) in descending order by commission.

"What If" Analysis   The real beauty of a spreadsheet is that if you change the value of a cell, all other affected cells are revised accordingly. This capability makes spreadsheet software the perfect tool for "what if" analysis. For example, B. J. McCue used the current data to assess how commissions might be affected if each of the rates of commission were increased by 0.5% (for example, from 5.5% to 6.0% for the Crown). The resulting spreadsheet in Figure 8–11 indicates that the salesperson earning the highest commission (G. Mann) would have earned almost $400 more—$5,493 versus $5,108—under the proposed commission rates.

Spreadsheet Graphics   Most commercial spreadsheet packages are *integrated packages* that combine spreadsheet, presentation graphics, and database capabilities. The graphics component enables users to present spreadsheet data as business graphs such as the graph shown in Figure 8–12. The user responds to a series of prompts to generate a graph. The first prompt asks the user to select the type of graph to be generated. The user then identifies the source of the data, enters labels and titles, and so on. In Figure 8–12 the sales figures for each region (Range C18..E20) are plotted in a stacked-bar graph. The resulting graph permits B. J. McCue to understand better the regional distribution of sales for each of the three products. Chapter 9, "Graphics, Multimedia, Communications, and Other PC Software," contains a detailed discussion of presentation graphics.

Database Capabilities of Spreadsheet Software   The database component of an integrated spreadsheet package provides the user with many features of a dedicated database package—all within the context of the rows and columns of a spreadsheet. When used as a database tool, spreadsheet software organizes fields, records, and files into columns, rows, and tables, respectively. With spreadsheet software, as with database software, you can retrieve, view, and print records based on preset conditions. These database capabilities are discussed in the next section.

FIGURE 8–11 Spreadsheet "What If" Analysis   *"What if" each of the commission rates were increased by 0.5%? This spreadsheet reflects the commissions that would have been earned had the increase been in effect.*

	A	B	C	D	E	F	G
1			MONTHLY SALES SUMMARY--MARCH				
2							
3			**** SALES SUMMARY BY REPRESENTATIVE ****				
4	NAME	REGION	CROWN	MONARCH	CURIO	TOTAL	COMMISSION
5	Rosco, R.	West	$18,750	$30,400	$12,000	$61,150	$3,945.00
6	Mann, G.	West	18,558	58,388	0	76,946	$5,492.58
7	Cox, B.	Middle	25,900	38,903	280	65,083	$4,484.33
8	Taylor, A.	Middle	15,570	32,005	730	48,305	$3,367.43
9	Allen, H.	East	22,460	32,055	5,050	59,565	$3,978.98
10	Hill, P.	East	28,087	24,660	26,440	78,167	$4,678.32
11							
12	TOTALS		$129,305	$216,411	$43,500	$389,216	$25,946.63
13							
14	COMMISSION RATE		6.0%	7.5%	4.5%		

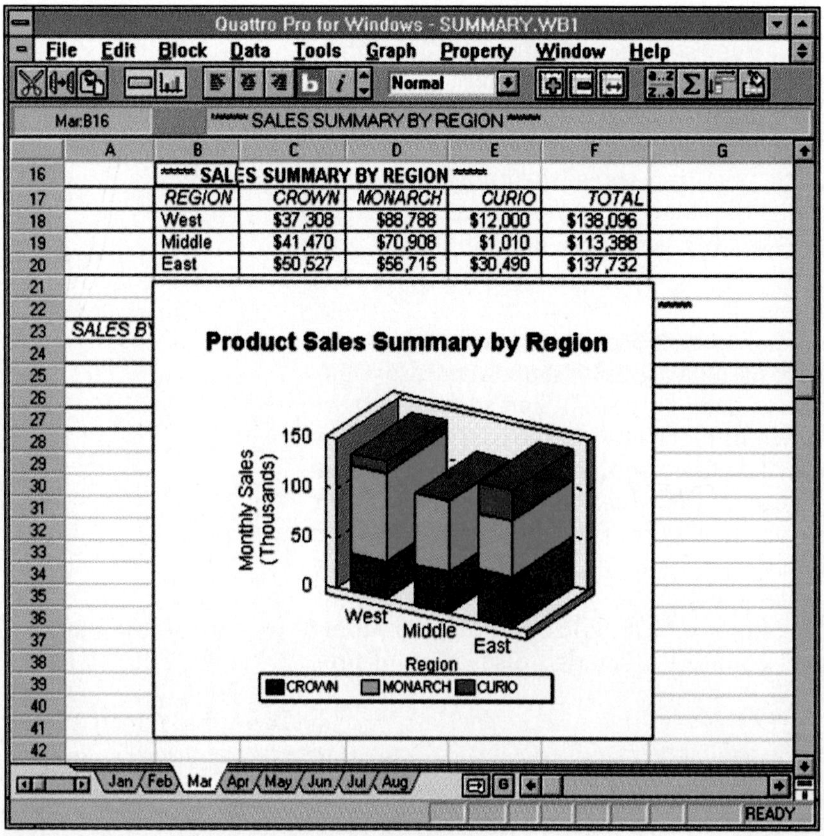

Quattro Pro for Windows - SUMMARY.WB1

File   Edit   Block   Data   Tools   Graph   Property   Window   Help

Normal

Mar:B16   ~~~~ SALES SUMMARY BY REGION ~~~~

	A	B	C	D	E	F	G
16		~~~~ SALES SUMMARY BY REGION ~~~~					
17		REGION	CROWN	MONARCH	CURIO	TOTAL	
18		West	$37,308	$88,788	$12,000	$138,096	
19		Middle	$41,470	$70,908	$1,010	$113,388	
20		East	$50,527	$56,715	$30,490	$137,732	
21							
22						~~~~	
23	SALES B\						

Product Sales Summary by Region

Monthly Sales (Thousands)

150 100 50 0

West   Middle   East

Region

■ CROWN   ■ MONARCH   ■ CURIO

Jan Feb Mar Apr May Jun Jul Aug

READY

FIGURE 8–12 Spreadsheet Graphs   *Regional sales for each of the three products (Range C18..E20) are represented in this stacked-bar graph. This graph can be displayed full screen or it can be printed.*

CD-ROM PUBLISHING LOWERS THE COST OF DISTRIBUTING DATA

For Shearson Lehman Brothers, Inc., it was a sobering realization. It was paying more than $1 million to use its PCs to access on-line financial information services that charge $20 to $400 an hour. Clearly, the company needed the data. An investment banker's recommendations are only as good as the data backing up those recommendations. But wasn't there a cheaper way to gather it? For Shearson Lehman and an increasing number of companies, research centers, universities, and libraries, CD-ROM publishing was the answer.

CD-ROM publishing refers to the collection and distribution of large financial, scientific, technical, legal, medical, and bibliographic databases, as well as reference works, catalogs, and manuals, on CD-ROM disks. Shearson Lehman's solution was to order a $30,000 subscription to One Source, a CD-ROM–based financial, business, and reference database from Lotus Development Corporation, which is updated weekly.

Information Service Offerings

One Source is just one of the more than 4000 databases offered on CD-ROM disks, often by the same information services that operate the on-line databases. Dialog Information Services, Inc., for example, offers many of its 400 databases both on-line and on CD-ROM. Other offerings include regularly updated databases on engineering developments, cancer research, and environmental issues surrounding pollution and hazardous wastes. Some of the databases contain bibliographic citations only; others contain the full text of articles, sometimes including all illustrations. And at many public libraries, the dog-eared *Reader's Guide to Periodical Literature* has been replaced by workstations that sport a CD-ROM drive, an ink-jet printer, and InfoTrac, a service from Information Access Company. InfoTrac is a collection of CD-ROM–based indexes for more than 1100 popular magazines and journals; about 800 business, management, and trade journals; and such leading newspapers as *The New York Times* and *The Wall Street Journal.* Other InfoTrac CD-ROM disks let users retrieve financial and investment data.

Users can search InfoTrac by key words, such as *computer graphics,* or they can conduct an extended search that combines key words, such as *computer graphics* and *medicine.* Highlighting a cross-reference whisks users to the related topic; another keystroke returns users to their original location in the database. Instead of scribbling down partial citations by hand, users can print out a complete citation and, in many cases, an abstract, simply by tapping the "print" key. All entries indicate whether the library subscribes to the publication, while an index number provides a cross-reference to InfoTrac's collection of microfilm cartridges.

CD-ROM–based databases are also available for specific industries. One example is Sabrevision, a national database for travel agencies that is updated quarterly.

Manuals, Catalogs, and Software

The federal government is turning to CD-ROM publishing as a cost-effective way to publish the thousands of manuals, specifications, and guidelines the government issues for its own use. An 800-page manual from the Army Corps of Engineers, for example, costs more than $6 to print on paper, weighs 4 pounds, and costs $6 to mail. The same information can be put on one CD-ROM disk for a fraction of the cost. As a bonus, the disk can be searched more quickly than a paper document.

Shop manuals and parts catalogs also lend themselves to CD-ROM publishing. The catalog from Intel Corporation, the major semiconductor manufacturer, delivers some 25,000 pages of technical data, wiring diagrams, schematics, and photographs to 300,000 design engineers worldwide. The massive amount of data can be stored on just two CD-ROM disks. Automobile and truck manufacturers also are providing parts catalogs to dealers on CD-ROM; the dealers find it faster and easier than going on-line to access a central mainframe.

Some software is also being shipped on CD-ROM disks to reduce the sheer number of magnetic disks required to deliver sophisticated programs. Corel-Draw, a popular draw program, is even shipped with a CD-ROM drive.

Computerworld **on CD-ROM**   Computerworld, *which has been a leading newsweekly for the computer industry for decades, is now being published on CD-ROM. CD-ROM subscribers receive a quarterly update that contains full-text articles for the previous four years. Users can search over 25,000 articles in 30 seconds for topics of interest.*

8–3   DATABASE: A DYNAMIC DATA TOOL

With database software you can create and maintain a database and extract information from it. To use database software, you first identify the format of the data, then design a display format that permits interactive entry and revision of the database. Once the database is created, its data can be deleted or revised and other data can be added.

All database software packages have these fundamental capabilities:

1. To create and maintain (add, delete, and revise records) a database
2. To extract and list all records or only those records that meet certain conditions
3. To make an inquiry (for example, "What is the total amount owed by all customers?")
4. To sort records in ascending or descending sequence by primary, secondary, and tertiary fields
5. To generate formatted reports with subtotals and totals

The more sophisticated packages include a variety of other features, such as spreadsheet-type computations, presentation graphics, and programming.

Concepts

Creating a Database with Database Software   Many similarities exist between word processing packages and spreadsheet packages. With word processing, you see and manipulate lines of text. With spreadsheets, you see and manipulate data in numbered rows and lettered columns. This is not so with database packages. What you see on the screen may be vastly different from one package to the next. However, the concepts behind these database packages are very similar. The database example we give here is generic and can be applied to all database packages. The displays in the accompanying figures are taken from Paradox for Windows (a product of Borland International).

The organization of the data in a microcomputer database is similar to the traditional hierarchy of data organization (see Chapter 5, "Data Storage and

Students use database software to keep records relating to a wide range of activities: expenses (item, amount, date); friends (name, address, phone); intramural scores (opponent, score, date); courses (title, instructor, credit hours, term, grade); and so on.

FIGURE 8–13 Education Database: COURSE Table and TRAINING Table *The COURSE table contains a record for each course that BrassCo Enterprises offers its employees. The TRAINING table contains a record for each BrassCo employee who is enrolled in or has taken a course. The fields for each table are described in the text.*

Organization). Related *fields,* such as employee, ID, and department, are grouped to form *records* (for example, the employee record in the TRAINING table in Figure 8–13). Most PC-based database packages use the *relational* approach to database management, which organizes data into *tables* in which a *row* is equivalent to a *record.* One or more tables comprise a database. (In database software terminology, *file* and *database* are often used interchangeably.) In contrast to the traditional flat-file approach to data management (discussed in Chapter 5), a **relational database** accesses data by *content* rather than by *address.* That is, a relational database uses the computer to search the database for the desired data rather than accessing data through a series of indices and physical addresses on a magnetic disk.

The best way to illustrate the concepts of database software is by example. Ed Rockford, BrassCo's education coordinator, uses a PC-based database software package to help him with his record-keeping tasks. To do this, Ed created an education database with two database tables: COURSE and TRAINING. The COURSE table (see Figure 8–13) contains a record for each course that BrassCo offers its employees and for several courses at the State University.

BrassCo provides tuition reimbursement for selected courses at the State University. Each record (row) in the COURSE table contains the following fields:

- IDentification number of course (supplied by BrassCo; provides cross-reference to the TRAINING table)
- TITLE of course
- TYPE of course (in-house seminar, multimedia, college, or vendor seminar)
- SOURCE of course (BrassCo staff or commercial supplier of course)
- DURATION of course (number of hours required for an employee to complete course)

The TRAINING table (see Figure 8–13) contains a record for each BrassCo employee who is enrolled in or has taken a course. Each record contains the following fields:

- EMPLOYEE (name of BrassCo employee; last name first)
- IDentification number of course taken by employee (provides cross-reference to COURSE table)
- DEPARTMENT (department affiliation of employee)
- START (date course was begun)
- STATUS (employee's status code: *I*=incomplete, *W*=withdrawn from course, *C*=completed course)

The structure of the database table. The first thing you do to set up a database table is to specify the *structure* of the database table. You do this by identifying the characteristics of each field in it. This is done interactively, with the system prompting you to enter the field name, field type, and so on (see Figure 8–14). For example, in the first row of Figure 8–14, the *field name* is ID; the *field type* is A for "alphanumeric"; and the *field size,* or field length, is five positions. The field names for the COURSE and TRAINING tables are listed at the top of each table in Figure 8–13 (ID, TITLE, TYPE, and so on). An *alphanumeric* field type can be a single word or any alphanumeric (numbers, letters, and special characters) phrase up to several hundred characters in length. For *numeric* field types, you can specify the number of decimal positions that you wish to have displayed. Because the course durations all are defined in whole hours, the DURATION field is displayed in whole numbers (see Figure 8–13).

Entering and editing a database. Once you have defined the structure of the database table you are ready to enter the data. The best way to enter data is to establish a *screen format* that allows convenient data entry. The data entry screen format is analogous to a hard-copy form that contains labels and blank

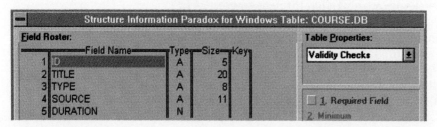

FIGURE 8–14 Structure of the COURSE Table *This display shows the structure of the COURSE table of Figure 8–13. The COURSE record has four alphanumeric (A) fields and one numeric (N) field.*

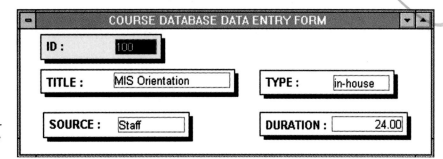

FIGURE 8–15 Data Entry Screen Format   *The screen format for entering, editing, and adding records to the COURSE table is illustrated.*

lines (for example, a medical questionnaire or an employment application). Data are entered and edited (added, deleted, or revised) one record at a time with database software as they are on hard-copy forms. The data entry screen format for the COURSE database table is shown in Figure 8–15. To enter the data for the COURSE table, the education coordinator issues a command that calls up the data entry screen in Figure 8–15, enters the data for the first record, then enters the second record, and so on. On most database systems, the records are automatically assigned a number as they are entered. Records can, of course, be added to the database and edited (deleted or revised) using the data entry screen in Figure 8–15.

Query by Example   Database software also permits you to retrieve, view, and print records based on **query by example (QBE)**. In query by example, you set conditions for the selection of records by composing one or more example *relational expressions*. A relational expression normally compares one or more field names to numbers or character strings using the **relational operators** (= [equal to], > [greater than], < [less than], and combinations of these operators). Several conditions can be combined with **logical operators** (*AND, OR,* and *NOT*). Commonly used relational and logical operators are summarized in Figure 8–16.

QBE: TYPE = in-house.   Ed Rockford wanted a listing of all in-house seminars; so he requested a list of all courses that meet the condition *TYPE = in-house* in the COURSE table (see Figure 8–13). The result is shown in Figure 8–17.

FIGURE 8–16 Relational and Logical Operators

Relational Operators	
COMPARISON	**OPERATOR**
Equal to	=
Less than	<
Greater than	>
Less than or equal to	<=
Greater than or equal to	>=
Not equal to	<>

Logical Operators AND and OR	
OPERATION	**OPERATOR**
For the condition to be true:	
Both subconditions must be true	AND
At least one subcondition must be true	OR

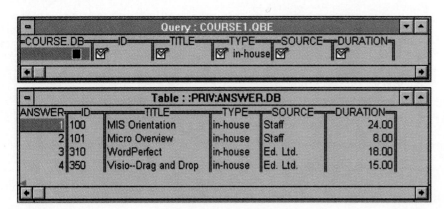

FIGURE 8–17 Query by Example, One Condition *All records in the COURSE table of Figure 8–13 that meet the condition TYPE = in-house (see criteria in top window) are displayed in the answer window (bottom).*

QBE: SOURCE = Staff OR TYPE = vendor. To produce the output in Figure 8–18, Ed Rockford set up his query by example to select only those courses that were taught by the BrassCo staff (SOURCE = staff) *OR* offered by a vendor (TYPE = vendor). In addition, the education coordinator can select which fields are to be displayed as a result of a query. For example, in Figure 8–18, Ed displayed only the TITLE, TYPE, and SOURCE fields. The OR operator can be applied between fields or within fields. For example, the query by example, *TYPE = college or in-house,* would display only the records of TYPE college or in-house.

QBE: Other examples. The following relational expressions establish conditions that will select or extract records (noted to the right of the expression) from the COURSE table in Figure 8–13.

QUERY BY EXAMPLE (COURSE table)	RECORDS DISPLAYED (ID)
TYPE=in-house *AND* DURATION=10	101
SOURCE=VidCourse *OR* =Takdel Inc.	202, 320, 330
DURATION>=15 *AND* <=25	100, 310, 330, 350
ID=CIS11	CIS11

These queries by example extract records from the TRAINING table in Figure 8–13.

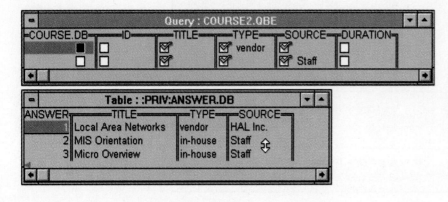

FIGURE 8–18 Query by Example, Two Conditions *All records in the COURSE table of Figure 8–13 that meet the condition SOURCE = Staff OR TYPE = vendor (see criteria in top window) are displayed in the answer window (bottom). In Paradox for Windows, the software package used in the database examples, expressions linked by the OR operator are placed on separate lines in the query by example window (top).*

QUERY BY EXAMPLE (TRAINING table)	RECORDS DISPLAYED (EMPLOYEE)
DEPARTMENT=Marketing	Adler, Bell, Johnson
START<=1/10/95	Johnson, Klein, Targa
STATUS=I *AND* DEPARTMENT=Finance	Austin, Fitz

Inquiries involving calculations.   Besides query by example, you can also make inquiries to the database that result in a display of calculated information. For example, Ed Rockford wants to know the total number of course hours taught by in-house staff. The query (SOURCE=Staff; DURATION: calc sum) and result (32 hours) are shown in Figure 8–19. The following table shows other queries involving calculations and their results.

QUERY BY EXAMPLE (COURSE table)	RESULTS
TYPE: calc count (count unique values)	4 (college, in-house, media, vendor)
TYPE=in-house; DURATION: calc average	16.25

Sorting Records   The records in a database table also can be sorted for display in a variety of formats. For example, the COURSE table in Figure 8–13 has been sorted and is displayed in ascending order by course identification number (ID). To obtain this sequencing of the database records, Ed Rockford selected ID as the *key field* and requested an ascending sort of the COURSE table. Database packages allow you to choose whether you want the *collating sequence* to be set up so that numbers are considered to be less than alphabetic characters, or vice versa. In Figure 8–13, the numeric IDs in the COURSE table are listed before those that begin with a letter.

Ed also wants a presentation of the COURSE table that is sorted by ID within TYPE. This involves the selection of a *primary* and a *secondary key field.* Secondary key fields are helpful when duplicates exist in the primary key field (for example, there are three records for TYPE=media). Ed selects TYPE as the primary key field, but he wants the courses offered by each TYPE to be listed in ascending order by ID. To achieve this record sequence, he selects ID as the secondary key field. A version of the COURSE table that has been sorted by ID within TYPE is shown in Figure 8–20. Notice in Figure 8–20 that the TYPE field entries are in alphabetical order and the three "media" records are in sequence by ID (202, 320, 330). If the need arises, Ed can perform sorts that require the identification of primary, secondary, and tertiary key fields.

FIGURE 8–19 Query by Example, Calculation with One Condition
The values in the DURATION field of the COURSE table of Figure 8–13 are summed for all records that meet the condition SOURCE = Staff (see criteria in top window). The result is displayed in the answer window (bottom).

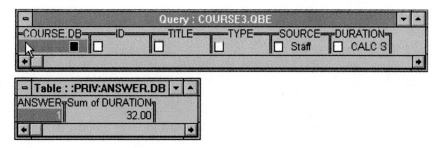

Table : SORT.DB

SORT	TYPE	ID	TITLE	SOURCE	DURATION
1	college	CIS11	Business COBOL	St. Univ.	45.00
2	college	CIS15	Mgt. Info. Systems	St. Univ.	45.00
3	in-house	100	MIS Orientation	Staff	24.00
4	in-house	101	Micro Overview	Staff	8.00
5	in-house	310	WordPerfect	Ed. Ltd.	18.00
6	in-house	350	Visio--Drag and Drop	Ed. Ltd.	15.00
7	media	202	4GL Programming	Takdel Inc.	35.00
8	media	320	Paradox for Windows	Takdel Inc.	30.00
9	media	330	Lotus 1-2-3	VidCourse	20.00
10	vendor	401	Local Area Networks	HAL Inc.	30.00

FIGURE 8–20 COURSE Table Sorted by ID within TYPE *This display is the result of a sort operation on the COURSE table with the TYPE field as the primary key field and the ID field as the secondary key field.*

FIGURE 8–21 Customized Report *This customized "Course Status Report" was compiled from the TRAINING table.*

STATUS: C

ID	EMPLOYEE
100	Johnson, Charles
100	Klein, Ellen
100	Targa, Phil
310	Day, Elizabeth
330	Targa, Phil

Count(STATUS): 5

STATUS: I

ID	EMPLOYEE
101	Massey, Rose
310	Fitz, Paula
330	Austin, Jill
330	Bell, Jim
CIS15	Mendez, Carlos

Count(STATUS): 5

STATUS: W

ID	EMPLOYEE
401	Adler, Phyllis

Count(STATUS): 1

Generating Reports A database is a source of information, and database software provides the facility to get at this information. A *report* is the presentation of information derived from one or more databases. The simple listings of selected and ordered records in Figures 8–17 through 8–20 are "quick and dirty" reports. Such reports are the bread and butter of database capabilities. These listings may not be fancy, but usually the user is more interested in the information than the format in which it is displayed.

Database software allows you to design the *layout* for and create customized, or formatted, reports. This means that you have some flexibility in spacing and can include titles, subtitles, column headings, separation lines, and other elements that make a report more readable. You describe the layout of the *customized* report interactively, then store it for later recall. The result of the description, usually called a *report file,* is recalled from disk storage and merged with a database to create the customized report. Managers often use this capability to generate periodic reports, such as a monthly status report.

Once a month Ed Rockford generates a "Course Status Report" from the TRAINING table (see Figure 8–13) that lists employees for each status: completed (C), incomplete (I), and withdrawn (W). The report can be displayed or printed as shown in Figure 8–21.

Putting Database Software to Work

Database software earns the "productivity tool" label by providing users with the capability of organizing data into an electronic database that can be maintained and queried (can allow user inquiries) easily. The examples illustrated and discussed in the "Concepts" section merely "scratch the surface" of the potential of database software. For example, databases with common fields can be linked to expand the information horizons its users (the ID field is common to COURSE and TRAINING databases). With relative ease, you can generate sophisticated reports that involve subtotals, calculations, and programming. In addition, data can be presented as a graph. You can even change the structure of a database (for example, add another field). The programming capability enables users to create their own microcomputer-based information systems.

8–4 PROGRAMMING

The discussions on spreadsheet and database software explain situations in which the user enters one instruction or selects one menu option at a time. Spreadsheet and database packages provide the capability to combine these instructions in a *program*. A spreadsheet or database program, like any other computer program, consists of a sequence of instructions executed one after another. These instructions are logically sequenced and assembled through the act of *programming*. **Programmers,** people who write programs, use a variety of **programming languages,** such as COBOL, BASIC, and dBASE IV language, to communicate instructions to the computer. Twenty years ago, nearly all programmers were computer specialists. Today, office managers, management consultants, engineers, politicians, and people in all walks of life write programs to meet business and domestic needs. And, some do it for fun.

An Example Database Program

One of the most popular database packages is dBASE IV. We will use the dBASE IV programming language together with the TRAINING database (Figure 8–13) as the basis for our discussion on programming. Every day, millions of dBASE IV programs manipulate databases, such as the COURSE and TRAINING databases in the examples in the last section.

Typically, a program will accept *input* (from the keyboard or a file), access disk *storage,* accomplish some *processing* activity, and provide some kind of *output* (to a disk file, a printer, or the monitor). The example program in Figure 8–22

- Allows the user to make an inquiry to the TRAINING database (*storage*) in Figure 8–13.
- Allows the user to enter (*input*) the name of an employee (for example, "Targa, Phil").
- Searches the file and identifies all records that involve the employee in question (*processing*).
- Displays a "Training History Report" (*output*) that contains all records that apply to the employee in question.

The Kurzweil VOICE system permits voice control of popular software applications, including spreadsheet, database, and word processing. VOICE has a 50,000 word capacity and is ready to recognize virtually any speaker's voice once installed. When using VOICE, spreadsheet and database users can enter data and commands verbally. For example, instead of entering the number 5483 via a keyboard, the user would simply say, "Five, four, eight, three."

```
****** TRAINING HISTORY PROGRAM (HISTORY.PRG) ******
*        This dBASE IV program allows the user to make an inquiry to the
*        TRAINING database.  The user enters an employee name to generate
*        an "EMPLOYEE TRAINING HISTORY" report for that employee.
******  ******  ******  ******

USE A:?\DB\TRAINING     && Activate TRAINING database
CLEAR                        && CLEAR the screen
@ 4, 20 SAY "EMPLOYEE TRAINING HISTORY"    && Display title
?                            && Insert 2 blank lines
?
ACCEPT"           Enter employee's name (Last, First): " TO NAME
CLEAR                        && Clear screen
@ 4,8 SAY "TRAINING HISTORY REPORT FOR:          " + NAME   && Display title
?
? "Department  Course ID  Status"  && Display header
? "======================================="

SET TALK OFF                 && Supress dBASE IV confirmation messages
GO TOP                       && Set record pointer to first record in database
****** Begin loop to search for records matching named employee
DO WHILE .NOT. EOF ()     && Do loop WHILE record is not end-of-file (EOF)
    IF EMPLOYEE = NAME  && Display dept., ID, and status of named employee
       ? DEPARTMENT + " " + ID + "        " + STATUS
    ENDIF
    SKIP                           && Advance record pointer to next record in file
ENDDO                         && End of loop
@ 11, 4 SAY "Status codes: C=complete; I=incomplete; W=withdrawn"
SET TALK ON                   && Restore default display settings
```

FIGURE 8–22 A dBASE IV Program *When executed, this database program enables a user to make an inquiry to the TRAINING database (Figure 8–13).*

Figure 8–23 shows an interactive session resulting from the execution of the program in Figure 8–22.

You could, of course, extract and display the information shown in Figure 8–23 by issuing a series of individual database software instructions. However, without a program, you would have to reenter the instructions each time you made a similar inquiry.

Problem Solving and Programming Logic

A single program addresses a particular problem, such as displaying a "Training History Report." In effect, when you write a program, you are solving a

```
                    EMPLOYMENT TRAINING HISTORY

        Enter employee's name (Last,First):   Targa, Phil
```

```
              TRAINING HISTORY REPORT FOR:  Targa, Phil

        Department                Course ID                Status
        =================================================================

        Finance                   100                      C
        Finance                   330                      C

        Status codes:  C=complete; I=incomplete; W=withdrawn
```

FIGURE 8–23 Program Input/ Output *These displays show the interactive session that results from the execution of the program in Figure 8–22.*

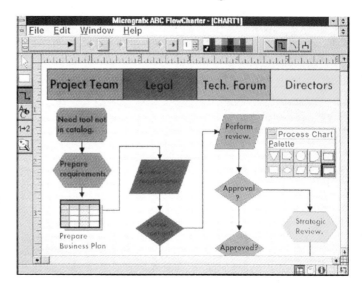

ABC FlowCharter, a Micrografx® product, helps to automate the flowcharting process. Flowcharting is used to document procedures (shown here) as well as programs. Symbols in a flowchart can be moved while maintaining the links between other symbols.

problem. To solve the problem you must derive a *solution.* And to do that, you must use your powers of *logic.*

A program is like the materials used to construct a building. Much of the brainwork involved in the construction of a building goes into the blueprint. The location, appearance, and function of a building are determined long before the first brick is laid. And so it is with programming. The design of a program, or its programming logic (the blueprint), is completed before the program is written.

Flowcharting

Several techniques are available to help programmers analyze a problem and design the logic of the program. One of the most popular techniques is **flowcharting**. **Flowcharts** are used to illustrate data, information, and work flow through the interconnection of *specialized symbols* with *flow lines*. The combination of symbols and flow lines portrays the logic of the program. The flowchart symbols commonly used for database programming are shown in Figure 8–24.

Each symbol in Figure 8–24 indicates the *type of operation to be performed,* and the flowchart (see Figure 8–25) graphically illustrates the *sequence in which the operations are to be performed.* The program flowchart of Figure 8–25 illustrates the use of these symbols by portraying the logic for the program in Figure 8–22.

Writing Programs

Over the next few years, you will gain experience with spreadsheet and database software in your working environment. Eventually you may find entering one instruction at a time to be too slow for your information and processing needs. When this happens, you or somebody else may need to write some programs to meet these needs. Each program is a project. There are certain steps a programmer takes to address a programming problem and write a program. These seven steps are summarized in Figure 8–26.

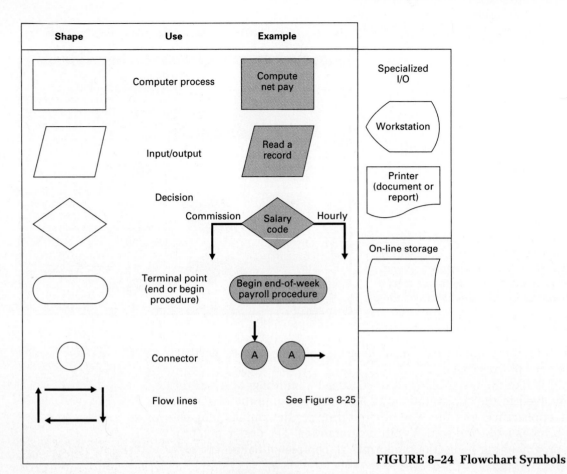

FIGURE 8–24 Flowchart Symbols

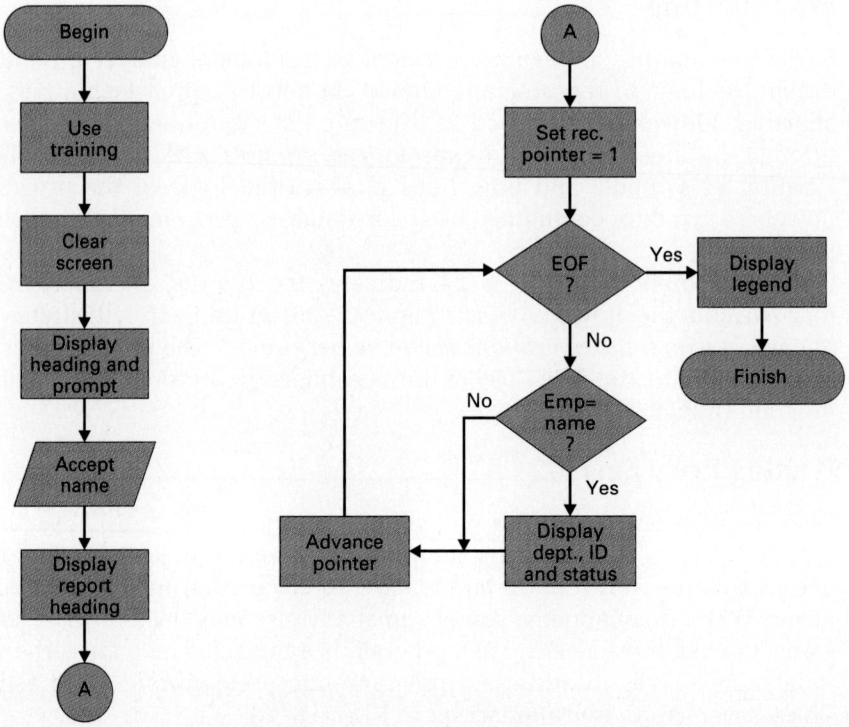

FIGURE 8–25 Program Flowchart *This flowchart graphically illustrates the logic of the dBASE IV program in Figure 8–22.*

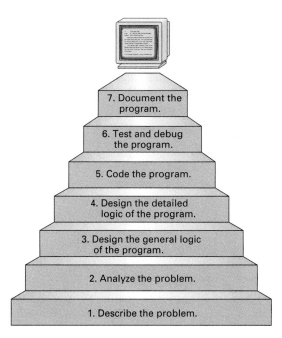

FIGURE 8–26 Steps in Writing a Program

IMPORTANT TERMS AND SUMMARY OUTLINE

absolute cell addressing	flowcharting	query by example (QBE)
argument	function	range
arithmetic operator	logical operator	relational database
cell	pointer	relational operator
cell address	programmers	relative cell addressing
flowchart	programming language	template

8–1 Data Management in Practice The background knowledge you learned earlier in this course can help you be an effective user of spreadsheet, database, and other data management software.

8–2 The Spreadsheet: The Magic Matrix Spreadsheets are simply an electronic alternative to thousands of manual tasks that involve rows and columns of data. The primary example used in this chapter illustrates spreadsheet concepts in a spreadsheet **template** of a monthly sales summary.

Spreadsheets are organized in a tabular structure of rows and columns. The intersection of a particular row and column designates a **cell**. During operations, data are referred to by their **cell addresses**. The **pointer** can be moved around the spreadsheet to any cell address with the arrow keys.

To make an entry, edit, or replace an entry in a spreadsheet, move the pointer to the appropriate cell.

When in edit mode, revise the entry in much the same way you would revise the text in a word processing document.

The four types of **ranges** are a single cell, all or part of a column of adjacent cells, all or part of a row of adjacent cells, and a rectangular block of cells. A particular range is depicted by the addresses of the endpoint cells (for example, C5..E10).

An entry to a cell is classified as label, numeric, formula, or date/time. A label entry is any string of alphanumeric text (spaces included) that occupies a particular cell. A numeric entry is any number. A cell may contain a formula, but it is the numeric results that are displayed in the spreadsheet. Spreadsheet formulas use standard programming notation for **arithmetic operators**.

The **relative cell address** is based on its position in relation to the cell containing the formula. When you copy, or replicate, a formula to another cell, the relative cell addresses in the formula are revised so they retain the same position in relation to the new location of the formula. When a formula is copied, the **absolute cell addresses** in the formula remain unchanged.

Predefined **functions** can be used to create formulas that perform mathematical, logical, statistical, financial, and character-string operations on spreadsheet data. The function's **argument** identifies the data to be operated on.

The appearance of data in a spreadsheet can be modified to enhance readability by adjusting the column width and formatting the individual numeric entries.

A spreadsheet template can be used over and over for different purposes by different people. If you change the value of a cell in a spreadsheet, all other affected cells are revised accordingly. This capability makes spreadsheet software the perfect tool for "what if" analysis.

Integrated spreadsheet packages include a presentation graphics software module. This capability enables users to create a variety of presentation graphics from data in a spreadsheet.

8–3 Database: A Dynamic Data Tool Database software lets users create and maintain a database and extract information from it. Once the database is created, its data can be deleted or revised, and other data can be added to it.

Database software uses the **relational database** approach to data management. Relational databases are organized in tables where a row is a record and a column is a field.

In database software, the user-defined structure of a database table identifies the characteristics of each field in it. Related fields are grouped to form records. The screen format for entering, editing, and adding records

to a database table is generated automatically from the specifications outlined in the structure of the database table.

Database software also permits you to retrieve, view, and print records based on **query by example (QBE)**. To do this, users set conditions for the selection of records by composing a relational expression containing **relational operators** that reflects the desired conditions. Several expressions can be combined into a single condition with **logical operators**.

Records in a database can be sorted for display in a variety of formats. To sort the records in a database, select a primary key field and, if needed, secondary key fields. In most database packages, issuing a sort command results in the compilation of a temporary database.

Database software can create customized, or formatted, reports. The user describes the layout of the customized report interactively, then stores it for later recall.

8–4 Programming Spreadsheet and database **programming language** instructions are logically sequenced and assembled through the act of programming. **Programmers** use a variety of programming languages to communicate instructions to the computer. A single program addresses a particular problem. A typical programming problem involves accepting input, accessing disk storage, doing some processing, and providing some kind of output.

Flowcharting helps programmers analyze a problem and design the logic of the program. **Flowcharts** are used to illustrate data, information, and work flow through the interconnection of specialized symbols with flow lines.

REVIEW EXERCISES

Concepts

1. Describe the layout of a spreadsheet.
2. Give an example of a cell address. Which portion of the address indicates the row and which portion the column?
3. Give an example of each of the four types of ranges.
4. Give examples of the three types of entries that can be made in a spreadsheet.
5. Write the equivalent formula for @AVG(A1..D1) without the use of functions.
6. If the formula B2*$B$1 is copied from C1 to E3, what is the formula in E3? If the formula in E3 is copied to D45, what is the formula in D45?

7. List three different descriptors for the range A4..P12.
8. What formula would be entered in A5 to add all numbers in the range A1..A4?
9. What is the purpose of setting conditions for a database?
10. What is the relationship between a field, a record, and the structure of a database table?
11. Give examples and descriptions of at least two other fields that might be added to the record for the TRAINING table (Figure 8–13).
12. If the COURSE table (Figure 8–13) were sorted so that the primary and secondary key fields were DURATION and TITLE, respectively, what is the

company name for the third record? Records are sorted in ascending order for both keys.

13. What records would be displayed if the selection condition for the COURSE table (Figure 8–13) were DURATION > 20 AND TYPE = media?

14. Draw the flowcharting symbols for computer process, terminal point, input/output, and decision.

Discussion

15. All commercial spreadsheet packages manipulate rows and columns of data in a similar manner. What makes one spreadsheet package more desirable than another?

16. If you were asked to create a micro-based inventory management system for a privately owned retail shoe store, would you use spreadsheet software, database software, or both? Why?

17. Describe two types of inquiries to a database that involve calculations.

18. Under what circumstances is a graphic representation of data more effective than a tabular presentation of the same data?

19. Discuss the difference between a program and a programming language.

SELF-TEST (BY SECTION)

8–1 Generally, people are better prepared for learning data management software than word processing software. (T/F)

8–2 a. The term *spreadsheet* was coined at the beginning of the personal computer boom. (T/F)

b. Data in a spreadsheet are referred to by their cell ___address___.

c. The spreadsheet pointer highlights the: (a) relative cell, (b) status cell, or (c) current cell?

d. D20..Z40 and Z20..D40 define the same spreadsheet range. (T/F)

e. When the spreadsheet formula +H4*$Z$18 is copied from A1 to A3, the formula in A3 is ___+H6*. $Z$18___

f. The spreadsheet formula @SUM(A1..A20) results in the computation of the sum of the values in the range A20..A1. (T/F)

g. A model of a spreadsheet designed for a particular application is sometimes called a ___template___.

8–3 a. If the COURSE database table in Figure 8–13 is sorted in descending order by ID, the third course record would be Local Area Networks. (T/F)

b. The definition of the structure of a database table would not include which of the following: (a) field names, (b) selection conditions for fields, (c) field lengths.

c. The relational operator for greater than or equal to is ___> =___.

d. Which record(s) would be selected from the COURSE table in Figure 8–13 for the condition SOURCE = VidCourse: (a) 310; (b) 330; or (c) no records are selected?

8–4 a. Programmers use a variety of ___programming languages___ to communicate instructions to the computer.

b. Flowcharting can be used to depict the logic of a program. (T/F)

Self-test answers.   **8–1** F. **8–2 (a)** F; **(b)** addresses; **(c)** c; **(d)** T; **(e)** +H6*$Z$18; **(f)** T; **(g)** template. **8–3 (a)** T; **(b)** b; **(c)** > =; **(d)** b. **8–4 (a)** programming languages; **(b)** T.

9

GRAPHICS, MULTIMEDIA, COMMUNICATIONS & OTHER PC SOFTWARE

OBJECTIVES

To understand graphics software concepts.

To describe the functions of different types of graphics software.

To understand multimedia concepts and applications.

To identify hardware and software associated with multimedia.

To describe the purpose, use, and applications of micro-based communications software.

To grasp the scope of available PC software.

9–1   PC SOFTWARE: EXPLORING THE POSSIBILITIES

Word processing, desktop publishing (Chapter 7), spreadsheet, and database software (Chapter 8) are wonderful tools. Indeed, you could become an effective PC user and never venture far from the capabilities of these four high-visibility products. However, there is an ever-growing world of PC software that can improve your productivity at work and at home; give you much needed information; expand your intellectual and cultural horizons; amaze you, your family, and your friends; and provide you with endless hours of enjoyment. This chapter gives you an opportunity to explore the possibilities.

The chapter is organized in four sections. The first section introduces you to an array of graphics software options to help you create and work with images. The second section introduces you to the exciting world of multimedia. Multimedia applications combine text, sound, graphics, motion video, and/or animation. The third section discusses communications software—how to use it and what it can do for you. In the last section, we explore the vast array of software available to the adventurous user.

9–2   GRAPHICS: CREATING AND WORKING WITH IMAGES

A dollar may not buy what it used to, but a picture is still worth a thousand words. This time-honored maxim may be one of the many reasons for the explosion of graphics software. Graphics software facilitates the creation and management of computer-based images. It can help you create pie graphs, line drawings, company logos, maps, clip art, blueprints, flowcharts, and just about anything else that can be drawn in the traditional manner.

With over 400,000 software products from which to choose, where do you begin? Many people begin at a retail software store, like Egghead Software (shown here), that specializes in the sale of PC software. Egghead Software stores sell hundreds of popular software packages. But what about the other 399,000 plus packages? There are literally hundreds of word processing packages and thousands of math education programs, but only a handful ever adorn the retailer's shelf. Shelf space is at a premium and retailers tend to stock those with established sales momentum and volume sales potential.

Reasonably priced workstations, such as these by Hewlett-Packard, and user-friendly graphics software are major contributors to the rapid growth of computer graphics applications. Workstations have the power necessary to enable users to work efficiently with high-resolution graphic images.

Six dominant categories of graphics software are

■ Paint
■ Draw
■ Drag-and-drop
■ Presentation graphics
■ Computer-aided design
■ Screen capture and graphics conversion

We describe the function, concepts, and use of each in this section. However, before you can fully understand the capabilities of the various categories of graphics software, first you need to know the fundamentals of how images are displayed.

Displaying and Printing Graphic Images

Depending on the software and hardware you are using, graphic images are maintained as **raster graphics** or **vector graphics.** In raster graphics, the image is composed of patterns of dots called *picture elements* or *pixels*. Pixels are introduced in Chapter 4, "Input/Output Devices." (The enlarged view shown in Figure 9–3 illustrates the pixel makeup of the original image.) In vector graphics, the image is composed of patterns of lines, points, and other geometric shapes (vectors). The naked eye cannot distinguish one method of graphics display from another; however, the differences are quite apparent when you try to manipulate them.

Raster Graphics   Raster graphics, displayed as dot patterns, are created by digital cameras, scanners, graphics paint software, presentation graphics software, and screen-capture software. Dots on the screen are arranged in rows and columns. The low-end PC monitor has about 300,000 pixels in 480 rows and 640 columns. Very high-resolution monitors will have thousands of rows and columns and millions of pixels. Each dot or pixel on a monitor is assigned a number that denotes its position on the screen grid (120th row and 323rd column) and its color. On a monochrome (one-color) monitor, the pixel denotes the position and a shade of one color.

As with all internal numbers in a computer system, the numbers that describe the pixel attributes (position and color) are binary bits (1s and 0s). The number of bits needed to describe a pixel increases with the monitor's resolution and the number of colors that can be presented. Because the image is projected, or "mapped," onto the screen based on binary bits, the image is said to be **bit-mapped.** In conversation, the term *bit-mapped* may be used more frequently than the term *raster graphics.*

A bit-mapped image and the display of a word processing document share many similarities. Just as you can replace one word with another in word processing, you can replace one color with another in a bit-mapped image. Carrying the analogy one step further, you also can do block operations—move, copy, and delete—on a user-defined area in a graphics display.

Like television, a bit-mapped image is continuously projected onto the screen, one line of dots at a time. Any changes in the display are reflected immediately. **Animation,** or movement, is accomplished by the rapid reposition-

MEMORY BITS

Graphic Images

■ Raster graphics
  Image as pixels
  Bit-mapped image
■ Vector graphics
  Image as line
    patterns and
    geometric shapes
  Permits
    manipulation of
    objects within
    image

ing (moving) of an area of the screen. For example, animation techniques give life to video-game characters.

Vector Graphics   Vectors, which are lines, points, and other geometric shapes, are configured to create the vector graphics image. The vector graphics display, in contrast to the raster graphics display, permits the user to work with objects, such as a drawing of a computer. Draw software and computer-aided design software use vector graphics to meet the need to manipulate individual objects on the screen.

Vector graphics images take up less storage than bit-mapped images. Each pixel in the bit-mapped image must be fully described, even the background colors. Vector graphics are defined in geometric shapes, each of which can define the attributes of many pixels.

Printing Graphics Images   In general, printers provide higher-resolution output than screen displays. The resolution of a 300-dpi page printer is four times that of a VGA monitor, and lines that may appear uneven on a monitor will be more uniform when printed.

Paint Software

Paint software provides the user with a sophisticated electronic canvas. Although you can perform amazing feats with paint software, one important similarity remains between it and the traditional canvas: Whatever you draw on either one becomes part of the whole drawing. Because the canvas is a bit map, you must erase or draw over any part with which you are dissatisfied. For example, suppose you draw a green circle. You would not be able simply to replace the circle with a blue square. The paint software does not remember the circle or any other representation of an object on the screen. To replace the circle with the square, you would have to draw over (or erase) the pixels that make up the green circle, then draw in the blue square.

The user interfaces of paint programs are similar. Once you are familiar with the six items in the user interface on a typical paint screen, you are ready to use the program. Paintbrush is a paint program distributed with Microsoft's Windows. The Paintbrush user interface is illustrated in Figure 9–1 and discussed here.

- *Drawing area.* The image is created in this area.
- *Graphics cursor.* A point-and-draw device, such as a mouse, is used to move the graphics cursor to draw images and to select options. When positioned in the drawing area, the graphics cursor takes on a variety of shapes, depending on the tool selected. Outside the drawing area, it is an arrow.
- *Main menu.* Pull-down menus appear when any of the items in the main bar menu (top of screen) are selected. Go to the main menu to load and save drawings, zoom in on a particular area for detailed editing, change the attributes of the screen fonts, copy parts of the screen, and so on.
- *Tool box.* One of the tools in the tool box is active at any given time. Use the

SimCity 2000 creators used vector graphics–based draw software to develop a simulation game that allows players to run a city without first getting elected to an office. The player governs a population of simulated citizens, with competing interests, and tries to keep the city's services running while balancing a budget. Players can build schools, libraries, universities, roads, hospitals, a prison, and so on to meet challenges. They can also dig underground traffic tunnels and lay pipe for transporting water. Scenario challenges include the 1991 Oakland fire, unemployment in Flint, Michigan, and Hurricane Hugo hitting Charleston.

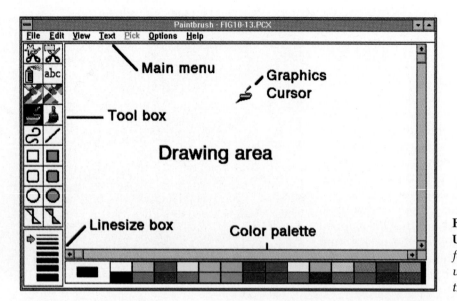

FIGURE 9–1 The Paint-Software User Interface   *The user interface for Paintbrush, which is distributed with Windows, is representative of paint programs.*

tools to draw; to move, copy, or delete parts of the screen; to create geometric shapes; to fill defined areas with colors; to add text; and to erase.

■ *Linesize box.* This box contains the width options for the drawing line.

■ *Color palette.* This box contains colors and patterns used with the drawing tools.

The examples in Figures 9–2, 9–3, and 9–4 illustrate some of the features of paint software. The screen in Figure 9–2 illustrates the steps in creating a PC image. Each step is described here.

Step A.   The *box* and *rounded box tools* (see tool box in Figure 9–1) are used to create the outlines for the monitor and the processor unit. Notice that Figure 9–2 used the *text tool* (denoted by "abc") to cross-reference the steps with letters.

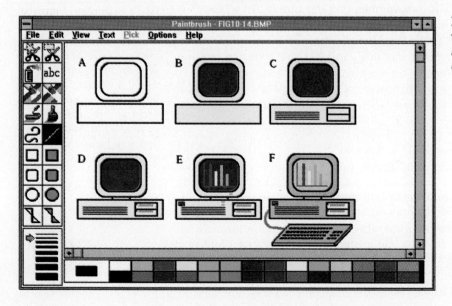

FIGURE 9–2 Creating an Image with Paint Software   *This screen shows various stages in the development of a PC image.*

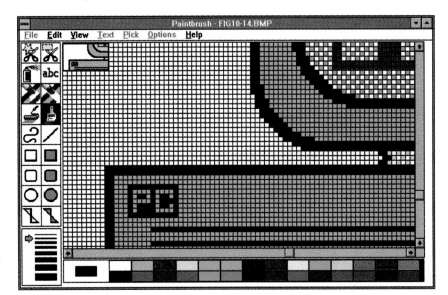

FIGURE 9–3 The Zoom Feature
In the illustration, the paint-software user has zoomed in on the upper-left corner of the processor box and the lower-right corner of the screen in the completed PC image in Figure 9–2 (Step F). Each square is a pixel. Any changes made in the enlarged version of the image are reflected in the window in the upper-left corner of the work area, which is the actual size, and in the actual image.

Step B.   The area containing the image created in Step A was *copied* to a position B, then the *paint roller tool* was used to fill in *background colors*. The image in each of the following steps was created from a copy of the image of the preceding step.

Step C.   The *line tool* is used to draw the vents on the front of the processor unit. Drag the graphics cursor from one point to another and release the mouse button to draw the line. The two box areas for the microdisks were created with the box and line tools.

Step D.   When the *brush tool* is active, the *foreground color* is drawn at the graphics cursor position. Use the brush tool for freehand drawing, such as the addition of the pedestal for the monitor. The microdisk slots and the disk-active lights are drawn with the line tool. Notice that the line width and the foreground color were changed to draw the disk slots and the lights.

FIGURE 9–4 The Shrink–Grow Feature   *The completed PC image in Figure 9–2 (Step F) is reduced and enlarged with the shrink–grow feature of paint software.*

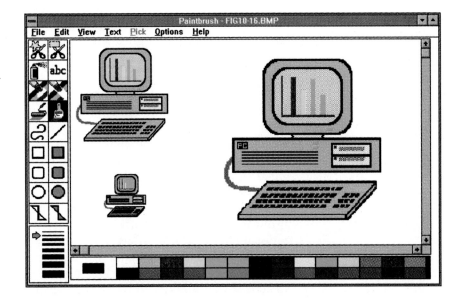

Step E. A logo (upper-left corner of processor box) and a bar graph are added. The *PC* in the black logo box was drawn one pixel at a time. The *zoom* feature explodes a small segment of the draw area to enable the user to draw one pixel at a time (see Figure 9–3). The bar graph is drawn with the line tool. Notice that each line is drawn with a different color from the color palette.

Step F. In this final step, the beige color is *erased* to gray. Paint software permits the user to selectively switch one color for another within a user-defined area or in the entire drawing area. The keyboard was drawn with the box, line, and erase tools, then *tilted* for a three-dimensional look.

Several other important paint-software features are illustrated in Figure 9–4. The medium-sized micro in the upper left corner of Figure 9–4 is an exact duplicate of the Step F bit-mapped image from Figure 9–2. The original image was selected with the *cutout tool,* then saved to disk. The stored image was then loaded from disk and displayed in a clear drawing area. The paint-software *shrink–grow* feature was employed to shrink and enlarge the image. Notice that parts of the image may be distorted when the image is shrunk (for example, the microdisk slots) and that image resolution suffers when the image is enlarged.

Once stored as a paint graphics file, images can be manipulated in many ways. For example, scanned images can be modified or colored. Even a frame from a video recording can be integrated into a paint drawing.

Draw Software

Both paint and **draw software** enable users to create imaginative images. Perhaps the best way to explain draw software is to address the differences between it and paint software. Consider the same example we used in the paint-software discussion—a drawing of a green circle, to be replaced with a blue square. As draw software permits you to isolate and manipulate representations of individual objects, you simply delete the entire green circle and copy a blue square to that position. This is not possible with paint software because it manipulates pixels, not objects.

Draw software relies on vector graphics, so a specific object can be moved, copied, deleted, rotated, tilted, flipped horizontally or vertically, stretched, and squeezed. Think of a screen image produced by draw software as a collage of one or more objects.

Drag-and-Drop Software

Paint and draw software demand that the user possess considerable drawing skills. That is, it is not enough to understand the use of the software, you also must be able to create the image from scratch. **Drag-and-drop software** is designed for those who have an ongoing need to create drawings and diagrams but are not graphics specialists and artists. With drag-and-drop software, users drag ready-made shapes from application-specific stencils to the desired position on the drawing area (see Figure 9–5). Each stencil addresses a particular application. For example, the user can select stencils for flowcharting, organizational charts, network diagrams, landscaping, maps, plant layout, bath and kitchen planning, various engineering schematics, marketing, project management, vehicle accident reporting, business graphics, and many more. Even stencils with dinosaurs and castles are available for child's play.

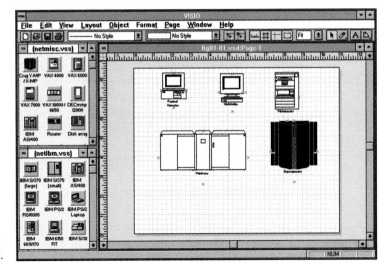

FIGURE 9–5 Drag-and-Drop Software
Visio, a product of Shapeware, Inc., lets you create professional looking drawings. Two Visio templates are open to the left of the drawing area. Images are chosen then dragged to the drawing area and dropped. Once positioned on the drawing area, images can be moved and resized to meet user needs.

In drag-and-drop software, the shapes are intelligent; that is, they can take on different forms, proportions, colors, and other properties, depending on the context in which they are used. Drag-and-drop software enables you to *glue* the shapes together such that the shapes stay connected even if one of them is moved.

Presentation Graphics

Using Technology to Make the Point Surprisingly, computer-generated business graphics is a fairly recent application of computers. With few exceptions, most computer-generated graphic outputs of 15 years ago were for engineers and researchers. Managers of business units who wanted a pie graph or a bar graph had it produced manually by the drafting department. This could take anywhere from a few days to weeks. Most managers, unwilling to wait, continued preparing reports and presentations in the traditional tabular manner—rows and columns of data.

Today, managers of business units have powerful microcomputers and user-friendly **presentation graphics software** that allow them to create in seconds a variety of visually appealing and informative presentation graphics. To capture and reproduce these graphic images, they use printers and desktop plotters (for paper and transparency acetates), desktop film recorders (for 35-mm slides), and screen image projectors (to project an image onto a large screen).

Output Options With presentation graphics software, you can create a variety of graphics from data in a spreadsheet or a database, or you can enter the data within the presentation graphics program. Among the most popular presentation graphics are **pie graphs** and **bar graphs** (see Figures 9–6 and 9–7). It is also possible to produce other types of graphs, range bar charts, and scatter diagrams, annotated with *titles, labels,* and *legends.*

Most spreadsheet and database packages come with presentation graphics software (see Figure 8–12 in Chapter 8). However, dedicated presentation graphics packages have a wider range of features that enable you to prepare

FIGURE 9–6 Pie Graph

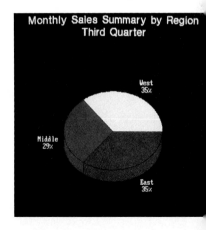

FIGURE 9–7 Bar Graph

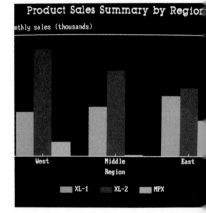

more dynamic and visually appealing graphics. Dedicated presentation graphics packages provide users with the tools they need to customize their graphs. For example, a transportation company can add another dimension to a sales-summary bar graph by topping the bars with clip art that represents the sales area (a bar of soap, an airplane, a refrigerator).

Besides traditional business graphs, presentation graphics software provides the ability to prepare *text charts* (see lists of key points in Figure 9–8), *organization charts* (such as the block charts in Figure 9–9 showing the hierarchical structure of an organization), and *maps.*

Besides offering the ability to prepare graphs and charts from user-supplied data, some presentation graphics packages let you create and store original drawings. This capability is functionally similar to that of paint and draw packages, but without their sophisticated features. Companies frequently use this capability to draw and store the image of their company logo to insert on memos, reports, and graphs.

Another recently introduced feature of presentation graphics software is the *dynamic show* capability. The dynamic show capability enables you to assemble presentation graphics in a synchronized demonstration. The show is usually presented to a small group on a single PC, or it is projected onto a large screen with a screen image projector. The dynamic show capability provides a visually interesting transition between the various graphics. For example, the current graph or image can be made to *fade out* (dissolve to a blank screen) while the next is fading in. Or the current image can be *wiped* away with the next.

The dynamic show can be further enhanced with rudimentary *animation.* Animating presentation graphics involves the rapid movement of an object, perhaps the image of an automobile, from one part of the screen to another. The animation is accomplished by moving the object in small increments of about 1/4 inch in rapid succession, giving the illusion of movement. The judicious use of this capability can enliven any presentation.

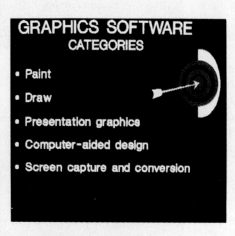

FIGURE 9–8 Text Chart

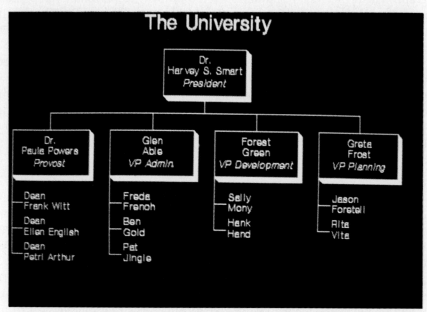

FIGURE 9–9 Organization Chart

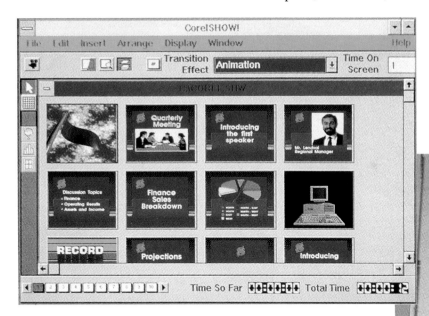

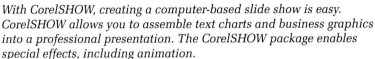

With CorelSHOW, creating a computer-based slide show is easy. CorelSHOW allows you to assemble text charts and business graphics into a professional presentation. The CorelSHOW package enables special effects, including animation.

Preparing a Business Graph   Usually the data needed to produce a graph already exist in a spreadsheet or a database. The graphics software leads you through a series of prompts, the first of which asks you what type of graph is to be produced—a bar graph, a pie graph, a line graph, and so on. You then select the data to be plotted. You can also enter names for the labels. Once you have identified the source of the data (perhaps a spreadsheet or a database), have entered the labels, and perhaps have added a title, you can display and print the graph.

Presenting a Graph   The use of sophisticated and colorful graphics adds an aura of professionalism to any report or presentation. The actual physical presentation of a graph depends on the available hardware (for example, color page printer). Computer-generated graphic images can be re-created on paper, transparency acetates, 35-mm slides, or they can be displayed on a monitor or projected onto a large screen. These output devices are discussed in Chapter 4, "Input/Output Devices."

Computer-Aided Design

Until recently, sophisticated **computer-aided design (CAD)** was not possible in the PC environment. Now high-performance micros can be configured with very high-resolution large-screen monitors, a variety of pointing and drawing devices, plotters (of any size), and whatever else is needed to produce computer-aided graphics design. Traditionally, CAD applications have been associated with engineers and scientists; however, today's PC-based CAD has opened the door to all who do design work.

Computer-based animation is finding its way into many applications, from Saturday morning cartoons to business presentations. Animation can be defined as a sequence of pictures presented in rapid succession to produce the effect of motion. The pictures are hand-drawn or are generated from a computer-based database. Much of today's animation is done with the help of computer and animation software. An animator created this frame for "The Adventures of Thomas and Nardo," which is seen on Liquid Television on MTV, with ElectronicImage™ Animation System, three-dimensional animation software.

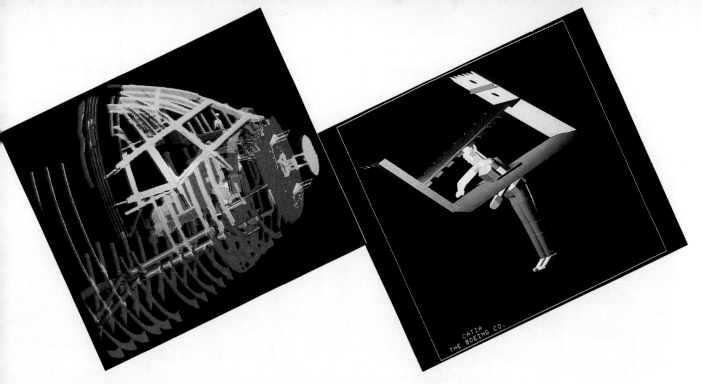

CAD has enabled Boeing to skip traditional physical prototypes. Boeing used a three-dimensional computerized modeling system to design its 777 transport, the largest product ever designed entirely by computer. The project uses eight mainframe computers and 2800 workstations to link the work of more than 7000 specialists on three continents. Although the project cost billions of dollars, the company expects that reduced reworking and time savings will cut costs by 20%. Computer simulations of solid three-dimensional models check for interferences between parts and, with the help of computer-generated human models, check the ergonomics, or the way the design and users interact. Here the system is being used to make sure a maintenance worker would have easy access to a vertical stabilizer.

Perhaps the best way to describe computer-aided design is visually, through its applications. Look at the photos above to see how engineers design parts and assemblies, how artists design logos for television programs, how architects design buildings, and how others use CAD. Although generic CAD packages can accommodate almost any design application, in some application areas they can be cumbersome. In those areas where CAD has become critical to success, specialized packages have emerged. For example, specialized CAD packages are available to help industrial engineers in plant layout, to help programmers and systems analysts with the design of an information system, to help architects with the design of buildings, and to help electrical engineers with the design of integrated circuits.

Screen Capture and Graphics Conversion

Screen-capture programs are memory-resident TSRs (terminate-and-stay-resident programs) that enable users to transfer all or part of the current screen image to a disk file. For example, you can capture the summary portion of a Lotus 1-2-3 display and integrate it into a report (a word processing document). The screen images in the figures in this chapter were captured by HiJaak Pro, a popular screen-capture program. A screen is captured as a bit-mapped image (pixel format). Once on disk, it can be recalled and manipulated with a paint program.

Unfortunately, there are no standards for the way graphic images are stored. Therefore, **graphics conversion programs** are needed so that graphics files can be passed between programs. Most of the popular programs that create graphic images (paint, draw, presentation graphics, spreadsheet graphics) do so in their own unique formats. Graphics conversion programs provide dozens of options. For example, you can convert an image created with a popular CAD program, AutoCAD (a vector graphics image), into Microsoft Windows Paintbrush (a bit-mapped image) for pixel-level editing. You also can convert a bit-mapped Harvard Graphics (presentation graphics program) file into a format that is compatible with a fax modem (an add-on board that can send and receive fax documents). If you do much work with graphics files, a good graphics conversion program is invaluable.

9–3   MULTIMEDIA: TEACHINGTHE COMPUTER TO SING AND DANCE

Probably no other computer "buzzword" is causing as much excitement today as *multimedia.* To understand the excitement, just consider the "show biz" appeal of these few examples.

- *Microsoft Bookshelf for Windows,* a single CD-ROM disk, contains seven reference works, including a "talking" dictionary that demonstrates correct pronunciations, a book of quotations that includes digitized recordings of such dignitaries as John F. Kennedy, an atlas that plays every country's national anthem, and a concise encyclopedia illustrated with high-resolution graphics and narrated animations showing how certain processes work. And, like any computer file, the CD-ROM can be searched by key word or phrase, taking a lot of the tedium out of research. *Bookshelf* is just one of a growing list of multimedia software titles that merge entertainment and education.
- A WordPerfect demonstration intersperses text promoting various films with what look like small color photographs. Click the mouse on any photo, though, and it comes to life, playing a "film clip." (Similar effects are already available for multimedia business presentations.)
- A computerized information kiosk at the Montreux Jazz Festival allowed

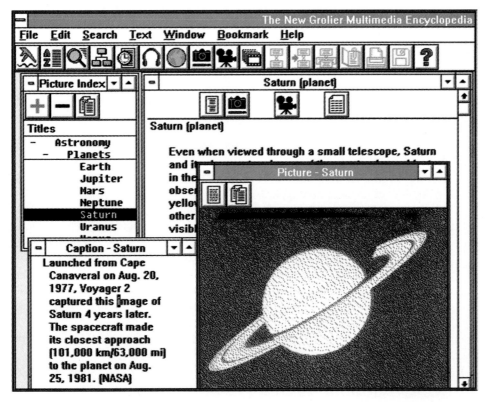

The multimedia encyclopedia is a good place to start your multimedia adventure. The New Grolier Multimedia Encyclopedia (shown here) contains over 10,000,000 words about thousands of people, places, and things. The CD-ROM encyclopedia uses the full capabilities of multimedia to enrich the presentation of information. For example, you can travel through time using maps that chart journeys filled with sights, sounds, and motion. How would you like to sail with Magellan or march with General Robert E. Lee? The encyclopedia offers narrated essays that use photos, music, and sound to explore such topics as the human body and space exploration. Thumbing through an encyclopedia will never be the same. In the example, the user searched for astronomy, selected planets, then Saturn. Open windows include a description of Saturn, a picture of Saturn, and a picture caption. The user can click on the movie camera icon for a motion video of Saturn.

users to call up biographies, photos, and performance videos of all the performers.

■ Thousands of workers are now learning Word, Lotus 1-2-3, and other popular applications via interactive multimedia tutorials that are enlivened with music, graphics, and motion. A 1990 Department of Defense study concluded that such tutorials take about a third less time, cost about a third less, and are more effective than traditional training methods.

The lure and range of such applications have sparked predictions that a multimedia revolution is just over the horizon.

Multimedia: A Definition

Multimedia is more sensual than traditional PC applications in that it tickles our senses while interacting with us and presenting us with information. In the multimedia environment, we can talk and listen to our PCs (in stereo). We can become part of the action as the screen comes alive with motion and sound. Multimedia has redefined what we can expect from our PCs, yet the term *multimedia* is frequently misused. You may see it used to describe everything from an animated, talking, and singing children's book on CD-ROM to a high-resolution monitor. Although there's no official definition, most computer experts agree that *multimedia* refers to a computer system that lets users access and interact with computer-based text, high-resolution still graphics, motion visuals, animation, and sound. Three elements in particular distinguish multimedia: sound, motion, and the opportunity for interaction.

Multimedia Hardware and Software: Making It Happen

What do you need to put the thrill of multimedia into your computing life? The answer depends, to a great extent, on what you want to do with multimedia. Most approach it in stages.

Getting Started with Multimedia   Do you want to experience multimedia? If so you will need the following hardware components.

■ *Personal computer.* You will need a PC with at least an Intel-386 level processor (see Chapter 3, "Inside the Computer").

■ *High-resolution monitor.* A VGA or better monitor is needed to provide vivid displays of images (see Chapter 4, "Input/Output Devices").

■ *CD-ROM drive.* The CD-ROM brings high-volume, low-cost storage to multimedia applications (see Chapter 5, "Data Storage and Organization").

■ *Sound card.* The sound card enables sounds to be captured and stored on disk and sounds to be played through external speakers (see Chapter 3).

■ *External speakers or headphones.* The sound card has a small amplifier that can play sounds directly to small speakers or headphones. If you wish to fill the room with sound, you can feed the sound from the sound card directly into your stereo system's amplifier.

■ *Microphone.* The microphone, which provides sound input directly to the sound card, lets you record sound in digitized format.

■ *Multimedia support software.* Starter multimedia software would normally include that which is distributed with the sound card. This may include a va-

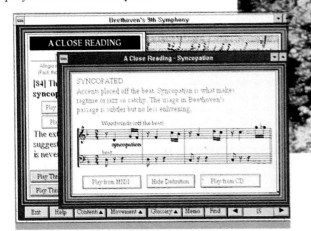

We can still learn a thing or two from the old masters. This multimedia presentation demonstrates how Ludwig van Beethoven used syncopation in his Ninth Symphony. *Selected passages are displayed, then played at the user's request.*

Through multimedia you can explore the coral reefs of the U.S. Virgin Islands without getting wet! In the illustration, a diver takes the user on a full-motion and sound tour of the coral reefs off St. Thomas.

riety of software. One type of software enables you to assemble sounds to be played in a user-defined sequence. Text-to-speech synthesizer software enables text on the screen to be read aloud to the user. *Authoring software* lets you create multimedia applications that integrate sound, motion, text, animation, and images. (Hypercard, an authoring software package, is bundled with all Macintosh computers.) Another software package lets you use your CD-ROM drive to play your audio CDs.

■ *Multimedia applications software.* Users can choose from over 10,000 CD-ROM titles, from flight simulators to encyclopedias. CD-ROM titles cost from $30 to $10,000. The lower priced CD-ROMs are for the mass market while the higher priced ones contain reference material, primarily for the corporate environment.

If you own any of the current Macintosh models, you already have most of the hardware needed to run multimedia applications. Just attach a *CD-ROM drive* and you're ready to go. If you already own a reasonably powerful IBM-PC compatible, look for a *multimedia upgrade kit.* These kits contain a CD-ROM drive, a sound card, multimedia software, external speakers, a microphone, and several CD-ROM titles. If your are planning to buy a new computer, consider paying 10% to 30% more for a PC configured with the basic multimedia components.

Growing with Multimedia The next stage of multimedia growth comes when you decide to *develop* multimedia applications—either your own multimedia title, a computer-based interactive tutorial, or a business presentation.

At this point, you may need to invest in some or all of the following hardware and software.

- *Video camera, videocassette recorder/player, audiocassette player, CD-audio player, and television.* These electronic devices are emerging as staples in many households. The video camera lets you capture motion video source material that can be integrated with multimedia applications. The videocassette recorder/player and audiocassette player are needed when you edit prerecorded motion video and sounds for inclusion in an application. The CD-audio player is handy when combining CD-based audio material with CD-ROM source material. The television provides an alternative output device.

- *Synthesizer.* A good synthesizer can reproduce a variety of special effects and sounds, including those of almost any musical instrument. A synthesizer with a keyboard can be played to create source music for inclusion in a multimedia application.

- *Video capture card.* This add-on card lets you capture full-motion color video with audio on magnetic disk (see Chapter 3).

- *Color scanner.* The color scanner is needed if you wish to capture images from hard-copy source material.

- *Applications development software.* If you wish to advance to developing sophisticated multimedia applications, you will need to upgrade to professional application development tools and authoring software. Figure 9–10 demonstrates how an authoring language uses design icons, each of which has a special meaning, to integrate multimedia elements into a logical sequence of events.

- *Source library.* The source library contains digitized versions of art, video, and audio that you can use as needed to complement a multimedia application.

A Confusion of Standards

Both consumers and software developers are confused by the lack of standards for multimedia. To a great extent, computer standards are forged in the

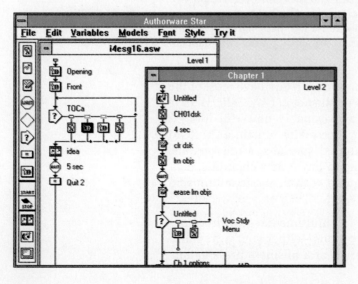

FIGURE 9–10 Authoring Software *Authoring software, such as Authorware Star, lets you integrate multimedia elements into a logical sequence of events.*

marketplace: The companies that garner the largest market share set a de facto standard that others follow. The IBM PC and Microsoft's MS-DOS are good examples of such standards. At this point a number of players are set to battle it out.

A highly publicized standard has been proposed by the Multimedia PC Marketing Council, a trade organization made up of Microsoft and a number of major hardware vendors. IBM is pursuing its own course, called Ultimedia.

Apple Computer maintains that its Macintosh models are multimedia-ready. With the bundled authoring system of HyperCard, many users are already developing their own multimedia applications. Macintosh multimedia applications have an especially strong presence in education.

In 1991, IBM and Apple shocked the computer world by announcing they would collaborate on a long-range five-point plan. One of the most significant points, at least for multimedia, is the creation of Kaleida, a company that will merge Apple and IBM research in animation, video, and multimedia, and create tiny multimedia machines that can run both Apple and IBM software.

The multimedia kiosk is popping up everywhere. This NoteStation™ kiosk is revolutionizing the way sheet music is selected, stocked, and sold. This music shopper is interacting with a touch screen monitor by simply touching the desired menu item (the "Change key" option in the photo). Kiosk users can choose to view, play, or print any of tens of thousands of titles.

Multimedia Summary   Multimedia possibilities stretch the human imagination to its limits. Already we see that multimedia will change the face of publishing. Many feel that *interactive books* based on multimedia technology have the potential to be more accessible and effective than traditional books, especially as learning tools. Early indications are that passive entertainment, such as TV and movies, may have to move aside to make way for interactive multimedia entertainment that involves the viewer in the action.

Multimedia applications touch our lives no matter which way we turn. They are in the malls to help us select the right product. Many magazines are delivered in multimedia format. The multimedia versions of board games look nothing like those of past generations. Multimedia products are beginning to invade classrooms from kindergarten to colleges. They help us learn Italian, appreciate music, and much more. We can explore the wonders of Tahiti, Kiev, or other exotic destinations simply by inserting a CD-ROM. It's amazing to think about what we can do now with multimedia. What we can do in the future boggles the mind.

9–4   MICRO-BASED COMMUNICATIONS SOFTWARE

The Function of Communications Software

Communications software is the key that unlocks the door to a new world of information. With communications software, a micro becomes more than a small stand-alone computer: It becomes capable of interacting with a remote computer, in the next room or in Japan.

Micro-based communications software performs two basic functions: terminal emulation and file transfer.

■ *Terminal emulation.* Communications software transforms a micro into a video display terminal (VDT) that can be linked to another computer. When an end user at a terminal logs-on to (establishes a link with) a host computer, the host immediately responds by asking the end user to enter the type of terminal being used. Of course a micro is not a terminal, but with the aid of communications software, a micro can emulate, or act like, one of the terminals that can interface with the host. When a micro is in **terminal emulation mode,** the keyboard, the monitor, and the data interface function like that of the terminal being emulated.

■ *File transfer.* Communications software enables the transfer of files between a micro and another computer. Once the link between the micro and host has been established, data, program, or text files can be downloaded from disk storage on the host computer to disk storage on the micro. Files also can be uploaded. The file transfer capability supported by communications software can be invaluable when you need to transfer files between computers.

Before accomplishing either of these functions, an electronic link must be established between the micro and the other computer. To establish this link the micro user initiates the *log-on procedure*. The log-on procedure, which is described in Chapter 2, "Interacting with Computers," requires the user to enter a preassigned *password* and *personal identification number,* or *PIN,* to gain access to a remote computer.

Preparing for an Interactive Session with a Remote Computer

When you use a PC, a modem, and data communications software to establish a link with another computer, the communications software will prompt you to specify the *telephone number* to be called and certain data communications parameters, or descriptors. These parameters may include

■ *Terminal emulation.* Specify the type of terminal to be emulated. The options might include the generic TTY, the DEC VT-100, DEC VT-52, IBM 3101, and others.

■ *Communications protocol.* Select protocol (for example, XON/XOFF, XMODEM).

■ *Data flow.* Select half- or full-duplex. Communication channels that transmit data in both directions, but not at the same time, are called **half-duplex.** A channel that transmits data in both directions at the same time is called **full-duplex.** Half-duplex channels do not permit the echoing of user keystrokes on the display screen.

■ *Data bits.* Specify the number of bits in the message (the bits within the start/stop bits). Typically, the character is transmitted with *seven* or *eight bits.*

■ *Parity checking.* In data communications, data in the form of coded characters are continuously transferred at high rates of speed. Both sending and receiving computers use a built-in checking procedure, called **parity checking,** to help ensure that the transmission is complete and accurate. This procedure checks to see if the number of bits transmitted equals the number received.

■ *Bits per second* (sometimes labeled as *baud*). Select the appropriate transmission rate: 300, 1200, 2400, 4800, or 9600 bps.

■ *Stop bits.* Stop is actually a misnomer in that it is actually a timing unit. Usually you would select *1* for micro-based data communications. Other options might be *1.5* or *2.*

While enjoying the comfort of home, this couple telecommutes to work. When they need access to their company's database or to check their E-mail, they run their communications software. The software enables their PC to emulate a VT-100 terminal so that they can establish an on-line link with their company's minicomputer.

■ *Echo.* Typically the host computer will **echo,** or return, the characters that are received from a micro; that is, the characters entered at the micro appear on the micro's monitor in the context of those originated by the host computer. In effect, the entire interactive session is displayed when the echo is on. When the host does not echo characters, the user will have to specify *local echo* to display characters entered via the keyboard.

Depending on the protocol and communications package, you may need to specify other parameters as well.

Communications software offers a variety of handy, time-saving features. For example, you can store the settings (parameters) for a particular bulletin board, information service, or mainframe computer in a *communications profile.* To establish a link with another computer, simply recall and activate the appropriate communications profile. From there, the communications software takes over and automatically dials and logs-on to the remote computer. It will even redial if it gets a busy signal. A micro with a modem and communications software can be on the receiving end as well: It can automatically answer "calls" from other computers.

Most communications software packages provide the feature that enables the micro to *capture* all input and output during an interactive session in an ASCII file on disk. At a later time the user can recall the session from disk storage with word processing software and browse through it at a more leisurely pace. Of course, all or part of the information gathered during an interactive session can be integrated into word processing documents, such as memos, letters, and reports.

Microcomputer Communications
Software in Practice

Personal computers that double as remote terminals can take advantage of a wide variety of communications-based applications.

Electronic Bulletin Boards   Most cities with a population of 25,000 or more have at least one electronic *bulletin-board system* (*BBS*), often sponsored by a local computer club. Members "post" messages, announcements, for-sale notices, and so on, "on" the computer bulletin board by transmitting them to a central computer—usually another micro. To scan the bulletin board, members again use communications software to link to the central computer. The person or group sponsoring the BBS is referred to as the **system operator,** or **sysop.**

There are hundreds of regional and national special-interest bulletin boards that focus on anything from matchmaking to UFOs. The Clean Air BBS deals with health and smoking topics. The U.S. Census Bureau sponsors several BBSs. People looking for jobs might scan the listings on the Employ-Net BBS. Catch up on which fish are biting and which are not by tapping into the Fly-Fishers Forum BBS. The do-it-yourselfer might want to log on to the Popular Mechanics Online BBS. Enter your own movie review on the Take 3 BBS. Lawyers talk with one another on the Ye Olde Bailey BBS. A Denver BBS is devoted to parapsychology. Some senators and members of Congress sponsor BBSs to facilitate communication with their constituents. A number of BBSs are devoted to religious topics.

The Internet is a global network that connects more than 40,000 networks, over a million host mainframe computers, and millions of users in more than 100 countries. Internet provides access for people in organizations with established networks and for individuals. Most colleges are on "The Net," as it is called. Individuals desiring access can obtain authorization to log onto a host or LAN with an Internet account or subscribe to a commercial information service, such as America Online (see screen capture examples), CompuServe, or Prodigy.

The Internet is the evolution of a national network that was founded over 20 years ago to link those interested in United States military research. In the early years, academic institutions were the foundation of The Net. Now all kinds of organiza-

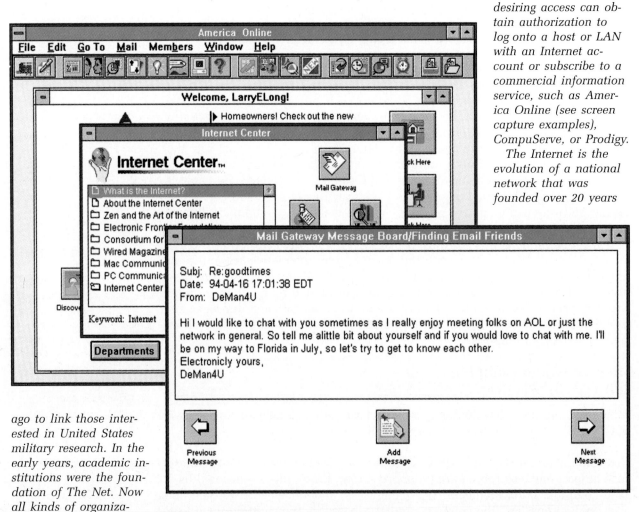

tions and people are on The Net. Traditionally, the Internet has supported three primary applications: electronic mail (E-mail), file transfer, and remote log on. E-mail can be sent from anyone to anyone or a group of people on the Internet. The message in the example (bottom) is an Internet E-Mail message from DeMan4U that was broadcast over one of the Internet's many electronic forums. The file transfer capability lets you send files from/to anywhere on the Internet. For example, you could send a spreadsheet file or a program. The remote log on capability lets users log onto a remote host or network. These applications remain the foundation of Internet services; however, applications are being added monthly. Hundreds of databases can be accessed via the Internet.

People on the Internet send/receive E-mail/files and interact with other networks through Internet addresses. The address has two parts and is separated by an @ symbol (for example, J_STUDENT@CIS.STATEUNIV.EDU). On the left is the user ID (usually the user's name). That portion to the right of the @ identifies the host or network. The host/network identifier follows the Domain Name System (DNS) hierarchy. At the top of the hierarchy are eight primary categories: EDU (education), COM (commercial), GOV (government), INT (international), and so on. Colleges are in the EDU category. At the next level might be the name of a college or business (STATEUNIV or XYZCORP). Large organizations might have subordinate identifiers (perhaps by department: CIS or PHYSICS). Note that the top level is on the right.

On-line Services   More and more PC users are subscribing to a commercial on-line service (also called an *information network*), such as CompuServe, America Online, GEnie, Prodigy, The Source, Dow Jones News/Retrieval Service, DIALOG, and NewsNet. The largest information services, CompuServe and Prodigy, have over a million subscribers each. These information services have one or several large computer systems that offer a variety of information services, from hotel reservations to daily horoscopes. Some, like Dow Jones News/Retrieval (financial news and information), offer specialized services.

In addition to a micro, to be able to take advantage of these information services all you need is a modem (the interface between the telephone line and a micro), a telephone line, and a few dollars. You normally pay a one-time fee and a monthly bill. For the initial fee, you get a password and personal identification number (PIN) that permit you to establish a communications link with the service. You also receive a booklet that lists the telephone numbers you dial to establish a link with the information service. If you live in a medium-to-large city, the telephone number you dial is usually local. Your monthly bill is based on how much you use the information service. Services provided by information networks are discussed in Chapter 1, "The World of Computers." These include news, weather, sports, entertainment, financial services, electronic mail, shop at home, reference, education, electronic bulletin boards, travel planning, and much, much more.

Telecommuting and the Cottage Industry   In the coming years, we will probably see business people carrying less work to and from the office. Why? With communications software and an ever-growing number of home computers, people won't need to lug their paperwork between home and office every day. A great many white-collar workers do much of their work on computers. Working at home is simply a matter of establishing a link between home and office computers. This is sometimes referred to as **telecommuting.** In the years to come, many white-collar workers will elect to telecommute at least one day a week.

The combination of microcomputers and communications software has also fueled the growth of *cottage industries.* The world has been made more compact with the computer revolution. Stockbrokers, financial planners, writers, programmers, buyers, and people from a variety of professions may not need to "go to the office," so they can live wherever they choose. Micros make it possible for these people to access needed information, communicate with their clients, and even deliver their work (programs, stories, reports, or recommendations) in electronic or hard-copy format.

Telecommuters use facsimile machines or fax modems (see Chapter 6, "Data Communications and Networking") in conjunction with communications software to fax

With about 2,000,000 paid subscribers in more than 135 countries, CompuServe is the largest of the on-line information services. CompuServe has over 2000 places for you to go and things for you to see. CompuServe's wide range of services includes an on-line look at the latest weather satellite photo (shown here), an electronic mall, hundreds of interactive forums, opportunities to download thousands of freeware and shareware packages, and much more. All on-line services support both Apple Macintosh (shown here) and IBM-PC–compatible computers. All information services offer access speeds up to 9.6 kbps. Some, like CompuServe, offer 14.4 kbps service.

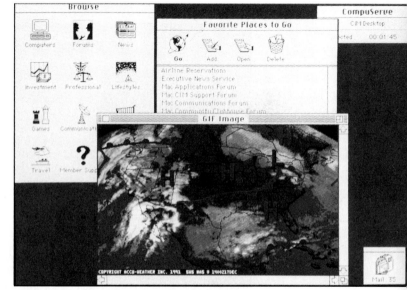

hard-copy material back and forth between the office. When using a PC to simulate a fax machine, the electronic image received via data communications can be viewed on the display, or if a hard copy is desired, it can be printed.

Summary   Microcomputers have placed the power of computers at our finger tips. Communications software expands that capability by enabling micro users to become a part of any number of computer networks. Once part of the network, a user can take advantage of the awesome power of mainframe computers, the information in their databases, and the opportunity to communicate electronically with others on the network.

9–5   PC SOFTWARE: THE REST OF THE STORY

The PC software story has no end. As you read this, tens of thousands of people are inventing new and better ways to use PCs. Today, there are over 400,000 commercial software products that cover everything from astrology to zoology. The following is but a tiny sample of what the world of PC software has to offer.

- *It's Legal.* Too often we put off preparing important legal documents because of the expense of involving a lawyer. It's Legal, from Parson Technology, helps you prepare a wide variety of binding legal documents, all of which are customized to your circumstances and the laws of your state. Save money by using It's Legal to create the legal documents for living wills (see Figure 9–11), health-care power of attorney, promissory notes, real estate leases, and much more.

- *Quicken.* Anyone who has attempted to balance a sadly out of kilter checkbook or consolidate tax information will appreciate Quicken for Windows (see Figure 9–12). Quicken is a comprehensive financial-management system

FIGURE 9–11 Preparing a Living Will   *You can pay an attorney $100 an hour to prepare a living will, or you can prepare it and many other legal documents yourself with* It's Legal, *a Parson's Technology product. The software prompts you to select those options to be included in the document.*

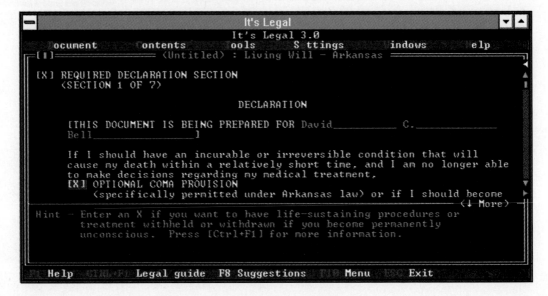

for both the home and small business. Quicken helps you manage your bills, bank accounts, investments, tax records, assets and liabilities, and much more. And best of all, you don't have to be an accountant to use it.

■ *World Atlas.* If you're looking for answers about the world we live in, then World Atlas, a product of Software Toolworks, Inc., is a good place to start looking (see Figure 9–13). It provides a geographic database filled with thousands of facts, statistics, images, and even national anthems for more than 200 countries. Information is organized in 11 major categories with more than 300 subtopics of interest from *animals* to *exchange rates.* Users can create new categories or subtopics and add their own information to the permanent database.

■ *Where in the World Is Carmen Sandiego?* Do you enjoy adventure, travel, and solving mysteries? If so, try chasing Carmen Sandiego (a Broderbund product) around the globe. Young sleuths follow clues to nab Carmen and her crew while learning geography (see Figure 9–14).

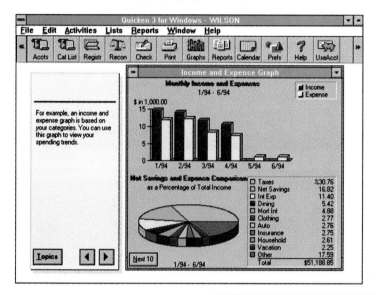

FIGURE 9–12 Quicken for Windows Tutorials   *Quicken for Windows, a popular financial-management package, helps you get up and running with on-line tutorials that walk you through various procedures, such as creating graphs and reports.*

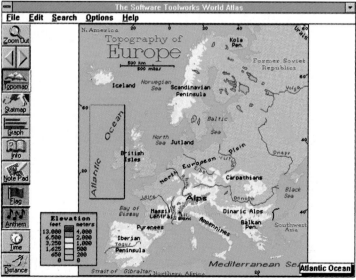

FIGURE 9–13 Topographic Map of Europe from World Atlas Software   *This topographical map is one of many in World Atlas. The map shows elevations throughout Europe.*

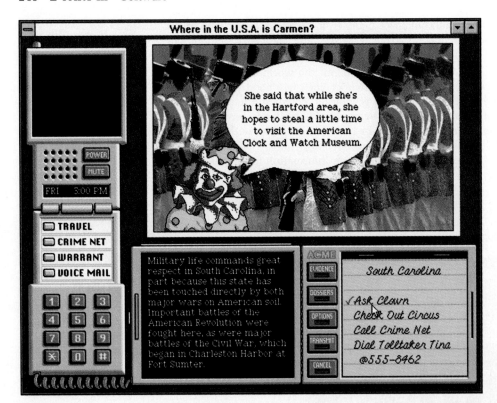

FIGURE 9–14 Where in
the U.S.A. Is Carmen
Sandiego? *Carmen
Sandiego, an elegant thief,
is the title character of the
popular computer game
that gives players clues
that can lead them to the
stolen goods.*

FIGURE 9–15 Studying
Anatomy on Computers
*Bodyworks gives you an
opportunity to view and
learn about all facets of the
human anatomy, from
head to toe.*

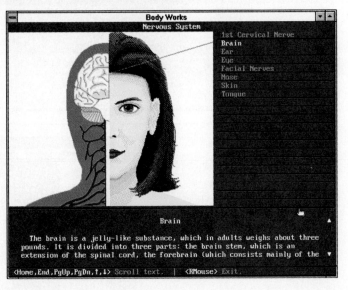

■ *Bodyworks.* We spend our lives looking at one another, but few of us ever
have an opportunity to look past the epidermis (skin). Bodyworks, from the
Software Marketing Corporation, takes you on an adventure in anatomy (see
Figure 9–15). You can you look inside the body at the skeletal, muscular, nervous, digestive, cardiovascular, reproductive, and other major systems.

■ *myHouse.* Are you considering remodeling your current home or building a
new one? Then perhaps your first stop should be myHouse (a product of
DesignWare). With myHouse (see Figure 9–16), you can create a three-

dimensional design of your kitchen, play with decorating ideas throughout the house, and even "walk through" the inside of the house to see if the design is what you want. myHouse takes the guesswork out of home remodeling and design so when you move in, you have exactly what you want.

■ *Personal Advocate.* Have you ever wanted to make a statement but did not know what to say or to whom to say it? Personal Advocate, from Parson Technology, helps you express your concerns in a forceful manner to the right people, whether consumer groups, government agencies, public officials, debtors, or others (see Figure 9–17).

FIGURE 9–16 Designing a Home *Not only can you design your own home with myHouse, you can also use virtual reality to take a personal walk through the project before you pound the first nail.*

FIGURE 9–17 Preparing Letter Requesting Removal of Your Name from Telephone Solicitation Lists *With Personal Advocate and a few keystrokes, you can reduce telephone solicitation, make yourself heard in Washington, collect money owed, register complaints, and much more.*

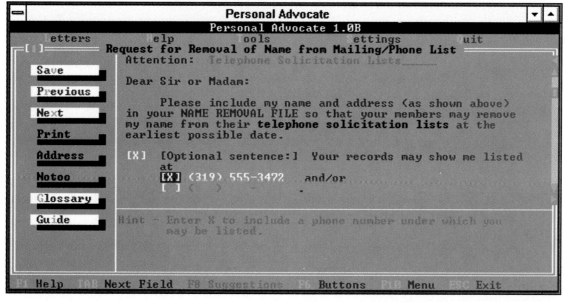

SHAREWARE: AFFORDABLE SOFTWARE

Thousands of software authors have created a wide variety of excellent programs, from business graphics to trivia games. However, most of these creative authors do not have the funds needed to launch their creations in the commercial software marketplace. (A million-dollar marketing campaign to launch a new software product would be considered minimal.) The alternative is to make their software available as *shareware.* Shareware is software made readily available to PC users via electronic bulletin boards, on-line services (Prodigy, CompuServe, and so on), and other low-cost distribution channels.

Here is how shareware works. A PC user logs-on (establishes a data communications link) to an electronic bulletin board or an on-line service, then downloads copies of the desired software to his or her system. Or, shareware diskettes can be ordered from any of the approximately 200 companies that specialize in the distribution of shareware. Shareware distribution companies sell diskettes containing shareware. You pay the same nominal amount for a diskette (from $1.75 to $5.00), no matter whether it contains a spreadsheet program or clip art. Or, you can order a CD-ROM containing about 1000 shareware programs from the Association of Shareware Professionals.

When you download or order shareware, it is implied that you will register the software with the developer if you like it and intend to use it. The registration fees vary from $10 for utility programs to $100 for full-featured word processing packages. Software developers use several methods to encourage registra-

tion of their software. At a minimum, developers provide technical support and update information to registered users. Some shareware is distributed with start-up documentation only: Complete documentation is sent to registered users. Some shareware developers make shareware enhancements available only to registered users.

A relatively small amount of the software available through electronic bulletin boards, on-line services, and software distribution companies is *public domain software.* Public domain software is not registered.

The Software Labs, one of the largest distributors of shareware, offers almost 2000 diskettes full of shareware and public domain software. Software authors submit their software creations to The Software Labs for distribution. Authors are compensated when they receive fees from users who register their software. You can get programs that print signs and banners, help you with your taxes, teach you to speak Japanese, help you manage projects, provide access to many delicious recipes, and suggest lottery numbers. You can get complete systems for church accounting, stamp collection, billing and invoicing, and investment management. You can get full-featured packages for word processing, spreadsheet, database, and graphics. And, if you're intimidated by the thought of learning a spreadsheet, why not try "Templates of Doom," a shareware program that uses an adventure game to teach spreadsheet basics. Scores of games are available from golf to martial arts. These are just the tip of the shareware iceberg.

■ *Print Shop.* All too often, the local greeting-card store has cards and announcements for everyone except you. When you want something special, try doing it yourself with Print Shop, from Broderbund. Print Shop lets you create imaginative banners, greeting cards, letterheads, calendars, announcements, and more (see Figure 9–18). You select the backdrop, size of paper, graphics, fonts, text box shape; then you supply the words.

■ *Windows accessories.* Microsoft's Windows GUI has many accessories you may find helpful. For example, use Calendar to keep an on-line calendar (see Figure 9–19), draw with Paintbrush, maintain a database with Cardfile, write a memo with Write, link up to an on-line information service with Terminal, calculate your earnings with Calculator, play CDs with Media Player, or record your voice with Recorder.

Somewhere among the 400,000 packages rests the answers to many of your processing and information needs as well as plenty of opportunities to have a great time. Explore the possibilities!

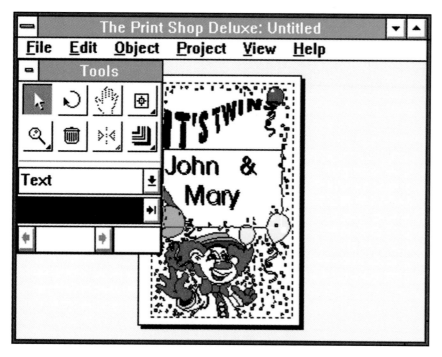

FIGURE 9–18 A Birth Announcement Created with Print Shop   *Print Shop, a Broderbund product, lets you do more than just sign cards—you create them.*

FIGURE 9–19 Calendar Software   *Calendar software enables you to view highlights of future events a month at a time (shown here). Details of events are displayed hour-by-hour for a given day. This calendar software is one of the many software accessories that comes with Microsoft's Windows.*

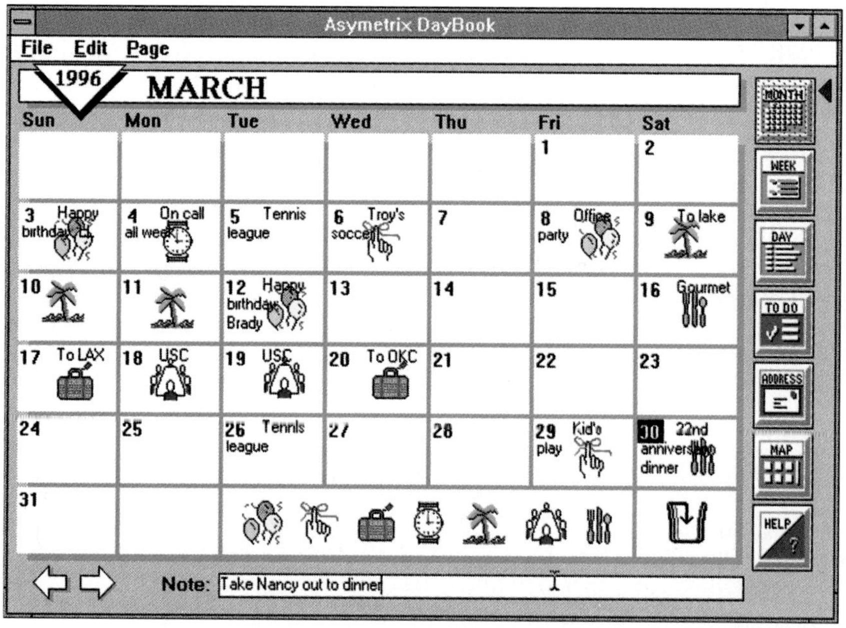

IMPORTANT TERMS AND SUMMARY OUTLINE

animation
bar graph
bit-mapped
computer-aided design (CAD)
drag-and-drop software
draw software
echo

full-duplex
graphics conversion program
half-duplex
paint software
parity checking
pie graph
presentation graphics software

raster graphics
screen-capture program
system operator (sysop)
telecommuting
terminal emulation mode
vector graphics

9–1 PC Software: Exploring the Possibilities There is an ever-growing world of PC software products designed to improve your productivity at work and at home, give you much needed information, expand your intellectual and cultural horizons, and provide you with endless hours of enjoyment.

9–2 Graphics: Creating and Working with Images Graphics software facilitates the creation and management of computer-based images. The six dominant categories of graphics software are paint, draw, drag-and-drop, presentation graphics, computer-aided design, and screen capture and graphics conversion.

Graphic images are presented as **raster graphics** or **vector graphics.** In raster, or **bit-mapped,** graphics, the image is composed of patterns of dots (pixels). **Animation,** or movement, is accomplished by the rapid repositioning of an area of the screen. In vector graphics, the image is composed of patterns of lines, points, and other geometric shapes (vectors).

Paint software provides the user with a sophisticated electronic canvas. Whatever you draw on either the traditional or the electronic canvas becomes part of the whole drawing. The six items in a paint program's user interface are the drawing area, the graphics cursor, the main menu, the tool box, the linesize box, and the color palette.

Draw software permits you to create a screen image, then isolate and manipulate representations of individual objects within the overall image. Draw software relies on vector graphics, so a specific object can be dealt with independently.

Drag-and-drop software allows users to drag ready-made shapes from application-specific stencils to the desired position on the drawing area. With drag-and-drop software, you can glue the shapes together such that the shapes stay connected even if one of them is moved.

User-friendly **presentation graphics software** enables users to create a wide variety of visually appealing and informative presentation graphics. Among the most popular are **pie graphs** and **bar graphs.** Presentation graphics software also permits the preparation of text charts, organization charts, maps, and original drawings. These graphic images are captured and reproduced on printers, desktop plotters, desktop film recorders, and screen image projectors. Some sophisticated packages allow you to present dynamic shows.

High-performance microcomputers that support **computer-aided design (CAD)** are configured with very high-resolution large-screen monitors, a variety of pointing and drawing devices, plotters, and sometimes other design-oriented devices. CAD applications include everything from television graphics to engineering design.

Screen-capture programs are TSRs that enable users to transfer all or part of the current screen image to a disk file. **Graphics conversion programs** help users pass graphics files between programs.

9–3 Multimedia: Teaching the Computer to Sing and Dance Multimedia refers to a computer system that lets users access and interact with computer-based text, high-resolution still graphics, motion visuals, animation, and sound. Three elements in particular distinguish multimedia: sound, motion, and the opportunity for interaction.

A basic multimedia system includes a PC, a high-resolution monitor, a CD-ROM drive, a sound card, external speakers or headphones, a microphone, multimedia support software, and multimedia applications software.

The next stage of multimedia growth would include some or all of the following hardware and software: a video camera, a videocassette recorder/player, an audio-cassette player, a CD-audio player, a television, a synthesizer, a video capture card, a color scanner, professional applications development software, and a source library.

Multimedia standards are still emerging.

9–4 Micro-Based Communications Software Communications software performs two basic functions: *terminal emulation* and *file transfer*. Typically, the log-on procedure involves dialing the remote computer and entering a password and a personal identification number, or PIN.

When a micro is in **terminal emulation mode,** the keyboard, the monitor, and the data interface are like that of the terminal being emulated.

When using communications software, specify the following parameters: type of terminal to be emulated, communications protocol, data flow (**half-duplex** or **full-duplex**), data bits, **parity checking** activated, bits per second (sometimes labeled as *baud*), stop bits, and **echo.**

A variety of information services are available to microcomputer owners with communications capabilities. Bulletin-board systems (BBSs) are popular throughout the country. The person or group sponsoring the BBS is referred to as the **system operator,** or **sysop.**

PC users can subscribe to a commercial on-line service. Some of the services are news, weather, sports, entertainment, games, home banking, financial information, brokerage services, bulletin boards, electronic mail, shop at home, reference, education, and much more.

In the years to come, many white-collar workers will elect to **telecommute** at least one day a week. The combination of microcomputers and communications software has fueled the growth of cottage industries.

9–5   PC Software: The Rest of the Story There are over 400,000 commercial software products and more being developed every day. There is software that helps us prepare legal documents, manage our finances, look up geographic information, create greeting cards, study anatomy, and much, much more.

REVIEW EXERCISES

Concepts

1. What term is frequently used in place of *raster graphics*?
2. Which type of graphics software package provides a computer-based version of the painter's canvas?
3. Which type of graphics software package enables the generation of a wide variety of presentation graphics?
4. Which presentation graphics software capability enables users to assemble presentation graphics in a synchronized show?
5. Which type of TSR program enables users to transfer all or part of the current screen image to a disk file?
6. Briefly describe two multimedia applications.
7. Name at least three devices over and above a standard PC configuration you might need to run multimedia applications.
8. What type of software lets you create multimedia applications that integrate sound, motion, text, animation, and images?
9. Name three common household electronic devices that a developer of multimedia applications might use when developing multimedia applications.
10. Which type of add-on card lets you capture full-motion color video with audio on magnetic disk?
11. What is the advantage of a communications profile?

12. What two basic functions are performed by micro-based communications software?
13. Name three data communications parameters that may need to be specified to establish a communications link between a PC and another computer.
14. If you were to sponsor a bulletin-board system, what would you be called?
15. The combination of microcomputers and communications software has also fueled the growth of what type of industries?

Discussion

16. What kind of work would you like to be doing in five years? Explain how you might telecommute to accomplish part or all of your work.
17. Describe the advantages of a multimedia-based encyclopedia over a traditional printed encyclopedia. Describe the advantages of a traditional printed encyclopedia over a multimedia-based encyclopedia.
18. A bar graph that was created with a presentation graphics package needs to be integrated into a report that is being created camera-ready with DTP software. The bar graph is in Lotus 1-2-3 PIC format, but the DTP package accepts only graphics files in PCX format. Describe how you might integrate the bar graph into the report.

246 PART III Software

SELF-TEST (BY SECTION)

9–1 As a rule of thumb, you cannot be an effective PC user without using at least 40 different software packages. (T/F)

9–2 a. Presentation graphics software allows users to create charts and line drawings. (T/F)

b. In raster graphics, the image is composed of patterns of: (a) vectors, (b) pictures, or (c) dots?

c. Which of the following would not be a tool in a paint program's tool box: (a) rectangle, (b) color palette, or (c) add text?

d. _____ charts show the hierarchical structure of an organization.

e. Bit-mapped files cannot be converted to a format that is compatible with fax modems. (T/F)

9–3 a. Which of the following would not be considered one of the major elements of multimedia:

(a) sound, (b) sequential access, or (c) the opportunity for interaction?

b. The _____ card has a small amplifier through which sound can be played.

9–4 a. Parity checking is not needed or used in data communications. (T/F)

b. A micro with a modem and communications software can make calls to other computers but it cannot receive calls. (T/F)

c. When acting like a terminal, the micro is said to be in _____ mode.

d. A channel that transmits data in both directions at the same time is called _____

9–5 PC software is available that can assist people in creating common legally binding documents. (T/F)

Self-test answers.   **9–1** F. **9–2 (a)** T; **(b)** c; **(c)** b; **(d)** Organization; **(e)** F. **9–3 (a)** b; **(b)** sound. **9–4 (a)** F; **(b)** F; **(c)** terminal emulation; **(d)** full-duplex. **9–5** T.

10

COMPUTERS IN SOCIETY: TODAY AND TOMORROW

OBJECTIVES

To put society's dependence on computers in perspective.

To explore ethical questions concerning the use of computers.

To identify causes of illegal information processing activity.

To identify points of security vulnerability for the computer center and for information systems.

To identify ergonomic considerations in the design of the knowledge worker's work place.

To identify possible applications for the emerging information superhighway.

10–1   INFORMATION TECHNOLOGY: CAN WE LIVE WITHOUT IT?

For decades, managers and executives have made critical decisions based on limited information. Some still do; however, the trend is toward a more strategic use of information. Tactician (shown here), a powerful marketing and mapping system, has enabled many managers and executives to take advantage of the age of information and realize a competitive advantage. For example, a manufacturer can use Tactician software to geographically isolate the strengths and weaknesses of its distribution coverage and market penetration (left). Tactician enables companies to build alliances through sharing marketing data for mutual profit and success (right). Anyone who has used a GIS (geographic information system) such as Tactician will readily admit that information technology has emerged as the weapon of choice in business wars.

Albert Einstein said that "concern for man himself and his fate must always form the chief interest of all technical endeavors." Some people believe that a rapidly advancing information technology exhibits little regard for "man himself and his fate." They contend that computers are overused, misused, and generally detrimental to society. This group argues that the computer is dehumanizing and is slowly forcing society into a pattern of mass conformity. To be sure, the age of information is presenting society with difficult and complex problems, but they can be overcome.

Information technology has enhanced our lifestyles to the point that most of us take it for granted. There is nothing wrong with this attitude, but we must recognize that society has made a real commitment to computers. Whether it is good or bad, society has reached the point of no return in its dependence on computers. Stiff business competition means their continued and growing use. On the more personal level, we are reluctant to forfeit the everyday conveniences made possible by computers. More and more of us find that our personal computers are an integral part of our daily activities.

Our dependence on food has evolved into the joy of eating gourmet food—and so it is or can be with information technology. Dependence is not necessarily bad as long as we keep it in perspective. However, we can't passively assume that information technology will continue to enhance the quality of our lives. It is our obligation to learn to understand computers so we can better direct their application for society's benefit. Only through understanding can we control the misuse or abuse of information technology. We, as a society, have a responsibility to weigh the benefits, burdens, and consequences of each successive level of automation. This chapter addresses our responsibilities as well as the opportunities and challenges that accompany our evolution into an information society.

10–2   THE QUESTION OF ETHICS

The computer revolution has generated intense controversy. This controversy has raised questions about what is and is not ethical with regard to activities involving information technology. In this section we discuss ethical conduct and the dominant ethical issues.

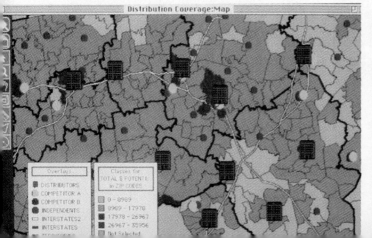

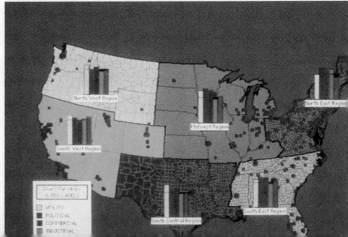

Standards of Conduct:
A Code of Ethics

About 20 years ago, one of the largest professional societies adopted a code of ethics. The code warns the members, who are mostly professionals in the information technology fields, that they can be expelled or censured if they violate it. To date, not one of the society's tens of thousands of members has been expelled or censured for violating the code. Other professional societies publish a code of ethics as well, and they, too, rarely or never take action against delinquent members. Does this mean there are no violations? Of course not. A carefully drafted code of ethics provides some guidelines for conduct, but professional societies cannot be expected to police the misdoings of their membership. In many instances, a code violation is also a violation of the law.

A code of ethics provides direction for computer professionals and users so that they act responsibly in their application of information technology. The following code of ethics is in keeping with the spirit of those encouraged by professional societies for people in the information technology fields.

It is more the rule than the exception that people who work with computer systems will have ready access to a broad range of sensitive information. Because of the potential for the abuse of this information, many organizations have adopted a code of ethics to help guide the actions of their employees. These people are meeting to design a test for Space Station Freedom's power system.

1. Maintain the highest standard of professional behavior.
2. Avoid situations that create a conflict of interest.
3. Do not violate the confidentiality of your employer or those you service.
4. Continue to learn so your knowledge keeps pace with the technology.
5. Never misrepresent or withhold information that is germane to a problem or situation of public concern.
6. Use information judiciously and maintain system integrity at all times.
7. Do not violate the rights or privacy of others.
8. Take appropriate action when exposed to unethical or illegal practices.
9. Do not exploit the shortcomings of an employer's computer system for personal gain.
10. Accomplish each task to the best of your ability.

If you follow this 10-point code, it is unlikely that anyone will question your ethics. Nevertheless, well-meaning people routinely violate this simple code because they are unaware of the tremendous detrimental impact of their actions. With the speed and power of computers, a minor code infraction easily can be magnified to a costly catastrophe. For this reason, the use of computers is raising new ethical questions, the most visible of which are discussed in the following sections.

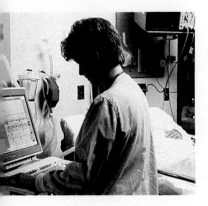

Progressive hospitals restrict staff access to patient medical histories on a need-to-know basis. An employee's personal identification number (PIN) and password determine what portions of the database can be accessed.

These stockbrokers use computer-based systems to complete buy and sell orders. In so doing, they add name, address, and other personal information to the client database. On average, each American is listed in about 60 government and 80 private-sector databases. On a typical day, each person's name is passed between computers 10 times. People who are socially, economically, and politically active may be listed in hundreds of databases.

The Misuse of Personal Information

Sources of Personal Data The issue with the greatest ethical overtones is the privacy of personal information. Some people fear that computer-based record-keeping offers too much of an opportunity for the invasion of an individual's privacy. There is indeed reason for concern. For example, credit-card users unknowingly leave a "trail" of activities and interests that, when examined and evaluated, can provide a surprisingly comprehensive personal profile.

The date and location of all credit-card transactions are recorded. In effect, when you charge lunch, gasoline, or clothing, you are creating a chronological record of where you have been and your spending habits. From this information, a good analyst could compile a very accurate profile of your lifestyle. For example, the analyst could predict how you dress by knowing the type of clothing stores you patronize. On a more personal level, records are kept that detail the duration, time, and numbers of all your telephone calls. With computers, these numbers easily can be matched to people, businesses, institutions, and telephone services. So each time you make a phone call, you also leave a record of whom or what you call. Enormous amounts of personal data are maintained on everyone by the IRS, your college, your employer, your creditors, your hospital, your insurance company, your broker, and on and on.

We hope that information about us is up-to-date and accurate. Unfortunately, much of it is not. Laws permit us to examine our records, but first we must find them. You cannot just write to the federal government and request to see your files. To be completely sure that you examine all your federal records for completeness and accuracy, you would have to write and probably visit more than 5000 agencies that each maintain computer-based files on individuals. The same is true of computer-based personal data maintained in the private sector.

Violating the Privacy of Personal Information Most will agree that the potential exists for abuse, but are these data being misused? Some say yes. Consider the states that sell lists of the addresses and data on their licensed drivers. At the request of a manager of several petite women's clothing stores, a state provided the manager with a list of all licensed drivers in the state who were women between the ages of 21 and 40, less than 5 feet 3 inches tall, and under 120 pounds. You be the judge. Is the sale of such a list an abuse of personal information? Does the state cross the line of what is considered ethical practice?

Personal information has become the product of a growing industry. Companies have been formed that do nothing but sell information about people. Not only are the people involved not asked for permission to use their data, they are seldom even told that their personal information is being sold! A great deal of personal data can be extracted from public records. For example, one company sends people to county courthouses all over the United States to gather publicly accessible data about people who have recently filed papers to purchase a home. Mailing lists are then sold to insurance companies, land-

scape companies, members of Congress seeking new votes, lawyers seeking new clients, and so on. Those placed on the mailing list eventually become targets of commerce and special-interest groups.

The use of personal information for profit and other purposes is growing so rapidly that the government has not been able to keep up with abuses. Antiquated laws, combined with judicial unfamiliarity with computers, make policing and prosecuting abuses of the privacy of personal information difficult and, in many cases, impossible.

Computer Matching In **computer matching,** separate databases are examined and individuals common to both are identified. The focus of most computer-matching applications is to identify people engaged in wrongdoing. For example, federal employees are being matched with those having delinquent student loans. Wages are then garnisheed to repay the loans. In another computer-matching case, a $30-million fraud was uncovered when questionable financial transactions were traced to common participants.

The Internal Revenue Service also uses computer matching to identify tax cheaters. The IRS gathers descriptive data, such as neighborhood and automobile type, then uses sophisticated models to create lifestyle profiles. These profiles are matched against reported income on tax returns to predict whether people seem to be underpaying taxes. When the income and projected lifestyle do not match, the return is audited.

Proponents of computer matching cite the potential to reduce criminal activity. Opponents of computer matching consider it an unethical invasion of privacy.

Securing the Integrity of Personal Information Computer experts feel that the integrity of personal data can be more secure in computer databases than in file cabinets. They contend that we can continue to be masters and not victims if we implement proper safeguards for the maintenance and release of this information and enact effective legislation to cope with the abuse of it.

Summary The ethical questions surrounding the privacy of personal information are extremely complex and difficult to resolve. For example, consider the position of the American Civil Liberties Union. On one hand, the ACLU is fighting to curb abuses of personal information and on the other, it is lobbying the government for greater access to government information. Are these goals in conflict?

As automation continues to enrich our lives, it also opens the door for abuses of personal information. Research is currently being done which may show that people with certain genetic and/or personality makeups have a statistical predisposition to a physical problem or a mental disorder, such as early heart failure or depression. Will employers use such information to screen potential employees?

By now it should be apparent to you that we may never resolve all of the ethical questions associated with the privacy of personal information. Just as the answer to one question becomes more clear, another is raised by an ever-growing number of applications that deal with personal information.

Computer Monitoring

One of the newest and most controversial applications of information technology is **computer monitoring**. In computer monitoring, computers continu-

Law enforcement officials, from FBI agents to local police, routinely use computer matching techniques to fight crime.

Anyone who records transactions on a computer system is a candidate for computer monitoring. Air traffic controllers, who simultaneously communicate with pilots and computers, are candidates.

ously gather and assimilate data on job activities to measure worker performance. Today computers monitor the job performance of more than 7 million American workers and millions more worldwide. Most of these workers interact with a mainframe computer system via terminals or work on a micro that is part of a local area network. Others work with electronic or mechanical equipment that is linked to a computer system.

Many clerical workers who use VDTs are evaluated by the number of documents they process per unit of time. At insurance companies, computer monitoring systems provide supervisors with information on the rate at which clerks process claims. Supervisors can request other information, such as time spent at the terminal and keying-error rate.

Computers also monitor the activities of many jobs that demand frequent use of the telephone. The number of inquiries handled by directory-assistance operators is logged by a computer. Some companies employ computers to monitor the use of telephones by all employees.

Although most computer monitoring is done at the clerical level, it is also being applied to higher-level positions such as commodities brokers, programmers, loan officers, and plant managers. For example, CIM (computer-integrated manufacturing) enables corporate executives to monitor the effectiveness of a plant manager on a real-time basis. At any given time executives can tap the system for productivity information, such as the rate of production for a particular assembly.

Not all computer monitoring is aimed at assessing ongoing job performance. For example, some organizations encourage management scrutiny of employee electronic mail. In this form of monitoring, management opens and reads employee E-mail to ensure that internal communications are work-related and of a certain level of quality. Many organized worker groups have complained that this form of monitoring is an unnecessary invasion of privacy and can actually be counterproductive.

Workers complain that being constantly observed and analyzed by a computer adds unnecessary stress to their jobs. However, management is reluctant to give up computer monitoring because it has proved itself a tool for increasing worker productivity. In general, affected workers are opposing any further intrusion into their professional privacy. On the other hand, management is equally vigilant in its quest for better information on worker performance.

Computer Crime

The ethical spectrum for computer issues runs from that which is ethical, to that which is unethical, to that which is against the law—a computer crime. There are many types of computer crimes, ranging from the use of an unauthorized password by a student to a billion-dollar insurance fraud. It is estimated that each year the total money lost from computer crime is greater than the sum total of that taken in all robberies. In fact, no one really knows the extent of computer crime because much of it is either undetected or unreported (more often the latter). In those cases involving banks, officers may elect to write off the loss rather than announce the crime and risk losing the good will of their customers.

Computers and the Law   Companies try to employ information technology within the boundaries of any applicable law. Unfortunately, the laws are not always clear because many legal questions involving the use of information technology are being debated for the first time. To no one's surprise, computer law is the fastest growing type of law practice.

Laws governing information technology are few, and those that do exist are subject to a variety of interpretations. At present, federal laws that address computer crime are limited, because they apply only to those computer systems that in some way reflect a federal interest. These laws make it a felony to gain unauthorized access to any computer system with a federal interest with the intent to obtain anything of value, to defraud the system, or to cause more than $1000 in damage. Although most states have adopted computer crime laws, they are only the skeleton of what is needed to direct an orderly and controlled growth of information technology applications.

Existing federal and state laws concerning the privacy of personal information are being updated every year. At the same time, new laws are written. Current federal laws outline the handling of credit information, restrict what information the IRS can obtain, restrict government access to financial information, permit individuals to view records maintained by federal agencies, restrict the use of education-related data, and regulate the matching of computer files. States have or are considering laws to deal with the handling of social security numbers, criminal records, telephone numbers, financial information, medical records, and other sensitive personal information.

Computer crime is a relatively recent phenomenon. As a result, legislation, the criminal justice system, and industry are not yet adequately prepared to cope with it. Only a handful of police and FBI agents in the entire country have been trained to handle cases involving computer crime. And when a case comes to court, few judges and even fewer jurors have the background necessary to understand the testimony.

Defrauding the System   Most computer crimes fall under the umbrella of computer fraud. These crimes involve a premeditated or conscious effort to defraud a computer-based system. For example, a U.S. Customs official modified a program to print $160,000 worth of unauthorized federal payroll checks payable to himself and his co-conspirators. A 17-year-old high school student tapped into an AT&T computer and stole more than $1 million worth of software. One person illegally transferred $10,200,000 from a U.S. bank to a Swiss bank. He probably would have gotten away with this electronic heist if he hadn't felt compelled to brag about it. These are all examples of fraud. Any illegal entry into a computer system for the purpose of personal gain is considered fraud. Over 50% of all computer frauds are internal; that is, they are committed by employees of the organization being defrauded. About 30% of those defrauding employees are computer specialists.

Attempts to defraud a computer system require the cooperation of an experienced computer specialist. A common street thug does not have the knowledge or the opportunity to be successful at this type of computer crime. The sophistication of the crime, however, makes it no less criminal.

Negligence and Incompetence   Not all computer crime is premeditated. Negligence or incompetence can cause someone outside the organization to be unnecessarily inconvenienced, and it is usually a result of poor input/output control. For example, after she paid in full, a woman was sent dunning notices continually and was visited by collection agencies for not making payments on her automobile. Although the records and procedures were in error, the company forcibly repossessed the automobile without thoroughly checking its procedures and the legal implications. The woman had to sue the company for the return of her automobile. The court ordered the automobile returned and the company to pay her a substantial sum as a penalty.

The Hacker Problem   Another problem is the criminal activities of overzealous hackers. These "electronic vandals" have tapped into everything from local credit agencies to top-secret defense systems. The evidence of unlawful entry, perhaps a revised record or access during nonoperating hours, is called a **footprint**. Some malicious hackers leave much more than a footprint—they infect the computer system with a virus. **Virus** software, which has been found at all levels of computing, "infects" other programs and databases. The virus is so named because it can spread from one system to another like a biological virus. Viruses are written by outlaw hackers and programmers to cause harm to the computer systems of unsuspecting victims. Left undetected a virus can result in loss of data and/or programs and even physical damage to the hardware. The types of viruses and the ways in which viruses are spread are covered in a box in this chapter. People are concerned that criminally oriented hackers are glorified by the media, creating heroes for a new generation of computer criminals.

Copyright laws protect literature, music, the design of a silicon chip, and software. A sophisticated circuit design may be the result of a multimillion-dollar research effort.

Software Piracy and the Theft of Intellectual Property   Software is protected by the Copyright Law of 1974, just as books are protected by copyright laws. This makes the duplication of copyright software illegal. The unlawful duplication of proprietary software, called **software piracy,** is making companies vulnerable to legal action by the affected vendors. The term **pilferage** is used to describe the situation where a company purchases a software product without a site-usage license agreement, then copies and distributes it throughout the company. Vendors of software for personal computers estimate that for every software product sold, two more are illegally copied. Software piracy is a serious problem, and software vendors are acting vigorously to prosecute people and companies who violate their copyrights.

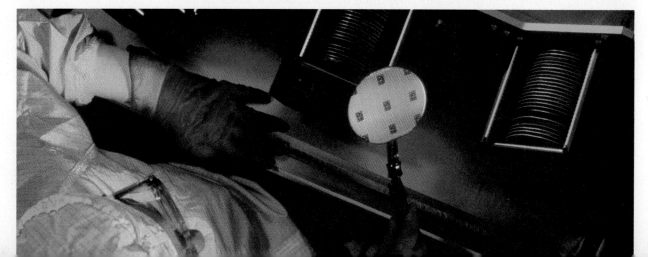

Some managers confront the issue head on and state bluntly that software piracy is a crime and offenders will be dismissed. This method has proven effective. Some, who are in reality accomplices, look the other way as subordinates copy software for office and personal use.

Other intellectual property, such as a chip design or a new concept in productivity software, is equally vulnerable to theft. Numerous cases involving intellectual property are currently being contested in the courts.

10–3   COMPUTER-CENTER AND SYSTEM SECURITY

The best way to minimize unethical abuses of information technology and computer crime is to build an envelope of security around hardware and to embed safeguards into the information systems. There are too many points of vulnerability and too much is at stake to overlook the threats to the security of a computer center and an information system. These threats take many forms—white-collar crime, natural disasters (earthquakes, floods), vandalism, and carelessness.

In this section we discuss commonly applied measures that can help to neutralize security threats to a computer center and an information system.

Computer-Center Security

Generally, enterprise-wide information systems are handled by minicomputers and mainframe computers located in centralized computer centers. **Enterprise-wide information systems** provide information and processing capabilities to workers throughout a given organization. An organization's computer center has a number of points of vulnerability; these are *hardware, software, files/databases, data communications,* and *personnel.* Each is discussed separately in this section and illustrated in Figure 10–1.

Hardware   If the hardware fails, the information system fails. The threat of failure can be minimized by implementing security precautions that prevent access by unauthorized personnel and by taking steps to keep all hardware operational.

Common approaches to securing the premises from unauthorized entry include closed-circuit TV monitors, alarm systems, and computer-controlled

People and computers must work around the clock to maintain the national flight weather database at Salt Lake City. To ensure continuous operation of the system, it is made fault-tolerant with duplicate processors and backup power supplies.

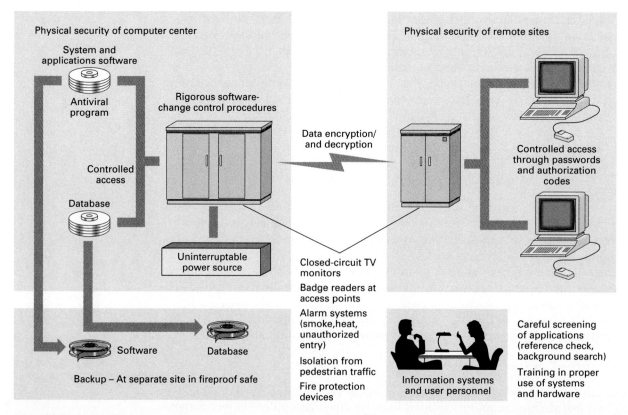

FIGURE 10–1 Security Precautions *Some or all of the security measures noted in the figure are in force in most computer centers. Each precaution helps minimize the risk of an information system's or a computer system's vulnerability to crime, disasters, and failure.*

devices that check employee badges, fingerprints, or voice prints before unlocking doors at access points. Computer centers also should be isolated from pedestrian traffic. Machine-room fires should be extinguished by a special chemical that douses the fire but does not destroy the files or equipment.

Computers, especially mainframe computers, must have a "clean," continuous source of power. To minimize the effects of "dirty" power or power outages, many computer centers have installed an **uninterruptible power source** (**UPS**). Dirty power, with sags and surges in power output or brownouts (low power), causes data transmission errors and program execution errors. A UPS system serves as a buffer between the external power source and the computer system. In a UPS system, the computer is powered by batteries that deliver clean power, which in turn are regenerated by an external power source. If the external power source fails, the UPS system permits operation to continue for a period of time after an outage. This allows operators to either "power down" normally or switch to a backup power source, usually a diesel-powered generator. Until recently UPS systems were associated only with mainframe computer systems. Now they are economically feasible for microcomputer systems.

Software   Unless properly controlled, the software for an information system can be modified for personal gain, or vandalized and rendered useless. Close control of software development and the documentation of an information system is needed to minimize the opportunity for computer crime and vandalism.

Unlawful modification of software.   Bank programmers certainly have opportunities to modify software for personal gain. In one case, a couple of programmers modified a savings system to make small deposits from other accounts to their own accounts. Here's how it worked: The interest for each savings account was compounded and credited daily; the calculated interest was rounded to the nearest penny before being credited to the savings account; programs were modified to round down all interest calculations and put the "extra" penny in one of the programmer's savings accounts. It may not seem like much, but a penny a day from thousands of accounts adds up to a lot of money. The "beauty" of the system was that the books balanced and depositors did not miss the 15 cents (an average of 1/2 cent per day for 30 days) that judiciously was taken from each account each month. Even auditors had difficulty detecting this crime because the total interest paid on all accounts was correct. However, the culprits got greedy and were apprehended when someone noticed that they repeatedly withdrew inordinately large sums of money from their own accounts. Unfortunately, other enterprising programmers in other industries have been equally imaginative.

Operational control procedures built into the design of an information system will constantly monitor processing accuracy. Unfortunately, cagey programmers have been known to get around some of them. Perhaps the best way to safeguard programs from unlawful tampering is to use rigorous change-control procedures. Such procedures make it difficult to modify a program for purposes of personal gain.

Viruses.   The growing threat of viruses has resulted in tightening software controls. Individuals and companies routinely run antiviral programs, called *vaccines,* to search for and destroy viruses before they can do their dirty work.

Files/Databases   The database contains the raw material for information. Often the files/databases are the lifeblood of a company. For example, how many companies can afford to lose their accounts receivable file, which documents who owes what? Having several *generations of backups* (backups to backups) to all files is not sufficient insurance against loss of files/databases. The backup and master files should be stored in fireproof safes in separate rooms, preferably in separate buildings.

Data Communications   Data communications applications are vulnerable because transmissions can be intercepted en route between locations. Companies address the data communications threat with encryption/decryption hardware and **cryptography** techniques. In effect, transmissions are scrambled such that only those with the software key can interpret them.

Personnel   The biggest threat to a company's security system is the dishonesty and/or incompetence of its own employees. Managers should pay close attention to who gets hired for positions with access to computer-based information systems and sensitive data. Many companies flash a message on each terminal display such as: "All information on this system is confidential and proprietary." It's not very user-friendly, but it gets the message across to employees that they may be fired if they abuse the system. Someone who is grossly incompetent can cause just as much harm as someone who is inherently dishonest.

Information Systems Security

Information systems security is classified as physical or logical. **Physical security** refers to hardware, facilities, magnetic disks, and other items that could be illegally accessed, stolen, or destroyed.

Logical security is built into the software by permitting only authorized persons to access and use the system. Logical security for on-line systems is achieved primarily by using *passwords* and *personal identification numbers* (*PINs*). Only those people with a need to know are told the password and given PINs. On occasion, however, these security codes fall into the wrong hands. When this happens, an unauthorized person can gain access to programs and sensitive files simply by dialing up the computer and entering the codes.

Keeping passwords and PINs from the computer criminal is not easy. One approach is to educate employees about techniques used to obtain passwords and PINs, such as tailgating. The *tailgating* technique is used by company outsiders to gain access to sensitive information. The perpetrator simply begins using the terminal or computer of an authorized user who has left the room without terminating his or her session.

COMPUTERS HAVE VIRUSES, TOO

Computers can get sick just like people. A variety of highly contagious "diseases" can spread from computer to computer, much the way biological viruses do among human beings. A *computer virus* is a program that literally "infects" other programs and databases upon contact. It can also hide duplicates of itself within legitimate programs, such as an operating system or a word processing program.

There are many types of viruses. Some act quickly by erasing user programs and databases. Others grow like a cancer, destroying small parts of a database each day. Some act like a time bomb. They lay dormant for days or months, but eventually are activated and wreak havoc on any software on the system. Many companies warn their micro users to back up all software prior to every Friday the thirteenth, a favorite date of those who write virus programs. Some viruses attack the hardware and have been known to throw the mechanical components of a computer system, such as disk-access arms, into costly spasms.

In the microcomputer environment, there are three primary sources of computer viruses (see figure opposite).

■ *Electronic bulletin-board systems.* The most common source of viral infection is the public electronic bulletin board on which users exchange software. Typically, a user logs onto the bulletin board and downloads what he or she thinks is a game, a utility program, or some other enticing piece of freeware, but gets a virus instead.

■ *Diskettes.* Viruses are also spread from one system to another via common diskettes. For example, a student with an infected application disk might infect several other laboratory computers with a virus which, in turn, infects the applications software of other students. Software companies have unknowingly distributed viruses with their proprietary software products.

■ *Computer networks.* In the minicomputer and mainframe environment, viruses generally are spread from one computer network to another.

How serious a problem are viruses? They have the potential of affecting an individual's career and even destroying companies. (A company that loses its accounts receivable records could be a candidate for bankruptcy.) Antiviral programs, also called *vaccines,* exist, but they can be circumvented by a persistent (and malicious) programmer. The best way to cope with viruses is to recognize their existence and to take precautionary measures.

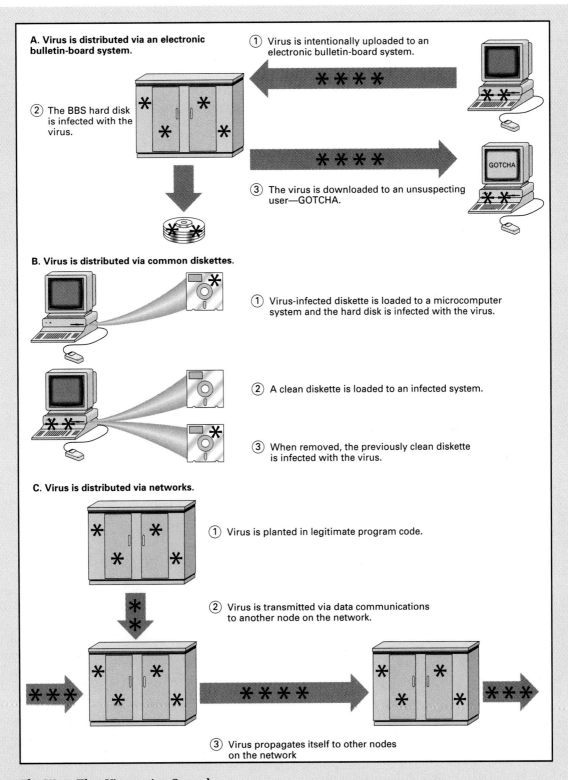

A. Virus is distributed via an electronic bulletin-board system.

① Virus is intentionally uploaded to an electronic bulletin-board system.

② The BBS hard disk is infected with the virus.

③ The virus is downloaded to an unsuspecting user—GOTCHA.

B. Virus is distributed via common diskettes.

① Virus-infected diskette is loaded to a microcomputer system and the hard disk is infected with the virus.

② A clean diskette is loaded to an infected system.

③ When removed, the previously clean diskette is infected with the virus.

C. Virus is distributed via networks.

① Virus is planted in legitimate program code.

② Virus is transmitted via data communications to another node on the network.

③ Virus propagates itself to other nodes on the network

The Ways That Viruses Are Spread

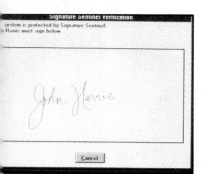

Now your signature can be a key to your PC as well as your checking account. Those who use pen-based computers or PCs configured with a tablet and pen can add an extra level of security by requiring the user to sign his or her name at the start of each session. Signature Sentinel (by Handwriter for Windows) learns your signature and how you write it, virtually locking out tracing and forgery attempts.

System Security in the PC Environment

Unlike mainframe computers, PCs literally are everywhere. Generally, each is readily accessible to its primary user and anyone else in the area. This ease of accessibility makes PC security a difficult problem to address. However, the conscientious PC user has several physical and logical security measures that can be used to safeguard valuable and/or sensitive information. The most frequently used physical tools include the lock and key and the badge reader. The lock and key, which come standard on most modern PCs, work like an automobile ignition switch. That is, the PC functions only when the lock is turned to the enable position. The badge reader is an optional peripheral device that reads magnetic stripes on badges, such as credit cards. The PC is disabled until an authorized card is inserted in and read by the badge reader.

Stand-alone PCs can be set up so users must enter passwords and PINs to gain access to programs and data. Often, users of LAN-based PCs must enter passwords and PINs before being allowed access to LAN resources. Individual files can be secured by assigning them unique passwords. For example, if you were using a word processing package to prepare personnel performance evaluations, you could secure these files by assigning each a password. To recall a file at a later session, you or anyone else would have to enter the name of the file and the associated password to gain access to it.

Level of Risk

No combination of security measures will completely remove the vulnerability of a computer center, an inormation system, a PC, or a file. Security systems are implemented in degrees. That is, an information system can be made marginally secure or very secure but never totally secure. Each company must determine the level of risk that it is willing to accept. Unfortunately, some corporations are willing to accept an enormous risk and hope that those rare instances of crime and disaster do not occur. Some of them have found out too late that *rarely* is not the same as *never*!

10–4 ERGONOMICS: THE HUMAN CONNECTION

For close to a hundred years, the design of automobiles was driven by two overwhelming considerations: marketing and functionality. Engineers were asked to design cars that had plenty of sales handles and could go from point A to point B. Surprisingly little attention was given to the human factor; that is, the connection between the driver and passengers and the automobile. About 20 years ago, executives discovered that they could boost sales and enhance functionality by improving this human connection; thus began the era of ergonomically designed automobiles. **Ergonomics** is the study of the relationships between people and their machines. Today, human factors engineers apply the principles of ergonomic design to ensure that the interface between people and cars is safe, comfortable, effective, and efficient.

The emergence of ergonomics is having a similar impact on the relationship between knowledge workers and their work places (see Figure 10–2). Engineers are applying ergonomic principles to both the elements of the work

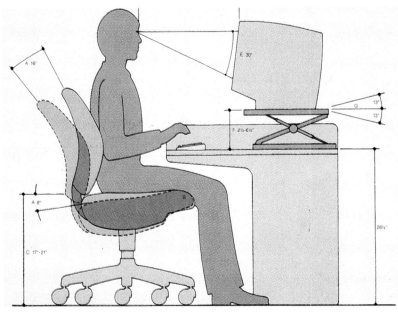

FIGURE 10–2 Ergonomically Designed Workstation *Because knowledge workers may spend four or more hours each day at a PC or terminal, hardware manufacturers are paying more attention to the ergonomics (efficiency of the person–machine interface) of the hardware, including chairs and desks. Features of an ergonomically designed PC or terminal include a high-resolution and non-glare display, tilt and swivel adjustments for the display, tilt adjustment for the keyboard, and noise-level adjustments for prompting alarms.*

place (for example, keyboards, chairs, lighting) and the overall work place. An ergonomically designed work place, like an ergonomically designed automobile, is *safe, comfortable, effective,* and *efficient.*

Reasons for Concern

Attention was focused on the knowledge worker's work place during the 1980s when workers began to blame headaches, depression, anxiety, nausea, fatigue, and irritability on prolonged interaction with a terminal or PC. These and other problems often associated with extended use of a terminal or PC are collectively referred to as *video operator's distress syndrome,* or *VODS.* However, there is little evidence to link these problems with using terminals or PCs. The same problems occur in work environments without VDTs, from the executive suite to the assembly line.

A poorly designed work place has the potential to cause *cumulative trauma disorder* (*CTD*), a condition that can lead to a permanent disability of motor skills. CTD typically occurs in key entry personnel who perform their duties day in and day out within working environments in which the human factor is ignored.

Much has been written about the health concerns associated with monitors. Talk about the radiation emitted by monitors has unduly frightened of-

The Kinesis Ergonomic Keyboard is contoured to fit the shape and movements of the human body. The design puts less stress and strain on muscles, reducing the user's risk of fatigue in hands, wrists, and arms. The keyboard also reduces risk factors for developing painful injuries, such as carpal tunnel syndrome, tendinitis, and cumulative trauma disorders (CTDs).

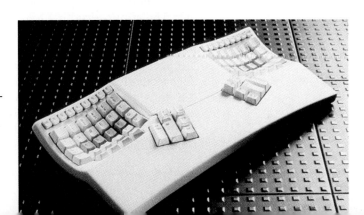

The knowledge worker's work place can and should be designed to meet user needs. This woman works as a database administrator at a computer-services company. Unable to use the keyboard, she uses voice input to enter comands and data. The availability of specially equipped terminals and PCs have made careers that rely heavily on working with computers particularly inviting to the physically disabled.

fice workers. A controversial, and apparently flawed, study in the late 1980s concluded that women who are exposed to the radiation emitted from terminals and PCs may have a higher rate of miscarriage that those who are not. A comprehensive four-year federal government study completed in 1991 concluded that women who work with terminals and PCs and those who do not have the same rate of miscarriage. A display screen does not emit any more radiation than the human body.

Work Place Design

Proper work place design, whether on the factory floor or in the office, is good business. Any good manager knows that a healthy, happy worker is a more productive worker. A good manager also knows that the leading cause of lost work time is back/shoulder/neck pain, all of which can result from poor work place design. The second leading cause of lost work time is CTD.

The key to designing a proper work place for the knowledge worker is *flexibility*. The knowledge worker's work place should be designed with enough flexibility to enable it to be custom-fitted to its worker. Every element of the work place should be designed to accommodate the physical profile of the person using it. For example, the keyboard should be a separate unit with tilt and height adjustments. Some workers like to use a wrist rest in conjunction with the keyboard. The monitor should have a high-resolution, non-glare display and be equipped with tilt and height adjustments. The chair should be on rollers and have seat and back adjustments for proper lumbar support.

Attention to the overall environment can reduce stress and increase worker performance. For example, equipping impact printers with acoustical enclosures can reduce the noise level. Indirect lighting can reduce glare. Proper ventilation eliminates health concerns caused by the ozone emitted by laser printers. (Excessive exposure to ozone can cause headaches and nausea.)

Each knowledge worker can contribute to the quality of his or her work place by following a few simple rules. First, make the adjustments necessary to custom fit your work place. Second, take several short breaks rather that one long break. Third, take periodic mini-breaks; that is, look away from the monitor and/or generally alter you body orientation for a few seconds (make a fist, turn you head from side to side, roll your shoulders, walk around your desk, wiggle your toes, and so on).

10–5   DOWN THE ROAD: INFORMATION SUPERHIGHWAYS

Let's gaze into the crystal ball and look into the future of information technology. The application that may have the greatest impact on the largest number of people may be what some people are calling the **information superhighway**. The information superhighway is a network of high-speed data communications links, primarily fiber optic technology, that eventually will connect virtually every facet of our society. The superhighway, which is still on the drawing board, will involve the integration of this *high-speed data communications network* with *computer* and *television* technologies. The information superhighway is a tool. You and other innovators will ultimately determine who and what drives along the information superhighway.

Travelers along the Information Superhighway

Traffic on the superhighway, which is expected to be heavy, will be anything that can be digitized. Digitized versions of text (perhaps the morning newspaper), graphic images (a CT scan of a brain tumor), motion video (a movie), still photographs (a picture of a friend), and sound (a hit recording) will be frequent travelers on the information superhighway.

Perhaps the best way to describe the information superhighway is in terms of its applications. A mind-boggling array of information and telecommunication services is planned for the information superhighway, some of which are described here.

The Electronic Family Reunion   The telephone as we know it will probably disappear. In the relatively near future, the function of the telephone will be incorporated into a video phone or, perhaps, into our computers so we can both hear and see the person on the other end of the line. Moreover, we will be able to pass data and information back and forth as if we were sitting at the same table.

You will be able to use the information superhighway, your television, and multiple video phone hookups to hold an electronic family reunion. Here is how it would work. You would dial the video phones of your relatives and a real-time video of each family would appear in a window on your wall-size television monitor. The conversation would be as if all families were in the same room. The members of each family would be able to see the members of the other families. You could even share photos and view family videos. Information superhighways will enable more frequent family reunions, but we will still have to travel on traditional highways to get real hugs and taste grandmother's cherry pie.

Entertainment Galore   Many of the initial offerings traveling the information superhighway will be aimed at entertaining us. We'll have *video-on-demand;* that is, you will be able to choose what television program or movie you want to watch and when you want to watch it. Your choices will encompass virtually all available video—really! You will be able to watch any movie, from the classic archives to first runs, at your convenience. The same is true of television programming. If you would prefer to watch this week's edition of *60 Min-*

Travelers along the information superhighway will pass through network control rooms, similar to this state-of-the-art facility. As busy as this network control room is, the superhighway network facility must be capable of handling a thousand times the traffic. For example, television options will jump from 50 to 500 channels.

It's a good bet that Nickelodeon will be one of those 500 viewing options coming down the information superhighway. Images such as this one are created using 3-D animation software. Computer-based animation and art are playing an ever-increasing role in TV production.

utes on Wednesday, rather than Sunday, you have that option. For that matter, you can elect to watch any past edition of *60 Minutes*. As you might expect, video stores and scheduled TV may become only memories in a few years.

The information superhighway opens the door for a more sophisticated form of entertainment. How about interactive soap operas? Yes, because of the two-way communication capabilities of your television/terminal, you can be an active participant in how a story unfolds. The soaps will be shot so that they can be pieced together in a variety of ways. Imagine—you can decide whether Michelle marries Clifton or Patrick!

If you like video arcades you will love what is coming down the superhighway. Your home entertainment center will become a video arcade, with immediate access to all games. You can hone your skills on an individual basis or test them against the best in the land.

The Home Library As the information superhighway begins to mature during the first decade of the twenty-first century, your home library may look more like that of the Library of Congress. Indeed, your personal library is that of the Library of Congress and much more. The information superhighway makes it possible for you to browse through virtually any book from your PC/terminal. Then, if you wish to purchase a hard-copy version of a book, it will be printed and bound on your high-speed color printer while you wait.

Certainly books, magazines, newspapers, and the printed word in general will prevail for casual reading and study. However, the information superhighway offers *soft-copy* publishing as an alternative to *hard-copy* publishing. We'll be able to receive virtually any printed matter—books, magazines, newspapers, and reference material—in electronic format. You can get newspapers electronically while the news is hot, no wait for printing and delivery. Your home is a newsstand in which you can obtain individual issues of any magazine or any newspaper. You can browse through electronic multimedia catalogs that are updated daily, not by the season.

Mail at the Speed of Light Jokes about the pace of postal delivery will gradually disappear with the emergence of the information superhighway. Most of what we now know as mail will travel electronically over the superhighway, even greeting cards and family photos. And, of course, we will continue to receive our share of electronic junk mail. We can store the mail and read it at our convenience and we will have the option to make hard copies, if we so desire.

The Cashless Society Each weekday, the financial institutions of the world use electronic funds transfer (EFT) to transfer more than one trillion dollars—that's

The information superhighway brings these periodicals and many more to your office or home. Mead Data Central provides LEXIS® and NEXIS®, a full-text legal, news, and business information service. These services include access to nearly 4700 databases. More than 650,000 documents are added each week to the more than 188 million documents currently on-line. Lawyers, accountants, financial analysts, journalists, public relations, marketing and information specialists, and other professionals routinely access LEXIS® and NEXIS® information, mostly from their PCs.

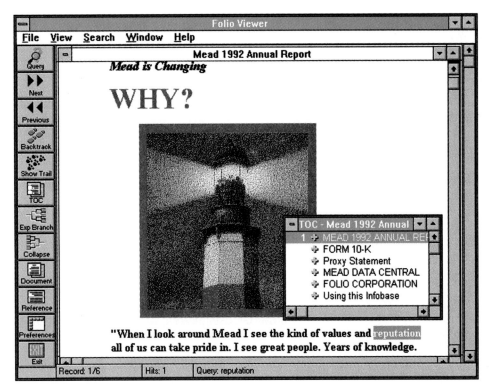

Publishers of all types of printed matter will make their materials available over the information superhighway. Perhaps, in time, the superhighway will be our magazine rack, bookshelf, and research center. Each year corporations distribute millions of printed annual reports to shareholders. As the information superhighway matures and becomes accessible to more people, look for companies to distribute computer-based versions of their annual reports, such as this one for Mead.

$1,000,000,000,000! Applications of EFT, such as ATMs and payroll transfer systems, are being implemented all around us. The implementation of the information superhighway may be the next step toward a *cashless society*. The information superhighway will provide the necessary link between individuals, businesses, and financial institutions. Should we move toward a cashless society, the administrative work associated with handling money and checks would be eliminated. We would no longer need to manufacture or carry money. Each purchase, no matter how small or large, would result in an immediate transfer of funds between buyer and seller. Think of it—rubber checks and counterfeit money would be eliminated. Moreover, with total EFT you would have a detailed and accurate record of all monetary transactions.

Shop at Home   The information superhighway will provide a direct visual and electronic link to mail-order companies and retail/wholesale establishments. Many people will opt to do much of their shopping electronically. Instead of walking down the aisle of a grocery store or thumbing through stacks of shirts, we will be able to use our personal computer or terminal in conjunction with the information superhighway to select and purchase almost anything, from paper clips to airplanes. In some cases the items selected will be automatically picked, packaged, and possibly delivered to our doorstep. This type of service will help speed the completion of routine activities, such as grocery shopping, and leave us more time for leisure, travel, and the things we enjoy.

First there was the automatic teller machine (ATM) and now there is the automated checkout machine (ACM). The move to self-checkout in supermarkets is gaining momentum. Shoppers scan their own groceries and receive visual and verbal confirmation of each purchase from the monitor. With ACMs, checkout is faster and less expensive. Checkout will be even faster and less expensive with the information superhighway.

The emergence of the information superhighway is already changing the way many of us shop. Several on-line information services such as Prodigy offer shop-at-home capabilities. Users can shop for everything from lingerie to pickup trucks. Purchases are charged to a credit card and delivered to your door—even a pickup.

Education will take on a new dimension with the coming of the information superhighway. While in the classroom students will be able to observe constellations with the astronomers, pursue criminals with law enforcement officers, or interpret Tchaikovsky with a conductor.

High-Tech Voting and Polling   Local, state, and federal elections might not require an army of volunteers. Politicians might not have to worry about low voter turnout on a rainy Election Day. In the not-too-distant future we will record our votes over the information superhighway. Such a system will reduce the costs of elections and encourage greater voter participation.

Television newscasters will be able to sample the thinking of tens of thousands, even millions, of people in a matter of minutes. After they ask the questions, we at home will register our responses over the information superhighway. Our responses will be sent immediately to a central computer for analysis, and the results reported almost instantaneously. In this way, television news programs will keep us abreast of public opinion on critical issues and the feeling toward political candidates on a day-to-day basis.

The National Database   The information superhighway will provide the electronic infrastructure needed to maintain a national database. A national database will be a central repository for all personal data for citizens. An individual would be assigned a unique identification number at birth. This ID number would replace the social security number, the driver's license number, the student identification number, and dozens of others.

A national database would consolidate the personal data now stored on tens of thousands of manual and computer-based files. It could contain an individual's name, past and present addresses, dependent data, work history, medical history, marital history, tax data, criminal record, military history, credit rating and history, and so on.

A national database has certain advantages. A national database could provide the capability of monitoring the activities of criminal suspects; virtually eliminating welfare fraud; quickly identifying illegal aliens; making an individual's medical history available at any hospital in the country; taking the 10-year Census almost automatically; and generating valuable information. Medical researchers could isolate geographical areas with inordinately high incidences of certain illnesses. The Bureau of Labor Statistics could monitor real, as opposed to reported, employment levels on a daily basis. The information possibilities are endless.

Summary

The information superhighway will enable people of all walks of life to interact with just about anyone else, with institutions, with businesses, and with vast amounts of data and information. The superhighway will, however, be very expensive and must be implemented in degrees over the next 15 years. Much of the technology is in place for a modest beginning. For example, many major cities are linked with high-speed fiber optic cable. Millions of homes have personal computers. Information services, such as CompuServe, Prodigy, and GEnie, are growing every day in the scope and variety of services they offer. However, to enable information services such as video-on-demand, high-speed lines must be extended to your home or place of business. At present, when high-speed intercity traffic exits from the information superhighway, it must travel slowly on low-speed lines. These low-speed lines are the weakest link in the information chain and, therefore, limit the variety and sophistication of applications that can be delivered to your electronic doorstep.

In time, we will be able to use our PCs or terminals to turn up the heat at home, call a taxi, buy shares of stock, request any movie ever made, take a college course, or make hotel reservations from virtually anywhere at any time. We'll even be able to talk with someone who is speaking a different language through an electronic interpreter. That time may be sooner than you think. Telecommunications, computer, and information services companies are jockeying for position to be a part of what forecasters predict will be the most lucrative industry of the twenty-first century—information services.

10–6   YOUR CHALLENGE

Congratulations. Your newly acquired base of knowledge has positioned you to mainstream into the information society. However, the computer learning process is ongoing. The dynamics of a rapidly advancing computer technology demands a constant updating of skills and expertise. By their very nature, computers bring about change. With the total amount of computing capacity in the world doubling every two years, we can expect even more dramatic change in the future. The cumulative effects of these changes are altering the basic constructs of society and the way we live, work, and play. Terminals and microcomputers have replaced calculators and ledger books; electronic mail speeds communication; word processing has virtually eliminated typewriters; computer-aided design has rendered the T square and compass obsolete; computer-based training has become a part of the teaching process; EFT may eventually eliminate the need for money; on-line shopping is affecting consumer buying habits . . . and the list goes on.

Francis Bacon said, "Knowledge is power." You now have a base of computer knowledge. Combine this knowledge with your innate creative abilities and you are poised to make a significant impact on whatever field you choose to pursue, be it in the business world, health care, government, education, or the arts.

We as a society are, in effect, trading a certain level of computer dependence for an improvement in the quality of life. This improvement in the way we live is not a foregone conclusion. It is our challenge to harness the power of the computer and direct it toward the benefit of society. To be an active participant in this age of information, we as a society and as individuals must continue to learn about and understand computers. Charles Lecht, an outspoken advocate of computers, is fond of saying, "What the lever is to the arm, the computer is to the mind."

Never before has such opportunity presented itself so vividly. This generation, *your generation,* has the technological foundation and capability of changing dreams into reality.

IMPORTANT TERMS AND SUMMARY OUTLINE

computer matching
computer monitoring
cryptography
enterprise-wide information system
ergonomics

footprint
information superhighway
logical security
physical security
pilferage

software piracy
uninterruptible power source (UPS)
virus

10–1 Information Technology: Can We Live Without It? Society has reached a point of no return with regard to dependence on computers. Business competition demands the use of computers. We are also reluctant to give up those personal conveniences made possible by computers. Only through understanding can we control the misuse or abuse of computer technology.

10–2 The Question of Ethics A code of ethics provides direction for computer professionals and users so they can apply computer technology responsibly.

The dominant ethical issue is the privacy of personal information. As automation continues to enrich our lives, it also opens the door for abuses of personal information. Personal information has become the product of a growing industry. Not only are the people involved not asked for permission to use their data, they are seldom even told that their personal information is being sold. **Computer matching** involves the examination of separate databases to identify individuals common to both. **Computer monitoring** is used to measure worker performance.

Computer crime is a relatively recent phenomenon; therefore, laws governing information technology are few, and those that do exist are subject to a variety of interpretations. Computer crimes are frequently a result of computer fraud, negligence, or incompetence. Overzealous hackers tap into computer systems and sometimes leave evidence of unlawful entry, called a **footprint,** or infect the computer system with a **virus,** which is intended to cause harm to the computer systems of unsuspecting victims. **Software piracy** and **pilferage** are computer crimes.

10–3 Computer-Center and System Security Generally, **enterprise-wide information systems** are handled by minicomputers and mainframe computers located in centralized computer centers. The threats to the security of computer centers and information systems call for precautionary measures. A computer center can be vulnerable in its hardware, software, files/databases, data communications, and personnel. Organizations use a variety of approaches to secure the computer center, including the installation of an **uninterruptible power source (UPS)** and the use of **cryptography** to scramble messages sent over data communications channels.

Information systems security is classified as **logical security** or **physical security**. Logical security for online systems is achieved primarily by using passwords and personal identification numbers (PINs).

Ease of accessibility makes PC security a difficult problem to address. However, the conscientious PC user can use several physical and logical security measures to safeguard valuable and/or sensitive information.

Security systems are implemented in degrees, and no computer center or system can be made totally secure.

10–4 Ergonomics: The Human Connection Human factors engineers are applying the principles of **ergonomic** design to ensure that the interface between knowledge worker and work place is safe, comfortable, effective, and efficient. The knowledge worker's work place should be designed with enough flexibility to enable it to be custom-fitted to its worker. Attention to the overall environment (lighting, noise, ventilation) can reduce stress and increase worker performance.

10–5 Down the Road: Information Superhighways The **information superhighway** is a network of high-speed data communications links that eventually will connect virtually every facet of our society. The superhighway will involve the integration of this high-speed data communications network with computer and television technologies. Traffic on the superhighway will be anything that can be digitized. A wide range of information and telecommunication services are planned for the information superhighway. These applications include video phones, video-on-demand, interactive television, video games, soft-copy publishing (with a hard-copy option), multimedia catalogs, electronic mail (including a video option), total electronic funds transfer (EFT), electronic shopping, electronic voting and polling, and a national database. The information superhighway will enable people to interact with just about anyone else, with institutions, with businesses, and with vast amounts of data and information.

10–6 Your Challenge The computer offers us the opportunity to improve the quality of our lives. It is our challenge to harness the power of the computer and direct it to the benefit of society.

REVIEW EXERCISES

Concepts

1. What precautions can be taken to minimize the effects of hardware failure?
2. What name is given to programs intended to damage the computer system of an unsuspecting victim?
3. Most computer monitoring takes place at which level of activity: clerical, operational, tactical, or strategic?
4. What is the objective of computer matching?
5. Briefly describe two types of computer crimes.
6. The implementation of the information superhighway will involve the integration of which three technologies?
7. Briefly describe video-on-demand, an information superhighway application.

Discussion

8. In the past, bank officers have been reluctant to report computer crimes. If you were a customer of a bank that made such a decision, how would you react?
9. Briefly describe how the business letter of the future will be composed and delivered.
10. Why would a judge sentence one person to 10 years in jail for an unarmed robbery of $25 from a convenience store and another to 18 months for computer fraud involving millions of dollars?
11. List and discuss at least one application, other than those mentioned in the text, of a national database.
12. Describe what yesterday would have been like if you had not used the capabilities of computers. Keep in mind that businesses with which you deal rely on computers and that many of your appliances are computer-based.
13. Argue for or against a cashless society.
14. Discuss the kinds of personal information that can be obtained by analyzing a person's credit-card transactions during the past year.
15. Speculate on what the consumer hardware for the information superhighway would look like in the year 2001.

SELF-TEST (BY SECTION)

10–1 a. It would take at least a month to retool a typical automobile assembly line so it could function without computers. (T/F)

b. If the number of computer applications continues to grow at the present rate, our computer-independent society will be dependent on computers by the year 2000. (T/F)

10–2 a. The number of federal government agencies that maintain computer-based files on individuals is between: (a) 50 and 100, (b) 500 and 1000, or (c) 5000 and 10,000?

b. In _____, computers continuously gather and assimilate data on worker activities for the purpose of measuring worker performance.

c. Gaining unauthorized access to any computer system with a federal interest with the intent of defrauding the system is a: (a) violation of public ethics, (b) misdemeanor, or (c) felony?

d. Many legal questions involving computers and information processing are yet to be incorporated into the federal laws. (T/F)

e. The evidence of unlawful entry to a computer system is called a _____ .

f. What law is violated when an organization duplicates proprietary software without permission: (a) civil rights, (b) antitrust, or (c) copyright?

10–3 a. Logical security for on-line systems is achieved primarily by _____ and PINs.

b. Virusology is the study of the assignment of security codes. (T/F)

10–4 a. The study of the relationships between people and their machines is called: (a) humanology, (b) human economics, or (c) ergonomics?

b. A display screen does not emit any more radiation than the human body. (T/F)

10–5 a. The primary transmission technology to be used for data communications along the information superhighway will be: (a) fiber optic cable, (b) satellite microwave, or (c) twisted-pair copper wire?

b. The volume of traditional mail handled by the postal service is expected to decrease as the information superhighway begins to mature. (T/F)

10–6 The total computing capacity in the world is increasing at slightly less than 5% per year. (T/F)

Self-test answers. **10–1 (a)** F; **(b)** F. **10–2 (a)** c; **(b)** computer monitoring; **(c)** c; **(d)** T; **(e)** footprint; **(f)** c. **10–3 (a)** passwords; **(b)** F. **10–4 (a)** c; **(b)** T. **10–5 (a)** a; **(b)** T. **10–6** F.

APPENDIX: USING WINDOWS

A-1 ABOUT WINDOWS

What Is Windows?

Windows is the dominant graphical user interface (GUI) for the IBM-PC–compatible environment. The name *Windows* describes basically how the software functions. It runs one or more applications in "windows"—rectangular areas displayed on the screen. Other Windows capabilities are described in this section.

The Windows Platform Windows, itself a commercial software package, is more than just another application for micros. It also defines a new platform for which other applications software packages are written. MS-DOS remains a popular platform, but it is about 15 years old and is not designed to take advantage of modern PC technology. Windows offers some inviting solutions to the limitations of MS-DOS.

1. *Windows is user-friendly.* Windows employs a graphical user interface (GUI). With a GUI the user "points" to the desired option, file, program, and so on with a mouse or other pointing device. In contrast, MS-DOS users must enter what are often cryptic commands to the microcomputer system via the keyboard. (Microsoft refers to Windows as a "graphical environment.")

2. *Windows enables multiple programs to be run simultaneously.* This multitasking feature permits a user to print out a WordPerfect report while engaged in a Lotus 1-2-3 session. Multitasking is the concurrent execution of more than one program at a time.

3. *Windows enables users to work with large files.* Databases, spreadsheet files, and word processing documents can be as big as available memory will permit. Some micros have as much as 32 MB of RAM. With Windows, the text in this book (about 1 MB of memory) and many other books could be loaded to RAM—simultaneously! Without Windows, a file containing one or two chapters of this book might not fit into available RAM.

4. *Windows permits information to be passed between applications.* With Windows, text in a word processing document can be transferred in seconds to a database record. A pie chart from a graphics program can be inserted into a word processing document just as easily. These types of information transfers, though not impossible, are cumbersome and time-consuming with MS-DOS.

Although Windows establishes a new platform, most of the thousands of applications software packages created for MS-DOS can run under Windows.

De Facto Standard Windows is being so wholeheartedly embraced by the microcomputer community, including software vendors, that the GUI, the terms, and the concepts introduced by Windows are emerging as de facto standards in the industry. Of course, the Windows platform uses many traditional tools (for example, the mouse) and techniques (such as windows, bar menus, and default options). However, Windows has introduced a number of new terms and concepts, all of which apply to the hundreds of software packages that have been and are being developed to run under Windows. These are discussed in this appendix.

Non-Windows versus Windows Applications

Non-Windows Applications Any software application that does not adhere to the Microsoft Windows Common User Access, or CUA, standard is a **non-Windows application.** Non-Windows applications will run under Windows, but these software packages cannot take advantage of many helpful Windows features.

Windows Applications Programs that adhere to Windows conventions are **Windows applications.** These conventions describe:

- *Type and style of window.* A window is a rectangular box superimposed over the screen image.
- *Arrangement and style of menus.*
- *Use of the keyboard and mouse.*
- *Format for screen-image display.* Windows is a graphics-based application (as opposed to text-based). In a graphics-based software package, the text and all images are made up of patterns of pixels. This permits tremendous flexibility in the integration and presentation of information.

The GUI for Windows versions of Word, Corel-DRAW, Quicken, Pagemaker, and all other Windows applications have the same look and feel. *When you learn the GUI for Windows, you also learn the GUI for hundreds of different software packages.*

The Windows graphical user interface employs both the mouse and the keyboard as input devices. Interaction with Windows or a Windows application is most efficient when options are chosen with a mouse and characters are entered via the keyboard. All Windows commands can be activated with the keyboard, but keyboard-only interaction can be slow and cumbersome for many operations.

When working with the mouse in Windows:

- Point and *click* the left button to **select** an item (an application program, a menu option, a box, and so on). When you select an item, the item is highlighted in some way. *Generally, selection does not result in the initiation of a processing activity.*
- Point and *double-click* the left button to **choose** an item. *Choosing an item results in some kind of action.*
- Point and *drag* to move or resize a window on the display screen.

When working with the keyboard in Windows:

- Enter text as needed (for example, a path for a file: **c:\wp\wp.exe**).
- Activate the current menu bar with function keys.
- Enter the underlined letter of the menu option in the active menu to choose that option.
- Use the arrow keys to highlight menu options in an active menu.
- Use shortcut key combinations (for example, ALT+F4) to highlight items and to navigate between applications.

A–2 WINDOWS CONCEPTS

The Desktop

The screen upon which icons, windows, and so on are displayed is known as the **desktop.** The Windows desktop may contain a *background, one ac-*

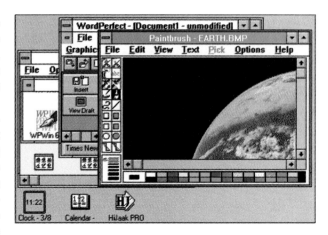

FIGURE A–1 The Windows Desktop *The appearance of the Windows desktop depends on the user's application mix and visual needs at a particular time. This user has three open application windows (Program Manager, WordPerfect, and Paintbrush, the active window) and three applications that have been shrunk to application icons (Clock, Calendar, and HiJaak PRO) at the bottom of the desktop.*

tive window, one or more inactive windows, and *icons* (see Figure A–1). The background can be anything from a single-color screen to an elaborate artistic image, such as a 3-D chessboard. The user can choose from a number of backgrounds. All windows and icons are superimposed over the background, be it plain or an artistic image.

The Windows Window A typical rectangular Windows **application window** is illustrated in Figure A–1. An application window contains a running application, such as Paintbrush or WordPerfect. Several applications can be running simultaneously, but there is only one **active window** at any given time. (Paintbrush is the active window in Figure A–1.) Commands issued via the keyboard or mouse apply to the active window, which is highlighted. The elements of an application window are:

- Title bar
- Menu bar
- Work space
- Scroll bars
- Corners and borders

Each is described in the following sections and illustrated in Figure A–2.

Control menu box
Menu bar
Title bar
Border
Corner

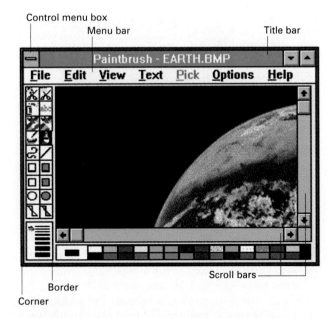

FIGURE A-2 Elements of an Application Window

Title bar. The horizontal **title bar** at the top of each window runs the width of the window. From left to right (see Figure A–2), the elements of the title bar are the *control menu box, window title and active filename,* and *maximize/minimize restore buttons.* Point and click the mouse on these elements to change the presentation of the window.

■ *Control menu box.* Point and click on the control menu box to display the pull-down control menu (see Figure A–3), which is also called the *system menu.* Most of the options on the control menu are available without having to dis-

FIGURE A-3 The Control Menu

play the menu. For example, one of the options is *Move.* To move a window, the user simply uses the mouse to point to the window title area, then drags the window to the desired location. The keyboard user would need to choose the *Move* option and use the cursor-control keys to move the window. Control menu options vary, depending on the type of application being displayed in the window, but most will have some or all of the following options.

Restore When available, users can restore an enlarged window to its previous size (a window or an icon). The *Restore* option is **dimmed** and not available unless the window is enlarged. The term *dimmed* is used to describe an option that is visible but not as dark as the available options. (*Restore* is dimmed in Figure A–3.)

Move The *Move* option enables the user to use the cursor-control keys to reposition the active window on the desktop.

Size The *Size* option enables the user to change the height or width of the active window with the cursor-control keys.

Minimize The *Minimize* option **shrinks** the active window to an icon at the bottom of the desktop (see Figure A–1). That is, the application in the window is deactivated and the window disappears from the screen, but the application remains open in the form of an icon.

Maximize The *Maximize* option enlarges the active window to fill the entire screen.

Close Choosing *Close* deactivates and removes the active window from the desktop.

Switch to Choosing the *Switch to* option results in the display of the Task List. The Task List lists open applications (see Figure A–4). Use the mouse to point, and double-click the application you want to make the active application.

Next Choose *Next* to rotate among active **document windows** and document windows that have been shrunk to icons. Document windows, which are explained and illustrated in the "File Manager" portion of Section A–3, are windows within application windows.

Edit Choosing *Edit* results in a **cascading menu** that permits users to transfer information between windows. A cascading menu is a pop-up menu that is displayed when a command from the active menu is chosen. Edit operations are discussed in Section A–4.

- *Window title and active filename.* The title of the application is contained in the center portion of the title bar ("Paintbrush" in Figure A–2). To the right of the title is the name of the file displayed in the application work space ("EARTH.BMP" in Figure A–2).
- *Maximize/minimize/restore buttons.* Mouse users can point and click on the maximize (▲) and minimize (▼) buttons (at the right end of the title bar in Figure A–2) to enlarge the window to fill the screen or to shrink it to an icon. The restore button (⬍) replaces the maximize button (▲) when the window is enlarged.

Menu bar. The **menu bar** for an application window runs the width of the window just below the title bar (see Figure A–2). The menu bar lists the menus available for that application. Choosing an option from the menu bar results in a pull-down menu. The *File, Edit,* and *Help* menus are available for most applications. Other menu options depend on the application.

Certain conventions apply to user interactions with any Windows menu, whether a menu bar, a pull-down menu, or a cascading menu.

- *Only the boldface options can be chosen.* Dimmed options are not available for the current circumstances. For example, the *Copy* option would not be available in an Edit menu if nothing had been identified to be copied.
- *Choosing a menu option followed by an ellipsis (. . .) results in a dialog box.* The text in the pop-up **dialog box** asks the user to choose parameters or enter further information. Often the dialog box appears when the user must choose among more options before the chosen menu option can be executed. For example, choosing the *Paste from* menu option from Figure A–5 produces a dialog box. In the box, the user is asked to enter the file specification of the source file (the file to be copied into the work space).

   The Task List in Figure A–4 provides another example of a dialog box. The Task List dialog box asks the user to choose one of the open applications in the active application.
- *Corresponding shortcut keys are presented adjacent to many options in Windows menus.* The **shortcut key** is a key combination that can be executed without displaying a menu. For example, the Cut option on the Edit menu in Figure A–5 can be executed by the Ctrl+X

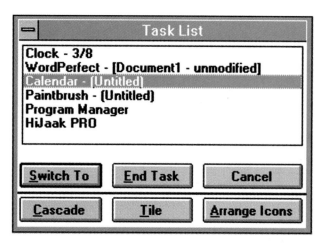

FIGURE A–4 The Task List *The Task List provides a list of open applications.*

shortcut key combination; that is, tap *X* while holding down *Ctrl.*

- *Choosing a menu option followed by an arrow (▶) results in a cascading menu.* For example, the Edit option on control menus for non-Windows applications results in a cascading menu (Cut, Copy, Paste, and so on).
- *A user-recorded check mark (✓) to the left of the menu option indicates that the option is active and applies to any related commands.* For example, in the Windows File Manager application, the View option lets the user check the options that apply when the files are listed (i.e., alphabetical *By Name* or *By File Type*).

FIGURE A–5 A Pull-Down Edit Menu *The Edit menu is pulled down from the Paintbrush menu bar. Point and click with the mouse or key the underlined letter to choose an option. Options followed by an ellipsis (. . .) result in a pop-up dialog box. Shortcut key combinations for* Undo *(Ctrl+Z),* Cut, Copy, *and* Paste *enable users to perform these activities from the keyboard without calling up the Edit menu.*

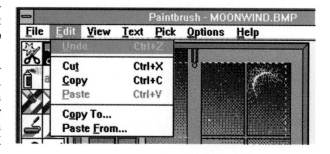

■ *There are three ways to choose a menu option.*
  1. Point and click the mouse on the option.
  2. Use the keyboard cursor-control keys to select (highlight) the option and tap the Enter key to choose it.
  3. Use the keyboard to enter the underlined letter of the menu option. For example, in Figure A–5, enter *T* (Cu*t*), *C* (*C*opy), and so on.

On most application windows, the last option on the menu bar is *Help.* Choose the on-line Help menu whenever you need context-sensitive information regarding basic Windows skills, key shortcuts, procedures, features, or commands.

Work space. The **work space** is the area in a window below the title bar or menu bar (see Figure A–2). Everything that relates to the application noted in the title bar is displayed in the work space. For example, in Figure A–2, an image of the earth as seen from space is in the work space of the Paintbrush paint program. The work space of a word processing program contains the word processing document.

Scroll bars. Depending on the size of a window, the entire application may not be visible. When this happens the window is outfitted with **vertical** and/or **horizontal scroll bars** (see Figure A–2). Each bar contains a **scroll box** and two **scroll arrows.** Use the mouse or keyboard to move a box up/down or left/right on a scroll bar to display other parts of the application. To move the scroll box with the mouse, simply drag it to another location on the scroll bar or click the scroll arrows.

Corners and borders. To resize a window, use the mouse and point to a window's border or corner. The graphics cursor changes to a double arrow when positioned over a border or corner. Drag the border or corner in the directions indicated by the double arrow to the desired shape. When dragging a corner, the two sides linked to the corner move. To resize with the keyboard, display the control menu and choose *Size.*

Types of Windows The three types of windows in the Windows graphical environment are the *application window,* the *document window,* and the *dialog box,* all of which have been introduced in earlier sections. The document window and the dialog box require further explanation.

Document windows, which are windows within an application window, are displayed in the parent application window's work space. For example, the Windows File Manager application normally will have document windows into which various directories are displayed. In Figure A–6, the title bars of four open directory windows are displayed (H:\, B:\, F:\ ESSNTIAL\CAPTURE, and C:\DR11\FIGURES\ANIMALS). Being a subordinate window, the document window does not have a menu bar. However, the menu bar for the active application is applicable to the active document window. Note in Figure A–6 that the title bars of both the active application (File Manager) and the active document window (C:\DR11\FIGURES\ANIMALS) are highlighted.

Typically, entries in the dialog box must be okayed or revised by the user before a command can be executed. The dialog box may contain any of these seven elements (see Figures A–7 and A–8).

1. *Text box.* Enter text information in the text box or accept the default entry that is displayed. Often the user is asked to enter a number (see Figure A–7) or the path for a file (C:\QUICKENW\QW.EXE).

2. *Command buttons.* Point and click to the *OK* rectangular command button to carry out the command with the information provided in the dialog box. Choose *Cancel* to retain the original information (see Figure A–7).

FIGURE A–6 Application and Document Windows
In this example display, the Windows File Manager application has four open document windows.

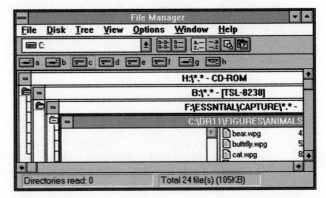

Drop-down list box with scroll bar

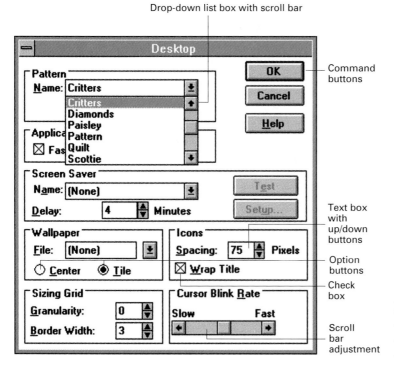

FIGURE A–7 Elements of a Dialog Box
Five of the seven dialog box elements are shown in the Desktop dialog box (see also Figure A–8).

3. *Option buttons.* Circular option buttons preface each item in a list of mutually exclusive items (only one can be marked). Point and click a button to insert a black dot in the button and activate the option (see Figure A–7).

4. *Drop-down list boxes.* The drop-down list box is used as an alternative to the list box (see Figure A–8 and Item 6, following) when the dialog box is too small for a list box to be displayed. The existence of a drop-down list box is indicated by a button containing an underlined down arrow. The button is positioned to the right of the current choice in the dialog box. Point and click on the button to display a drop-down list box (see Figure A–7).

5. *Scroll bar adjustment.* The scroll bar adjustment enables users to change parameters with an infinite number of possible settings, such as the speed at which the cursor blinks (see Figure A–7).

6. *List boxes.* A list box displays a list of available choices for a particular option. For example, one list box lists the printers that are installed on the system (see Figure A–8). Long lists will have a vertical scroll bar. In contrast with the drop-down list box (see Figure A–7

and Item 4, above), the list box is part of the original dialog box display. The drop-down list box must be requested by the user.

7. *Check boxes.* Check boxes preface options that can be switched off or on as needed. Point and click on a box to insert an *X* and activate the option (see Figure A–8).

FIGURE A–8 Elements of a Dialog Box   *The list box and check box dialog box elements are shown in the Printers dialog box (see also Figure A–7).*

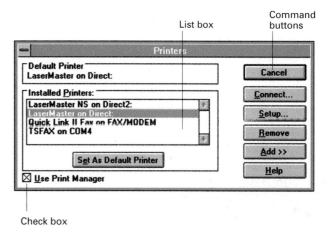

Icons   Icons, the graphical representation of a Windows element, play a major role in the Windows environment. The most commonly used icons are in the following four categories: *application and program-item icons, document icons, disk-drive icons,* and *file icons.*

Application and program-item icons.   An active application window can be minimized, or shrunk, to an **application icon,** thereby making it inactive. The application icon, usually a graphic rendering of the software package's logo, is positioned at the bottom of the desktop (see Figure A–1). Point and double-click on the icon to restore the window and the application to active status. Typically, you would minimize application windows that may not be needed for a while to make room on the desktop for other windows.

An application icon that has not been opened is called a **program-item icon.** An application icon and a program-item icon for a particular application, such as Paintbrush, look exactly the same. Their location indicates whether the application is opened or closed. Program-item icons are discussed and illustrated in the Program Manager portion of Section A–3.

Document icons.   The active document window, which is a window within an application window, can be minimized to a **document icon.** For example in Figure A–9, three of the document windows in Figure A–6 are minimized to document icons in the File Manager application window. The graphic for the document-window icon usually provides some insight into the function of the document window. For example, in the File Manager application window of Figure A–9, the directory icons look like lists. Point and double-click on the document icon to restore the document window.

Disk-drive icons.   The disk-drive icons graphically represent five disk-drive options: floppy, hard, network (hard), RAM, and CD-ROM. The floppy (A, B, and G), hard-disk (C through F), and CD-ROM (H) icons shown in Figure A–9 resemble the faceplates of the disk drives. Typically, PCs have only one or two floppy drives, assigned to A and B. This system is unique in that it has a very high-density floptical disk drive assigned to G.

File icons.   File icons are found in the document windows within the Windows File Manager application (see Figures A–6 and A–9). These windows typically list disk content. The four types of file icons are:

FIGURE A–9 Document Icons   *Windows uses a variety of icons to represent everything from disk drives to applications. In this File Manager example, three directory windows in Figure A–6 are minimized to document icons.*

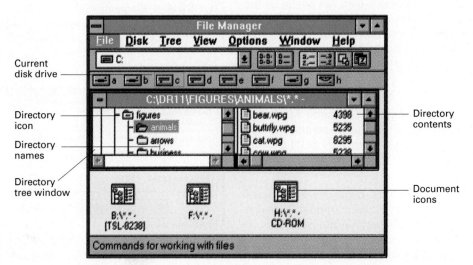

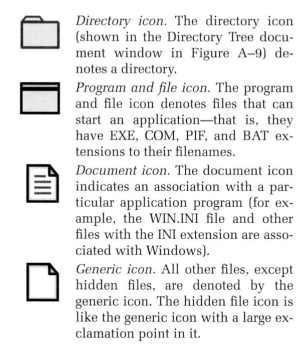 *Directory icon.* The directory icon (shown in the Directory Tree document window in Figure A–9) denotes a directory.

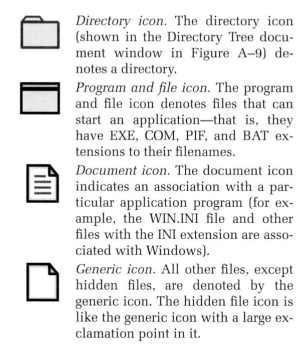 *Program and file icon.* The program and file icon denotes files that can start an application—that is, they have EXE, COM, PIF, and BAT extensions to their filenames.

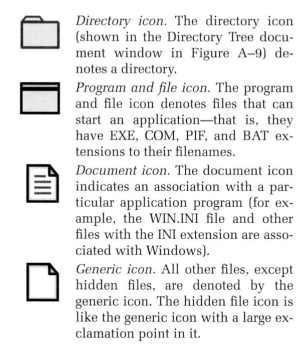 *Document icon.* The document icon indicates an association with a particular application program (for example, the WIN.INI file and other files with the INI extension are associated with Windows).

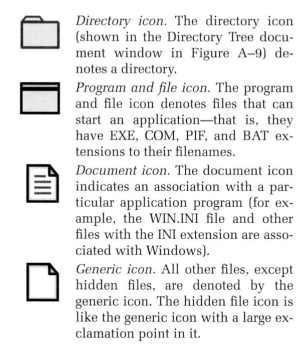 *Generic icon.* All other files, except hidden files, are denoted by the generic icon. The hidden file icon is like the generic icon with a large exclamation point in it.

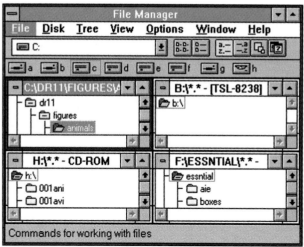

FIGURE A–10 The Tile Arrangement of Windows
The File Manager document windows in Figure A–6 are shown in a tile arrangement. Contrast this arrangement with the cascade arrangement in Figure A–6.

Viewing Windows   Windows is designed so you can view multiple applications in windows on the desktop display. An application window can be opened in several ways, usually by pointing and clicking on the application icon in the Program Manager window. Once open, a window can be resized, shrunk (and restored), maximized (and restored), and, finally, closed.

Essentially, any applications software written to run under Windows can be:

■ Viewed and run in a window, the shape and size of which is determined by the user.

■ Run full-screen; that is, filling the entire screen, with no other application windows or icons showing.

Some non-Windows applications run only as full-screen applications and cannot be run in a window. When multiple applications are running, the user can use the Move and Resize capabilities to arrange and size the windows to meet viewing needs. Of course, open windows can be minimized to free viewing space on the desktop.

Within a given application window, such as the Program Manager, multiple document windows can be sized, shrunk, and arranged by the user within the work space. As an alternative, the user can request that the document windows be automatically presented as **cascading windows** (see Figure A–6) or **tiled windows** (see Figure A–10). Choose these options from the Windows menu option in the menu bar. The Cascade option overlaps open document windows so all title bars are visible. The Tile option fills the work space in such a way that no document window overlaps another. Scroll bars are provided on those document windows for which the space is not adequate to display the windows' content.

A–3 WINDOWS APPLICATIONS

The Microsoft Windows software package comes with a number of applications, two of which are integral to running the program: Program Manager and File Manager.

Program Manager

The Program Manager is the nucleus of the Windows operating environment. When you start Windows, the Program Manager is opened as the active window and remains open until you exit Windows. The Program Manager window contains document windows, each of which may be displayed or minimized to a document icon (see Fig-

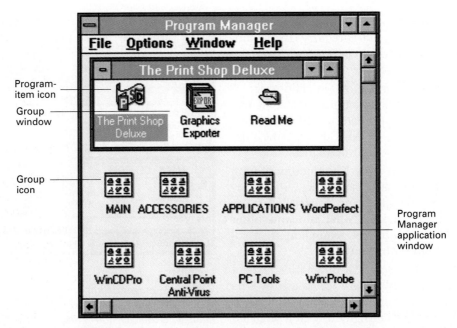

FIGURE A–11 The Program Manager Window *In the example, The Print Shop Deluxe application group window is open within the Program Manager application. All other application groups are presented as group icons.*

ure A–11). Each document window contains icons for a group of related applications. For example, one document window might contain those icons for applications that are related to The Print Shop Deluxe, a popular package for creating greeting cards, banners, and so on (see Figure A–11). These icons are called *program-item icons.* When opened, they become application windows, which can be minimized to *application icons.* Program-item icons represent dormant applications. The document windows within the Program Manager sometimes are called **group windows** because they contain groups of program-item icons.

Normally you will find these predefined group windows in the Program Manager.

- *Main group.* The main group includes Windows system applications, such as the File Manager and DOS Prompt.
- *Accessories group.* This group contains several helpful applications that do not relate directly to the running of Windows applications, such as the clock, calendar, drawing, and so on.
- *Games group.* Microsoft includes several fun and instructive games.

Windows permits program items to be added to, deleted from, or moved between group windows. In addition, users can define their own groups. For example, in Figure A–11, a group window is defined for "PC Tools."

To run an application from the Program Manager, open the appropriate group window by pointing and double-clicking the icon. Then point and double-click the desired program-item icon. When you exit an application, such as The Print Shop Deluxe, its application window is removed from the desktop.

To exit Windows, close all open applications except the Program Manager (which cannot be closed), then point and double-click the menu control box on the Program Manager title bar. A *confirmation dialog box* asks you for confirmation in this and many other circumstances that may result in loss of data.

File Manager

The Windows File Manager application is a user-friendly file-management tool. Users who are familiar with the cryptic, command-driven MS-DOS approach to file management will appreciate the ease with which File Manager allows files to be moved, copied, deleted, and generally organized for more efficient retrieval. The File Manager application is opened from the Main group window within the Program Manager application (see Figure A–11).

A File Manager document window is divided in two sections.

- *Directory tree.* The left side of the window graphically illustrates the organization of directories and subdirectories for a particular disk drive (see Figure A–12).
- *Contents list.* The right side lists the contents of a user-selected directory or subdirectory (see Figure A–12).

Files and directories are listed next to four types of icons: directory icon, program- and batch-file icon, document-file icon, and generic file icon (see Figure A–12). You can open as many document windows as you need by simply pointing and double-clicking on the desired disk-drive icon.

The Directory Tree   In Figure A–12 the disk-drive icons under the title bar of the directory tree window show the available lettered root directories and the disk-drive type associated with each root directory. Point and click the desired disk-drive icon to display the corresponding directory window. When displayed, the "tree" (left side) looks more like a list of directories. It becomes a tree when one or more directories with subdirectories are *expanded* to show the subdirectories (see Figure A–12). Directories with one or more subdirectories are marked with a "+" within the icon. Point and click the already selected directory icon to expand it. Or, select the tree menu-bar option to expand or *collapse* the entire directory. Directory icons that have been expanded to show subdirectories are marked with a "-" (see Figure A–12).

Contents List   Point and double-click a directory icon in the directory tree to show the files for that directory (see Figure A–12). The contents list contains a list of all files and subdirectories in the selected directory.

FIGURE A–12 The File Manager Window and the Directory Document Window   *In the directory section, directories with subordinate directories can be expanded (indicated with a "-") or collapsed (indicated with a "+") to meet the needs of the user. The active document window is shown with file details.*

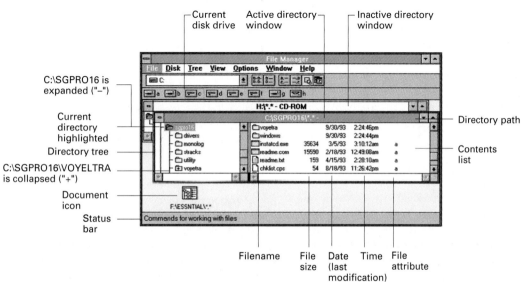

The user has the option of displaying all files and subdirectories in the directory, or he or she can use check boxes to tell the system which types to display (directories, programs, documents, and/or others). The user also can request that file details be displayed (see Figure A–12) or only the filename. The file-details list can include any or all of the following along with the filename.

- Size of file (in bytes)
- Last modification date
- Last modification time
- File attributes (hidden or not available to the user, read-only, archive, or system files)

The File Manager permits the user to choose the order in which files are displayed in the directory window. The View option in the menu bar gives you four mutually exclusive options from which to choose (*Name, Type* of file, *Size,* and last modification *Date*). Figure A–12 illustrates a directory that contains all file details and is sorted by size.

Working with File Manager Document Windows
The File Manager's menu bar is applicable to the active document window.

The File menu. Choosing the File Manager menu bar's File option presents the user with several important file-management capabilities. Most options require that a file or files be selected before the command can be executed. Typically, choosing an option in the pull-down File menu results in a pop-up dialog box (see Figure A–13) in which the user is asked to enter information and/or to confirm that the selected file is correct. The most frequently used File menu commands are:

- Run (execute a program)
- Print
- Search (for a user-specified file or files)
- Move (files or directories)
- Copy (files or directories)
- Delete (files or directories)
- Rename (files or directories)
- Create directory

A quick way to execute a program file is to open the directory window containing the file, then point and double-click the desired file.

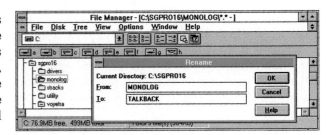

FIGURE A–13 Pop-Up Dialog Box *Choosing* Rename *in the* File *menu results in a pop-up dialog box.*

Perhaps the most efficient way to move and copy files/directories is to open the desired directory windows, then choose the tile window arrangement (see Figure A–10) so that the source and destination directory windows are visible. If you want to move a particular file in the source directory to a different directory, point to the selected file icon and drag it with the mouse to the destination directory while holding down the ALT key. Copy a file(s) in a similar manner, except that you simply drag the desired icon(s) between source and destination directories. In keeping with the user-friendly philosophy of Windows, a *confirmation message* asks users to confirm most file operations.

The Disk menu. Choosing the menu bar's Disk option presents the user with commands that enable the maintenance of hard disks and diskettes. The most frequently used commands in the Disk menu are the *Format Disk* and *Copy Disk* commands. The format command prepares the disk in the designated drive to store MS-DOS files. Copy Disk performs the same function as the MS-DOS diskcopy command; that is, it permits the entire contents of a diskette to be copied to a like disk (of the same size and density). These commands result in the destruction of all data on the formatted disk and the destination disk, so caution is recommended when using these commands.

A–4 WINDOWS IN PRACTICE

Windows is designed to be easy to learn and easy to use, but, like any other skill, you need a solid understanding of its underlying principles as well as plenty of practice.

The Help Feature

When using Windows, your best source of information about common operations is the Help command. The on-line Help feature is available whenever the Help command button is displayed or whenever the Help option is included in the menu bar. In any Help window display (see Figure A–14), point and click any green item (on color monitors) to get detailed information on that topic. Of course, Help information applies to the active application. Standard options found on the pull-down help menu include the following.

- *Contents.* A list of Help topics.
- *Search for Help On.* Prompts you to enter a key word, then provides you with a list of related help screens.
- *Commands.* Command explanations.
- *Procedures.* Step-by-step explanations of application procedures.
- *Using Help.* Information on how to use help. (This option explains how to navigate within the Help window.)

Switching between Windows

Windows allows users to open as many applications as available RAM will permit. It is not un-

FIGURE A–14 The Help Window *Help windows are context-sensitive; that is, they apply to the active application. Choose Contents in the main help menu, then in the pull-down menu (not shown) choose* Using Help *to learn more about using help within a particular application.*

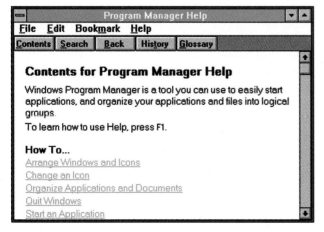

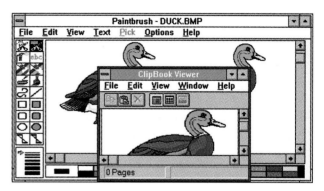

FIGURE A–15 The Windows Clipboard *In a* Cut *or* Copy *operation, information is transferred to the Windows clipboard. In the example, a Paintbrush image of a duck is copied to the clipboard, then* Pasted *from the clipboard to the original Paintbrush image to complete the* Copy *operation.*

usual for Windows users to have from two to ten applications running at any given time. For example, a user might open these applications and keep them open during the working day: Program Manager, File Manager, WordPerfect, CorelDRAW, Calculator, Clock, and Calendar. When running multiple applications, the user can elect to display them as windows or application icons. In Figure A–1, several open applications are shrunk to application icons and restored to windows as needed.

The active window is always highlighted in the **foreground.** When in the foreground all parts of the window are visible. Other open windows are in the **background,** or behind the foreground (see Figure A–15). There are three ways to switch between open applications.

- Point and click anywhere on the desired inactive window or point and double-click the desired application icon.
- Tap ALT+ESC to toggle between open windows and application icons.
- Tap CTRL+ESC to display the Task List box (see Figure A–4); then point and click the name of the application you want to make the active window.

Transferring Information between Applications

One of the most inviting aspects of the Windows environment is the ability to copy and move information (text, graphics, or a combination) from one application to another. This is done via the Windows clipboard and the Edit option. Edit is an option in the menu bar of most Windows-based applications and an option in the control menu of most non-Windows applications. Choosing Edit results in a pull-down menu from the bar menu and a cascading menu from the control menu. Options common to most Edit menus are Cut, Copy, Paste, and Delete. The source and destination windows can contain dissimilar applications. For example, text in a word processing document can be copied into a cell in a spreadsheet. As another example, a block of text from a WordPerfect document can be copied into a Paintbrush work space.

The procedure for transferring information is as follows.

1. *Mark the information.* Point and hold the mouse button on one corner of the information to be cut or copied, then drag the graphics cursor to the opposite corner of the area and release the mouse button. The information to be transferred is highlighted.

2. *Cut or copy the marked information to the clipboard.* Choose Edit in the source application's bar menu or control menu to display the options (usually Cut and/or Copy). Choosing the Cut option causes the specified information to be removed from the source application and placed on the Windows clipboard. (Think of the clipboard as an intermediate holding area for information en route to another application.) The Copy option causes the specified information in the source application to be placed on the Windows clipboard, leaving the source application unchanged.

3. *Switch to the destination application and place the graphics cursor at the desired insertion point.*

4. *Paste the marked information.* Choose Edit in the destination application's bar menu or control menu to display the applicable options. Choosing the Paste option causes the contents of the clipboard to be copied to the cursor position in the destination application. The clipboard contents remain unchanged and can be pasted as many times as needed.

The clipboard also can be used to move or copy information within a single application (see Figure A–15). The clipboard window does not have to be opened to perform information transfers.

Terminating an Application and a Windows Session

Perform three operations before ending a Windows session.

1. *Save your work.* Most applications offer two options on the File menu: *Save* and *Save as.* More often than not, users work with existing files. The Save option updates the existing file to reflect the changes made during the session. The Save as option allows users to save the current file under another filename. This feature is handy when you want to retain the working file in its original format (as it was at the beginning of the session).

2. *Close all open windows (except Program Manager).* After saving your work, exit each window by pointing and double-clicking the control menu box in the title bar.

3. *Exit the Program Manager application and Windows.* After all windows are closed, only the Program Manager remains. Close it and exit Windows.

Summary

This Windows overview is intended to introduce you to fundamental Windows concepts, terminology, and capabilities. Thousands of software packages written specifically for the Windows environment have adopted the same concepts and terminology and are designed to take advantage of Windows capabilities. Once you understand the Windows environment, you will feel comfortable with the user interfaces of all software written for Microsoft Windows.

Use the Help feature and what you have learned in these pages to learn the use and operation of Windows and Windows applications. Once you gain familiarity with the environment, you may wish to customize Windows to meet your computing needs and maximize system throughput.

REVIEW EXERCISES

1. How is a Windows item, such as an application program or a menu option, selected with a mouse? How is the item chosen?

2. In Windows, what is the screen area called upon which icons, windows, and so on are displayed?

3. List four elements of the Windows application window.

4. Briefly describe what happens when the Minimize option in the Windows control menu is chosen.

5. What area is just below the Windows title bar or menu bar?

6. What is displayed in a Windows Program Manager group window?

7. Name the three types of windows in the Windows graphical environment.

8. Name four categories of Windows icons.

9. What results when a Windows menu option followed by an ellipsis (. . .) is chosen?

10. Which window arrangement in Windows enables the user to view at least a portion of the content of each window?

11. Briefly describe how a menu option is chosen from the keyboard.

12. What are the two sections of the document windows in the Windows File Manager?

13. When using a mouse to move a selected file from one Windows File Manager document window to another, which key is held down during the drag operation?

14. Is the active Windows window highlighted in the foreground or the background?

15. What is the intermediate holding area called through which information is transferred between Windows applications?

GLOSSARY

Absolute cell address A cell address in a spreadsheet that always refers to the same cell.

Access arm The disk drive mechanism used to position the read/write heads over the appropriate track.

Access time The time interval between the instant a computer makes a request for a transfer of data from a secondary storage device and the instant this operation is completed.

Accumulator The computer register in which the result of an arithmetic or logic operation is formed. (Related to *arithmetic and logic unit*.)

Add-on boards Circuit boards that contain the electronic circuitry for a wide variety of computer-related functions (also called *add-on cards*).

Add-on cards See *add-on boards*.

Address (1) A name, numeral, or label that designates a particular location in primary or secondary storage. (2) A location identifier for nodes in a computer network.

AIX A spinoff of the UNIX operating system.

Alpha A reference to the letters of the alphabet. (Compare with *numeric* and *alphanumeric*.)

Alphanumeric Pertaining to a character set that contains letters, digits, punctuation, and special symbols. (Related to *alpha* and *numeric*.)

Animation The rapid repositioning of an area of a display to create movement within the display.

Applications software Software designed and written to address a specific personal, business, or processing task.

Architecture The design of a computer system.

Argument That portion of a function which identifies the data to be operated on.

Arithmetic and logic unit That portion of the computer that performs arithmetic and logic operations. (Related to *accumulator*.)

Arithmetic operators Mathematical operators (add [+], subtract [−], multiply [*], divide [/], and exponentiation [^]) used in spreadsheet and database software for computations.

Artificial intelligence (AI) The ability of a computer to reason, to learn, to strive for self-improvement, and to simulate human sensory capabilities.

ASCII [American Standard Code for Information Interchange] An encoding system.

ASCII file A generic text file that is stripped of program-specific control characters.

ASCII-8 An 8-bit version of the ASCII encoding system.

Automatic teller machine (ATM) An automated deposit/withdrawal device used in banking.

Backbone A system of routers and the associated transmission media that facilitates the interconnection of computer networks.

Background (1) That part of RAM that contains the lowest priority programs. (2) In Windows, the area of the display over which the foreground is superimposed. (Contrast with *foreground*.)

Backup Pertaining to equipment, procedures, or databases that can be used to restart the system in the event of system failure.

Backup file Duplicate of an existing file.

Badge reader An input device that reads data on badges and cards. (Related to *magnetic stripe*.)

Bar code A graphic encoding technique in which vertical bars of varying widths are used to represent data.

Bar graph A graph that contains vertical bars that represent specified numeric values.

Batch processing A technique in which transactions and/or jobs are collected into groups (batched) and processed together.

Baud (1) A measure of the maximum number of electronic signals that can be transmitted via a communications channel. (2) Bits per second (common-use definition).

Binary A base-2 numbering system.

Bit A *bi*nary digi*t* (0 or 1).

Bit-mapped   Referring to an image that has been projected to a screen based on binary bits.

Bits per second (bps)   The number of bits that can be transmitted per second over a communications channel.

Boilerplate   Existing text in a word processing file that can in some way be customized to be used in a variety of word processing applications.

Boot   The procedure for loading the operating system to primary storage and readying a computer system for use.

BPI   [*Bytes Per Inch*] A measure of data-recording density on secondary storage.

Bubble memory   Nonvolatile solid-state memory.

Bug   A logic or syntax error in a program, a logic error in the design of a computer system, or a hardware fault. (See *debug*.)

Bulletin-board system (BBS)   The electronic counterpart of a wall-mounted bulletin board that enables end users in a computer network to exchange ideas and information via a centralized database.

Bus   An electrical pathway through which the processor sends data and commands to RAM and all peripheral devices.

Bus architecture   See *open architecture*.

Bus topology   A computer network that permits the connection of terminals, peripheral devices, and microcomputers along an open-ended central cable.

Byte   A group of adjacent bits configured to represent a character.

Bytes per inch   See *bpi*.

C   A transportable programming language that can be used to develop software.

C++   An object-oriented version of the C programming language.

Cache memory   High-speed solid-state memory for program instructions and data.

CAD   See *computer-aided design*.

Carrier   Standard-sized pin connectors that permit chips to be attached to a circuit board.

Carrier, common   [in data communications] A company that furnishes data communications services to the general public.

Cathode-ray tube   See *CRT*.

CBT   See *computer-based training*.

CD-ROM disk   [*Compact-Disk–Read-Only Memory disk*] A type of optical laser storage media.

Cell   The intersection of a particular row and column in a spreadsheet.

Cell address   The location—column and row—of a cell in a spreadsheet.

Central processing unit (CPU)   See *processor*.

Centronics connector   A 36-pin connector that is used for the electronic interconnection of computers, modems, and other peripheral devices.

Channel   The facility by which data are transmitted between locations in a computer network (e.g., terminal to host, host to printer).

Channel capacity   The number of bits that can be transmitted over a communications channel per second.

Chip   See *integrated circuit*.

CISC   [*Complex Instruction Set Computer*] A computer-designed architecture that offers programmers a wide variety of instructions. (Contrast with *RISC*.)

Click   A single tap on a mouse's button.

Client/server computing   A computing environment in which processing capabilities are distributed throughout a network such that a client computer requests processing or some other type of service from a server computer.

Clip art   Prepackaged electronic images that are stored on disk to be used as needed in word processing or desktop publishing documents.

Clone   A hardware device or a software package that emulates a product with an established reputation and market acceptance.

Closed architecture   Refers to micros with a fixed, unalterable configuration. (Contrast with *open architecture*.)

Coaxial cable   A shielded wire used as a medium to transmit data between computers and between computers and peripheral devices.

Code   (1) The rules used to translate a bit configuration into alphanumeric characters. (2) The process of compiling computer instructions into the form of a computer program. (3) The actual computer program.

Command   An instruction to a computer that invokes the execution of a preprogrammed sequence of instructions.

Common carrier   [in data communications] See *carrier, common*.

Common User Access (CUA)   The standard by which all software applications designed to be run under Microsoft's Windows must adhere.

Communications   See *data communications*.

Communications channel   The facility by which data are transmitted between locations in a computer network.

Communications protocols   Rules established to govern the way data in a computer network are transmitted.

Communications server   The LAN component that provides external communications links.

Communications software   (1) Software that enables a microcomputer to emulate a terminal and to transfer files between a micro and another computer. (2) Software that enables communication between remote devices in a computer network.

Compatibility   (1) Pertaining to the ability of one computer to execute programs of, access the database of, and communicate with another computer. (2) Pertaining to the ability of a particular hardware device to interface with a particular computer.

Computer   An electronic device capable of interpreting and executing programmed commands for input, output, computation, and logic operations.

Computer competency   A fundamental understanding of the technology, operation, applications, and issues surrounding computers.

Computer matching   The procedure whereby separate databases are examined and individuals common to both are identified.

Computer monitoring   Observing and regulating employee activities and job performance through the use of computers.

Computer network   An integration of computer systems, terminals, and communications links.

Computer system   A collective reference to all interconnected computing hardware, including processors, storage devices, input/output devices, and communications equipment.

Computer-aided design (CAD)   Use of computer graphics in design, drafting, and documentation in product and manufacturing engineering.

Computer-based training (CBT)   Using computer technologies for training and education.

Configuration   The computer and its peripheral devices.

Connectivity   Pertains to the degree to which hardware devices, software, and databases can be functionally linked to one another.

Context-sensitive Referring to an on-screen explanation that relates to a user's current software activity.

Control field See *key field.*

Control unit The portion of the processor that interprets program instructions, directs internal operations, and directs the flow of input/output to or from main memory.

Cooperative processing An environment in which organizations cooperate internally and externally to take full advantage of available information and to obtain meaningful, accurate, and timely information. (See also *intracompany networking.*)

Cottage industry People who do work-for-profit from their homes.

CPU The main processor in a computer system. (See also *host processor.*)

CRT [*Cathode-Ray Tube*] The video monitor component of a terminal.

Cryptography A communications crime-prevention technology that uses methods of data encryption and decryption to scramble codes sent over communications channels.

Current window The window in which the user can manipulate text, data, or graphics.

Cursor, graphics Typically an arrow or a cross hair which can be moved about a monitor's screen by an input device to create a graphic image or select an item from a menu. (See also *cursor, text.*)

Cursor, text A blinking character that indicates the location of the next keyed-in character on the display screen. (See also *cursor, graphics.*)

Cursor-control keys The arrow keys on the keyboard that move the text cursor vertically a line at a time and horizontally a character at a time.

Custom code Software written to handle situations unique to a particular processing environment.

Cyberphobia The irrational fear of, and aversion to, computers.

Cylinder A disk storage concept. A cylinder is that portion of the disk that can be read in any given position of the access arm. (Contrast with *sector.*)

DASD [*Direct-Access Storage Device*] A random-access secondary storage device.

Data Representations of facts. Raw material for information. (Plural of *datum.*)

Data bits A data communications parameter that refers to the number of bits in a message.

Data cartridge Magnetic tape storage in cassette format.

Data communications The collection and distribution of the electronic representation of information from and to remote facilities.

Data entry The transcription of source data into a machine-readable format.

Data item The value of a field. (Compare with *field.*)

Data path The electronic channel through which data flows within a computer system.

Data processing (DP) Using the computer to perform operations on data.

Data transfer rate The rate at which data are read/written from/to secondary storage to RAM.

Database (1) An organization's data resource for all computer-based information processing in which the data are integrated and related to minimize data redundancy. (2) An alternative term for microcomputer-based data management software. (3) Same as a file in the context of microcomputer usage.

Database record Related data that are read from, or written to, the database as a unit.

Database software Software that permits users to create and maintain a database and to extract information from the database.

Debug To eliminate bugs in a program or system. (See *bug.*)

Decode To reverse the encoding process. (Contrast with *encode.*)

Decoder That portion of a processor's control unit that interprets instructions.

Default options Preset software options that are assumed valid unless specified otherwise by the user.

Density The number of bytes per linear length or unit area of a recording medium.

Desktop film recorders An output device that permits the reproduction of high-resolution computer-generated graphic images on 35-mm film.

Desktop PC Any computer that can be placed conveniently on the top of a desk. (Contrast with *laptop PC* and *tower PC.*)

Desktop publishing (DTP) Refers to the hardware and software capability of producing near-typeset-quality copy from the confines of a desktop.

Dialog box A window that is displayed when the user must choose parameters or enter further information before the chosen menu option can be executed.

Dictionary See *information repository.*

Digitize To translate data or an image into a discrete format that can be interpreted by computers.

Digitizing tablet A pressure-sensitive tablet with the same x–y coordinates as a computer-generated screen. The outline of an image drawn on a tablet with a stylus (pen) or puck is reproduced on the display.

Dimmed A menu option, which is usually gray, that is disabled or unavailable.

Direct access See *random access.*

Direct-access file See *random file.*

Direct-access processing See *random processing.*

Direct-access storage device See *DASD.*

Disk, magnetic A secondary storage medium for random-access data storage available in permanently installed or interchangeable formats.

Disk address The physical location of a particular set of data or a program on a magnetic disk.

Disk caching A hardware/software technique in which frequently referenced disk-based data are placed in an area of RAM that simulates disk storage. (See also *RAM disk.*)

Disk cartridge An environmentally sealed interchangeable disk module that contains one or more hard disk platters.

Disk density The number of bits that can be stored per unit of area on the disk-face surface.

Disk drive, magnetic A magnetic storage device that records data on flat rotating disks. (Compare with *tape drive, magnetic.*)

Diskette A thin interchangeable disk for secondary random-access data storage (same as *floppy disk* and *flexible disk*).

Document-conversion program Software that converts files generated on one software package into a format consistent with another.

DOS [*Disk Operating System*] A generic reference to a disk-based operating system.

Dot-matrix printer A printer that arranges printed dots to form characters and images.

Double click Tapping a button on a point-and-draw device twice in rapid succession.

Down-line processor A computer that collects data from a number of low-speed devices, then transmits "concentrated" data over a single communications channel (also called *multiplexer*).

Download The transmission of data from a mainframe computer to a terminal.

Downsizing Used to describe the trend toward increased reliance on smaller computers for personal as well as enterprise-wide processing tasks.

Downtime The time during which a computer system is not operational.

DP See *data processing.*

Drag A mouse-based procedure by which an object is moved or a contiguous area on the display is marked for processing.

Drag-and-drop software Software that lets users drag ready-made shapes from application-specific stencils to the desired position on the drawing area to do drawings for flowcharting, landscaping, business graphics, and other applications.

Draw software Software that enables users to create electronic images. Resultant images are stored as vector graphics images.

Driver module The program module that calls other subordinate program modules to be executed as they are needed (also called a *main program*).

DTP See *desktop publishing.*

E-mail See *electronic mail.*

E-time See *execution time.*

EBCDIC [*Extended Binary Coded Decimal Interchange Code*] An encoding system.

Echo A host computer's retransmission of characters back to the sending device.

EFT [*Electronic Funds Transfer*] A computer-based system allowing electronic transfer of money from one account to another.

EGA [*Enhanced Graphics Adapter*] A circuit board that enables the interfacing of high-resolution monitors to microcomputers.

EISA [*Extended Industry Standard Architecture*] An architecture for microcomputers that use the Intel microprocessors.

Electronic data interchange (EDI) The use of computers and data communications to transmit data electronically between companies (*also called intercompany networking.*)

Electronic dictionary A disk-based dictionary used in conjunction with a spelling-checker program to verify the spelling of words in a word processing document.

Electronic funds transfer See *EFT.*

Electronic mail A computer application whereby messages are transmitted via data communications to "electronic mailboxes" (also called *E-mail*). (Contrast with *voice message switching.*)

Electronic messaging A workgroup computing application that enables electronic mail to be associated with other workgroup applications.

Encode To apply the rules of a code. (Contrast with *decode.*)

Encoding system A system that permits alphanumeric characters to be coded in terms of bits.

End user The individual providing input to the computer or using computer output (same as *user*).

End user computing A computing environment in which the end users handle both the technical and functional tasks of the information systems projects.

Ergonomics The study of the relationships between people and machines.

Execution time The elapsed time it takes to execute a computer instruction and store the results (also called *E-time*).

Expansion slots Slots within the processing component of a microcomputer into which optional add-on circuit boards may be inserted.

Expert system An interactive knowledge-based system that responds to questions, asks for clarification, makes recommendations, and generally helps users make complex decisions.

Export The process of converting a database in the format of the current program to a format that can be used by another program. (Contrast with *import.*)

Facsimile Equipment that transfers images of hard-copy documents via telephone lines to another office.

Fax See *facsimile.*

Fax modem A modem that enables a PC to emulate a facsimile machine. (See also *modem.*)

Feedback loop A closed loop in which a computer-controlled process generates data that become input to the computer.

Fetch instruction That part of the instruction cycle in which the control unit retrieves a program instruction from main memory and loads it to the processor.

Fiber optic cable A data transmission medium that carries data in the form of light in very thin transparent fibers.

Field The smallest logical unit of data. Examples are employee number, first name, and price. (Compare with *data item.*)

File (1) A collection of related records. (2) A named area on a secondary storage device that contains a program, data, or textual material.

File server A micro with a high-capacity disk for storing the data and programs shared by the users on a LAN.

Fixed magnetic disk See *hard disk.*

Flash memory A type of programmable read-only memory that can be altered easily by the end user.

Flat files A traditional file structure in which records are related to no other files.

Flat-panel monitor A monitor, thin from front to back, that uses liquid crystal and gas plasma technology.

Flexible disk See *diskette.*

Floppy disk See *diskette.*

FLOPS Floating point operations per second.

Floptical disk drive A disk drive that uses optical technology to read and write to 20-MB diskettes as well as the standard 3-inch diskettes.

Flowchart A diagram that illustrates data, information, and work flow via specialized symbols which, when connected by flow lines, portray the logic of a system or program.

Flowcharting The act of creating a flowchart.

Font A typeface that is described by its letter style, its height in points, and its presentation attribute.

Footprint The evidence of unlawful entry or use of a computer system.

Foreground (1) That part of RAM that contains the highest priority program. (2) In Windows, the area of the display containing the active window. (Contrast with *background.*)

Frame A rectangular area in a desktop publishing–produced document that holds the text or an image of a particular file.

Front-end processor A processor used to offload certain data communications tasks from the host processor.

Full-duplex line A communications channel that transmits data in both directions at the same time. (Contrast with *half-duplex line.*)

Full-screen editing This word processing feature permits the user to move the cursor to any position in the document to insert or replace text.

Function A predefined operation that performs mathematical, logical, statistical, financial, and character-string operations on data in a spreadsheet or a database.

Function key A special-function key on the keyboard that can be used to instruct the computer to perform a specific operation (also called *soft key*).

Gb See *gigabit*.

GB See *gigabyte*.

General-purpose computer Computer systems that are designed with the flexibility to do a variety of tasks, such as CAI, payroll processing, climate control, and so on.

General-purpose software Software that provides the framework for a number of business and personal applications.

Geosynchronous orbit An orbit that permits a communications satellite to maintain a fixed position relative to the surface of the earth (also known as *geostationary orbit*).

GFLOPS A billion floating operation points per second.

Gigabit (Gb) One billion bits.

Gigabyte (GB) One billion bytes.

Graceful exit Quitting a program according to normal procedures and returning to a higher-level program.

Grammar checker An add-on program to word processing software that highlights grammatical concerns and deviations from conventions in a word processing document.

Graphical user interface (GUI) Software that permits users to select processing options simply by positioning an arrow over a graphic representation of the desired function or program.

Graphics cursor A symbol on a display screen which can be positioned anywhere on a display screen by a light pen, a joystick, a track ball, a digitizing tablet and pen, or a mouse to initiate action or to draw.

Graphics mode One of two modes of operation for PC monitors. (Contrast with *text mode*.)

Graphics software Software that enables you to create line drawings, art, and presentation graphics.

Graphics-conversion program Software that enables files containing graphic images to be passed between programs.

Gray scales The number of shades of a color that can be presented on a monochrome monitor's screen or on a monochrome printer's output.

Groupware Software whose application is designed to benefit a group of people. (Related to *workgroup computing*.)

Hacker A computer enthusiast who uses the computer as a source of recreation.

Half-duplex line A communications channel that transmits data in one direction at the same time. (Contrast with *full-duplex line*.)

Half-size expansion board An add-on board that fits in half an expansion slot.

Handshaking The process by which both sending and receiving devices in a computer network maintain and coordinate data communications.

Hard copy A readable printed copy of computer output. (Contrast with *soft copy*.)

Hard disk A permanently installed, continuously spinning magnetic storage medium made up of one or more rigid disk platters. (Same as *fixed magnetic disk;* contrast with *interchangeable magnetic disk*. See also *Winchester disk*).

Hardware The physical devices that comprise a computer system. (Contrast with *software*.)

Help command A software feature that provides an on-line explanation of or instruction on how to proceed.

Hertz One cycle per second.

Host computer See *host processor*.

Host processor The processor responsible for the overall control of a computer system. The host processor is the focal point of a communications-based system (also called *host computer*).

Hotkey A seldom used key combination that, when activated, causes the computer to perform the function associated with the key combination.

Hydra printer Multifunction machines that can handle several paper-related tasks such as computer-based printing, facsimile, scanning, and copying.

Hypermedia Software that enables the integration of data, text, graphics, sounds of all kinds, and full-motion video. (See also *hypertext*.)

Hypertext Data management software that provides links between key words in the unstructured text-based documents. (See also *hypermedia*.)

I/O [Input/Output] Input or output or both.

I-time See *instruction time*.

IBM Personal Computer (IBM PC) IBM's first personal computer (1981).

Icons Pictographs used in place of words or phrases on screen displays.

Idea processor A software productivity tool that allows the user to organize and document thoughts and ideas usually in outline form.

Image processing A reference to computer applications in which digitized images are retrieved, displayed, altered, merged with text, stored, and sent via data communications to one or several remote locations.

Image scanner A device which uses a camera to scan and digitize an image that can be stored on a disk and manipulated by a computer.

Impact printer A printer that uses some type of hammer or hammers to hit the ribbon and the paper.

Import The process of converting data in one format to a format that is compatible with the calling program. (Contrast with *export*.)

Information Data that have been collected and processed into a meaningful form.

Information network Same as *on-line service*.

Information society A society in which the generation and dissemination of information becomes the central focus of commerce.

Information superhighway A network of high-speed data communication links that will eventually connect virtually every facet of our society.

Information system A computer-based system that provides both data processing capability and information for managerial decision making.

Information technology A collective reference to the combined fields of computers and information systems.

Input Data to be processed by a computer system.

Input/output A generic reference to input and/or output to a computer.

Input/output—bound operation The amount of work that can be performed by the computer system is limited primarily by the speeds of the I/O devices.

Insert mode A data entry mode in which the character entered is inserted at the cursor position.

Instruction A programming language statement that specifies a particular computer operation to be performed.

Instruction register The register that contains the instruction being executed.

Instruction time The elapsed time it takes to fetch and decode a computer instruction (also called *I-time*).

Integrated circuit (IC) Thousands of electronic components that are etched into a tiny silicon chip in the form of a special-function electronic circuit.

Interactive Pertaining to on-line and immediate communication between the end user and the computer.

Interchangeable magnetic disk A magnetic disk that can be stored off-line and loaded to the magnetic disk drive as it is needed. (Contrast with *hard disk*, or *fixed magnetic disk*.)

Intercompany networking See *electronic data interchange*.

Intracompany networking The use of computers and data communications to transmit data electronically within a company. (See also *cooperative processing*.)

Invoke Execute a command or a macro.

Joystick A single vertical stick that moves the cursor on a screen in the direction in which the stick is pushed.

Kb See *kilobit*.

KB See *kilobyte*.

Key field The field in a record that is used as an identifier for accessing, sorting, and collating records (same as *control field*).

Key pad That portion of a keyboard that permits rapid numeric data entry.

Keyboard A device used for key data entry.

Keyboard templates Typically, a plastic keyboard overlay that indicates which commands are assigned to particular function keys.

Kilobit (Kb) 1024, or about 1000, bits.

Kilobyte (KB) 1024, or about 1000, bytes.

Knowledge base The foundation of a knowledge-based system that contains facts, rules, inferences, and procedures.

Knowledge worker Someone whose job function revolves around the use, manipulation, and dissemination of information.

Knowledge-based system A computer-based system, often associated with artificial intelligence, that helps users make decisions by enabling them to interact with a knowledge base.

LAN operating system The operating system for a local area network.

Landscape Referring to the orientation of the print on the page. Printed lines run parallel to the longer side of the page. (Contrast with *portrait*.)

Laptop PC Portable PC that can operate without an external power source. (Contrast with *desktop PC* and *tower PC*.)

Line printer A printer that prints a line at a time.

Load To transfer programs or data from secondary to primary storage.

Local area network (LAN or local net) A system of hardware, software, and communications channels that connects devices on the local premises. (Contrast with *wide area network*.)

Local net See *local area network*.

Log off The procedure by which a user terminates a communications link with a remote computer. (Contrast with *log-on*.)

Log-on The procedure by which a user establishes a communications link with a remote computer. (Contrast with *log off*.)

Logical operators Used to combine relational expressions logically in spreadsheet and database software (such as AND, OR). (See also *relational operators*.)

Logical security That aspect of computer-center security that deals with user access to systems and data.

Loop A sequence of program instructions executed repeatedly until a particular condition is met.

Machine cycle The cycle of operations performed by the processor to process a single program instruction: fetch, decode, execute, and place result in memory.

Machine language The programming language that is interpreted and executed directly by the computer.

Machine-independent Pertaining to programs that can be executed on computers of different designs.

Macintosh Apple Computer's mainline personal computer.

Macintosh System The operating system for the Apple Macintosh line of personal computers.

Macro A sequence of frequently used operations or keystrokes that can be recalled and invoked to help speed user interaction with microcomputer productivity software.

Magnetic disk See *disk, magnetic*.

Magnetic disk drive See *disk drive, magnetic*.

Magnetic stripe A magnetic storage medium for low-volume storage of data on badges and cards. (Related to *badge reader*.)

Magnetic tape See *tape, magnetic*.

Magnetic tape cartridge Cartridge-based magnetic tape storage media.

Magnetic tape drive See *tape drive, magnetic*.

Magneto-optical disk An optical laser disk with read and write capabilities.

Mail merge A computer application in which text generated by word processing is merged with data from a database (e.g., a form letter with an address).

Main memory See *RAM*.

Main menu The highest-level menu in a menu tree.

Mainframe computer A large computer that can service many users simultaneously.

Master file The permanent source of data for a particular computer application area.

Mb See *megabit*.

MB See *megabyte*.

MCA [*M*icro *C*hannel *A*rchitecture] The architecture of the high-end IBM PS/2 line of microcomputers.

Megabit (Mb) 1,048,576, or about one million, bits.

Megabyte (MB) Referring to one million bytes of primary or secondary storage capacity.

Memory See *RAM*.

Menu A display with a list of processing choices from which an end user may select.

Menu bar A menu in which the options are displayed across the screen.

Menu tree A hierarchy of menus.

Message A series of bits sent from a terminal to a computer, or vice versa.

MHz [*megahertz*] One million hertz.

Microcomputer (or micro) A small computer (same as *desktop PC, personal computer, PC*).

Microprocessor A computer on a single chip. The processing component of a microcomputer.

Microsecond One millionth of a second.

Microwave radio signal A high-frequency line-of-sight electromagnetic wave used in communications satellites.

Millisecond One thousandth of a second.

Minicomputer (or mini) A midsized computer.

MIPS Millions of instructions per second.

Mnemonics Symbols that represent instructions in assembler languages.

Modem [*MOdulator-DEModulator*] A device used to convert computer-compatible signals to signals suitable for data transmission facilities, and vice versa.

Monitor A televisionlike display for soft-copy output in a computer system.

Motherboard Same as *system board.*

Mouse A small device that, when moved across a desktop a particular distance and direction, causes the same movement of the cursor on a screen.

MS-DOS [*MicroSoft–Disk Operating System*] A microcomputer operating system.

Multifunction add-on board An add-on circuit board that performs more than one function.

Multimedia Computer applications that involve the integration of text, sound, graphics, motion video, and animation.

Multiplexer See *down-line processor.*

Multiplexing The simultaneous transmission of multiple transmissions of data over a single communications channel.

Multitasking The concurrent execution of more than one program at a time.

Multiuser microcomputer A microcomputer that can serve more than one user at any given time.

Nanosecond One billionth of a second.

Natural language A programming language in which the programmer writes specifications without regard to the computer's instruction format or syntax—essentially, using everyday human language to program.

Navigation Movement within and between a software application's work areas.

Network, computer See *computer network.*

Network topology The configuration of interconnection between the nodes in a communications network.

Node An endpoint in a computer network.

Nondestructive read A read operation in which the program and/or data that are loaded to RAM from secondary storage reside in both RAM (temporarily) and secondary storage (permanently).

Nonimpact printer A printer that uses chemicals, lasers, or heat to form the images on the paper.

Nonvolatile memory Solid-state RAM that retains its contents after an electrical interruption. (Contrast with *volatile memory.*)

Notebook PC A notebook-size laptop PC.

NuBus The architecture of high-end Apple Macintosh computers.

Numeric A reference to any of the digits 0–9. (Compare with *alpha* and *alphanumeric.*)

OCR scanner A light-sensitive input device that bounces a beam of light off an image to interpret the image.

Off-line Pertaining to data that are not accessible by, or hardware devices that are not connected to, a computer system. (Contrast with *on-line.*)

On-line Pertaining to data and/or hardware devices accessible to and under the control of a computer system. (Contrast with *off-line.*)

On-line service An on-line commercial information network that provides remote users with access to a variety of information services (same as *information network*).

On-line thesaurus Software that enables a user to request synonyms interactively during a word processing session.

Opcode Pertaining to that portion of a computer machine-language instruction that designates the operation to be performed. Short for *operation code.* (Related to *operand.*)

Open architecture Refers to micros that give users the flexibility to configure the system with a variety of peripheral devices. (Contrast with *closed architecture;* also called *bus architecture.*)

Operand Pertaining to that portion of a computer machine-language instruction that designates the address of the data to be operated on. (Related to *opcode.*)

Operating system The software that controls the execution of all applications and system software programs.

Operation code See *opcode.*

Operator console The machine-room operator's terminal.

Optical character recognition (OCR) A data entry technique that permits original-source data entry. Coded symbols or characters are scanned to retrieve the data.

Optical laser disk A secondary storage medium that uses laser technology to score the surface of a disk to represent a bit.

OS/2 A multitasking PC operating system.

Output Data transferred from primary storage to an output device.

Page printer A printer that prints a page at a time.

Paint software Software that enables users to "paint" electronic images. Resultant images are stored as raster graphics images.

Palmtop PC See *pocket PC.*

Parallel Pertaining to processing data in groups of bits versus one bit at a time. (Contrast with *serial.*)

Parallel port A direct link with the microcomputer's bus that facilitates the parallel transmission of data, usually one byte at a time.

Parallel processing A processing procedure in which one main processor examines the programming problem and determines what portions, if any, of the problem can be solved in pieces by other subordinate processors.

Parameter A descriptor that can take on different values.

Parity bit A bit appended to a bit configuration (byte) that is used to check the accuracy of data transmission from one hardware device to another (related to *parity checking* and *parity error*).

Parity checking A built-in checking procedure in a computer system to help ensure that the transmission of data is complete and accurate. (Related to *parity bit* and *parity error.*)

Parity error Occurs when a bit is dropped in the transmission of data from one hardware device to another. (Related to *parity bit* and *parity checking.*)

Password A word or phrase known only to the end user. When entered, it permits the end user to gain access to the system.

PC [Personal Computer] See *desktop PC* and *microcomputer.*

PC card Same as *PCMCIA card.*

PCMCIA card A credit-card–sized module that is inserted into a PCMCIA-compliant interface to offer add-on capabilities such as expanded memory, fax modem, and so on.

Peer-to-peer LAN A local area network in which all PCs on the network are functionally equal.

Pen-based computing Computer applications that rely on the pen-based PCs for processing capability.

Pen-based PC A personal computer that uses an electronic pen in lieu of a keyboard for input.

Peripheral device Any hardware device other than the processor.

Personal computer (PC) See *microcomputer.*

Personal computing   A computing environment in which individuals use microcomputers for both domestic and business applications.

Personal digital assistant (PDA)   Hand-held personal computers that support a variety of personal information systems.

Personal identification number (PIN)   A code or number that is used in conjunction with a password to permit the end user to gain access to a computer system.

Physical security   That aspect of computer-center security that deals with access to computers and peripheral devices.

Picosecond   One trillionth of a second.

Picture element   See *pixel.*

Pie graph   A circular graph that illustrates each "piece" of datum in its proper relationship to the whole "pie."

Pilferage   A special case of software piracy whereby a company purchases a software product without a site-usage license agreement, then copies and distributes it throughout the company.

Pixel   [*picture element*] An addressable point on a display screen to which light can be directed under program control.

Platform   A definition of the standards followed by those who create proprietary software packages.

Pocket PC   A hand-held personal computer (also called *palmtop PC*).

Pointer   The highlighted area in a spreadsheet display that indicates the current cell.

Polling   A line-control procedure in which each terminal is "polled" in rotation to determine whether a message is ready to be sent.

Pop-out menu   See *pop-up menu.*

Pop-up menu   A menu that is superimposed in a window over whatever is currently being displayed on the monitor (also called *pop-out menu*).

Port   An access point in a computer system that permits communication between the computer and a peripheral device.

Portrait   Referring to the orientation of the print on the page. Printed lines run parallel to the shorter side of the page. (Contrast with *landscape.*)

Power down   To turn off the electrical power to a computer system.

Power up   To turn on the electrical power to a computer system.

Presentation graphics   Business graphics, such as pie graphs and bar graphs, that are used to present information in a graphic format in meetings, reports, and oral presentations.

Presentation graphics software   User-friendly software that allow users to create a variety of visually appealing and informative presentation graphics.

Primary storage   See *RAM.*

Print server   A LAN-based PC that handles LAN user print jobs and controls at least one printer.

Printer   A device used to prepare hard-copy output.

Process/device control   Using the computer to control an ongoing process or device in a continuous feedback loop.

Processor   The logical component of a computer system that interprets and executes program instructions.

Processor-bound operation   The amount of work that can be performed by the computer system is limited primarily by the speed of the computer.

Program   (1) Computer instructions structured and ordered in a manner that, when executed, causes a computer to perform a particular function. (2) The act of producing computer software. (Related to *software.*)

Program register   The register that contains the address of the next instruction to be executed.

Programmable read-only memory   Programmable ROM. (See *ROM.*)

Programmer   One who writes computer programs.

Programming   The act of writing a computer program.

Programming language   A language programmers use to communicate instructions to a computer.

PROM   [*Programmable Read-Only Memory*] ROM in which the user can load read-only programs and data. (See *EPROM.*)

Prompt   A program-generated message describing what should be entered by the end user operator at a PC or terminal.

Protocols   See *communications protocols.*

Pull-down menu   A menu that is "pulled down" and superimposed in a window over whatever is currently being displayed on a monitor.

Query by example (QBE)   A method of database inquiry in which the user sets conditions for the selection of records by composing one or more example relational expressions.

RAM   [*Random-Access Memory*] The memory area in which all programs and data must reside before programs can be executed or data manipulated. (Same as *main memory, memory,* and *primary storage;* compare with *secondary storage.*)

RAM disk   That area of RAM that facilitates disk caching. (See also *disk caching.*)

Random access   Direct access to records, regardless of their physical location on the storage medium. (Contrast with *sequential access.*)

Random file   A collection of records that can be processed randomly. (Same as *direct-access file.*)

Random processing   Processing data and records randomly. (Same as *direct-access processing;* contrast with *sequential processing.*)

Range   A cell or a rectangular group of adjacent cells in a spreadsheet.

Raster graphics   A method for maintaining a screen image as patterns of dots.

Read   The process by which a record or a portion of a record is accessed from the magnetic storage medium (tape or disk) of a secondary storage device and transferred to primary storage for processing. (Contrast with *write.*)

Read/write head   That component of a disk drive or tape drive that reads from and writes to its respective magnetic storage medium.

Read-only memory (ROM)   A memory chip with contents permanently loaded by the manufacturer for read-only applications.

Record   A collection of related fields (such as an employee record) describing an event or an item.

Register   A small high-speed storage area in which data pertaining to the execution of a particular instruction are stored. Data stored in a specific register have a special meaning to the logic of the computer.

Relational database   A database in which data are accessed by content rather than by address.

Relational operators   Used in spreadsheet and database formulas to show the equality relationship between two expressions (= [equal to], < [less than], > [greater than], ≤ [less than or equal to], ≥ [greater than or equal to], ≠ [not equal to]). (See also *logical operators.*)

Relative cell address   Refers to a cell's position in a spreadsheet in relation to the cell containing the formula in which the address is used.

Resident font   A font that is accessed directly from the printer's built-in read-only memory.

Resolution Referring to the number of addressable points on a monitor's screen. The greater the number of points, the higher the resolution.

Reverse video Characters on a video display terminal presented as black on a light background; used for highlighting.

RGB monitor Color monitors that mix red, green, and blue to achieve a spectrum of colors.

Ring topology A computer network that involves computer systems connected in a closed loop, with no one computer system the focal point of the network.

RISC [*R*educed *I*nstruction *S*et *C*omputer] A computer-designed architecture based on a limited instruction set. (Contrast with *CISC.*)

Robot A computer-controlled manipulator capable of locomotion and/or moving items through a variety of spatial motions.

Robotics The integration of computers and industrial robots.

ROM [*R*ead-*O*nly *M*emory] RAM that can be read only, not written to.

Root directory The directory at the highest level of a hierarchy of directories.

Routers Communications hardware that enables communications links between LANs and WANs by performing the necessary protocol conversions.

RS-232C connector A 9-pin or 25-pin plug that is used for the electronic interconnection of computers, modems, and other peripheral devices.

Run The continuous execution of one or more logically related programs (such as printing payroll checks).

Scalable typeface An outline-based typeface from which fonts of any point size can be created.

Screen image projector An output device that can project a computer-generated image onto a large screen.

Screen-capture programs Memory-resident programs that enable users to transfer all or part of the current screen image to a disk file.

Scrolling Using the cursor keys to view parts of a word processing document or a spreadsheet that extends past the bottom or top or sides of the screen.

Secondary storage Permanent data storage on magnetic disk and/or tape. (Compare with *primary storage* and *RAM.*)

Sector A disk storage concept of a pie-shaped portion of a disk or diskette in which records are stored and subsequently retrieved. (Contrast with *cylinder.*)

Sector organization Magnetic disk organization in which the recording surface is divided into pie-shaped sectors.

Sequential access Accessing records in the order in which they are stored. (Contrast with *random access.*)

Sequential files Files containing records that are ordered according to a key field.

Sequential processing Processing of files that are ordered numerically or alphabetically by a key field. (Contrast with *direct-access processing* or *random processing.*)

Serial Pertaining to processing data one bit at a time. (Contrast with *parallel.*)

Serial port A direct link with the microcomputer's bus that facilitates the serial transmission of data, one bit at a time.

Serial printer A printer that prints one character at a time.

Serial representation The storing of bits one after another on a secondary storage medium.

Serpentine A magnetic tape storage scheme in which data are recorded serially in tracks.

Server A LAN component that can be shared by users on a LAN.

Shell Software that provides a graphical user interface alternative to command-driven software.

Simultaneous click Tapping both buttons on a point-and-draw device at the same time.

Smart card A card or badge with an embedded microprocessor.

Soft copy Temporary output that can be interpreted visually, as on a monitor. (Contrast with *hard copy.*)

Soft font An electronic description of a font that is retrieved from disk storage and downloaded to the printer's memory.

Soft key See *function key.*

Software The programs used to direct the functions of a computer system. (Contrast with *hardware; related to program.*)

Software package One or more programs designed to perform a particular processing task.

Software piracy The unlawful duplication of proprietary software. (Related to *pilferage.*)

Sort The rearrangement of fields or records in an ordered sequence by a key field.

Source data Original data that usually involve the recording of a transaction or the documenting of an event or an item.

Source data automation Entering data directly to a computer system at the source without the need for key entry transcription.

Speech synthesizers Devices that convert raw data into electronically produced speech.

Speech-recognition system A device that permits voice input to a computer system.

Spelling checker An add-on program to word processing that checks the spelling of every word in a word processing document against an electronic dictionary.

Spreadsheet software Refers to software that permits users to work with rows and columns of data.

Star topology A computer network that involves a centralized host computer connected to a number of smaller computer systems.

Style checker An add-on program to word processing software that identifies deviations from effective writing style in a word processing document (for example, long, complex sentences).

Supercomputer The category that includes the largest and most powerful computers.

Syntax The rules that govern the formulation of the instructions in a computer program.

Sysop [*system op*erator] The sponsor who provides the hardware and software support for an electronic bulletin-board system.

System Any group of components (functions, people, activities, events, and so on) that interface with and complement one another to achieve one or more predefined goals.

System board A microcomputer circuit board that contains the microprocessor, electronic circuitry for handling such tasks as input/output signals from peripheral devices, and memory chips (same as *motherboard*).

System check An internal verification of the operational capabilities of a computer's electronic components.

System operator See *sysop.*

System prompt A visual prompt to the user to enter a system command.

System software Software that is independent of any specific applications area.

Tape, magnetic A secondary storage medium for sequential data storage. Available as a reel or as a cartridge.

Tape backup unit (TBU) A magnetic tape drive design to provide backup for data and programs.

Tape density   The number of bits that can be stored per linear length of a magnetic tape.

Tape drive, magnetic   The hardware device that contains the read/write mechanism for the magnetic tape storage medium. (Compare with *disk drive, magnetic*.)

Task   The basic unit of work for a processor.

Telecommunications   Communication between remote devices.

Telecommuting   "Commuting" via a communications link between home and office.

Template   A model for a particular microcomputer software application.

Terminal   Any device capable of sending and receiving data over a communications channel.

Terminal emulation mode   The software transformation of a microcomputer so that its keyboard, monitor, and data interface emulate that of a terminal.

Text cursor   A blinking character on a display screen that indicates the location of the next keyed-in character on the screen.

Text mode   One of two modes of operation for PC monitors. (Contrast with *graphics mode*.)

Thesaurus, on-line   See *on-line thesaurus*.

Throughput   A measure of computer system efficiency; the rate at which work can be performed by a computer system.

Toggle   The action of pressing a single key on a keyboard to switch between two or more modes of operation, such as insert and replace.

Total connectivity   The networking of all hardware, software, and databases in an organization.

Touch screen monitors   Monitors with touch-sensitive screens that enable users to choose from available options by simply touching the desired icon or menu item with their finger.

Tower PC   A vertical PC that is designed to rest on the floor. (Contrast with *laptop PC* and *desktop PC*.)

Track, disk   That portion of a magnetic disk-face surface that can be accessed in any given setting of a single read/write head. Tracks are configured in concentric circles.

Track, tape   That portion of a magnetic tape that can be accessed by any one of the tape drives read/write heads. A track runs the length of the tape.

Trackball   A ball mounted in a box that, when moved, results in a similar movement of the cursor on a display screen.

Tracks per inch (TPI)   A measure of the recording density, or spacing, of tracks on a magnetic disk.

Transaction   A procedural event in a system that prompts manual or computer-based activity.

Transaction file   A file containing records of data activity (transactions); used to update the master file.

Transaction-oriented processing   Transactions are recorded and entered as they occur.

Transmission medium   The central cable along which terminals, peripheral devices, and microcomputers are connected in a bus topology.

Transparent   A reference to a procedure or activity that occurs automatically. It does not have to be considered in the use or design of a program or an information system.

Typeface   A set of characters that are of the same type style.

Typeover mode   A data entry mode in which the character entered overstrikes the character at the cursor position.

Uninterruptible power source (UPS)   A buffer between an external power source and a computer system that supplies clean, continuous power.

Universal product code (UPC)   A 10-digit machine-readable bar code placed on consumer products.

UNIX   A multiuser operating system.

Upload   The transmission of data from a PC or a terminal to the mainframe computer.

Uptime   That time when the computer system is in operation.

User   See *end user*.

User interface   A reference to the software, method, or displays that enable interaction between the user and the applications or system software being used.

User-friendly   Pertaining to an on-line system that permits a person with relatively little experience to interact successfully with the system.

Utility program   An often-used service routine, such as a program to sort records.

Vaccine   An antiviral program.

VDT   [*Video Display Terminal*] A terminal on which printed and graphic information are displayed on a televisionlike monitor and into which data are entered on a typewriterlike keyboard.

Vector graphics   A method for maintaining a screen image as patterns of lines, points, and other geometric shapes.

VGA   [*Video Graphics Array*] A circuit board that enables the interfacing of very high-resolution monitors to microcomputers.

Video display terminal   See *VDT*.

Virus   A program written with malicious intent and loaded to the computer system of an unsuspecting victim. Ultimately, the program destroys or introduces errors in programs and databases.

Vision-input systems   A device that enables limited visual input to a computer system.

Voice message switching   Using computers, the telephone system, and other electronic means to store and forward voice messages. (Contrast with *electronic mail*.)

Voice-response unit   A device that enables output from a computer system in the form of user-recorded words, phrases, music, alarms, or anything that might be recorded on tape.

Volatile memory   Solid-state semiconductor RAM in which the data are lost when the electrical current is turned off or interrupted. (Contrast with *nonvolatile memory*.)

Wand scanner   Hand-held OCR scanner.

Wide area network (WAN)   A computer network that connects nodes in widely dispersed geographic areas. (Contrast with *local area network*.)

Winchester disk   Permanently installed, continuously spinning magnetic storage medium that is made up of one or more rigid disk platters. (See also *hard disk*.)

Window   (1) A rectangular section of a display screen that is dedicated to a specific activity or application. (2) In integrated software, a "view" of a designated area of a worksheet, such as a spreadsheet or word processing text.

Window panes   Simultaneous display of subareas of a particular window.

Windows   A software product by Microsoft Corporation that provides a graphical user interface and multitasking capabilities for the MS-DOS environment.

Word   For a given computer, an established number of bits that are handled as a unit.

Word processing   Using the computer to enter, store, manipulate, and print text.

Word wrap   A word processing feature that automatically moves, or "wraps," text to the next line when that text would otherwise exceed the right margin limit.

Workgroup computing Computer applications that involve cooperation among people linked by a computer network. (Related to *groupware*.)

Workstation A high-performance single-user computer system with sophisticated input/output devices that can be easily networked with other workstations or computers.

Worm A program that erases data and/or programs from a computer system's memory, usually with malicious intent.

WORM disk [*Write-Once Read-Many* disk] An optical laser disk that can be read many times after the data are written to it, but the data cannot be changed or erased.

Write To record data on the output medium of a particular I/O device (tape, hard copy, PC display). (Contrast with *read*.)

WYSIWYG [*What You See Is What You Get*] A word processing package in which what is displayed on the screen is very similar in appearance to what you get when the document is printed.

X terminals Terminals that enable the user to interact via a graphical user interface (GUI).

XENIX A spinoff of the UNIX operating system.

Zoom An integrated software command that expands a window to fill the entire screen.

INDEX

PHOTO ACKNOWLEDGMENTS

International Business Machines Corporation; **150:** Ericsson; **151:** (top left) NASA; **151:** (top right) Courtesy of Harris Corporation; **151:** (bottom) Courtesy of E-Systems; **154:** Photo provided by GRiD Systems Corporation; **155:** Courtesy of International Business Machines Corporation; **156:** (top) Courtesy of Harris Corporation; **156:** (bottom) Courtesy of International Business Machines Corporation; **157:** Courtesy Home Shopping Network; **160:** Courtesy of International Business Machines Corporation.

CHAPTER 7 **164:** Courtesy of International Business Machines Corporation; **165:** Courtesy of International Business Machines Corporation; **168:** Courtesy of Kerr-McGee; **171:** Used by permission, Gannet Co., Inc.; **179:** Courtesy Software Studios, Inc.; **182:** Courtesy of Digital Equipment Corporation; **183:** (top) Courtesy Logitech; **185:** Screen shot provided courtesy of Micrografx Incorporated.

CHAPTER 8 **190:** Courtesy of International Business Machines Corporation; **191:** Courtesy of International Business Machines Corporation; **204:** Courtesy of International Business Machines Corporation; **211:** Kurzweil AI-MLS/A; **213:** Screen shot provided courtesy of Micrografx Incorporated.

CHAPTER 9 **218:** Microtime, Inc.; **219:** Courtesy of Egghead Software; **220:** Photo courtesy of Hewlett-Packard Company; **221:** Courtesy of Maxis; **227:** (left) Created using Corel DRAW 2.0. Corel Corporation, Ottawa, Canada.; **227:** (right) Courtesy of Colossal Pictures Liquid Television (MTV), Computer Animations by Hutchison/Fernalld. Rendered in ElectricImage Animation System.; **228:** Courtesy Boeing Company; **231:** (top) Courtesy of International Business Machines Corporation; **231:** (bottom) Microsoft Corporation; **233:** Courtesy of MusicWriter, Inc.; **234:** Courtesy of International Business Machines Corporation; **237:** Courtesy CompuServe.

CHAPTER 10 **247:** Courtesy of Ranger Productions, Inc. "Slingship entering Fort Hope." Rendered in ElectricImage Animation System; **248:** Courtesy of Tactics International Limited, 16 Haverhill St., Andover, MA 01810; **249:** Rockwell International/David Perry; **250:** (top) Photo courtesy of Hewlett-Packard Company; **250:** (bottom) Courtesy Sun Microsystems; **251:** Courtesy Zenith Data Systems; **252:** Courtesy of Harris Corporation; **254:** Courtesy of Harris Corporation; **255:** Courtesy of E-Systems; **260:** Courtesy Communication Intelligence Corporation; **261:** Courtesy of Kinesis(tm) Corporation; **262:** Courtesy of International Business Machines Corporation; **263:** Courtesy of Harris Corporation; **264:** (top) "Powerful TV" Nickelodeon-MTV Networks, Director Malcolm MacNeill, Animation, Jim Ludtke, Ludtke Design. Rendered in ElectricImage Animation System.; **264:** (bottom) Courtesy of Mead Data Central, Inc.; **265:** CheckRobot Automated Checkout Machines; **266:** (top) Courtesy Prodigy Services Company; **266:** (bottom) Courtesy of International Business Machines Corporation; **267:** Photo Courtesy of Ashland Oil, Inc.